The major characters

THE SCHULZ FAMILY

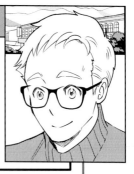

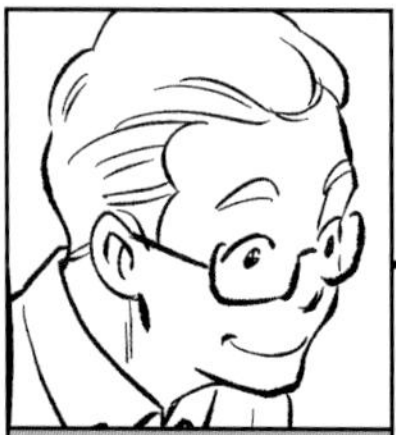

Father
Carl Schulz

Schulz's comics-loving father. He runs a barbershop. He's earnest and hardworking.

Charles M. Schulz

The creator of *Peanuts*. His nickname is "Sparky". He has loved newspaper comic strips since childhood, which inspired him to become a cartoonist.

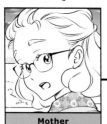

Mother
Dena Schulz

Schulz's mother. She supports Charles' aspirations to become a cartoonist.

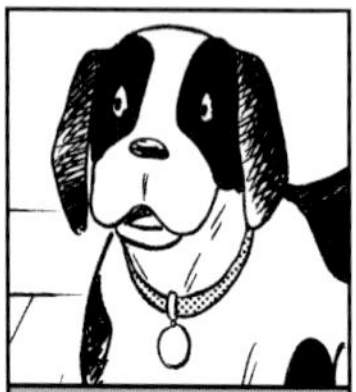

Spike

Schulz's beloved and incredibly intelligent dog. Snoopy is based on Spike.

His first love

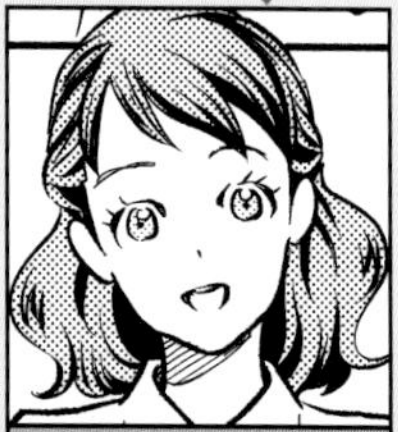

Donna Mae
Johnson

A woman Schulz meets at his workplace. He falls in love with her and eventually proposes.

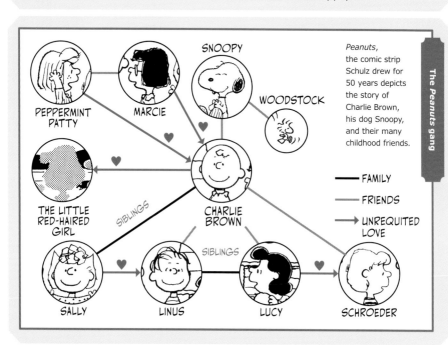

The *Peanuts* gang

Peanuts, the comic strip Schulz drew for 50 years depicts the story of Charlie Brown, his dog Snoopy, and their many childhood friends.

PEPPERMINT PATTY
MARCIE
SNOOPY
WOODSTOCK
THE LITTLE RED-HAIRED GIRL
CHARLIE BROWN
SIBLINGS
SIBLINGS
SALLY
LINUS
LUCY
SCHROEDER
FAMILY
FRIENDS
UNREQUITED LOVE

CHAPTER 1
A FUTURE CARTOONIST... AND A GREAT ONE AT THAT!

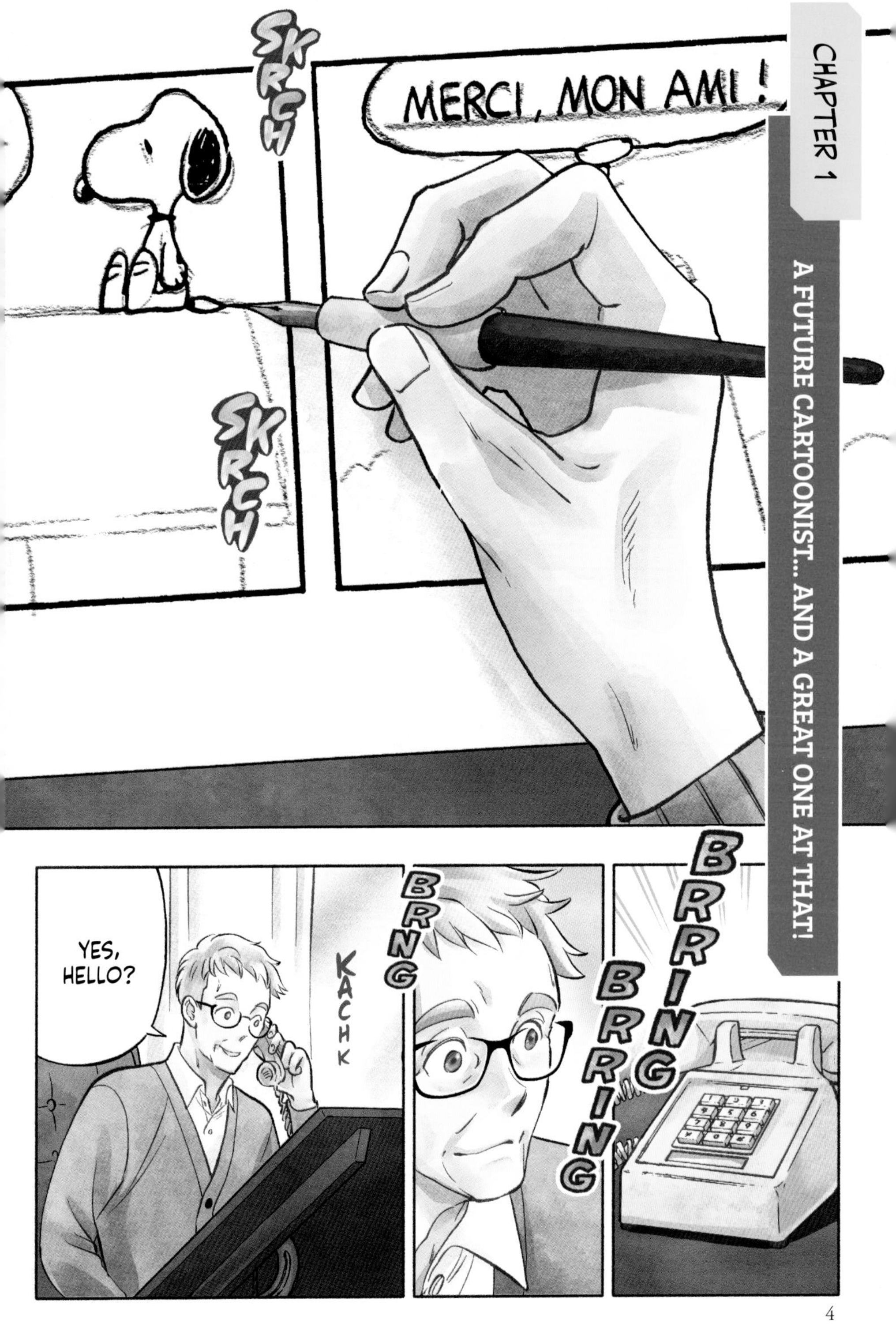

MERCI, MON AMI!
SKRCH
SKRCH
BRRRING
BRRING
BRNG
KACHK
YES, HELLO?

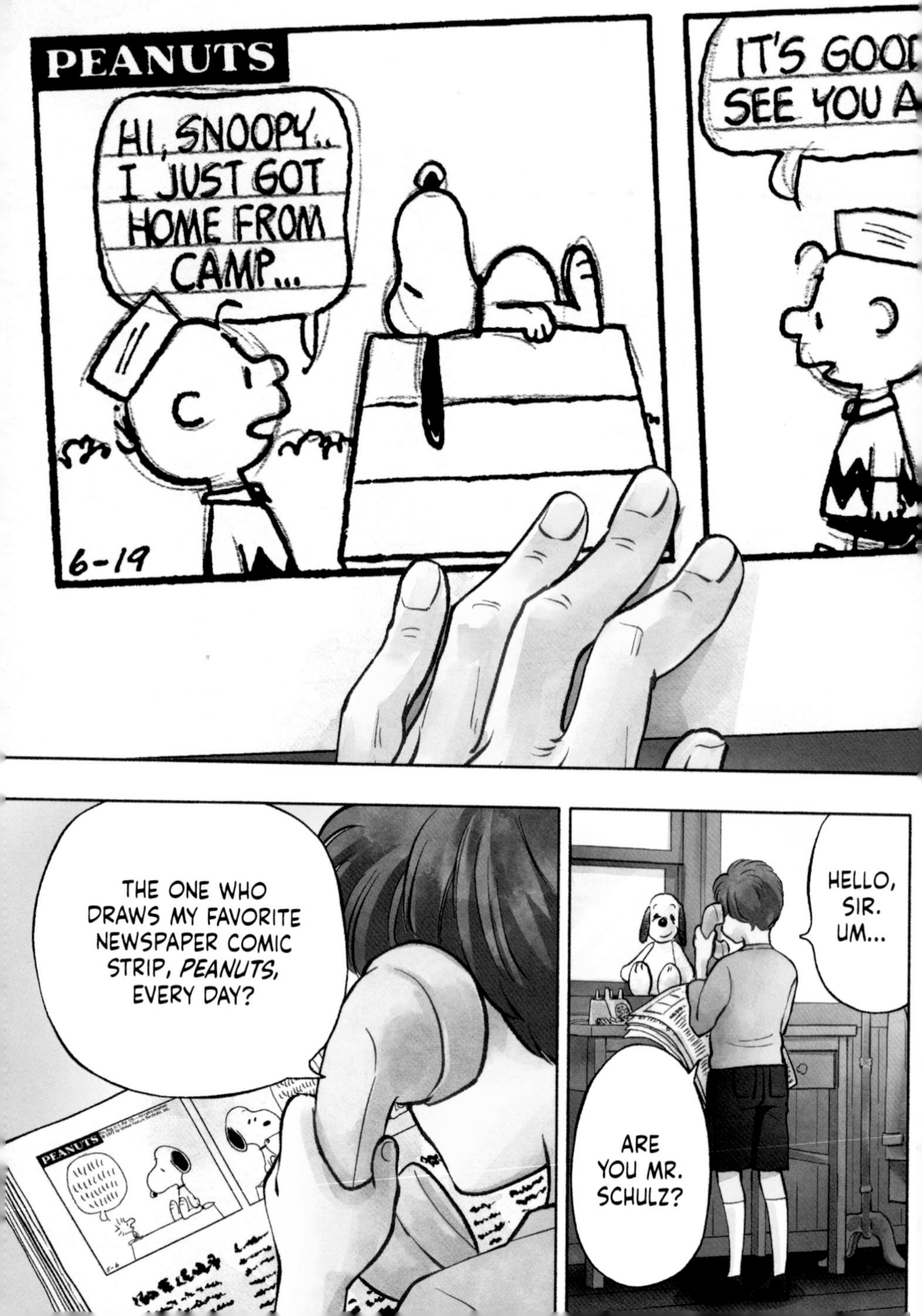
PEANUTS
IT'S GOOD SEE YOU A
HI, SNOOPY.. I JUST GOT HOME FROM CAMP...
6-19
HELLO, SIR. UM...
ARE YOU MR. SCHULZ?
THE ONE WHO DRAWS MY FAVORITE NEWSPAPER COMIC STRIP, *PEANUTS*, EVERY DAY?
PEANUTS

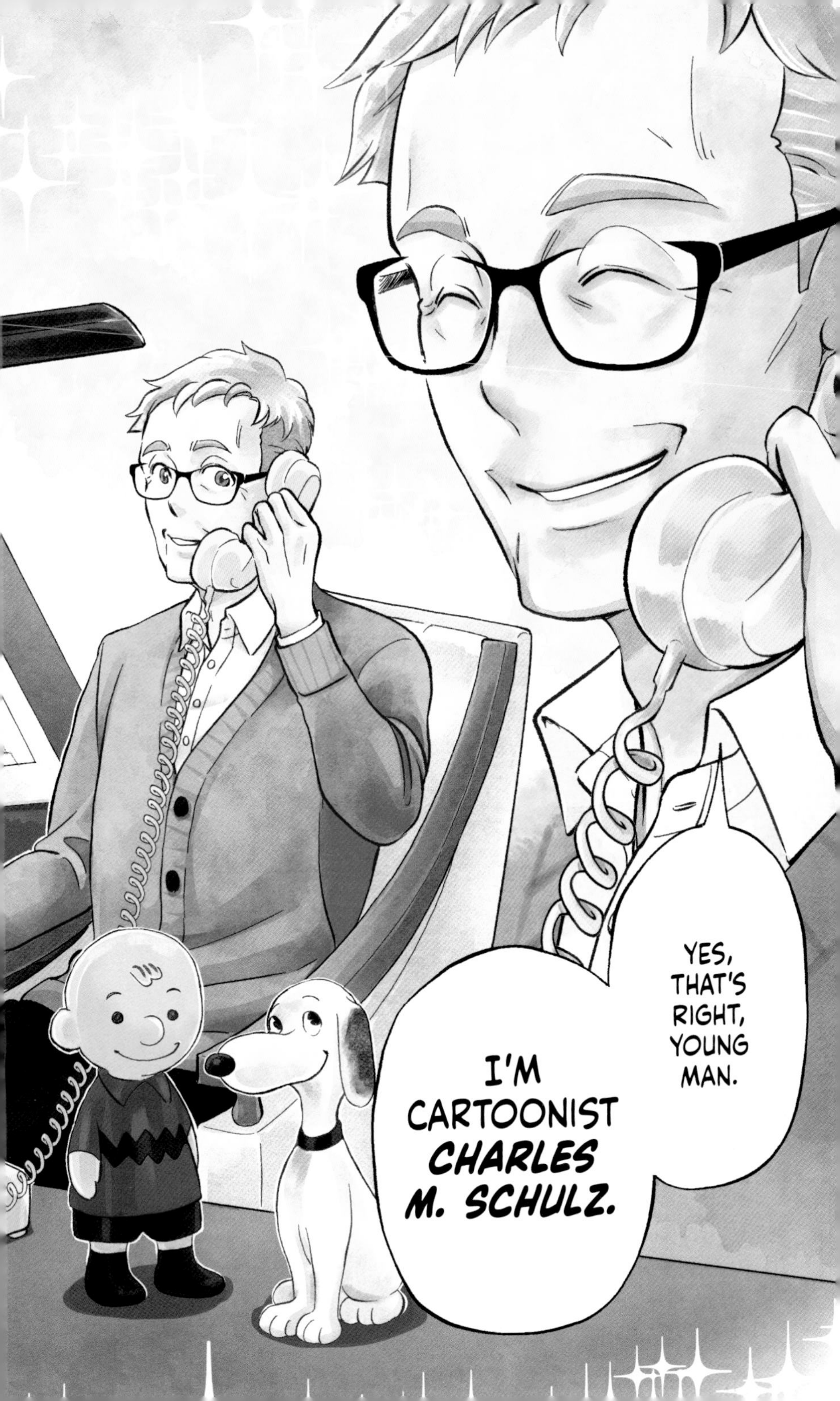
YES, THAT'S RIGHT, YOUNG MAN.
I'M CARTOONIST CHARLES M. SCHULZ.

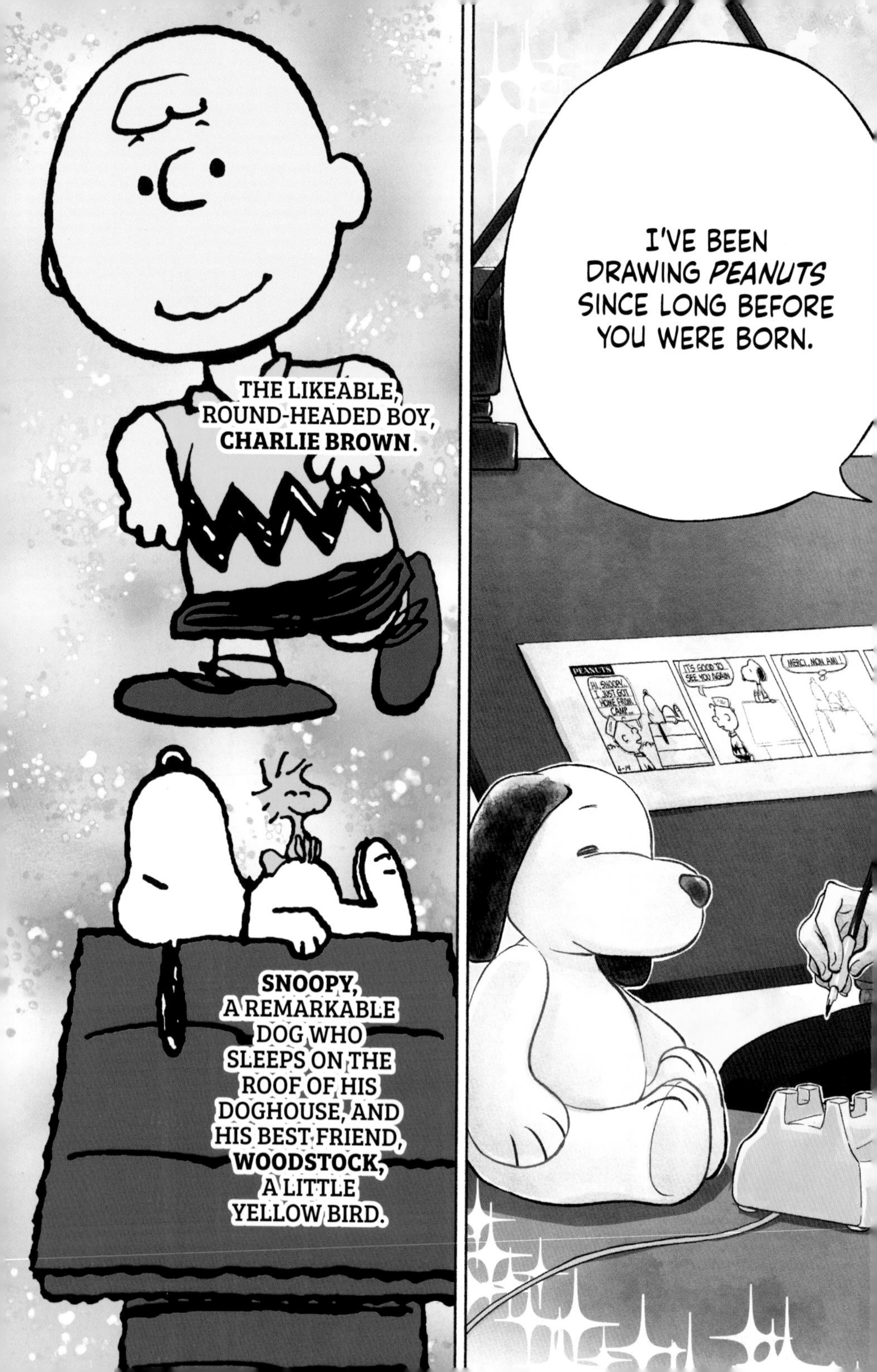
I'VE BEEN DRAWING *PEANUTS* SINCE LONG BEFORE YOU WERE BORN.
PEANUTS
HI, SNOOPY, I JUST GOT HOME FROM CAMP...
IT'S GOOD TO SEE YOU AGAIN
MERCI, MON AMI!
THE LIKEABLE, ROUND-HEADED BOY, **CHARLIE BROWN**.
SNOOPY, A REMARKABLE DOG WHO SLEEPS ON THE ROOF OF HIS DOGHOUSE, AND HIS BEST FRIEND, **WOODSTOCK**, A LITTLE YELLOW BIRD.

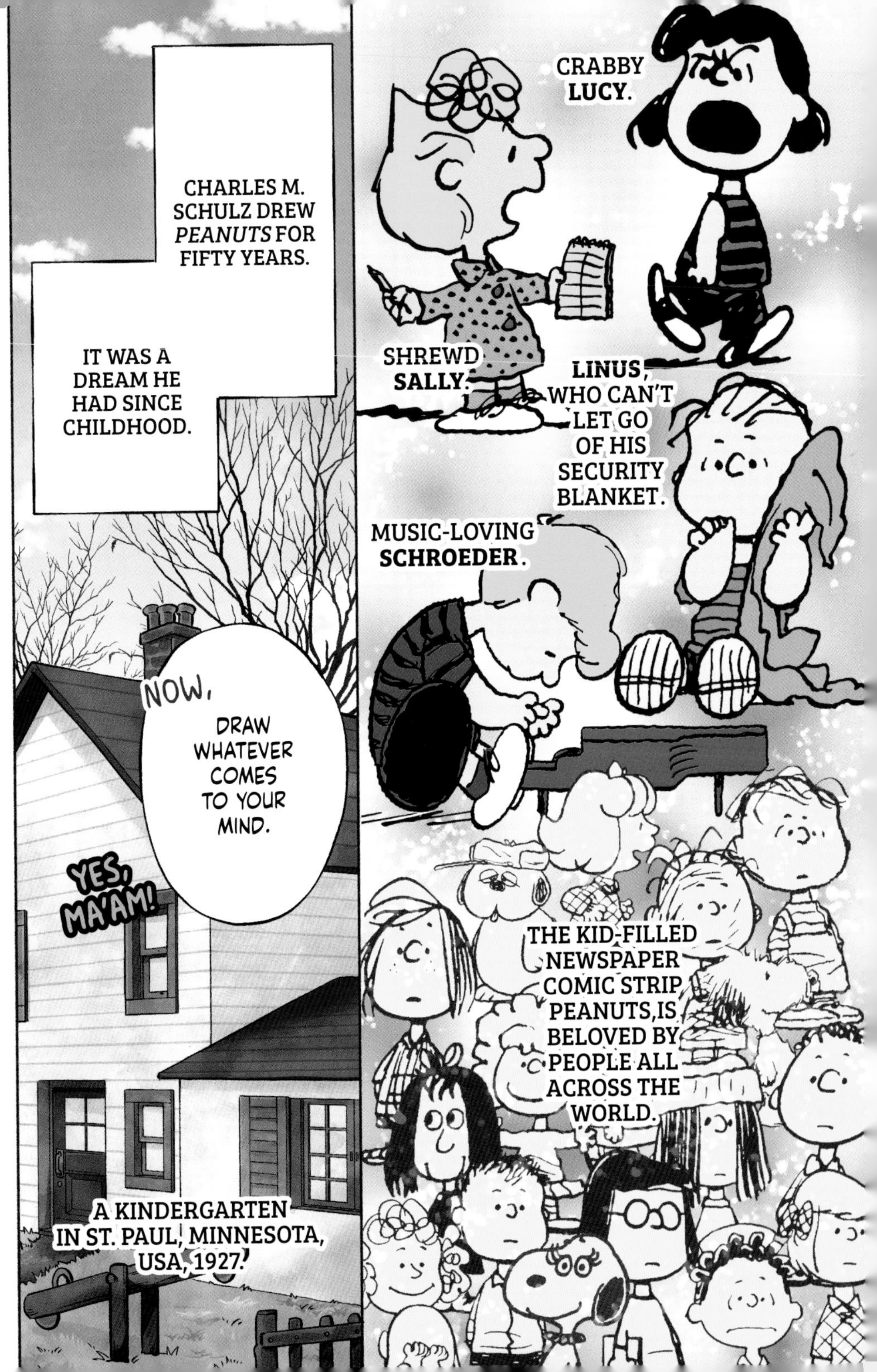
CRABBY LUCY.
SHREWD SALLY.
LINUS, WHO CAN'T LET GO OF HIS SECURITY BLANKET.
MUSIC-LOVING SCHROEDER.
THE KID-FILLED NEWSPAPER COMIC STRIP PEANUTS,IS BELOVED BY PEOPLE ALL ACROSS THE WORLD.
CHARLES M. SCHULZ DREW *PEANUTS* FOR FIFTY YEARS.
IT WAS A DREAM HE HAD SINCE CHILDHOOD.
NOW, DRAW WHATEVER COMES TO YOUR MIND.
YES, MA'AM!
A KINDERGARTEN IN ST. PAUL, MINNESOTA, USA, 1927.

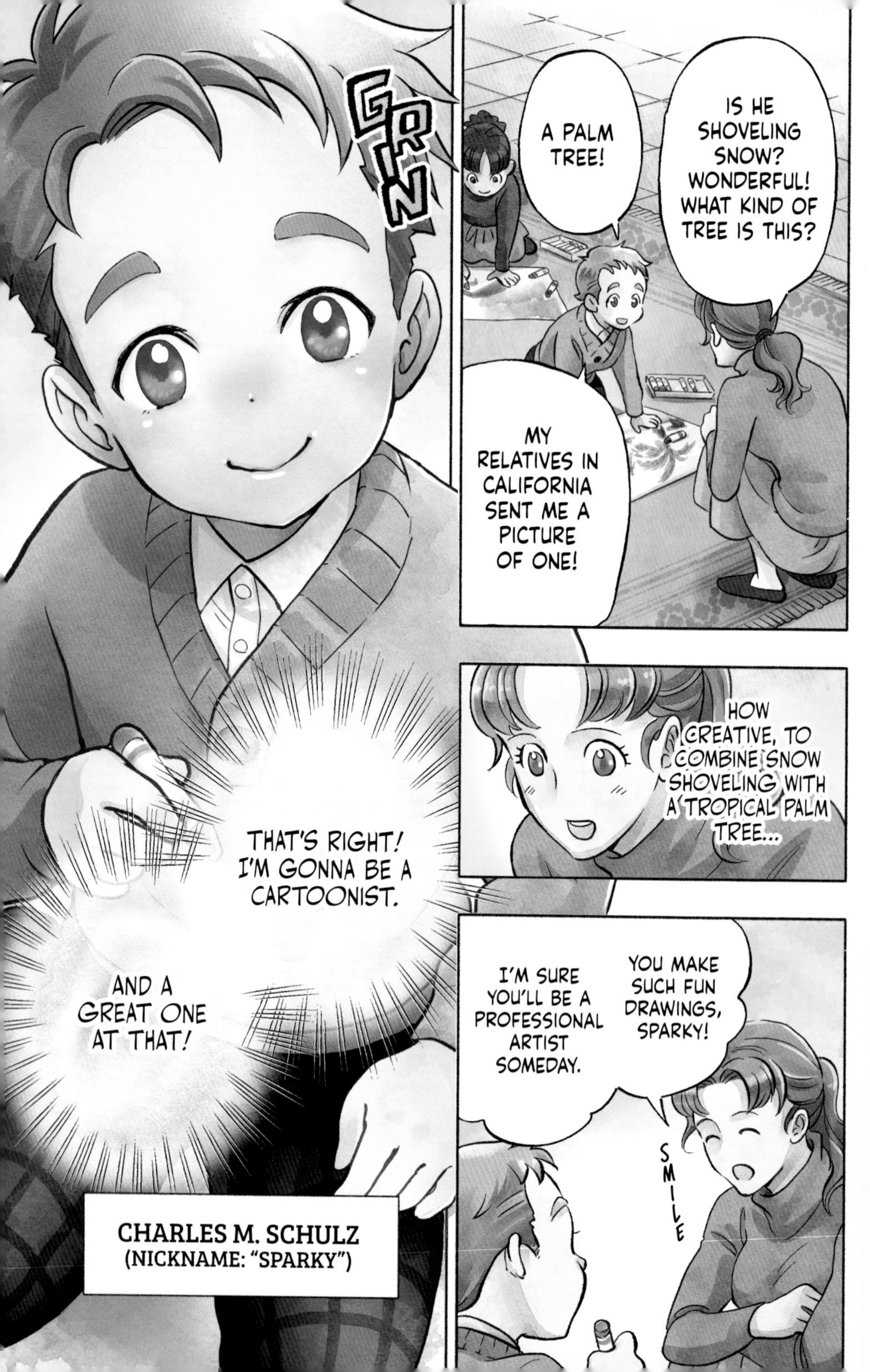
IS HE SHOVELING SNOW? WONDERFUL! WHAT KIND OF TREE IS THIS?
A PALM TREE!
MY RELATIVES IN CALIFORNIA SENT ME A PICTURE OF ONE!
HOW CREATIVE, TO COMBINE SNOW SHOVELING WITH A TROPICAL PALM TREE...
YOU MAKE SUCH FUN DRAWINGS, SPARKY!
I'M SURE YOU'LL BE A PROFESSIONAL ARTIST SOMEDAY.
SMILE
GRIN
THAT'S RIGHT! I'M GONNA BE A CARTOONIST.
AND A GREAT ONE AT THAT!
CHARLES M. SCHULZ
(NICKNAME: "SPARKY")

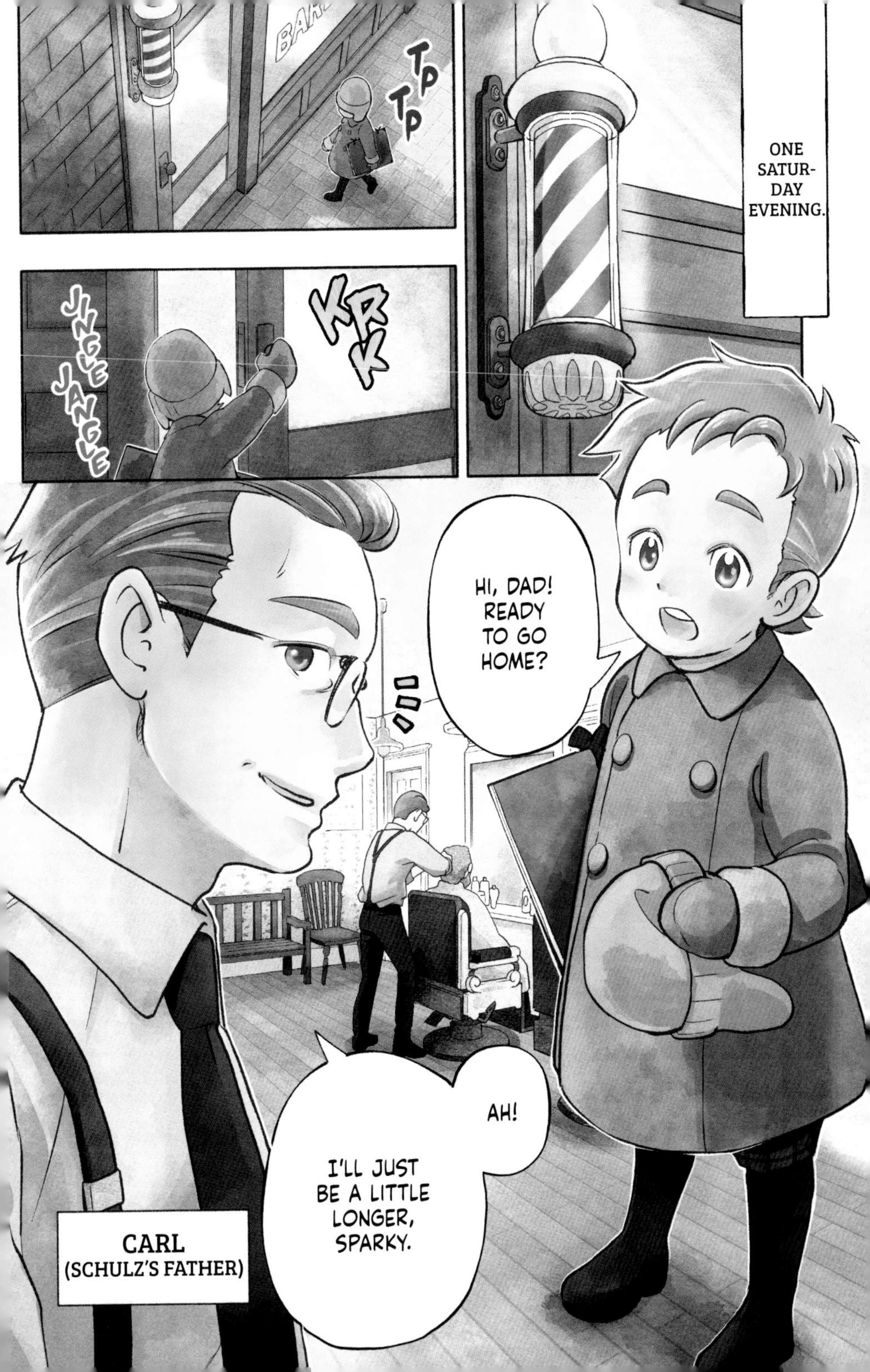
ONE SATUR-DAY EVENING.
TP TP
KRK
JINGLE JANGLE
HI, DAD! READY TO GO HOME?
AH!
I'LL JUST BE A LITTLE LONGER, SPARKY.
CARL (SCHULZ'S FATHER)

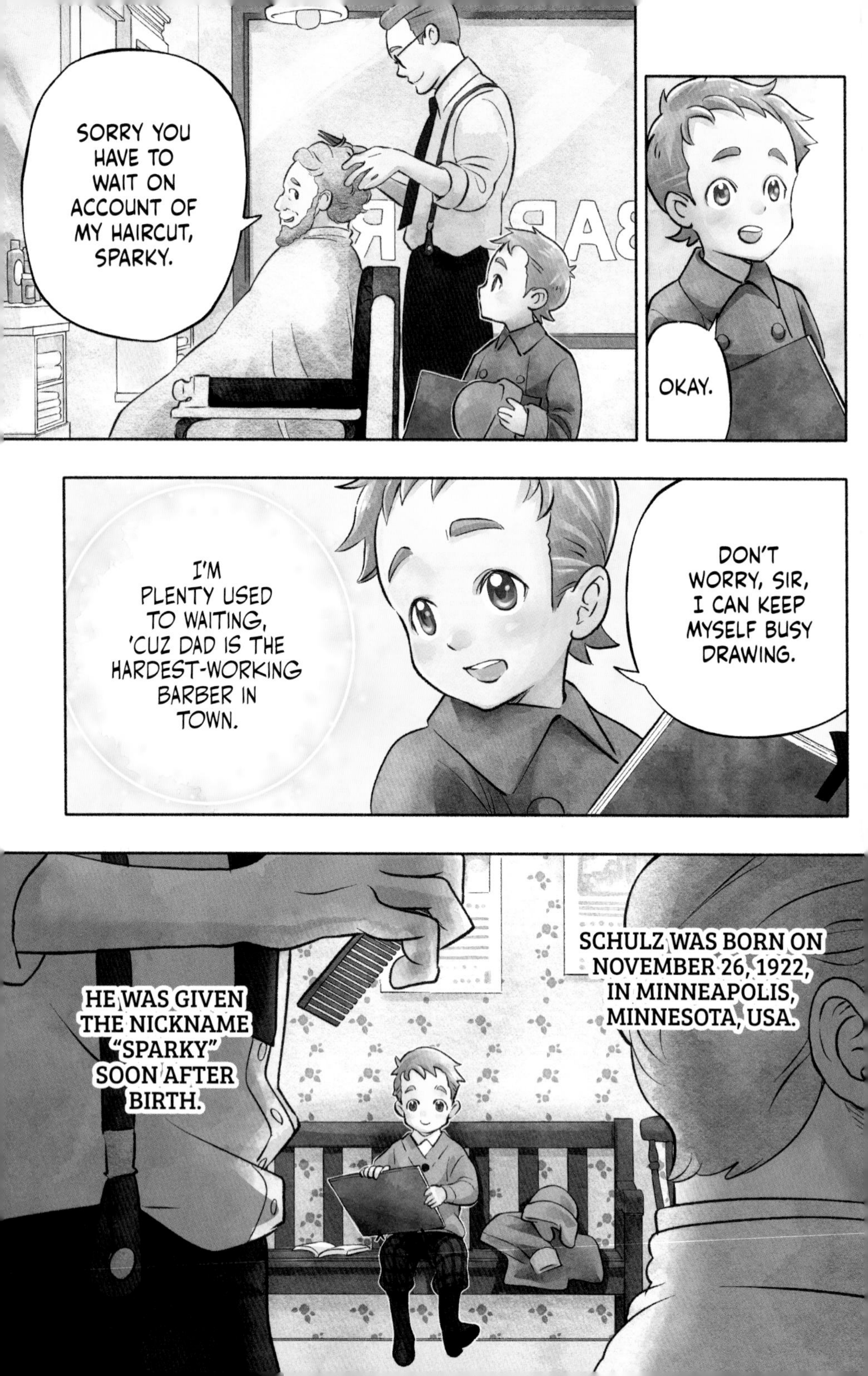
OKAY.
SORRY YOU HAVE TO WAIT ON ACCOUNT OF MY HAIRCUT, SPARKY.
DON'T WORRY, SIR, I CAN KEEP MYSELF BUSY DRAWING.
I'M PLENTY USED TO WAITING, 'CUZ DAD IS THE HARDEST-WORKING BARBER IN TOWN.
SCHULZ WAS BORN ON NOVEMBER 26, 1922, IN MINNEAPOLIS, MINNESOTA, USA.
HE WAS GIVEN THE NICKNAME "SPARKY" SOON AFTER BIRTH.

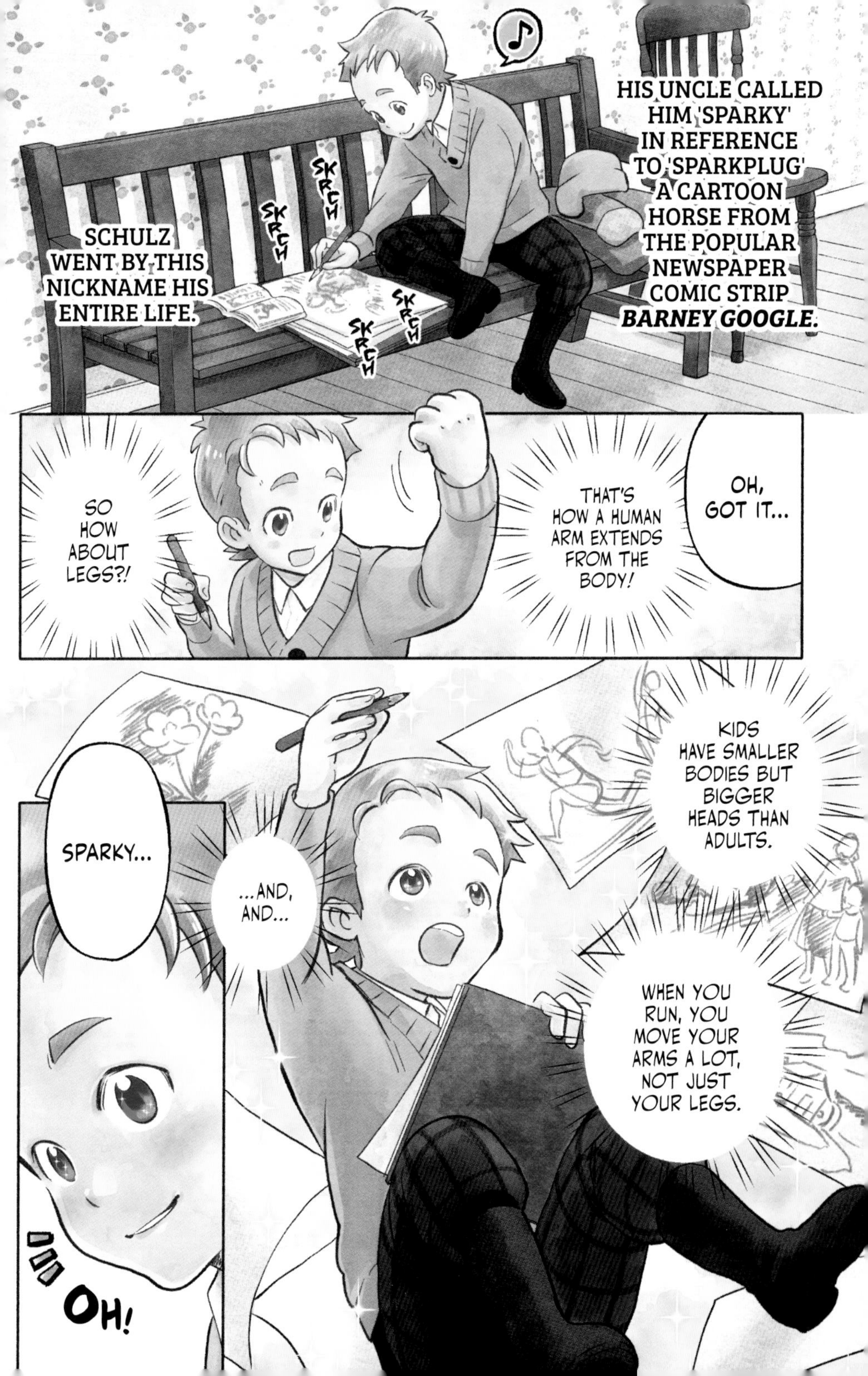
♪
HIS UNCLE CALLED HIM 'SPARKY' IN REFERENCE TO 'SPARKPLUG' A CARTOON HORSE FROM THE POPULAR NEWSPAPER COMIC STRIP ***BARNEY GOOGLE.***
SKRCH
SKRCH
SCHULZ WENT BY THIS NICKNAME HIS ENTIRE LIFE.
SKRCH
SKRCH
OH, GOT IT...
THAT'S HOW A HUMAN ARM EXTENDS FROM THE BODY!
SO HOW ABOUT LEGS?!
KIDS HAVE SMALLER BODIES BUT BIGGER HEADS THAN ADULTS.
...AND, AND...
WHEN YOU RUN, YOU MOVE YOUR ARMS A LOT, NOT JUST YOUR LEGS.
SPARKY...
OH!

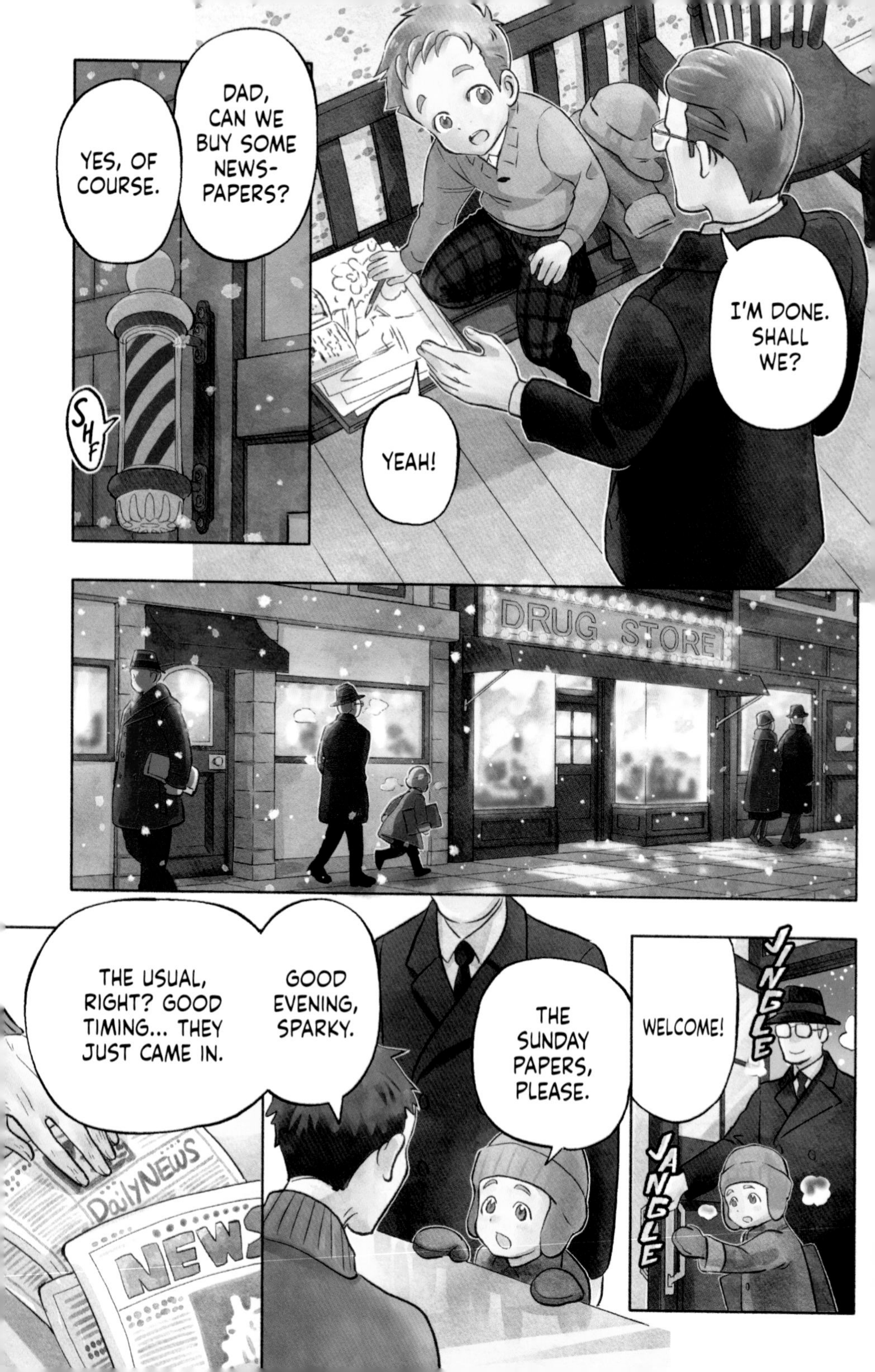
I'M DONE. SHALL WE?
YEAH!
DAD, CAN WE BUY SOME NEWS-PAPERS?
YES, OF COURSE.
SHF
DRUG STORE
JINGLE
WELCOME!
JANGLE
THE SUNDAY PAPERS, PLEASE.
GOOD EVENING, SPARKY.
THE USUAL, RIGHT? GOOD TIMING... THEY JUST CAME IN.
DailyNEWS
NEWS

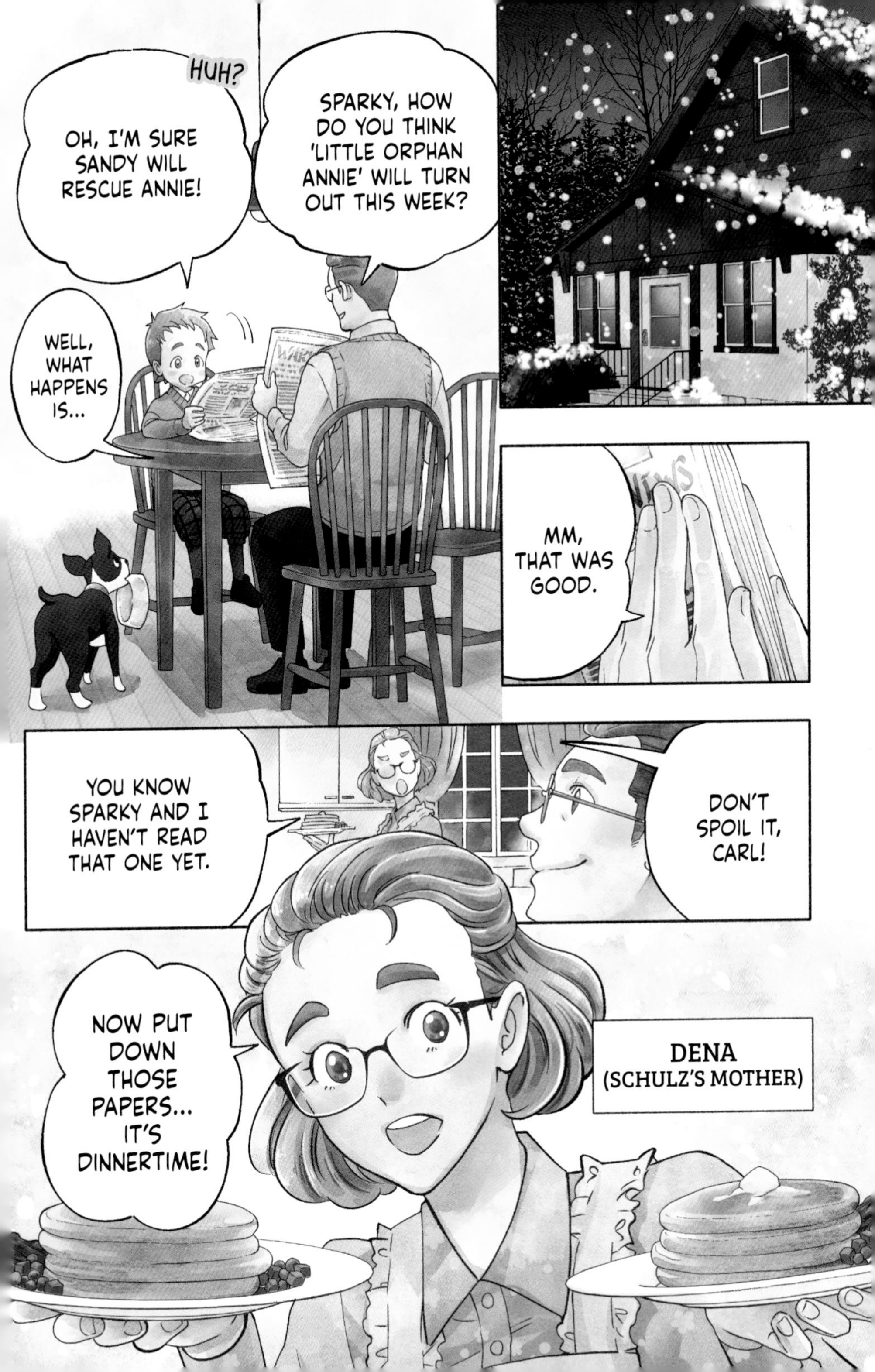
MM, THAT WAS GOOD.
SPARKY, HOW DO YOU THINK 'LITTLE ORPHAN ANNIE' WILL TURN OUT THIS WEEK?
HUH?
OH, I'M SURE SANDY WILL RESCUE ANNIE!
WELL, WHAT HAPPENS IS...
DON'T SPOIL IT, CARL!
YOU KNOW SPARKY AND I HAVEN'T READ THAT ONE YET.
DENA (SCHULZ'S MOTHER)
NOW PUT DOWN THOSE PAPERS... IT'S DINNERTIME!

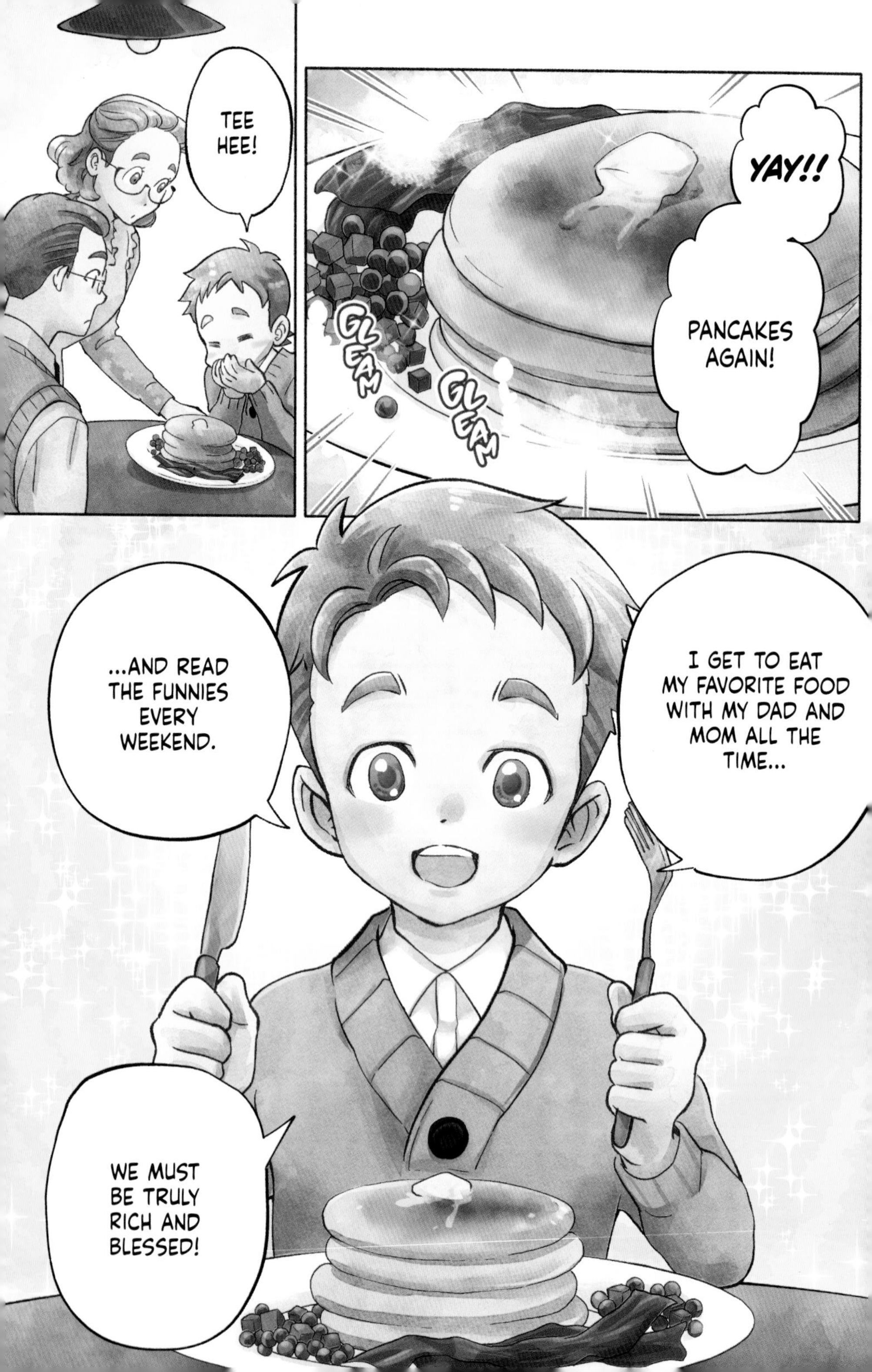
YAY!!
PANCAKES AGAIN!
GLEAM
GLEAM
TEE HEE!
I GET TO EAT MY FAVORITE FOOD WITH MY DAD AND MOM ALL THE TIME...
...AND READ THE FUNNIES EVERY WEEKEND.
WE MUST BE TRULY RICH AND BLESSED!

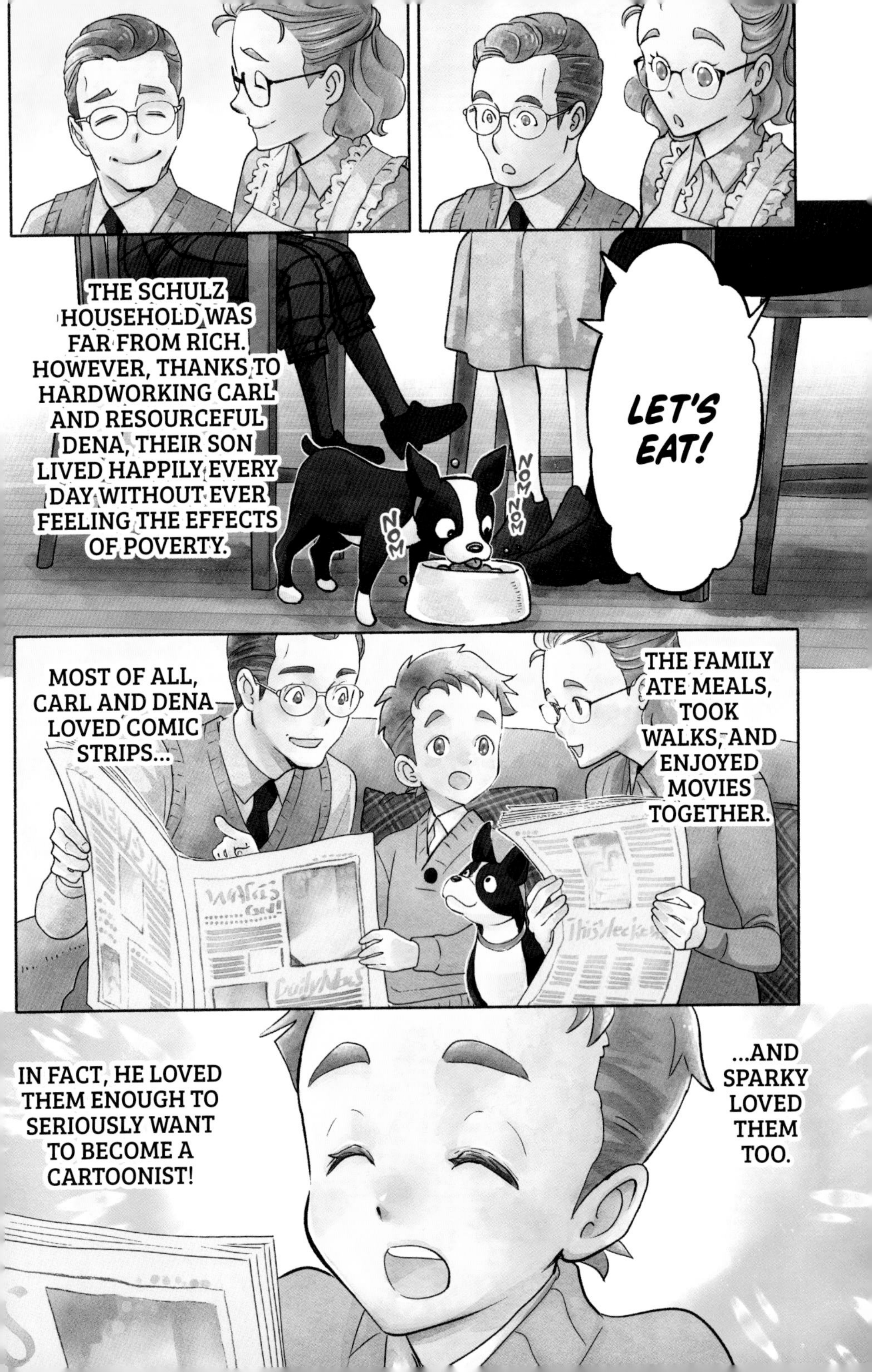
LET'S EAT!
NOM NOM
NOM
THE SCHULZ HOUSEHOLD WAS FAR FROM RICH. HOWEVER, THANKS TO HARDWORKING CARL AND RESOURCEFUL DENA, THEIR SON LIVED HAPPILY EVERY DAY WITHOUT EVER FEELING THE EFFECTS OF POVERTY.
THE FAMILY ATE MEALS, TOOK WALKS, AND ENJOYED MOVIES TOGETHER.
MOST OF ALL, CARL AND DENA LOVED COMIC STRIPS...
...AND SPARKY LOVED THEM TOO.
IN FACT, HE LOVED THEM ENOUGH TO SERIOUSLY WANT TO BECOME A CARTOONIST!

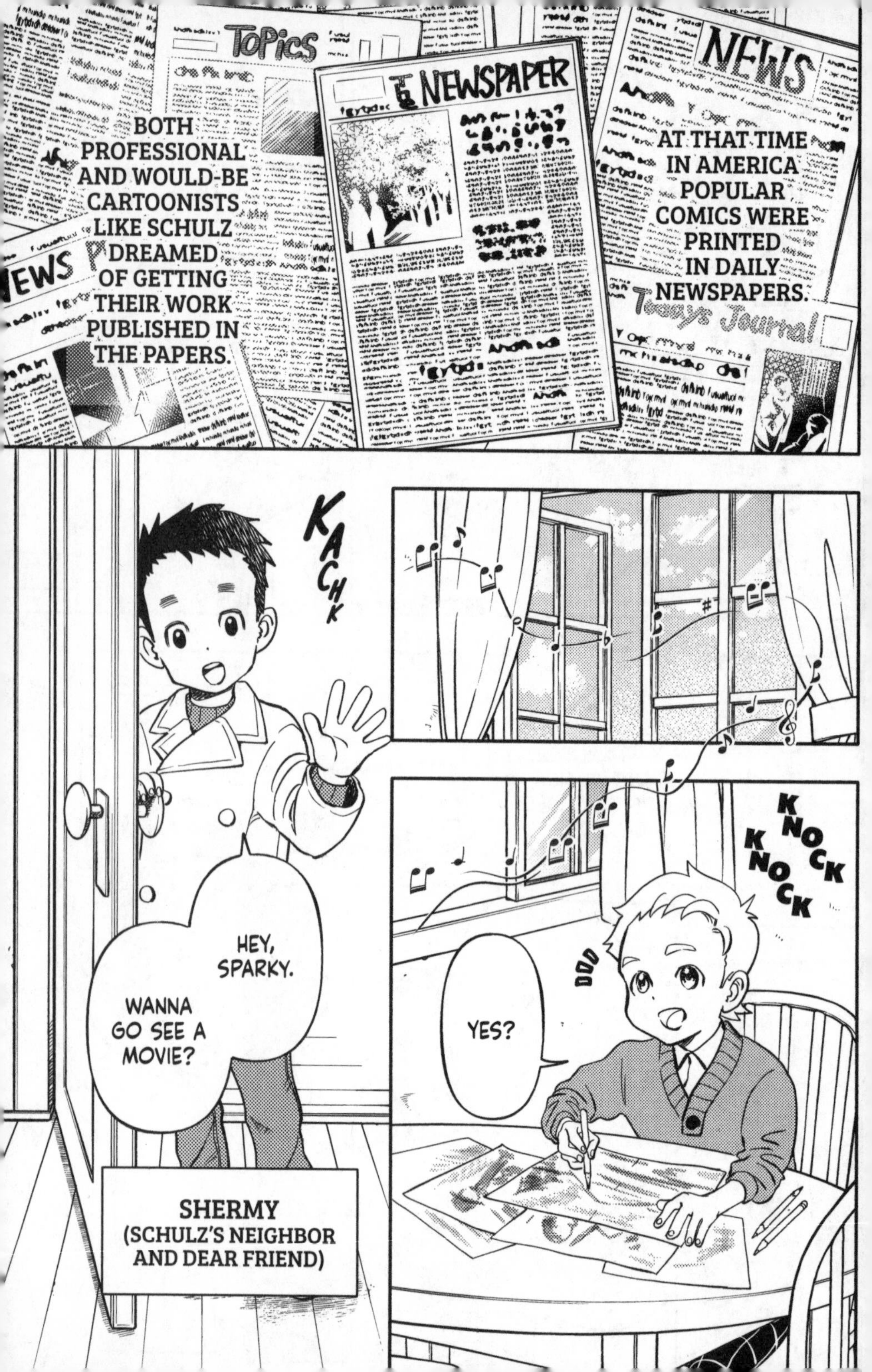
NEWS
THE NEWSPAPER
TOPICS
AT THAT TIME IN AMERICA POPULAR COMICS WERE PRINTED IN DAILY NEWSPAPERS.
BOTH PROFESSIONAL AND WOULD-BE CARTOONISTS LIKE SCHULZ DREAMED OF GETTING THEIR WORK PUBLISHED IN THE PAPERS.
KNOCK KNOCK
YES?
KACHK
HEY, SPARKY.
WANNA GO SEE A MOVIE?
SHERMY (SCHULZ'S NEIGHBOR AND DEAR FRIEND)

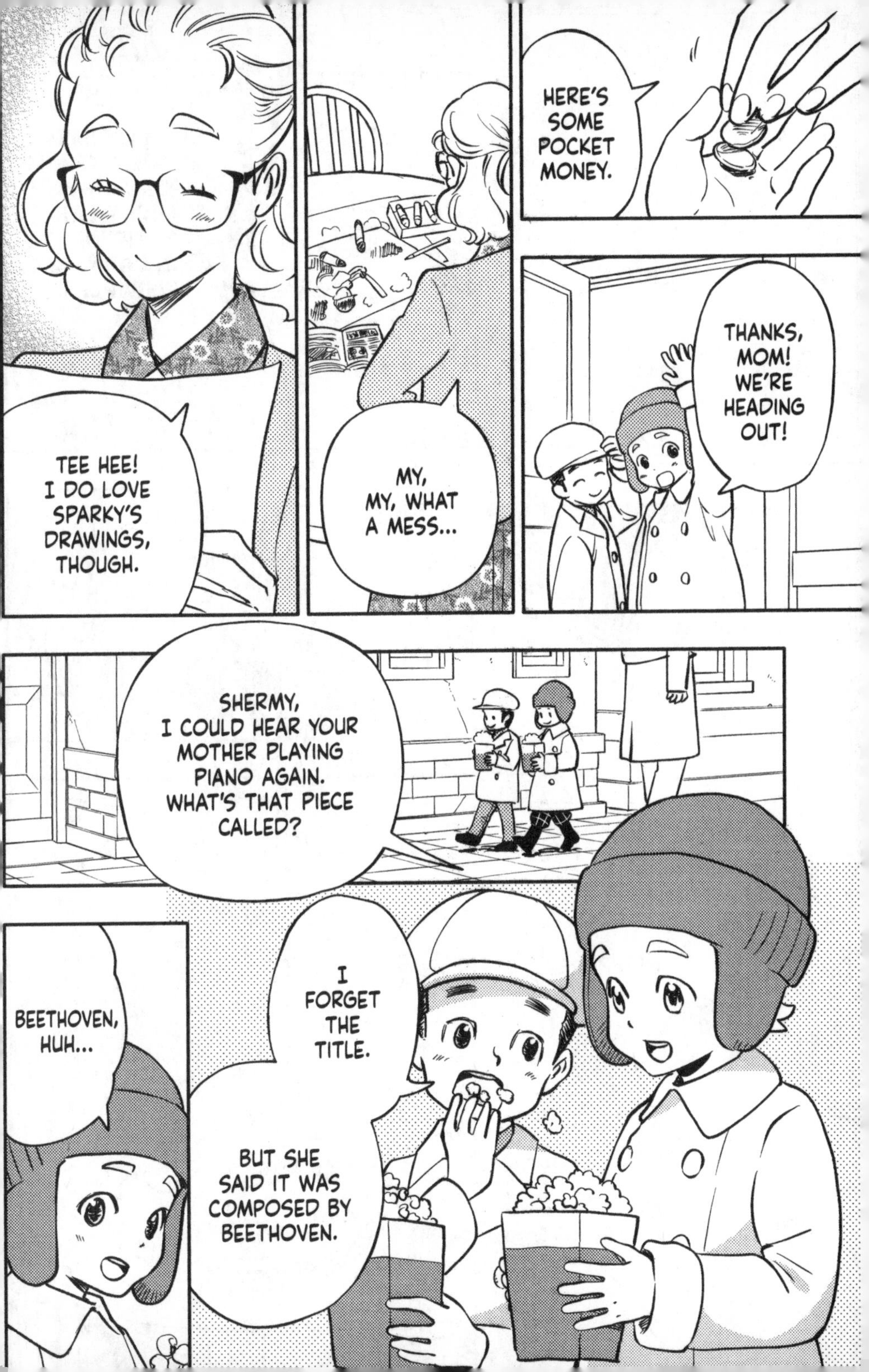
HERE'S SOME POCKET MONEY.
THANKS, MOM! WE'RE HEADING OUT!
MY, MY, WHAT A MESS...
TEE HEE! I DO LOVE SPARKY'S DRAWINGS, THOUGH.
SHERMY, I COULD HEAR YOUR MOTHER PLAYING PIANO AGAIN. WHAT'S THAT PIECE CALLED?
I FORGET THE TITLE.
BUT SHE SAID IT WAS COMPOSED BY BEETHOVEN.
BEETHOVEN, HUH...

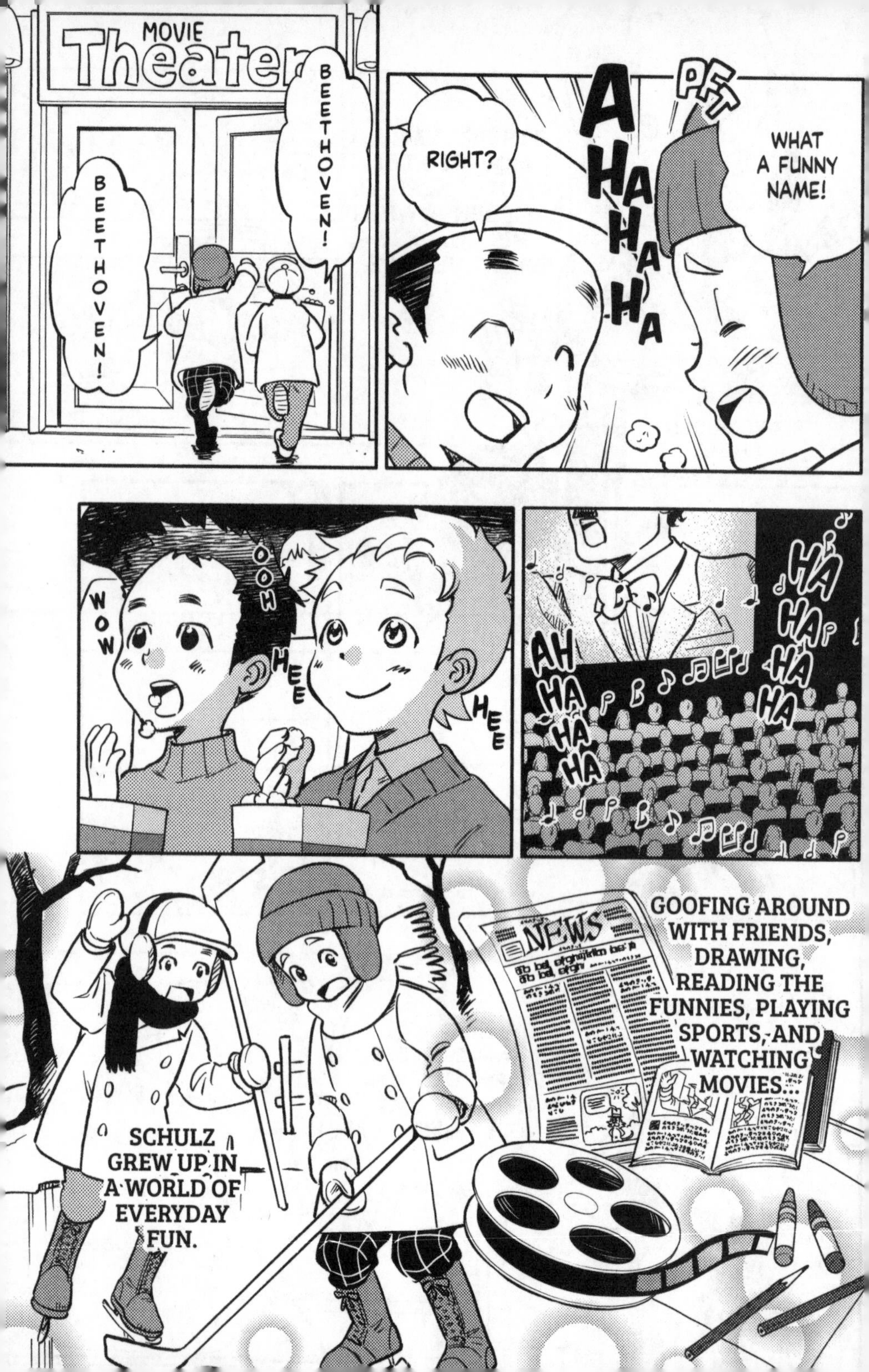
PFT
WHAT A FUNNY NAME!
AHAHAHAHA
RIGHT?
MOVIE Theater
BEETHOVEN!
BEETHOVEN!
HAHAHAHAHA
AHHAHAHAHA
HEE
OOH
HEE
WOW
GOOFING AROUND WITH FRIENDS, DRAWING, READING THE FUNNIES, PLAYING SPORTS, AND WATCHING MOVIES...
NEWS
SCHULZ GREW UP IN A WORLD OF EVERYDAY FUN.

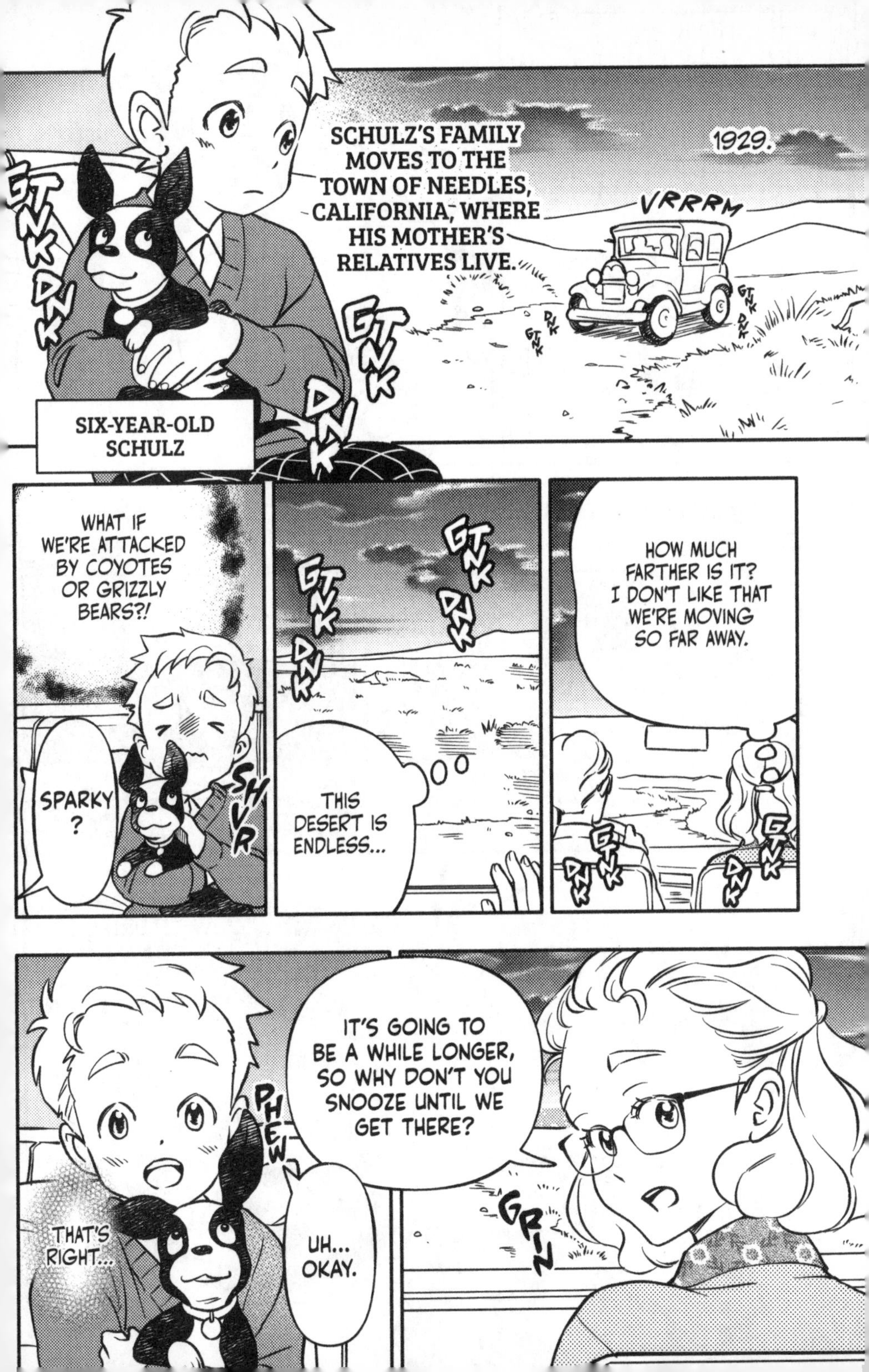
1929.
VRRRM
SCHULZ'S FAMILY MOVES TO THE TOWN OF NEEDLES, CALIFORNIA, WHERE HIS MOTHER'S RELATIVES LIVE.
GTNK DNK
GTNK DNK
SIX-YEAR-OLD SCHULZ
HOW MUCH FARTHER IS IT? I DON'T LIKE THAT WE'RE MOVING SO FAR AWAY.
GTNK DNK
GTNK DNK
GTNK DNK
GTNK DNK
THIS DESERT IS ENDLESS...
WHAT IF WE'RE ATTACKED BY COYOTES OR GRIZZLY BEARS?!
SHVR
SPARKY ?
IT'S GOING TO BE A WHILE LONGER, SO WHY DON'T YOU SNOOZE UNTIL WE GET THERE?
GRIN
PHEW
UH... OKAY.
THAT'S RIGHT...

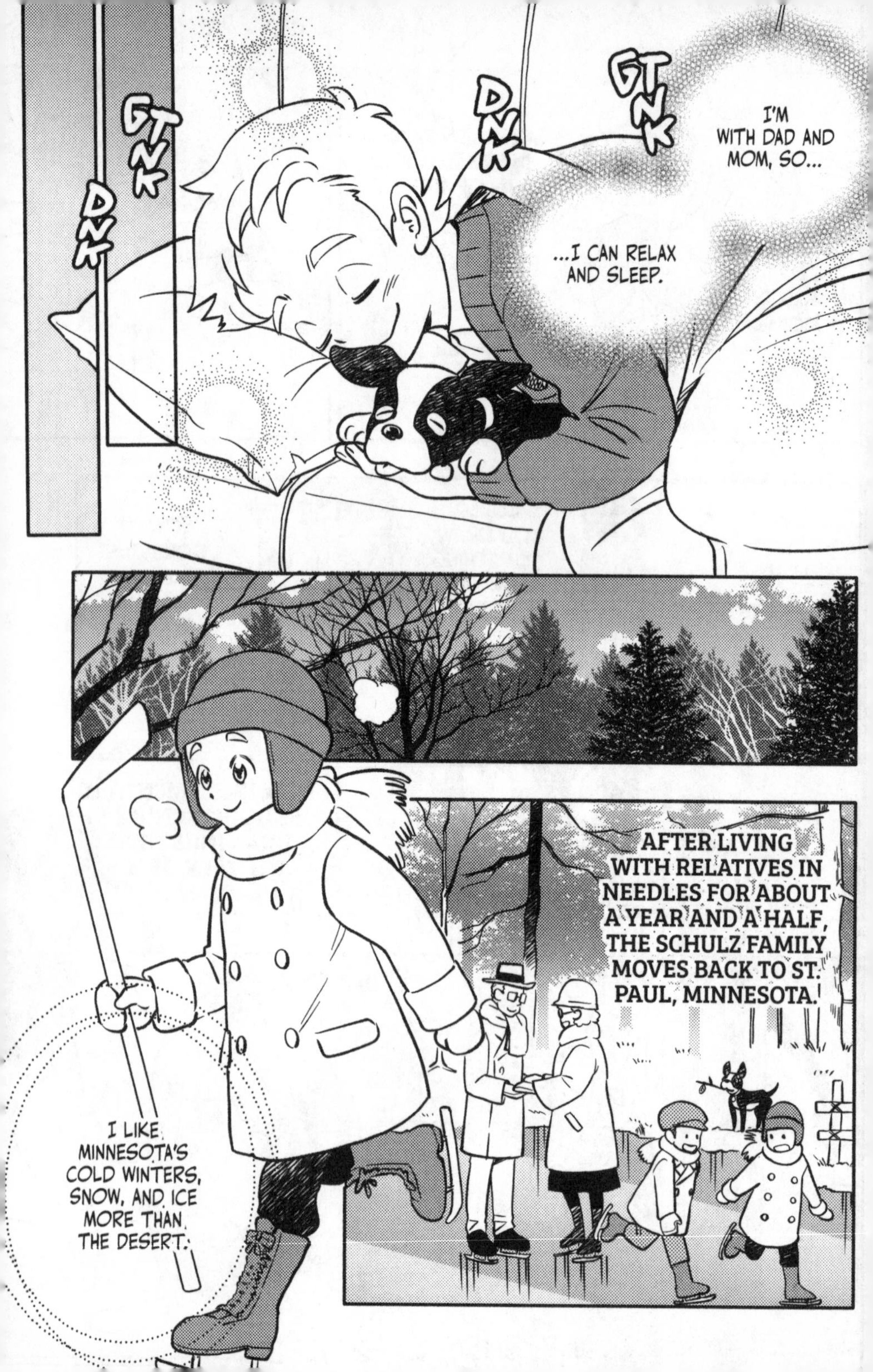
GTNK
I'M WITH DAD AND MOM, SO...
DNK
...I CAN RELAX AND SLEEP.
GTNK
DNK
AFTER LIVING WITH RELATIVES IN NEEDLES FOR ABOUT A YEAR AND A HALF, THE SCHULZ FAMILY MOVES BACK TO ST. PAUL, MINNESOTA.
I LIKE MINNESOTA'S COLD WINTERS, SNOW, AND ICE MORE THAN THE DESERT.

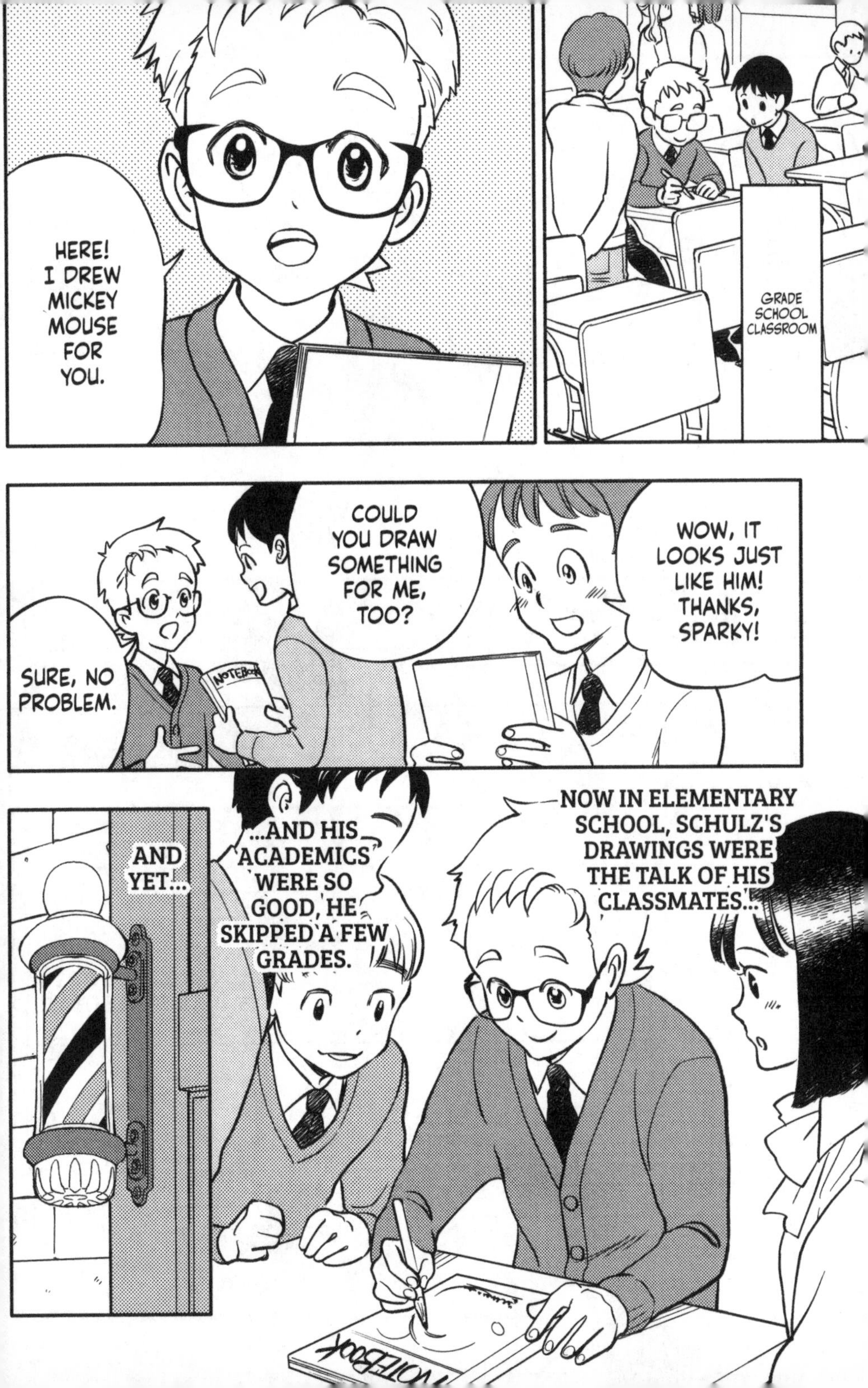
GRADE SCHOOL CLASSROOM
HERE! I DREW MICKEY MOUSE FOR YOU.
WOW, IT LOOKS JUST LIKE HIM! THANKS, SPARKY!
COULD YOU DRAW SOMETHING FOR ME, TOO?
SURE, NO PROBLEM.
NOW IN ELEMENTARY SCHOOL, SCHULZ'S DRAWINGS WERE THE TALK OF HIS CLASSMATES...
...AND HIS ACADEMICS WERE SO GOOD, HE SKIPPED A FEW GRADES.
AND YET...

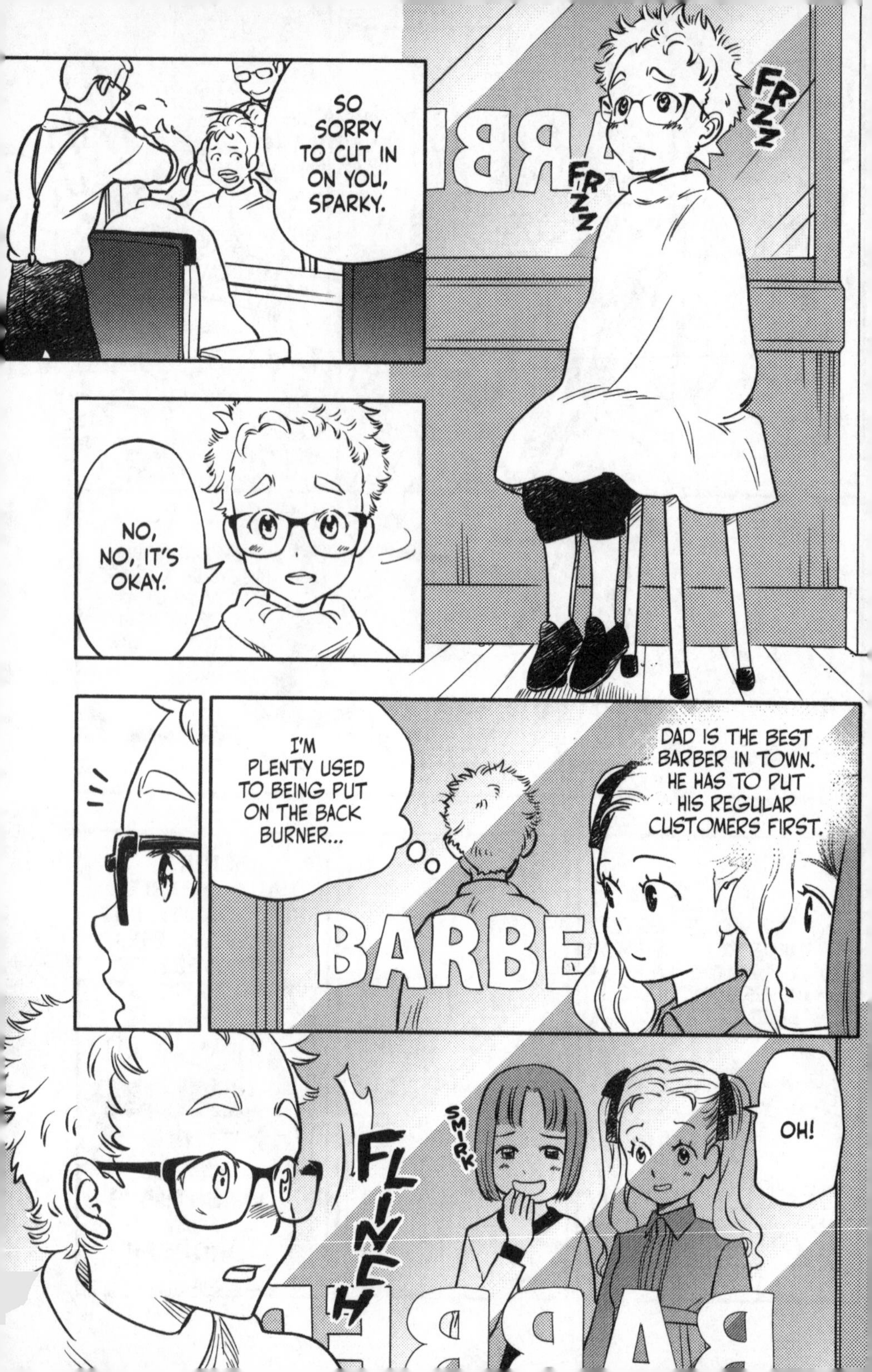
FRZZ
FRZZ
SO SORRY TO CUT IN ON YOU, SPARKY.
NO, NO, IT'S OKAY.
DAD IS THE BEST BARBER IN TOWN. HE HAS TO PUT HIS REGULAR CUSTOMERS FIRST.
I'M PLENTY USED TO BEING PUT ON THE BACK BURNER...
BARBE
OH!
SMIRK
FLINCH

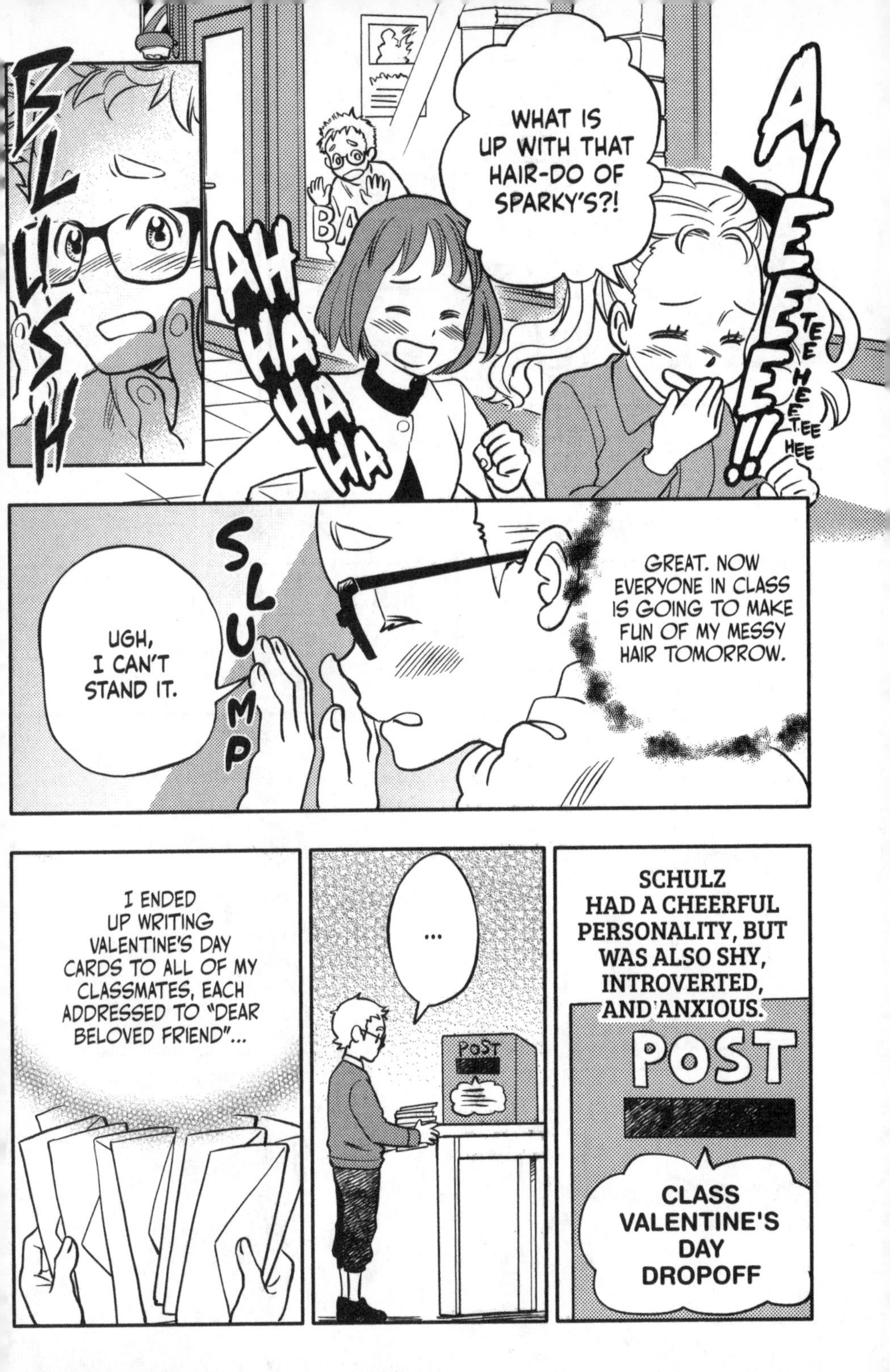
AIEEEEE!!
TEE HEE HEE TEE HEE
WHAT IS UP WITH THAT HAIR-DO OF SPARKY'S?!
AH HA HA HA HA
BA
BLUSH
GREAT. NOW EVERYONE IN CLASS IS GOING TO MAKE FUN OF MY MESSY HAIR TOMORROW.
SLUMP
UGH, I CAN'T STAND IT.
SCHULZ HAD A CHEERFUL PERSONALITY, BUT WAS ALSO SHY, INTROVERTED, AND ANXIOUS.
POST
CLASS VALENTINE'S DAY DROPOFF
...
POST
I ENDED UP WRITING VALENTINE'S DAY CARDS TO ALL OF MY CLASSMATES, EACH ADDRESSED TO "DEAR BELOVED FRIEND"...

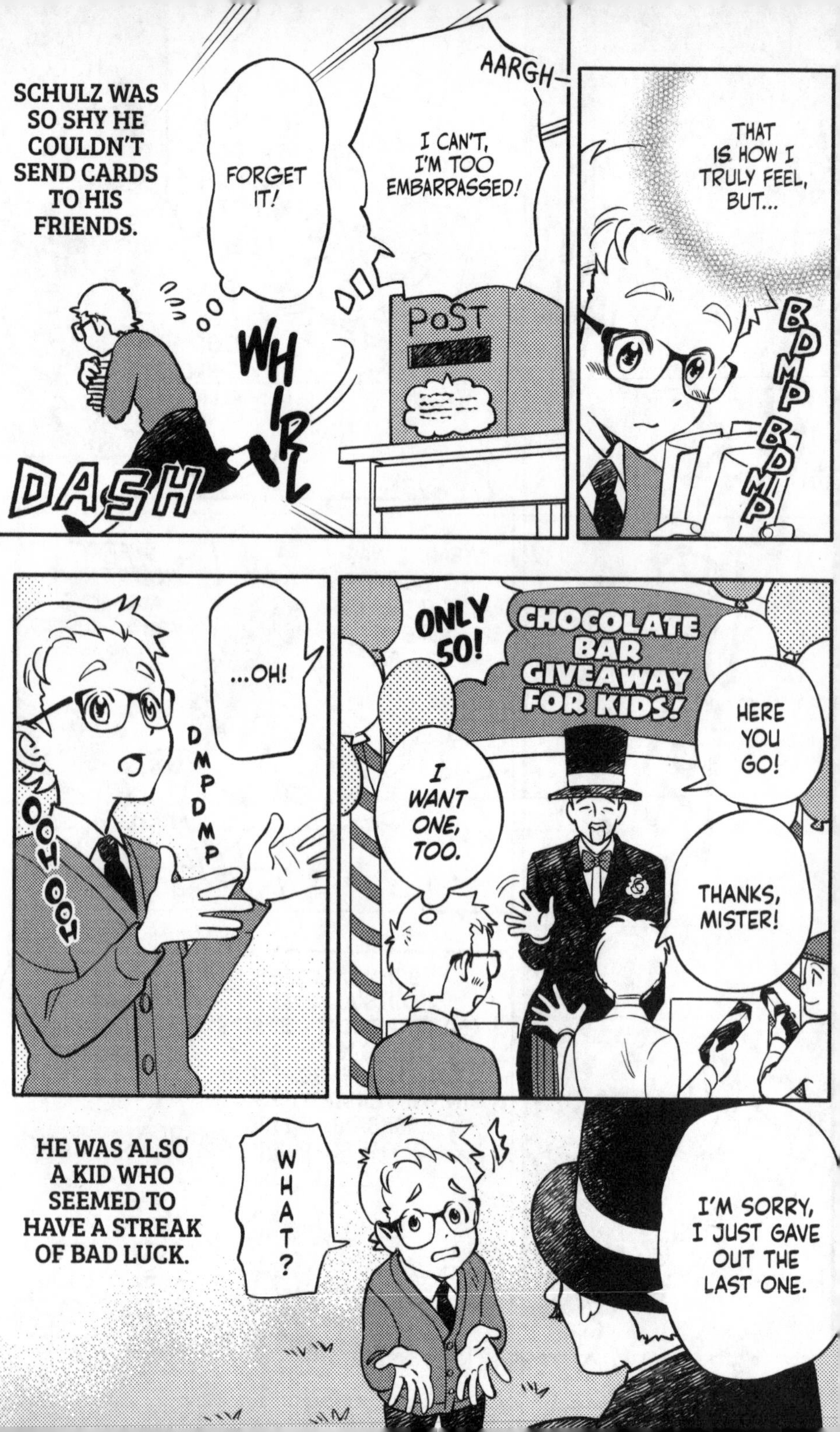
THAT IS HOW I TRULY FEEL, BUT...
BDMP BDMP
AARGH—
I CAN'T, I'M TOO EMBARRASSED!
FORGET IT!
SCHULZ WAS SO SHY HE COULDN'T SEND CARDS TO HIS FRIENDS.
POST
WHIRL
DASH
CHOCOLATE BAR GIVEAWAY FOR KIDS!
ONLY 50!
HERE YOU GO!
THANKS, MISTER!
I WANT ONE, TOO.
...OH!
DMP DMP
OOH OOH
I'M SORRY, I JUST GAVE OUT THE LAST ONE.
WHAT?
HE WAS ALSO A KID WHO SEEMED TO HAVE A STREAK OF BAD LUCK.

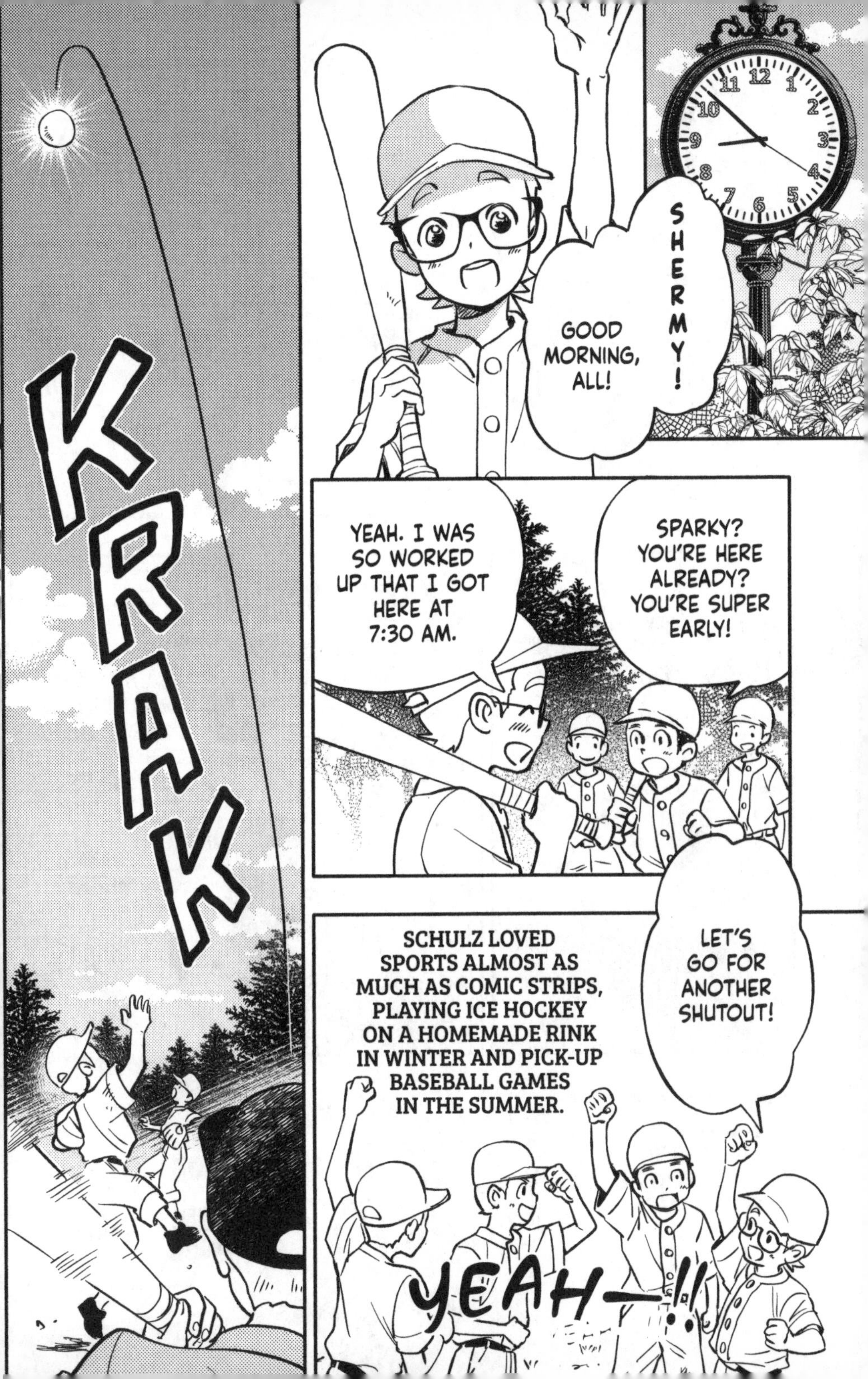
SHERMY!
GOOD MORNING, ALL!
SPARKY? YOU'RE HERE ALREADY? YOU'RE SUPER EARLY!
YEAH. I WAS SO WORKED UP THAT I GOT HERE AT 7:30 AM.
LET'S GO FOR ANOTHER SHUTOUT!
SCHULZ LOVED SPORTS ALMOST AS MUCH AS COMIC STRIPS, PLAYING ICE HOCKEY ON A HOMEMADE RINK IN WINTER AND PICK-UP BASEBALL GAMES IN THE SUMMER.
YEAH—!!
KRAK

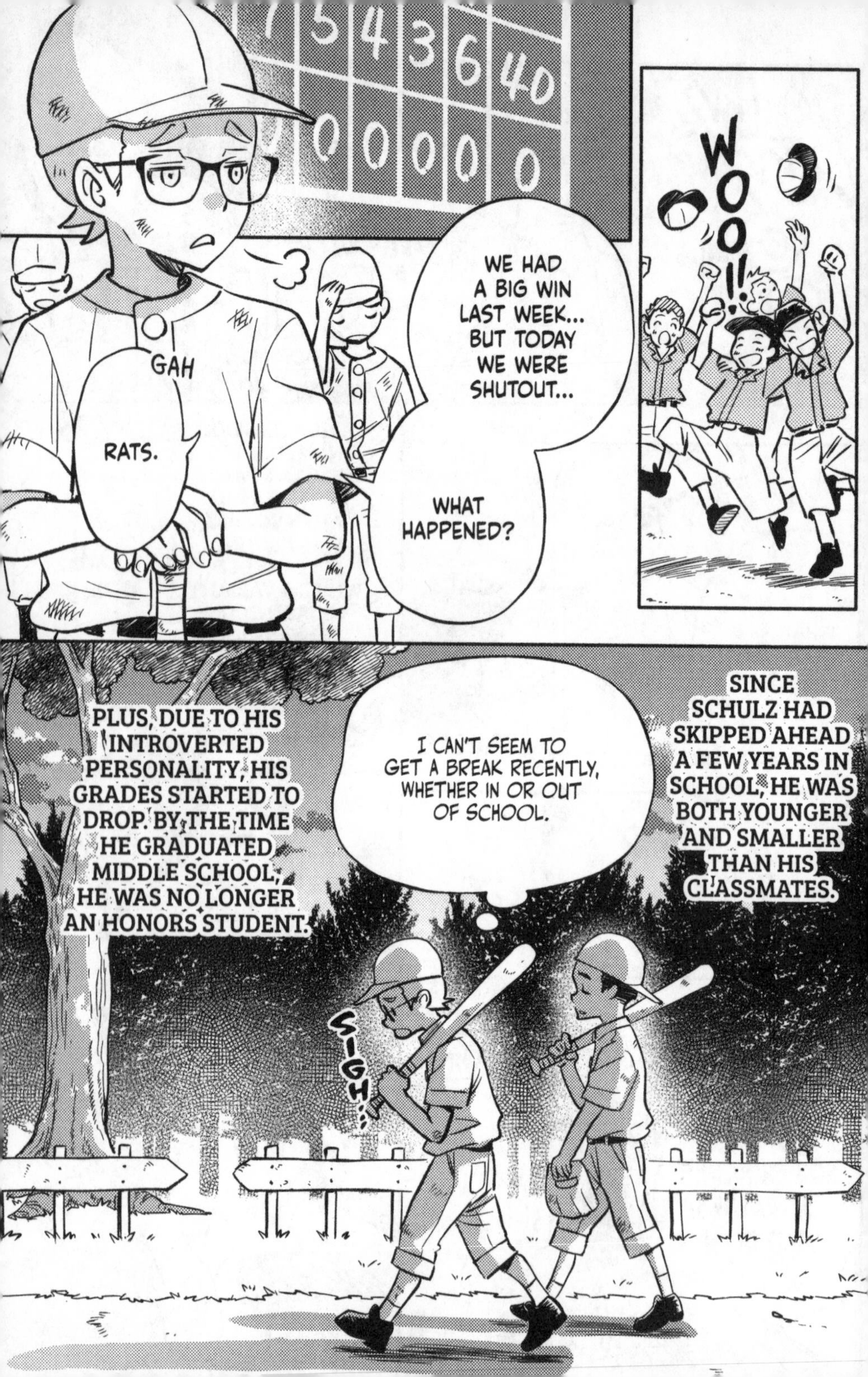
WOOO!!
WE HAD A BIG WIN LAST WEEK... BUT TODAY WE WERE SHUTOUT...
WHAT HAPPENED?
GAH
RATS.
SINCE SCHULZ HAD SKIPPED AHEAD A FEW YEARS IN SCHOOL, HE WAS BOTH YOUNGER AND SMALLER THAN HIS CLASSMATES.
I CAN'T SEEM TO GET A BREAK RECENTLY, WHETHER IN OR OUT OF SCHOOL.
PLUS, DUE TO HIS INTROVERTED PERSONALITY, HIS GRADES STARTED TO DROP. BY THE TIME HE GRADUATED MIDDLE SCHOOL, HE WAS NO LONGER AN HONORS STUDENT.
SIGH...

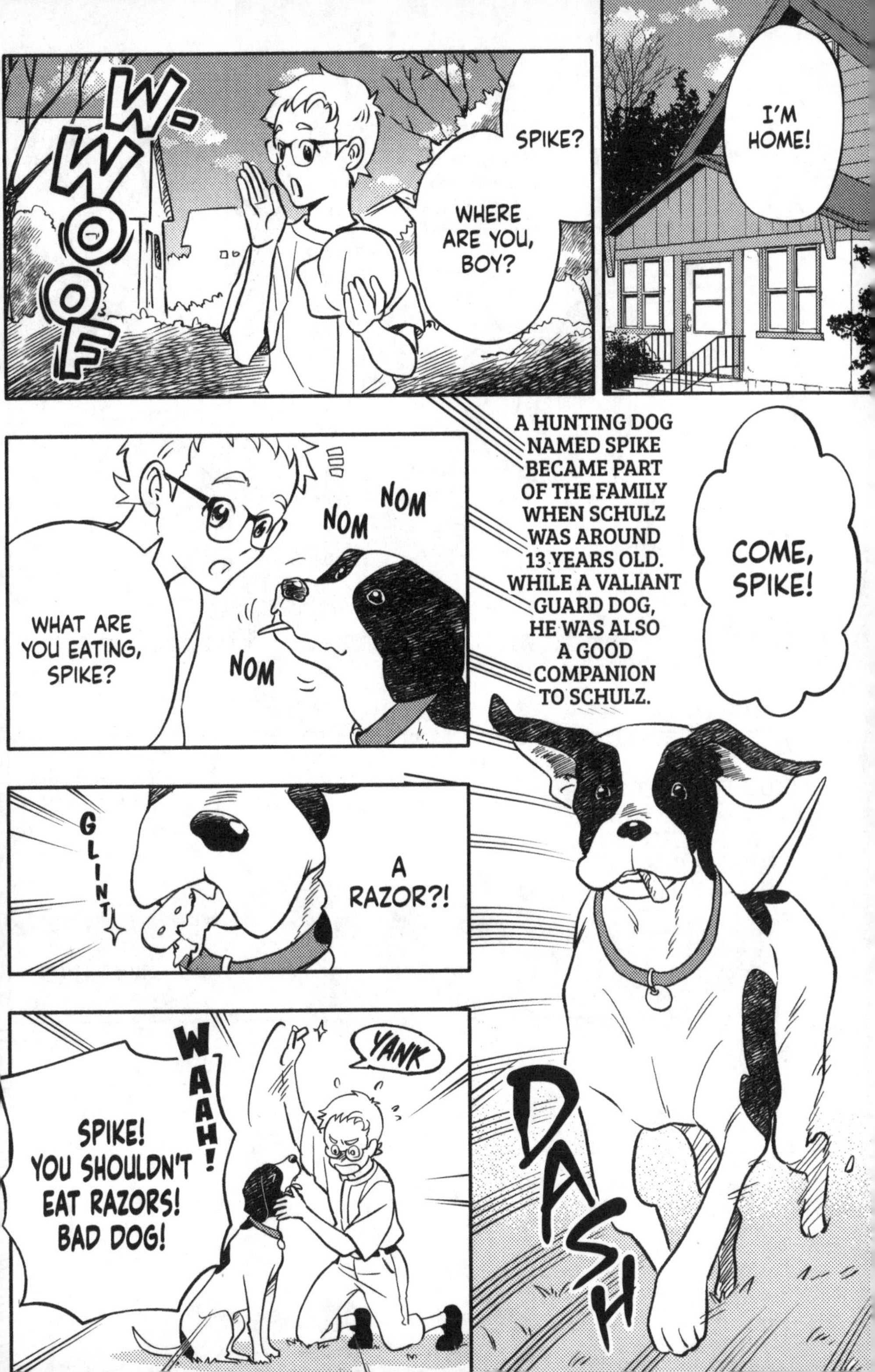
I'M HOME!
SPIKE?
WHERE ARE YOU, BOY?
W-WOOF
COME, SPIKE!
A HUNTING DOG NAMED SPIKE BECAME PART OF THE FAMILY WHEN SCHULZ WAS AROUND 13 YEARS OLD. WHILE A VALIANT GUARD DOG, HE WAS ALSO A GOOD COMPANION TO SCHULZ.
DASH
NOM
NOM
NOM
WHAT ARE YOU EATING, SPIKE?
A RAZOR?!
GLINT
YANK
WAAH!
SPIKE! YOU SHOULDN'T EAT RAZORS! BAD DOG!

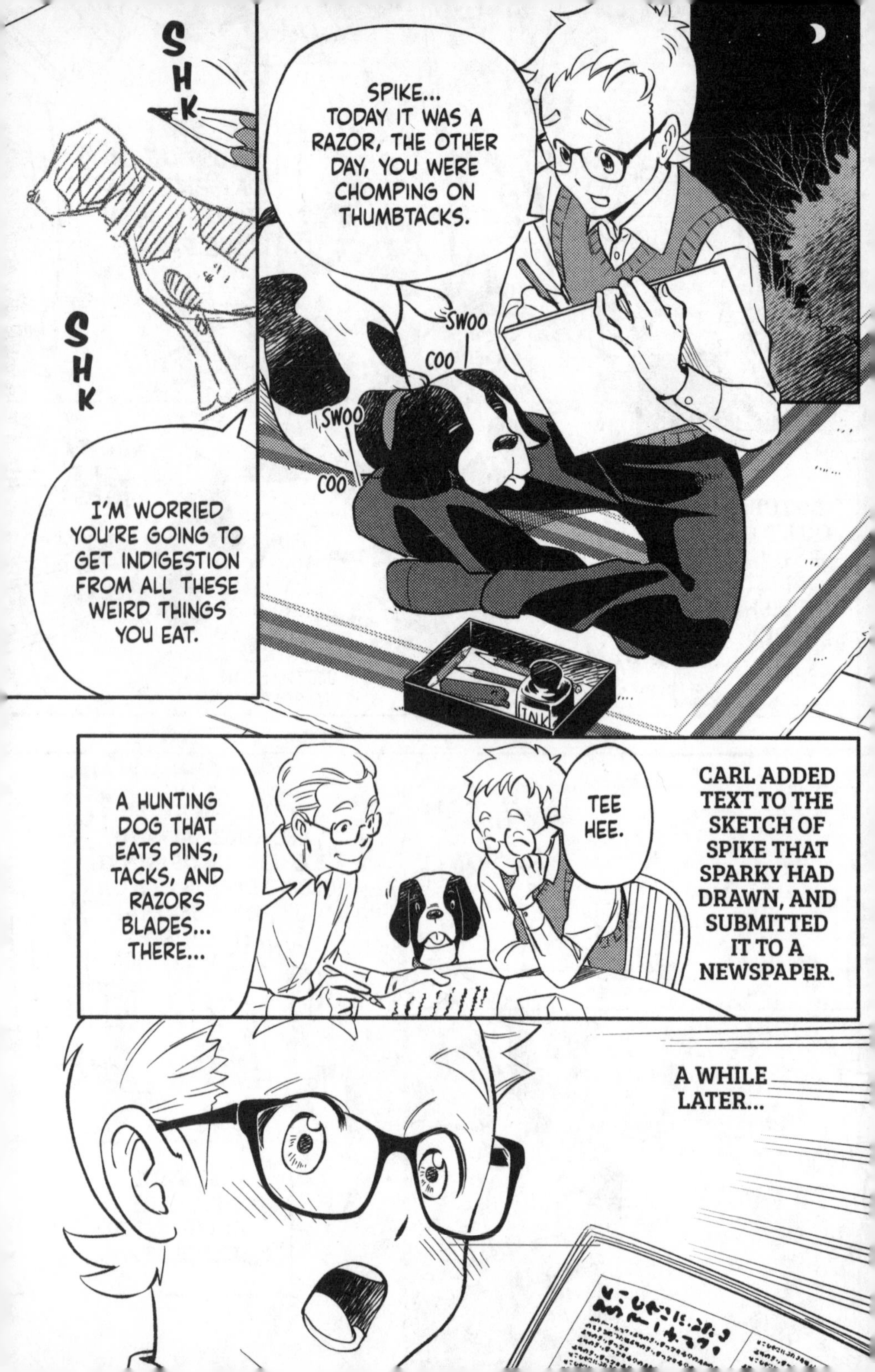

SPIKE... TODAY IT WAS A RAZOR, THE OTHER DAY, YOU WERE CHOMPING ON THUMBTACKS.
SWOO
COO
SWOO
COO
SHK
SHK
I'M WORRIED YOU'RE GOING TO GET INDIGESTION FROM ALL THESE WEIRD THINGS YOU EAT.
INK
CARL ADDED TEXT TO THE SKETCH OF SPIKE THAT SPARKY HAD DRAWN, AND SUBMITTED IT TO A NEWSPAPER.
TEE HEE.
A HUNTING DOG THAT EATS PINS, TACKS, AND RAZORS BLADES... THERE...
A WHILE LATER...

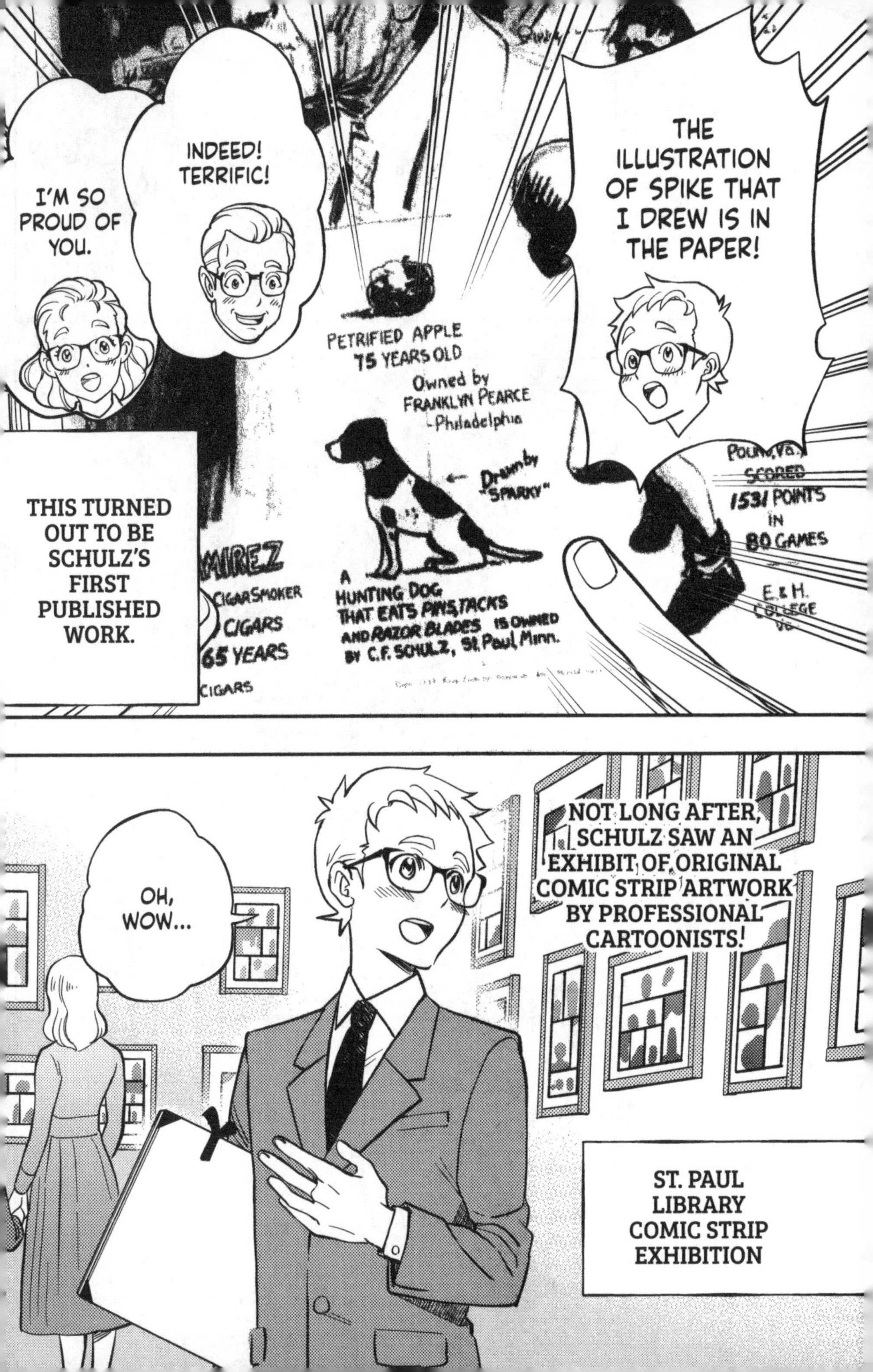
THE ILLUSTRATION OF SPIKE THAT I DREW IS IN THE PAPER!
INDEED! TERRIFIC!
I'M SO PROUD OF YOU.
PETRIFIED APPLE 75 YEARS OLD
Owned by FRANKLYN PEARCE -Philadelphia
Drawn by "SPARKY"
A HUNTING DOG THAT EATS PINS, TACKS AND RAZOR BLADES IS OWNED BY C.F. SCHULZ, St. Paul, Minn.
SCORED 1531 POINTS IN 80 GAMES
CIGAR SMOKER
CIGARS
65 YEARS
CIGARS
THIS TURNED OUT TO BE SCHULZ'S FIRST PUBLISHED WORK.
NOT LONG AFTER, SCHULZ SAW AN EXHIBIT OF ORIGINAL COMIC STRIP ARTWORK BY PROFESSIONAL CARTOONISTS!
ST. PAUL LIBRARY COMIC STRIP EXHIBITION
OH, WOW...

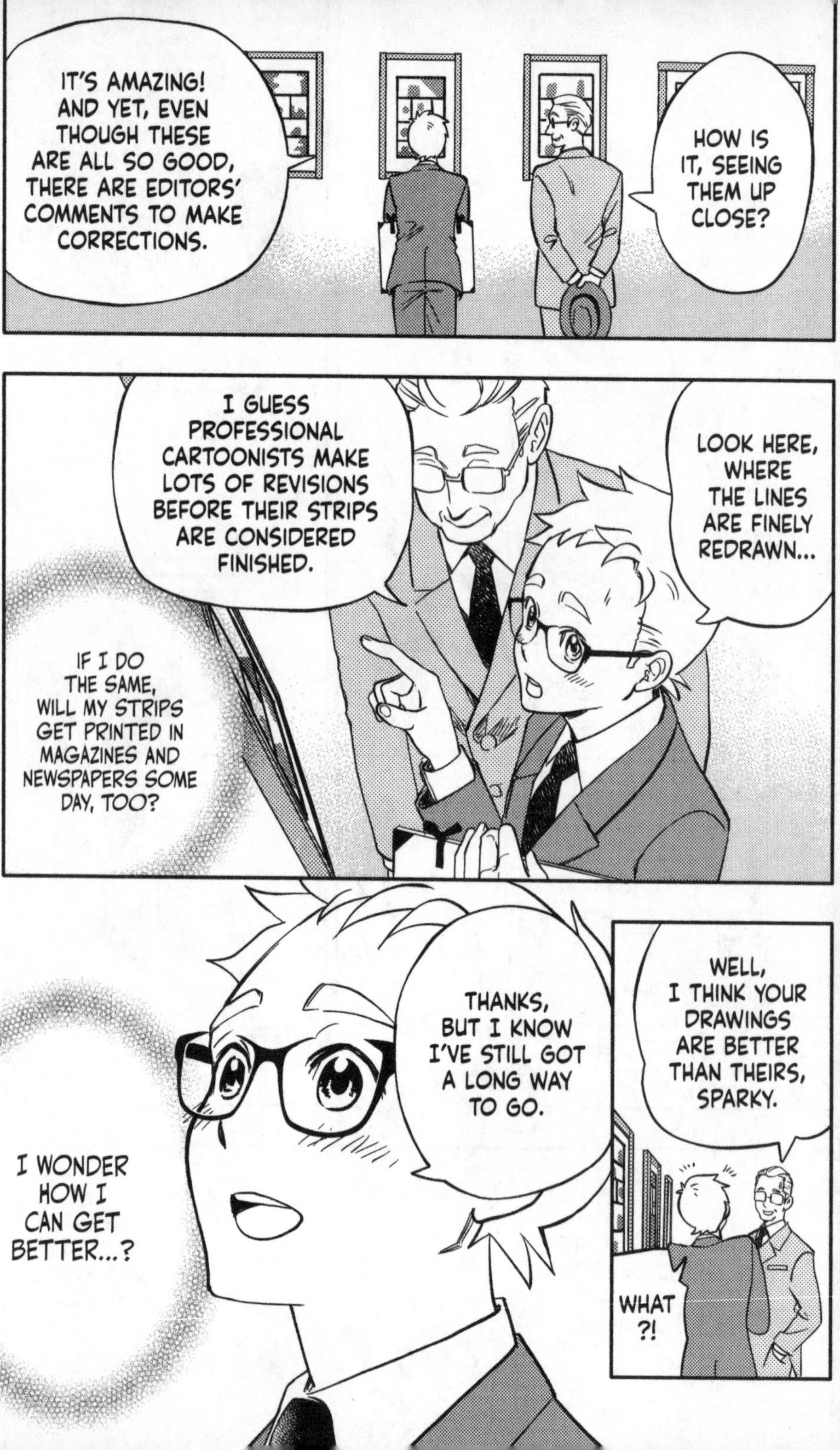
HOW IS IT, SEEING THEM UP CLOSE?
IT'S AMAZING! AND YET, EVEN THOUGH THESE ARE ALL SO GOOD, THERE ARE EDITORS' COMMENTS TO MAKE CORRECTIONS.
LOOK HERE, WHERE THE LINES ARE FINELY REDRAWN...
I GUESS PROFESSIONAL CARTOONISTS MAKE LOTS OF REVISIONS BEFORE THEIR STRIPS ARE CONSIDERED FINISHED.
IF I DO THE SAME, WILL MY STRIPS GET PRINTED IN MAGAZINES AND NEWSPAPERS SOME DAY, TOO?
WELL, I THINK YOUR DRAWINGS ARE BETTER THAN THEIRS, SPARKY.
WHAT ?!
THANKS, BUT I KNOW I'VE STILL GOT A LONG WAY TO GO.
I WONDER HOW I CAN GET BETTER...?

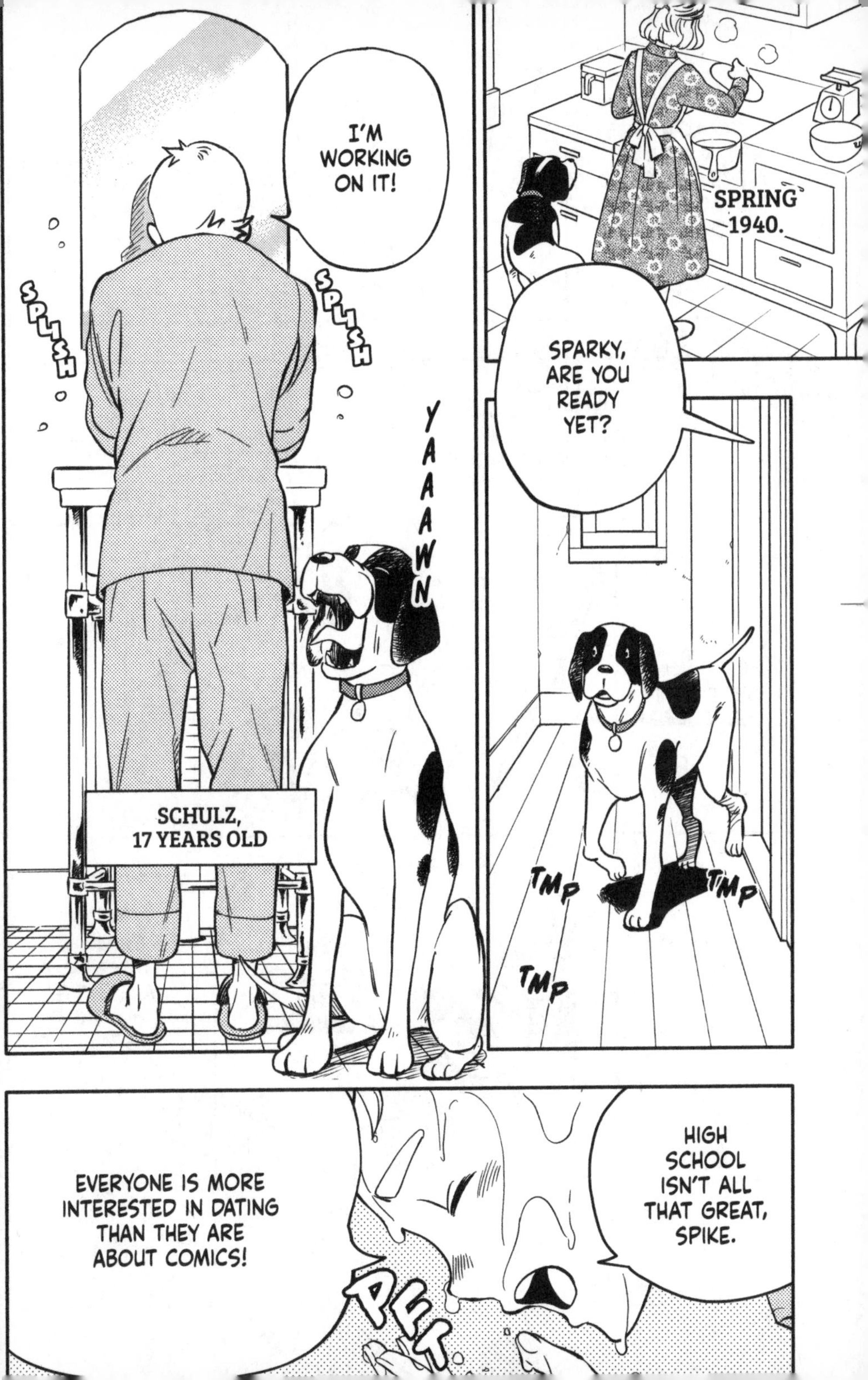

SPRING 1940.
SPARKY, ARE YOU READY YET?
TMP
TMP
TMP
I'M WORKING ON IT!
SPLISH
SPLISH
YAAAAWN
SCHULZ, 17 YEARS OLD
HIGH SCHOOL ISN'T ALL THAT GREAT, SPIKE.
EVERYONE IS MORE INTERESTED IN DATING THAN THEY ARE ABOUT COMICS!
PET

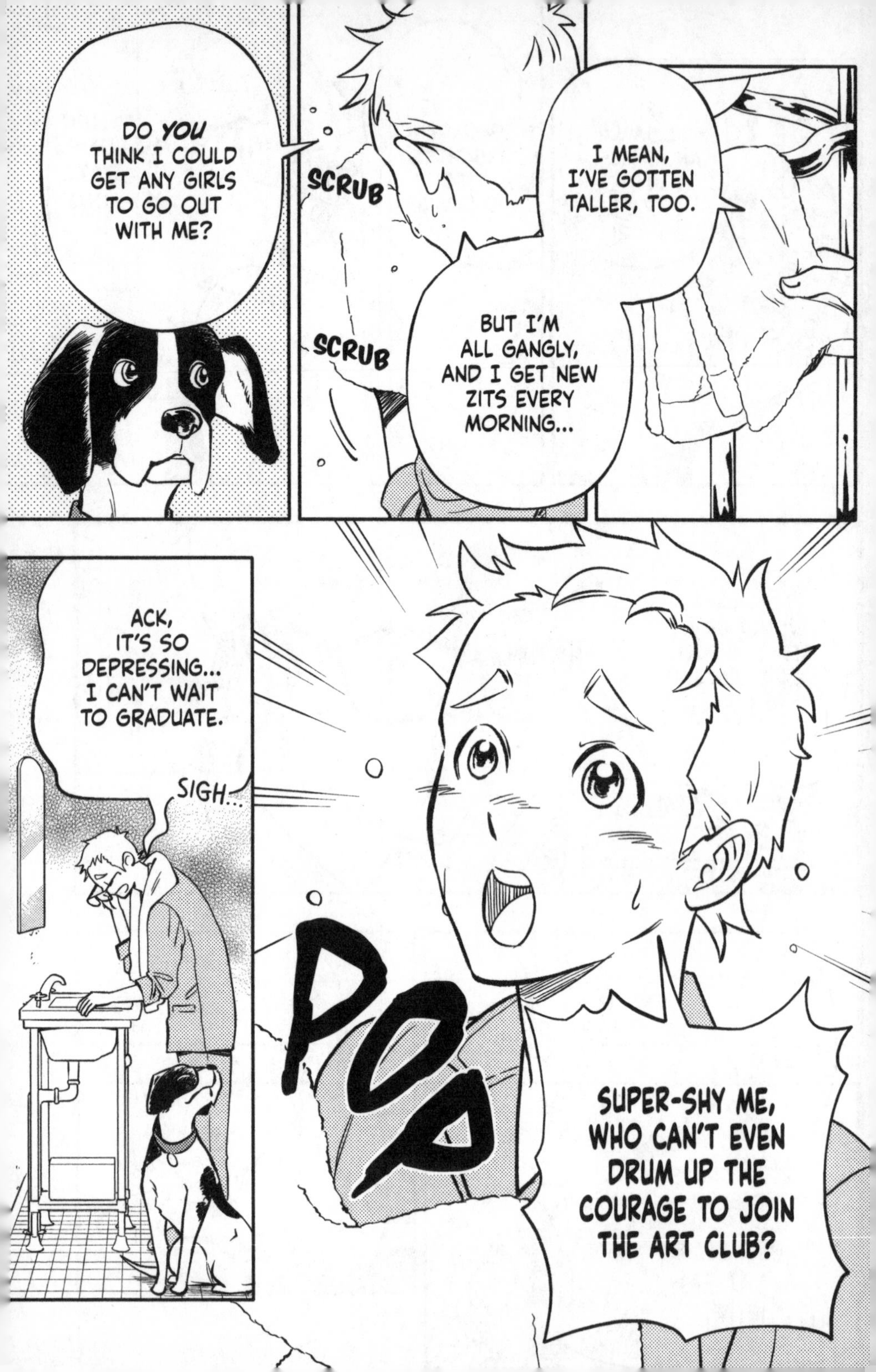
I MEAN, I'VE GOTTEN TALLER, TOO.
SCRUB
SCRUB
BUT I'M ALL GANGLY, AND I GET NEW ZITS EVERY MORNING...
DO *YOU* THINK I COULD GET ANY GIRLS TO GO OUT WITH ME?
POP
SUPER-SHY ME, WHO CAN'T EVEN DRUM UP THE COURAGE TO JOIN THE ART CLUB?
ACK, IT'S SO DEPRESSING... I CAN'T WAIT TO GRADUATE.
SIGH...

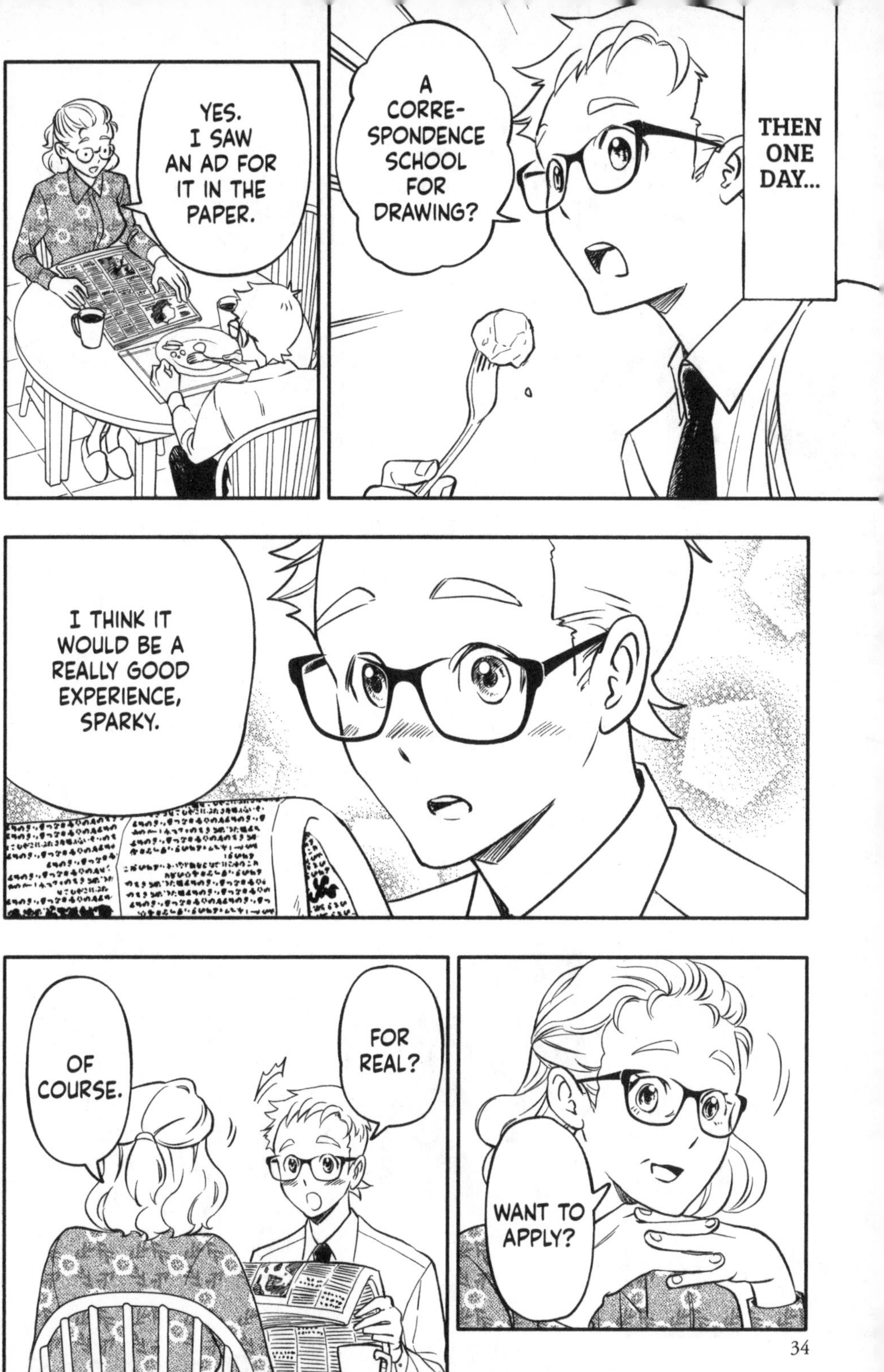
THEN ONE DAY...
A CORRE-SPONDENCE SCHOOL FOR DRAWING?
YES. I SAW AN AD FOR IT IN THE PAPER.
I THINK IT WOULD BE A REALLY GOOD EXPERIENCE, SPARKY.
WANT TO APPLY?
FOR REAL?
OF COURSE.

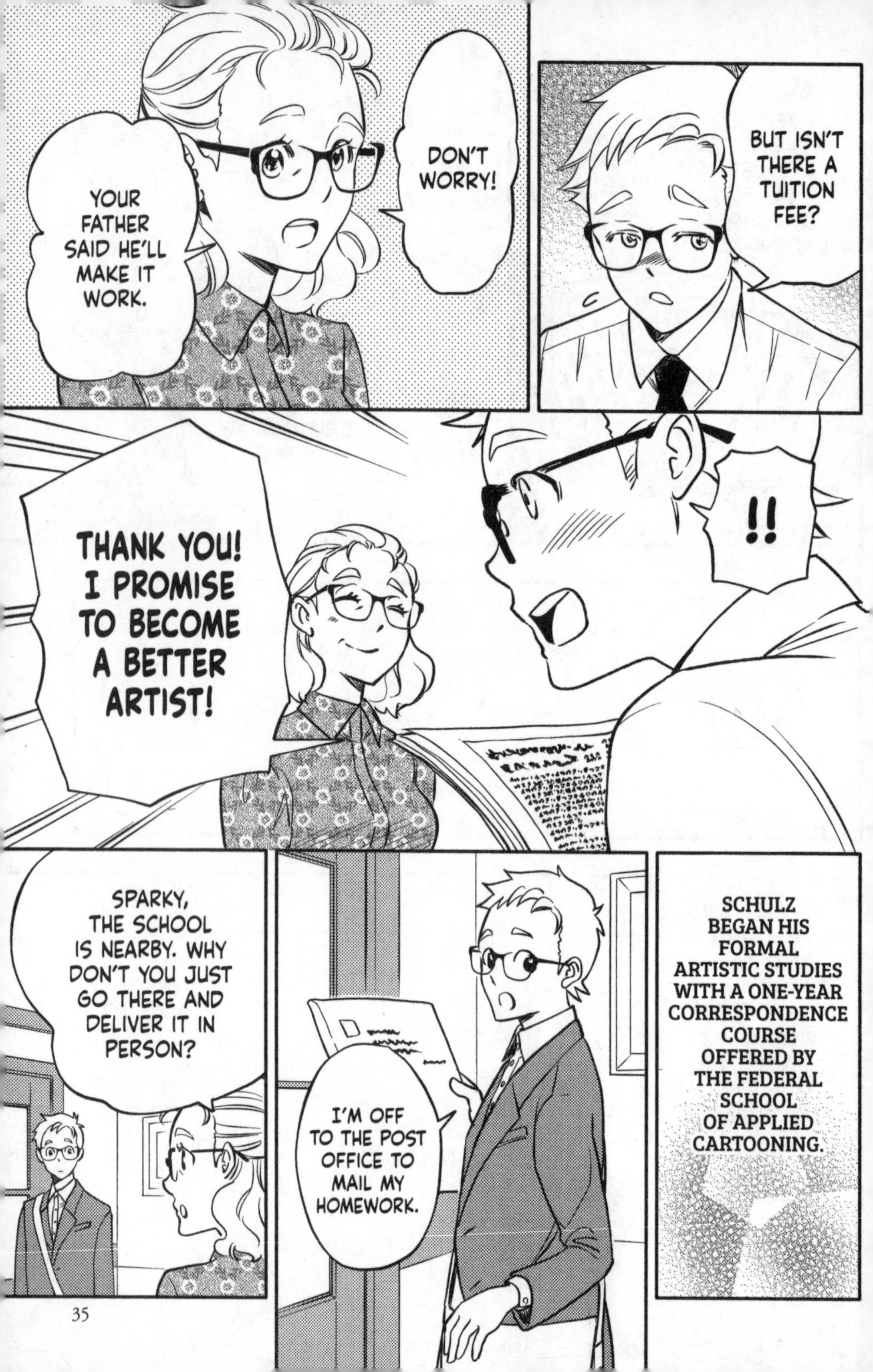
BUT ISN'T THERE A TUITION FEE?
DON'T WORRY!
YOUR FATHER SAID HE'LL MAKE IT WORK.
!!
THANK YOU! I PROMISE TO BECOME A BETTER ARTIST!
SCHULZ BEGAN HIS FORMAL ARTISTIC STUDIES WITH A ONE-YEAR CORRESPONDENCE COURSE OFFERED BY THE FEDERAL SCHOOL OF APPLIED CARTOONING.
I'M OFF TO THE POST OFFICE TO MAIL MY HOMEWORK.
SPARKY, THE SCHOOL IS NEARBY. WHY DON'T YOU JUST GO THERE AND DELIVER IT IN PERSON?

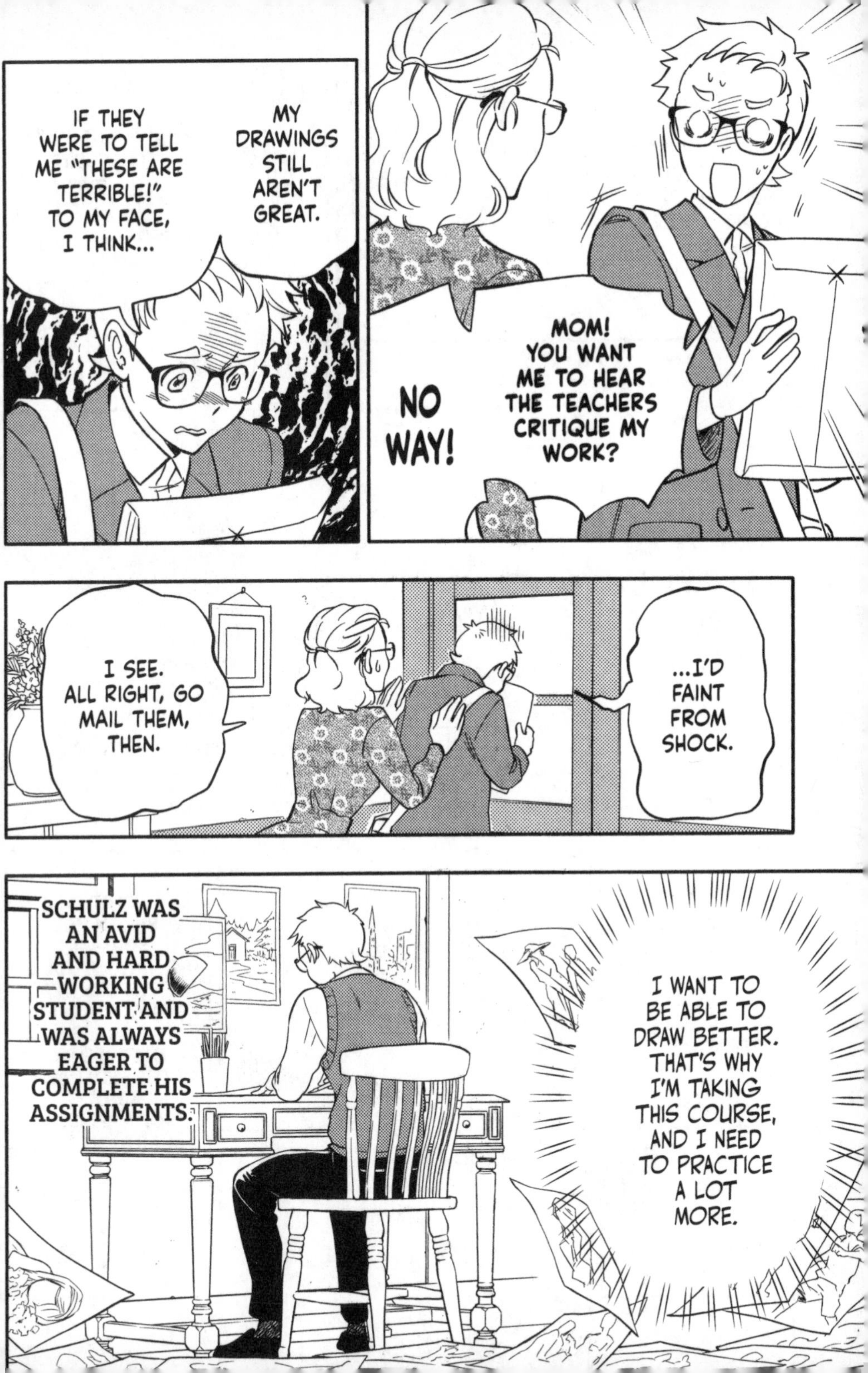
MOM! YOU WANT ME TO HEAR THE TEACHERS CRITIQUE MY WORK?
NO WAY!
MY DRAWINGS STILL AREN'T GREAT.
IF THEY WERE TO TELL ME "THESE ARE TERRIBLE!" TO MY FACE, I THINK...
...I'D FAINT FROM SHOCK.
I SEE. ALL RIGHT, GO MAIL THEM, THEN.
I WANT TO BE ABLE TO DRAW BETTER. THAT'S WHY I'M TAKING THIS COURSE, AND I NEED TO PRACTICE A LOT MORE.
SCHULZ WAS AN AVID AND HARD WORKING STUDENT AND WAS ALWAYS EAGER TO COMPLETE HIS ASSIGNMENTS.

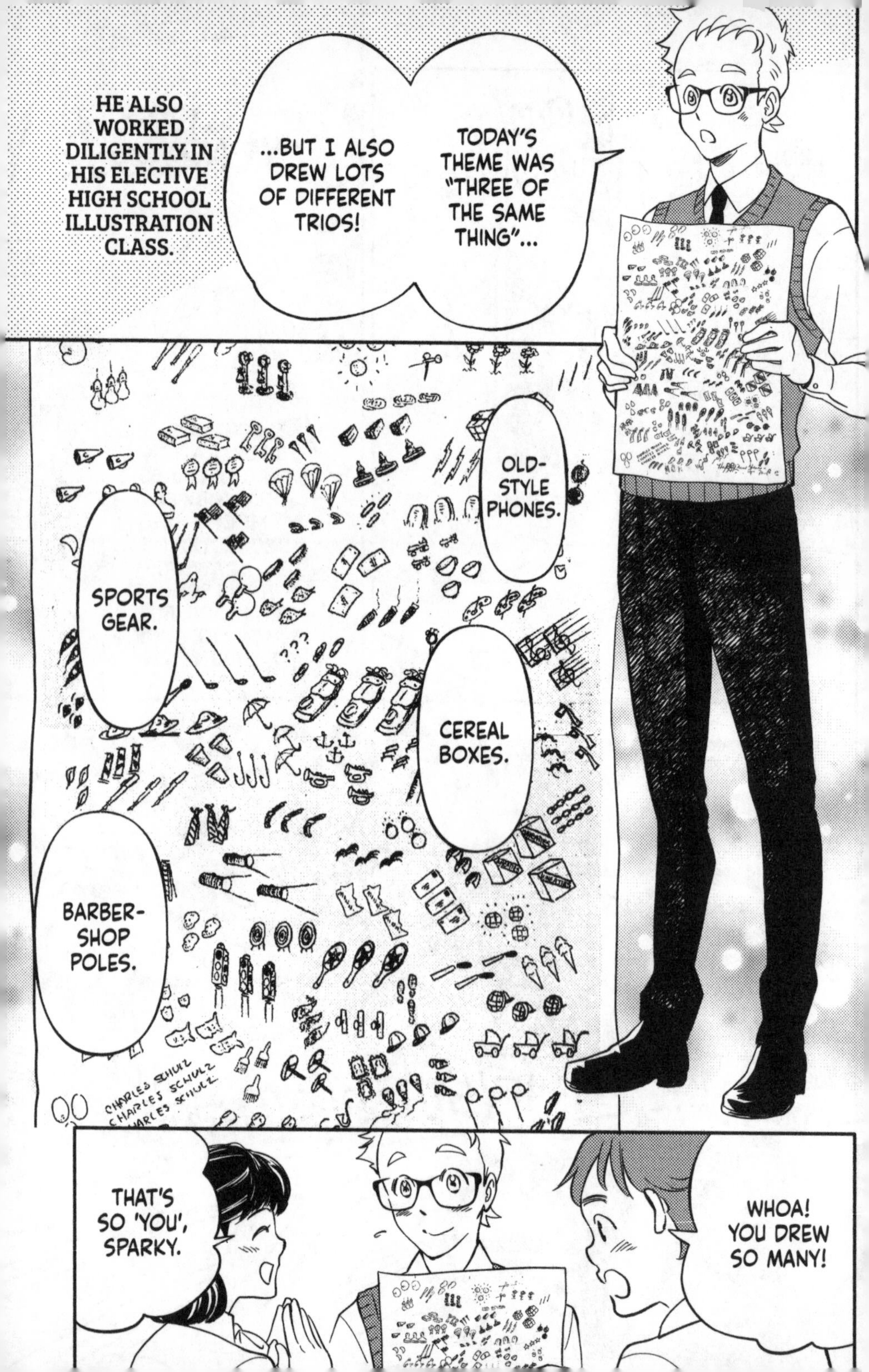
TODAY'S THEME WAS "THREE OF THE SAME THING"...
...BUT I ALSO DREW LOTS OF DIFFERENT TRIOS!
HE ALSO WORKED DILIGENTLY IN HIS ELECTIVE HIGH SCHOOL ILLUSTRATION CLASS.
OLD-STYLE PHONES.
SPORTS GEAR.
CEREAL BOXES.
BARBER-SHOP POLES.
CHARLES SCHULZ
CHARLES SCHULZ
CHARLES SCHULZ
WHOA! YOU DREW SO MANY!
THAT'S SO 'YOU', SPARKY.

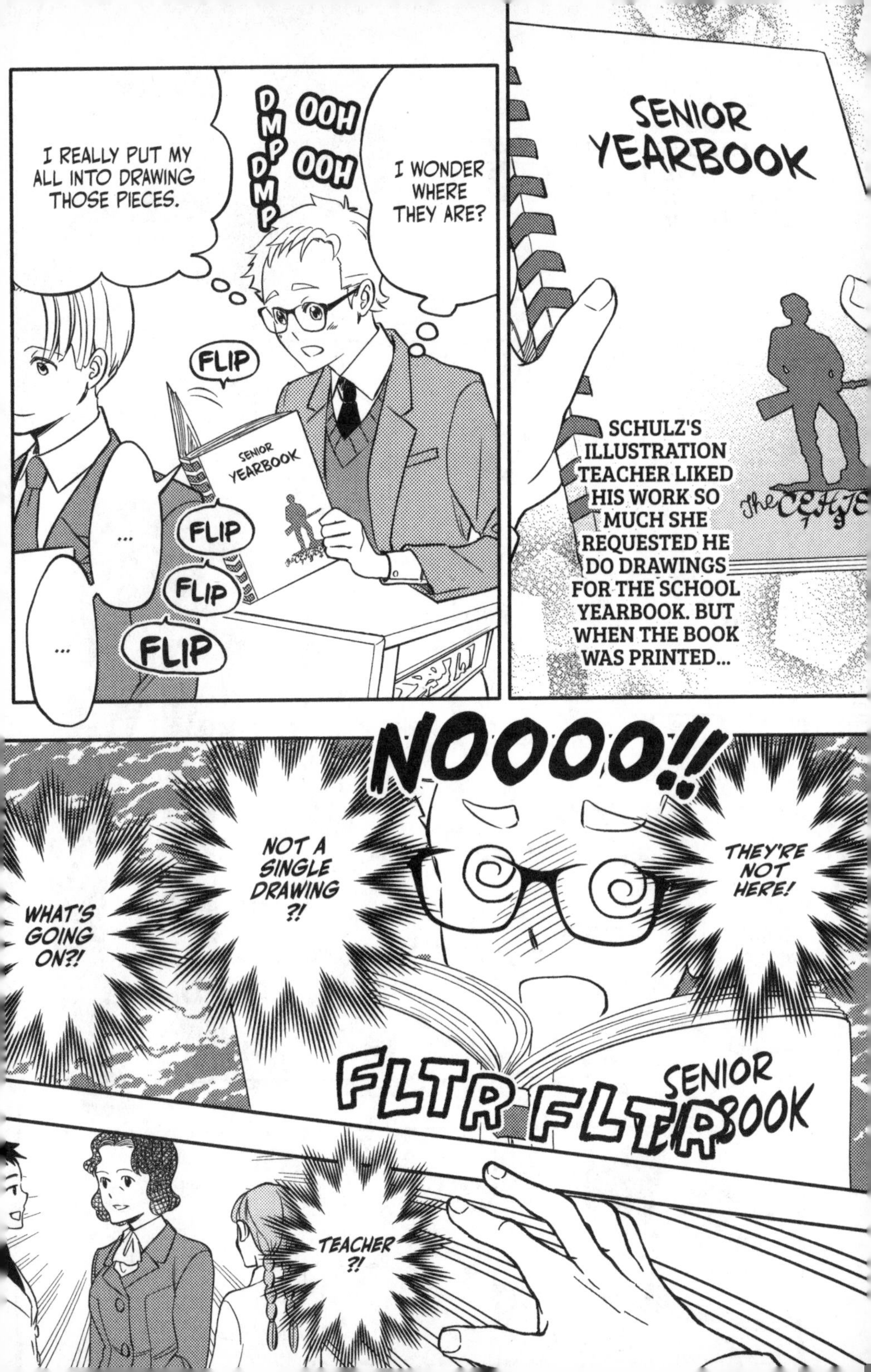
SENIOR YEARBOOK
SCHULZ'S ILLUSTRATION TEACHER LIKED HIS WORK SO MUCH SHE REQUESTED HE DO DRAWINGS FOR THE SCHOOL YEARBOOK. BUT WHEN THE BOOK WAS PRINTED...
I WONDER WHERE THEY ARE?
OOH OOH
DMP DMP
I REALLY PUT MY ALL INTO DRAWING THOSE PIECES.
FLIP
SENIOR YEARBOOK
FLIP
FLIP
FLIP
...
...
NOOOO!!
THEY'RE NOT HERE!
NOT A SINGLE DRAWING?!
WHAT'S GOING ON?!
SENIOR
BOOK
FLTR FLTR
TEACHER?!

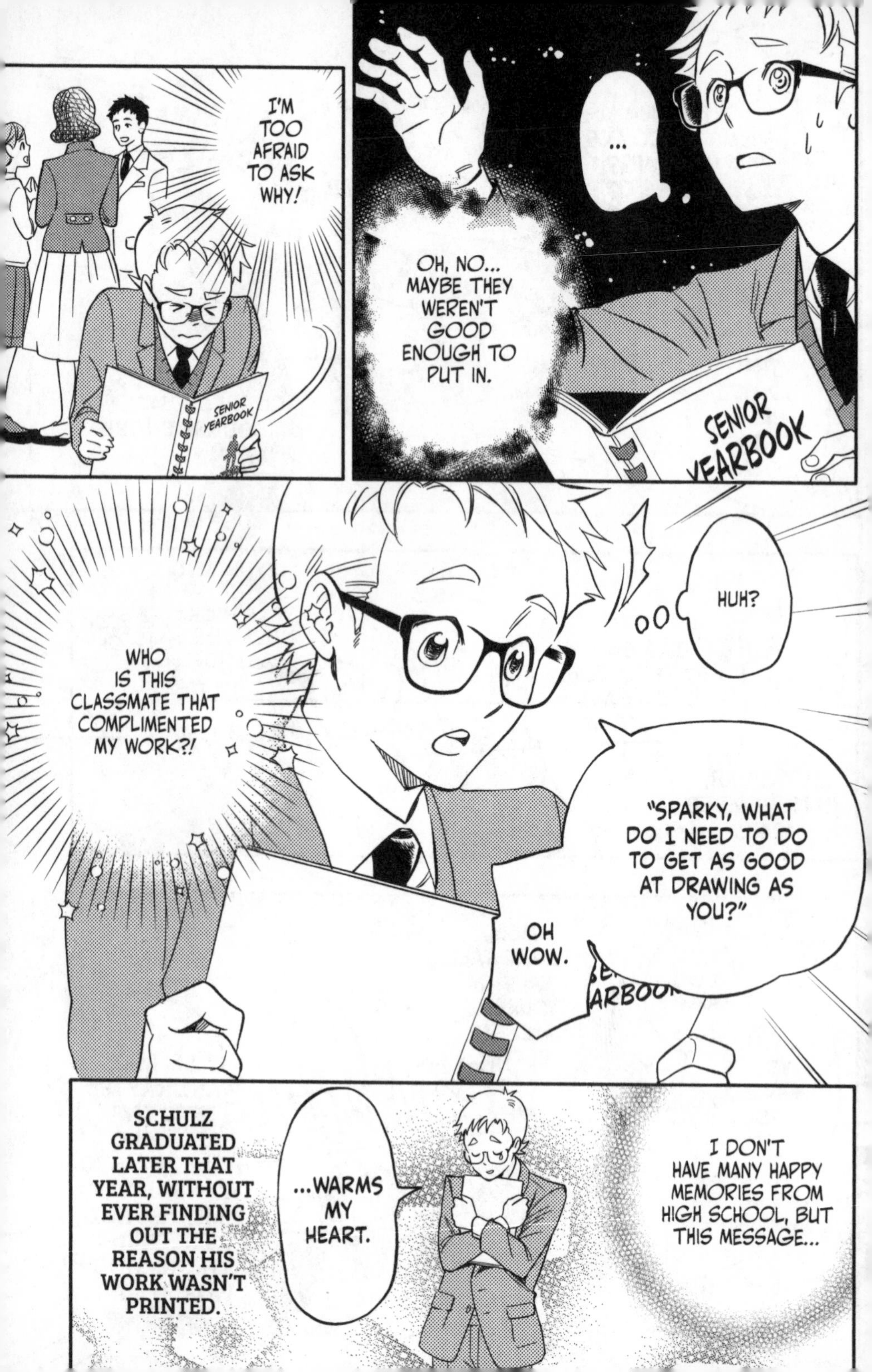
...
OH, NO... MAYBE THEY WEREN'T GOOD ENOUGH TO PUT IN.
SENIOR YEARBOOK
I'M TOO AFRAID TO ASK WHY!
SENIOR YEARBOOK
HUH?
"SPARKY, WHAT DO I NEED TO DO TO GET AS GOOD AT DRAWING AS YOU?"
OH WOW.
WHO IS THIS CLASSMATE THAT COMPLIMENTED MY WORK?!
I DON'T HAVE MANY HAPPY MEMORIES FROM HIGH SCHOOL, BUT THIS MESSAGE...
...WARMS MY HEART.
SCHULZ GRADUATED LATER THAT YEAR, WITHOUT EVER FINDING OUT THE REASON HIS WORK WASN'T PRINTED.

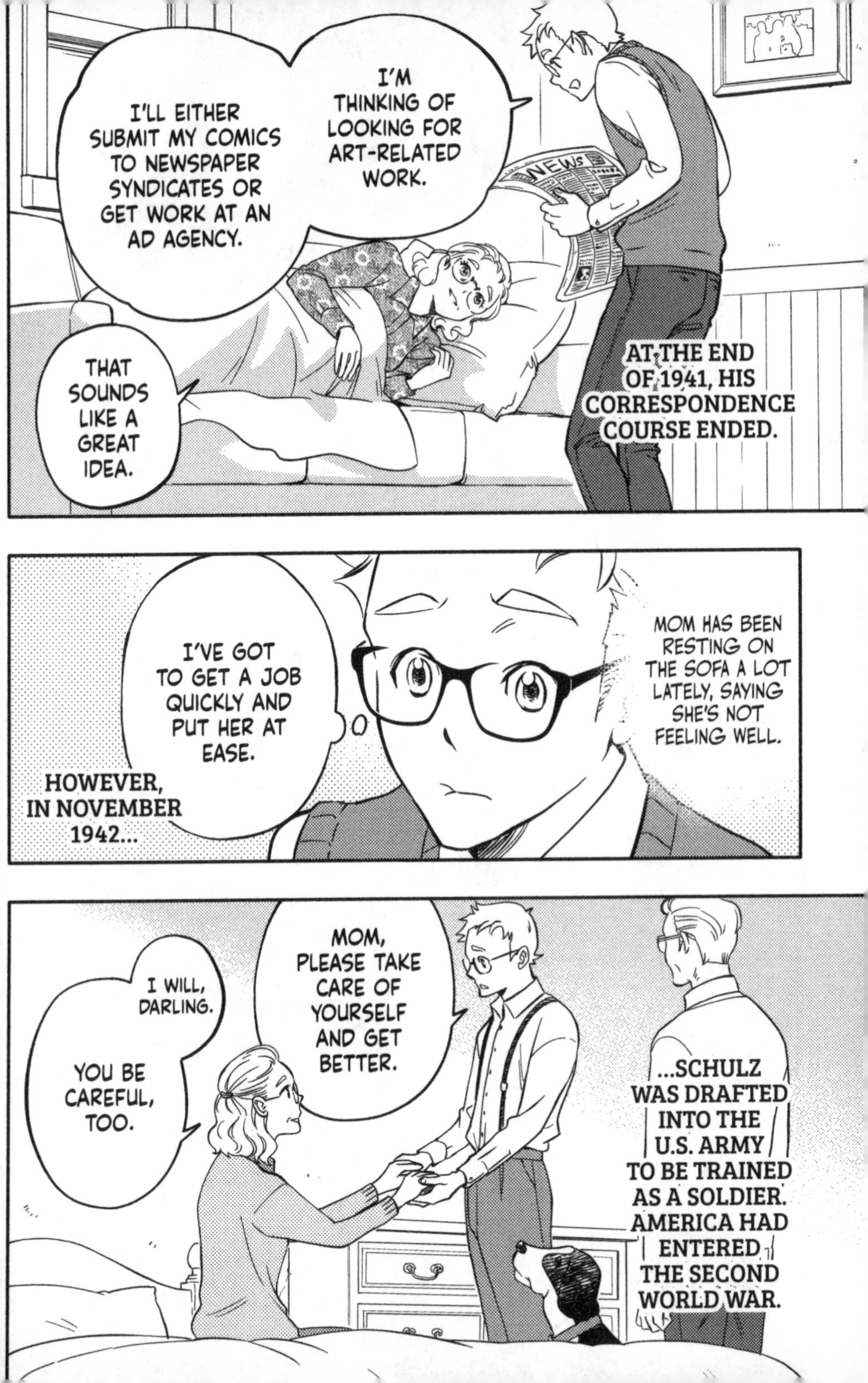
I'M THINKING OF LOOKING FOR ART-RELATED WORK.
I'LL EITHER SUBMIT MY COMICS TO NEWSPAPER SYNDICATES OR GET WORK AT AN AD AGENCY.
AT THE END OF 1941, HIS CORRESPONDENCE COURSE ENDED.
THAT SOUNDS LIKE A GREAT IDEA.
MOM HAS BEEN RESTING ON THE SOFA A LOT LATELY, SAYING SHE'S NOT FEELING WELL.
I'VE GOT TO GET A JOB QUICKLY AND PUT HER AT EASE.
HOWEVER, IN NOVEMBER 1942...
...SCHULZ WAS DRAFTED INTO THE U.S. ARMY TO BE TRAINED AS A SOLDIER. AMERICA HAD ENTERED THE SECOND WORLD WAR.
MOM, PLEASE TAKE CARE OF YOURSELF AND GET BETTER.
I WILL, DARLING.
YOU BE CAREFUL, TOO.

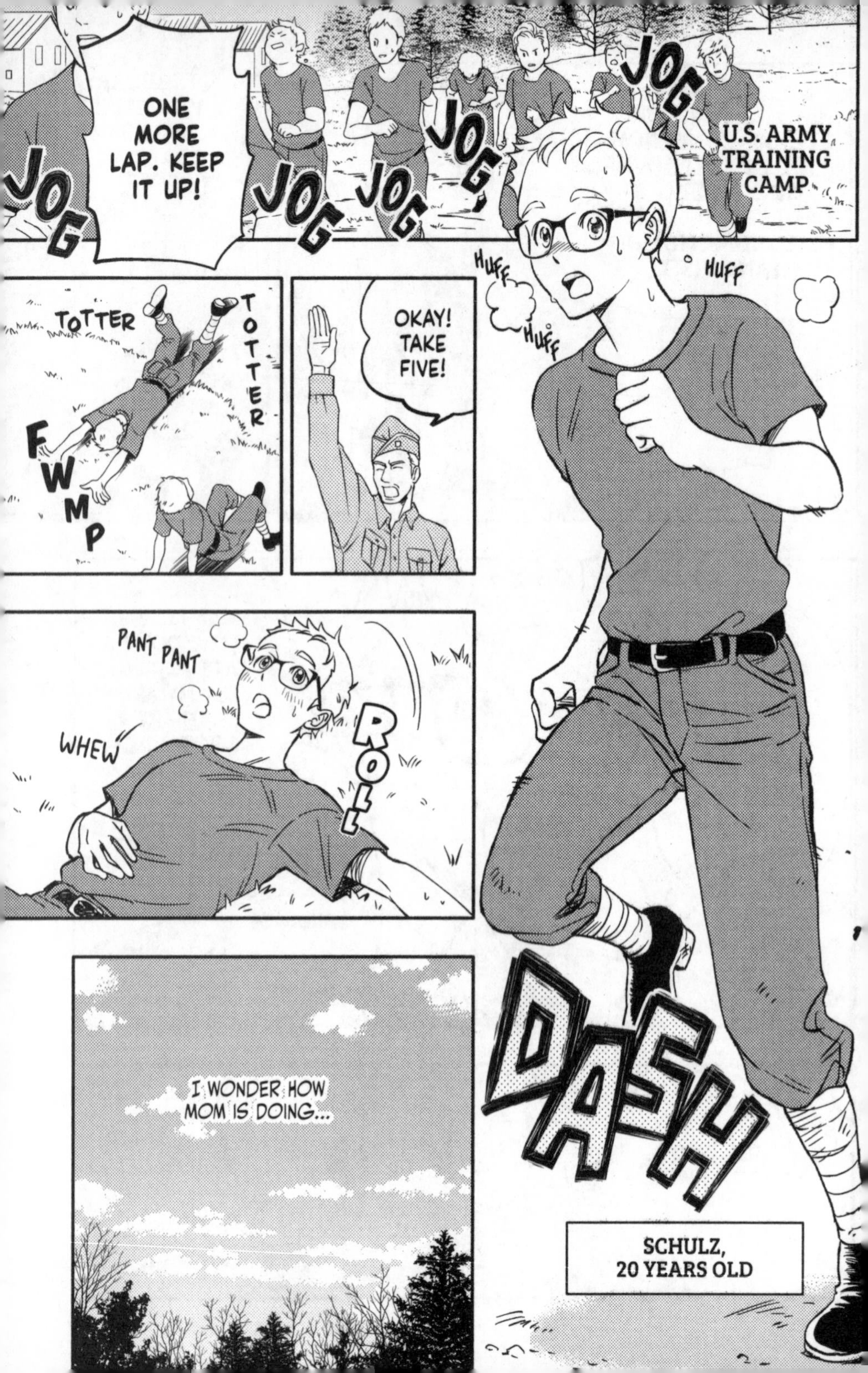
U.S. ARMY TRAINING CAMP
JOG
JOG
JOG
JOG
JOG
ONE MORE LAP. KEEP IT UP!
JOG
HUFF
HUFF
HUFF
DASH
SCHULZ, 20 YEARS OLD
OKAY! TAKE FIVE!
TOTTER
TOTTER
FWMP
ROLL
PANT PANT
WHEW
I WONDER HOW MOM IS DOING...

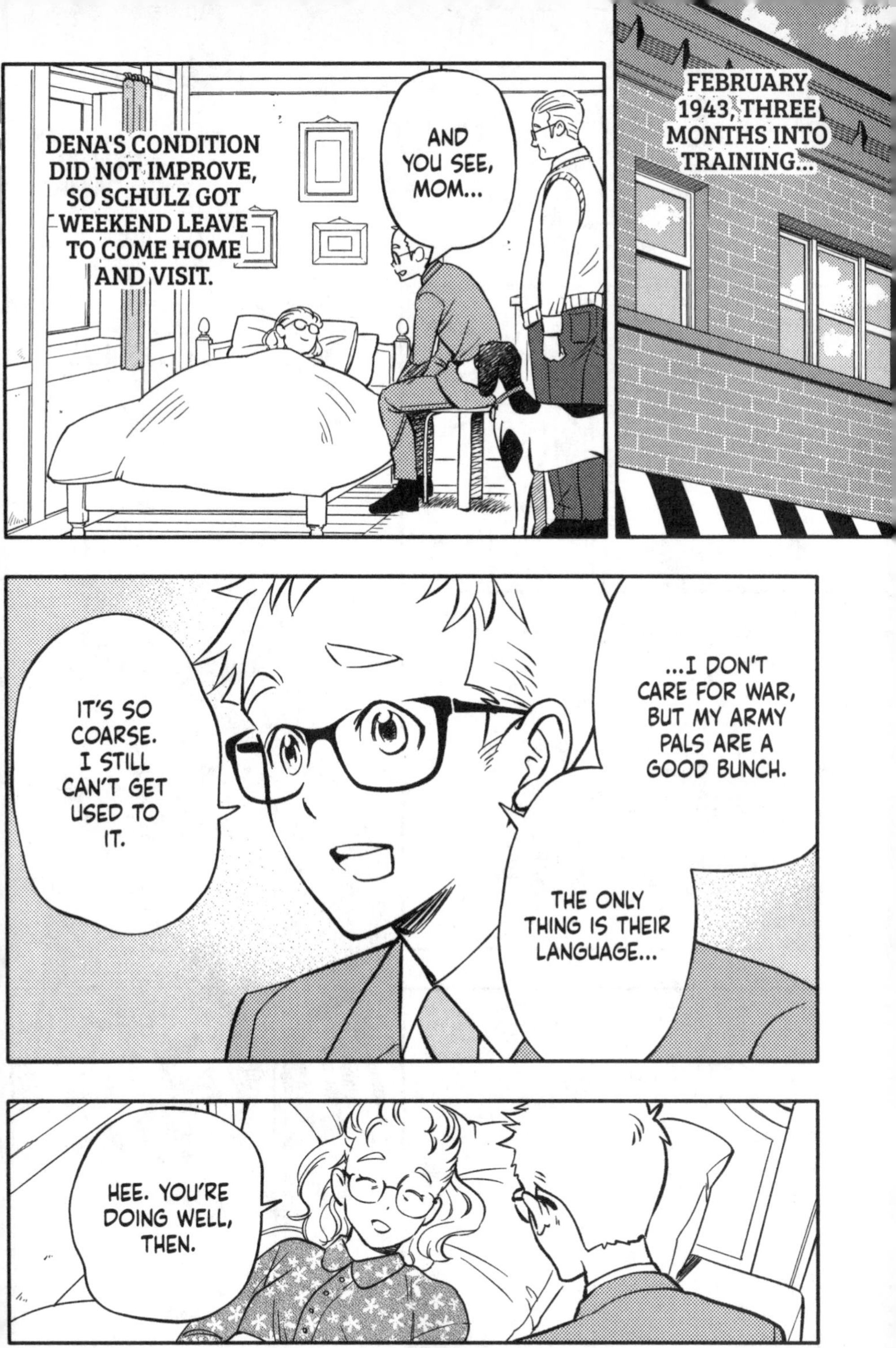
FEBRUARY 1943, THREE MONTHS INTO TRAINING...
AND YOU SEE, MOM...
DENA'S CONDITION DID NOT IMPROVE, SO SCHULZ GOT WEEKEND LEAVE TO COME HOME AND VISIT.
...I DON'T CARE FOR WAR, BUT MY ARMY PALS ARE A GOOD BUNCH.
THE ONLY THING IS THEIR LANGUAGE...
IT'S SO COARSE. I STILL CAN'T GET USED TO IT.
HEE. YOU'RE DOING WELL, THEN.

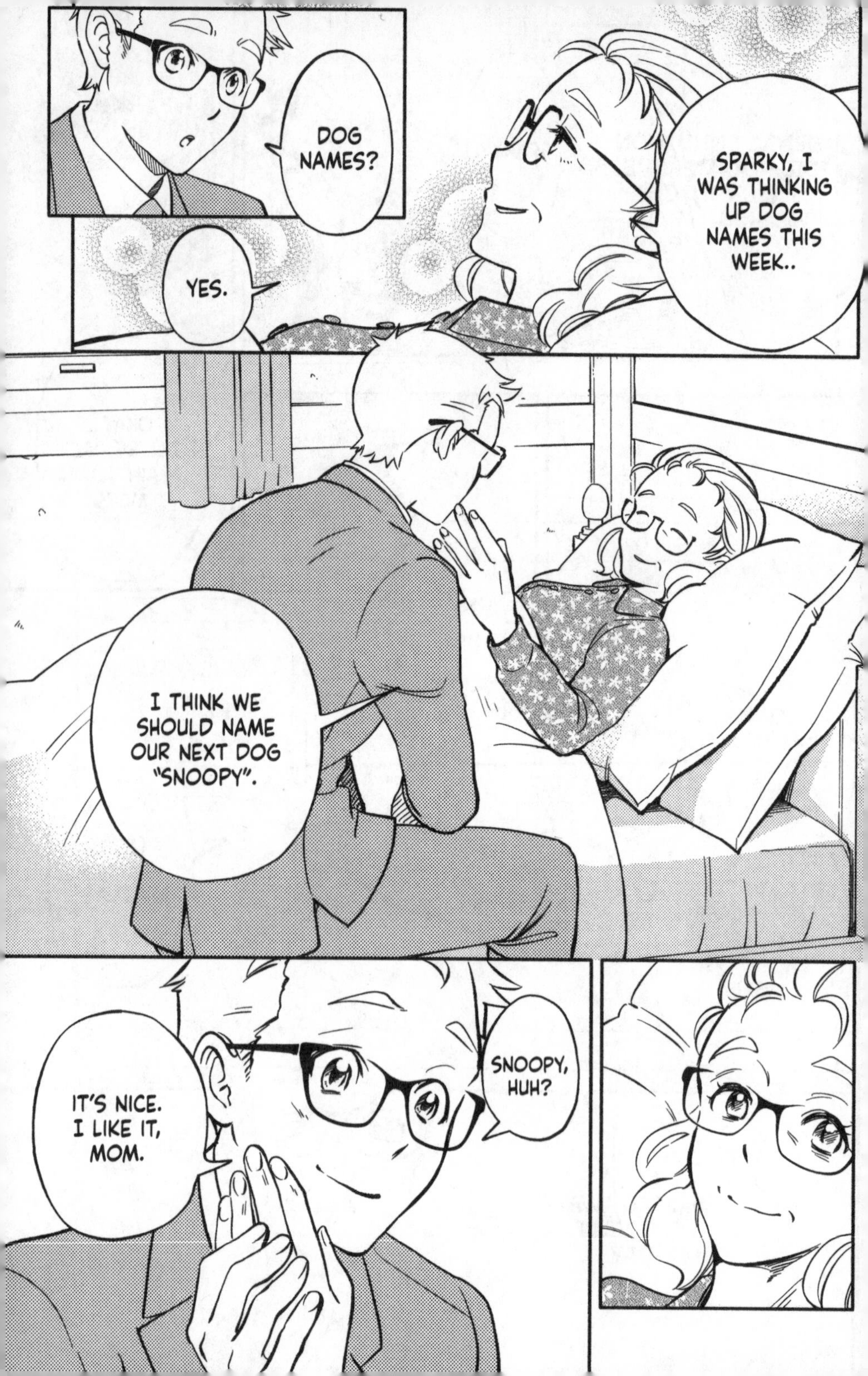
SPARKY, I WAS THINKING UP DOG NAMES THIS WEEK..
DOG NAMES?
YES.
I THINK WE SHOULD NAME OUR NEXT DOG "SNOOPY".
SNOOPY, HUH?
IT'S NICE. I LIKE IT, MOM.

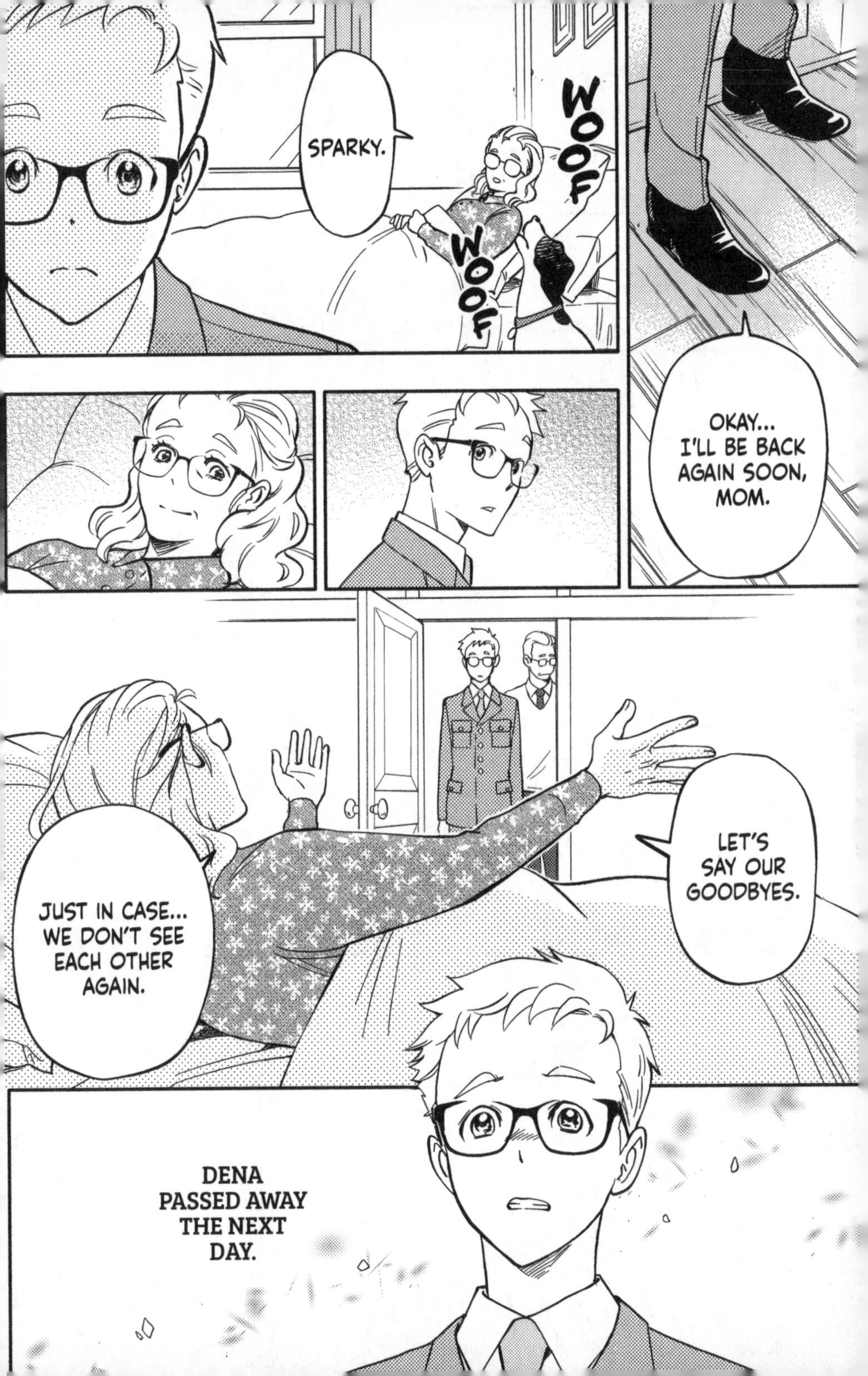
OKAY... I'LL BE BACK AGAIN SOON, MOM.
WOOF WOOF
SPARKY.
WOOF WOOF
LET'S SAY OUR GOODBYES.
JUST IN CASE... WE DON'T SEE EACH OTHER AGAIN.
DENA PASSED AWAY THE NEXT DAY.

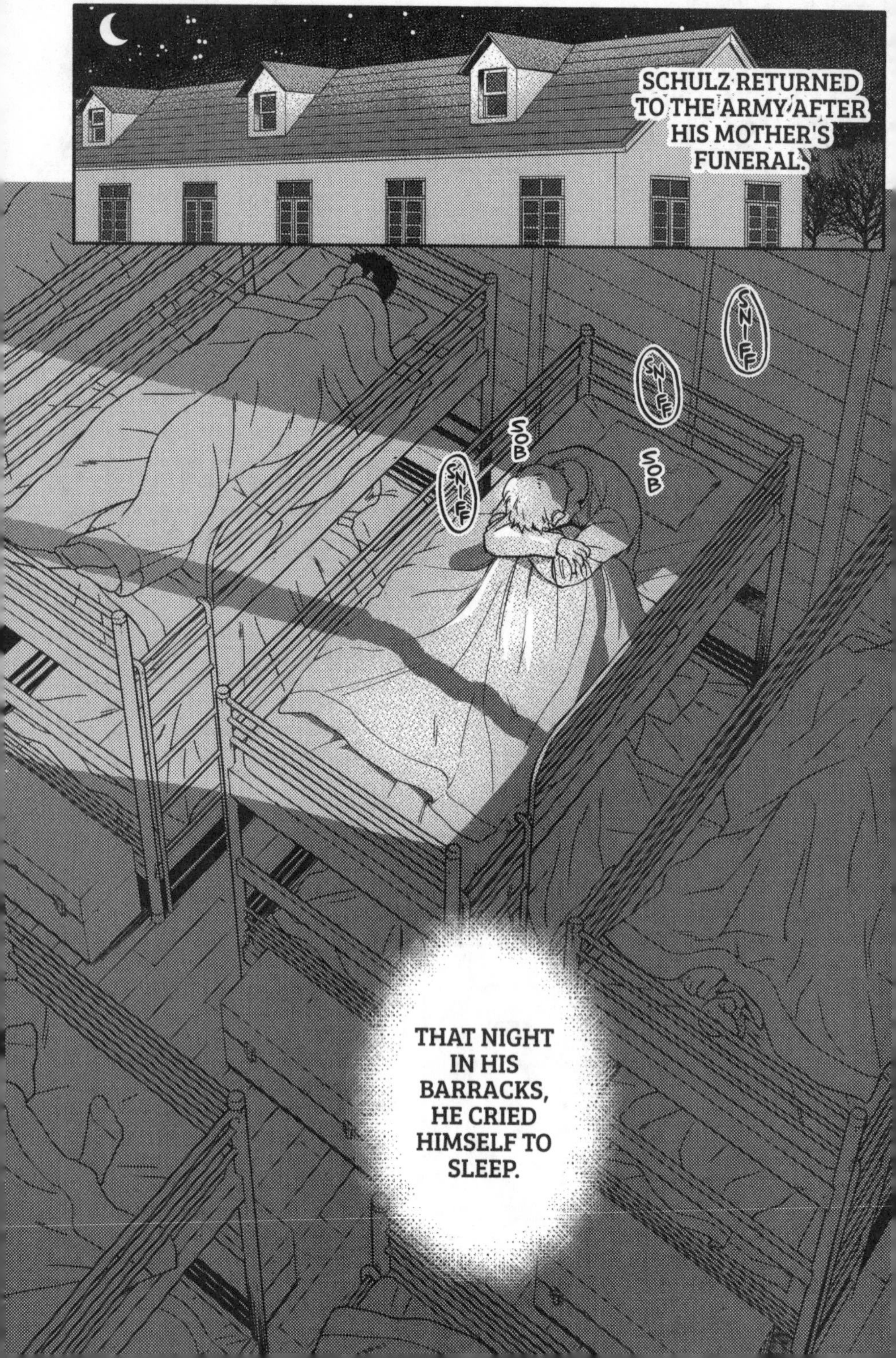
SCHULZ RETURNED TO THE ARMY AFTER HIS MOTHER'S FUNERAL.
SNIFF
SNIFF
SOB
SOB
SNIFF
THAT NIGHT IN HIS BARRACKS, HE CRIED HIMSELF TO SLEEP.

CHAPTER 2

WORK, LOVE, COMICS, & MORE COMICS!

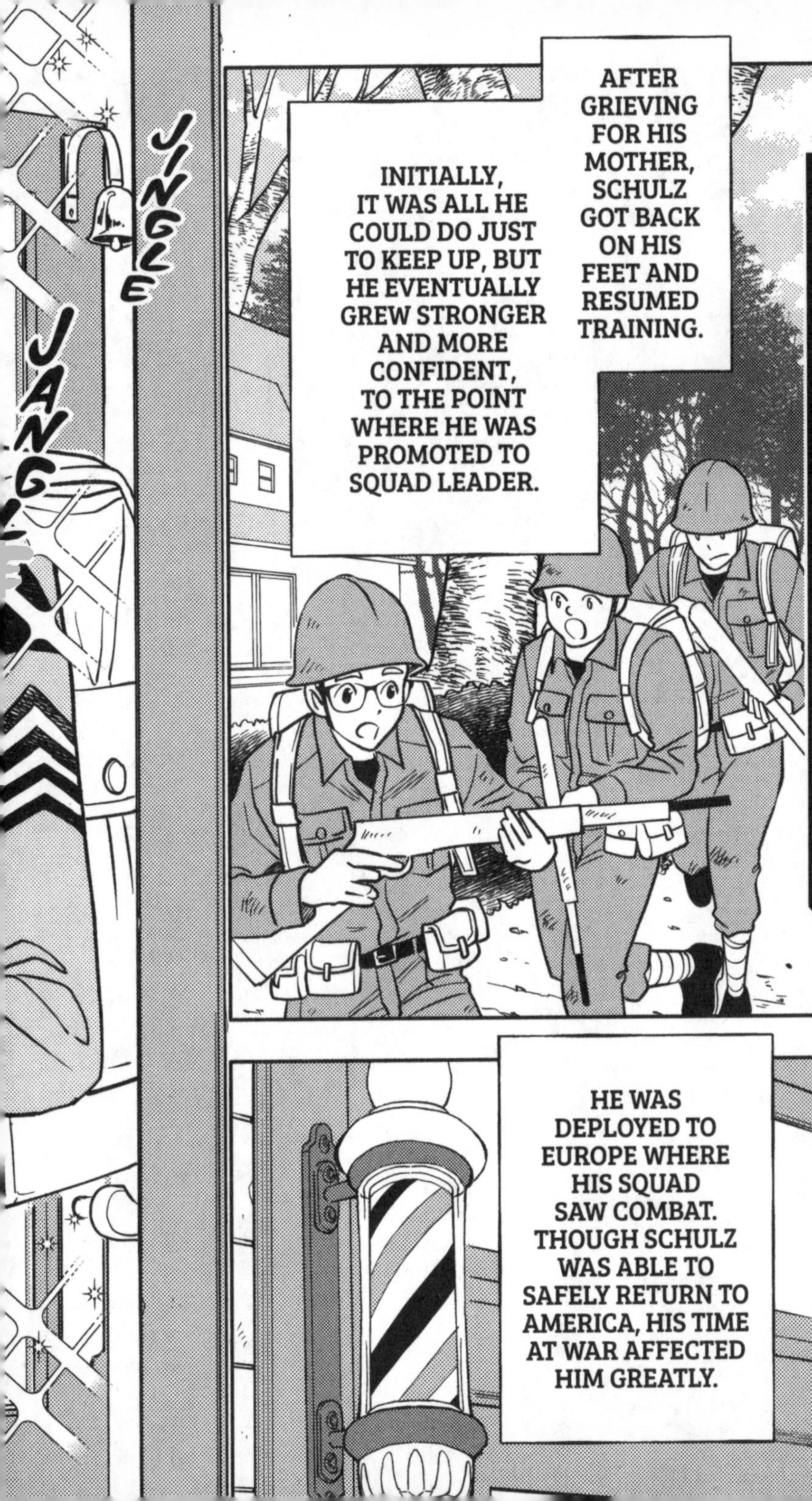
AFTER GRIEVING FOR HIS MOTHER, SCHULZ GOT BACK ON HIS FEET AND RESUMED TRAINING.
INITIALLY, IT WAS ALL HE COULD DO JUST TO KEEP UP, BUT HE EVENTUALLY GREW STRONGER AND MORE CONFIDENT, TO THE POINT WHERE HE WAS PROMOTED TO SQUAD LEADER.
HE WAS DEPLOYED TO EUROPE WHERE HIS SQUAD SAW COMBAT. THOUGH SCHULZ WAS ABLE TO SAFELY RETURN TO AMERICA, HIS TIME AT WAR AFFECTED HIM GREATLY.
JINGLE
JANGLE

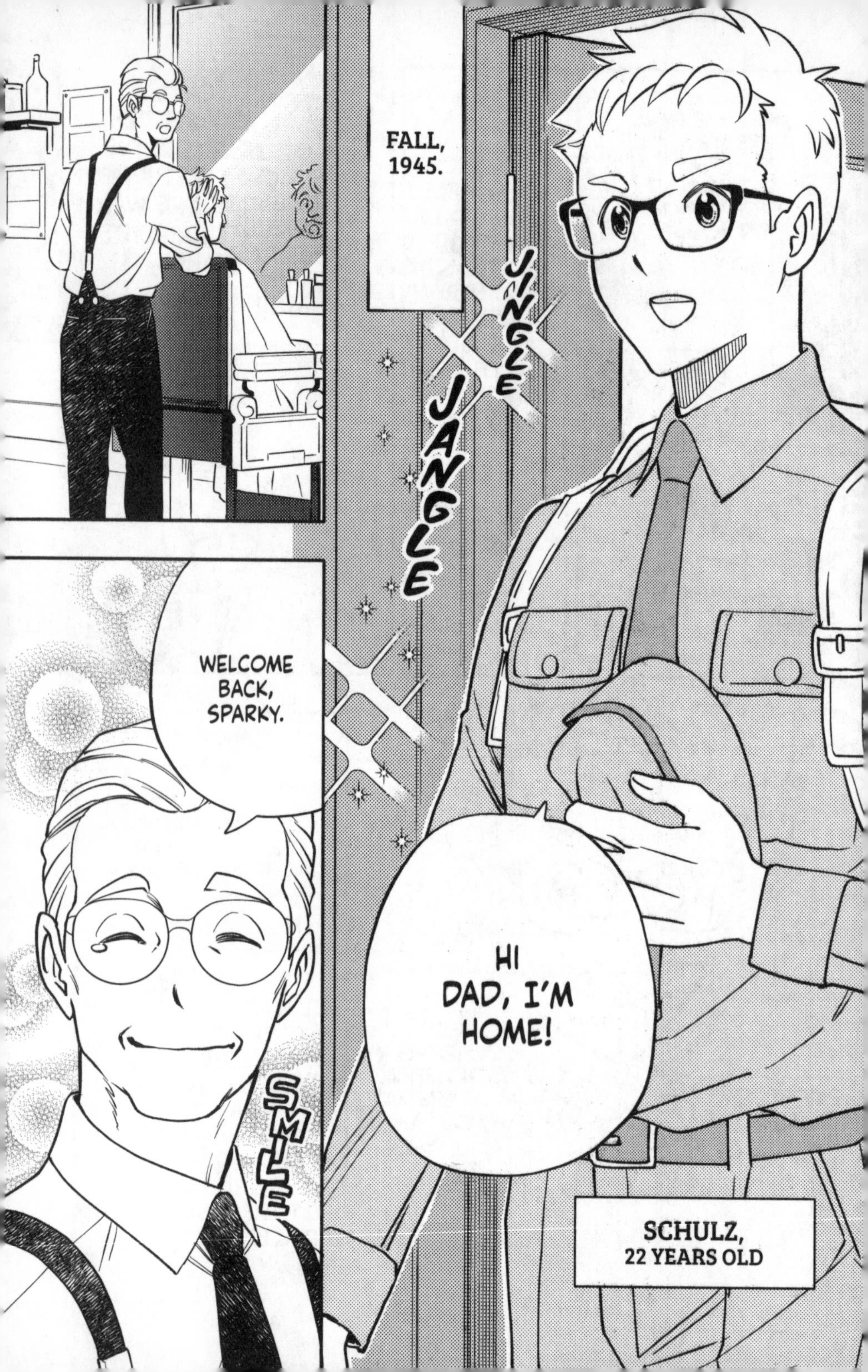
FALL, 1945.
JINGLE
JANGLE
HI DAD, I'M HOME!
SCHULZ, 22 YEARS OLD
WELCOME BACK, SPARKY.
SMILE

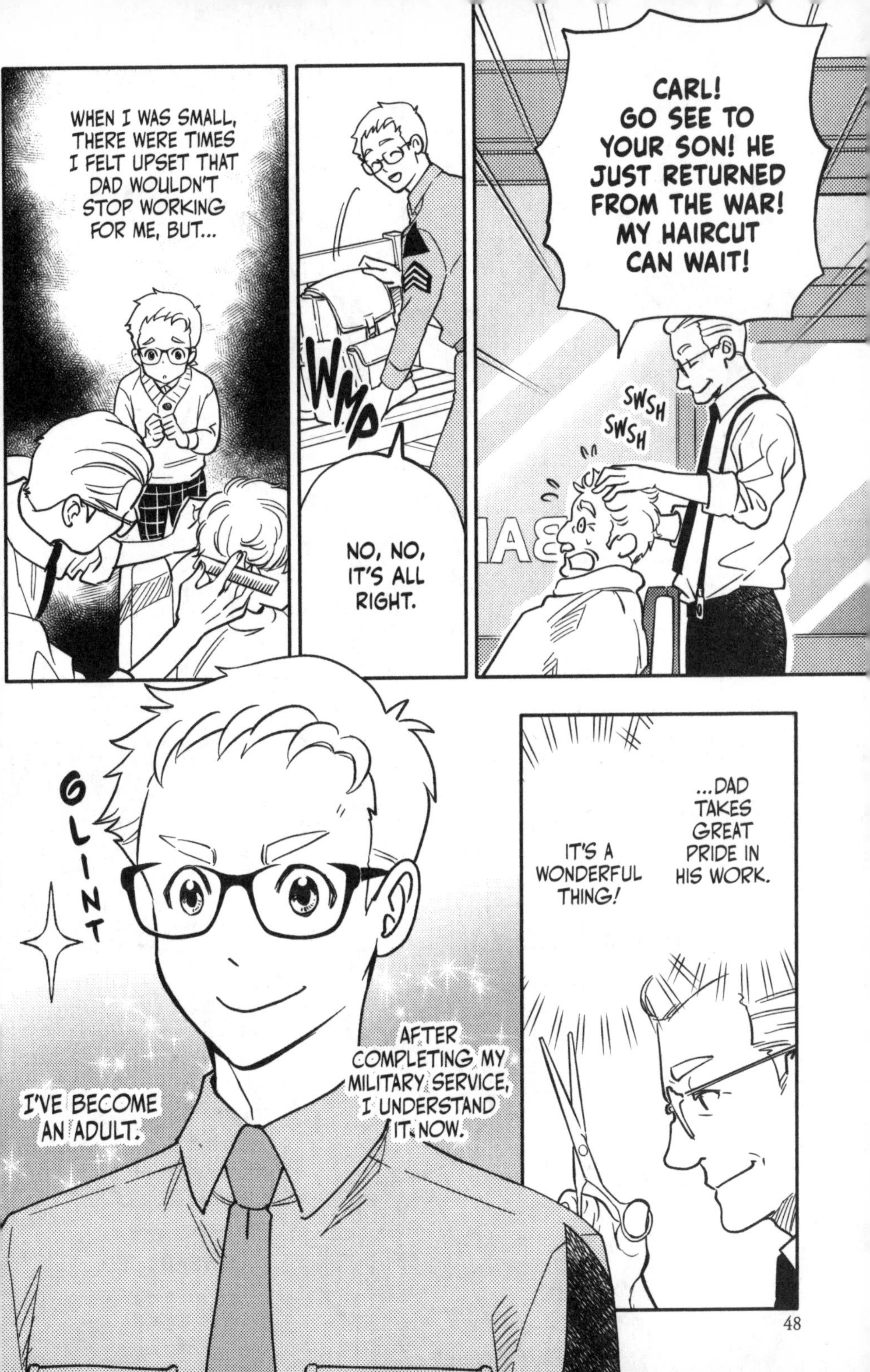

CARL! GO SEE TO YOUR SON! HE JUST RETURNED FROM THE WAR! MY HAIRCUT CAN WAIT!
SWSH SWSH
WMP
NO, NO, IT'S ALL RIGHT.
WHEN I WAS SMALL, THERE WERE TIMES I FELT UPSET THAT DAD WOULDN'T STOP WORKING FOR ME, BUT...
...DAD TAKES GREAT PRIDE IN HIS WORK.
IT'S A WONDERFUL THING!
AFTER COMPLETING MY MILITARY SERVICE, I UNDERSTAND IT NOW.
I'VE BECOME AN ADULT.
GLINT

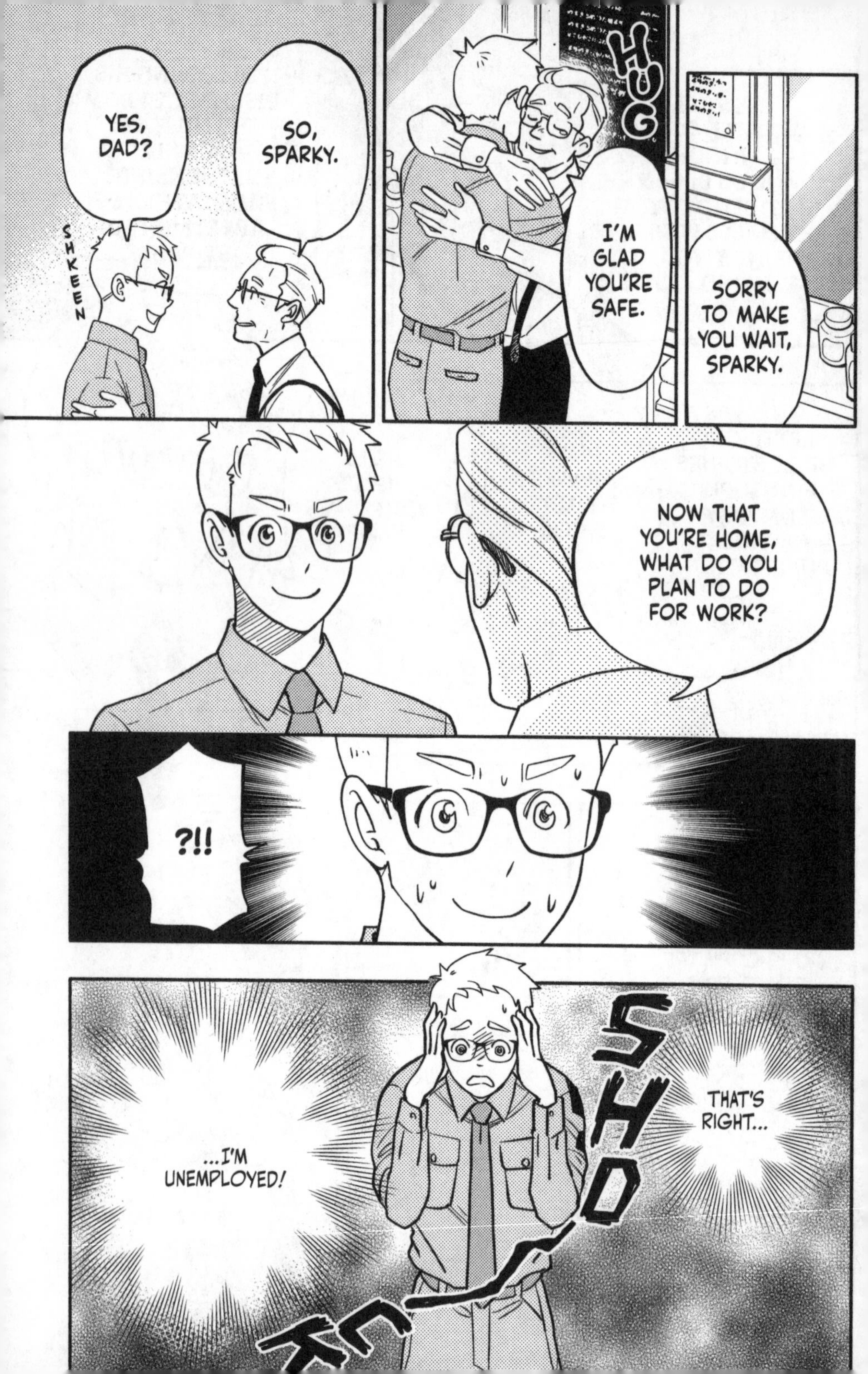
SORRY TO MAKE YOU WAIT, SPARKY.
HUG
I'M GLAD YOU'RE SAFE.
SO, SPARKY.
YES, DAD?
SHKEEN
NOW THAT YOU'RE HOME, WHAT DO YOU PLAN TO DO FOR WORK?
?!!
THAT'S RIGHT...
...I'M UNEMPLOYED!
SHOCK

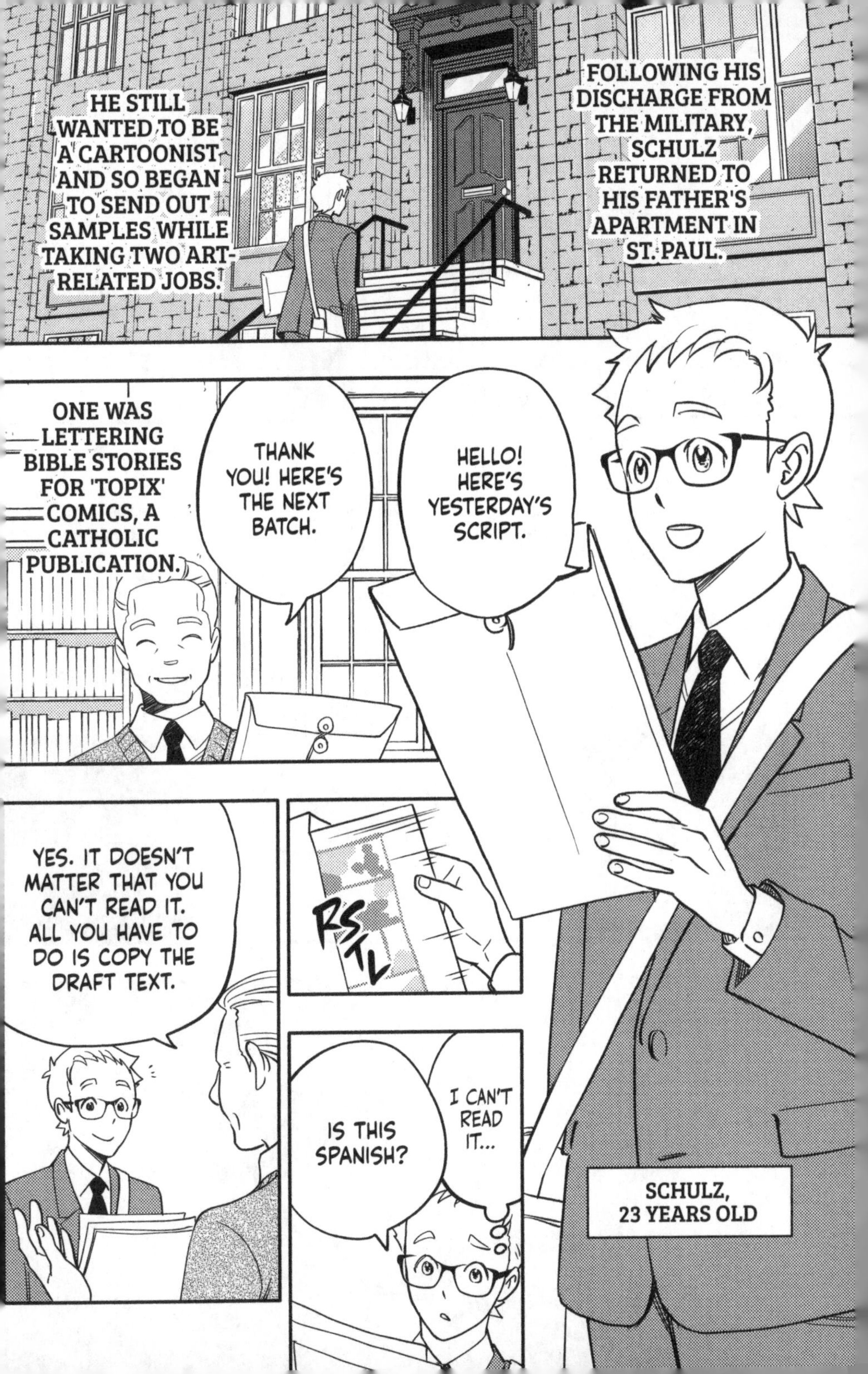
FOLLOWING HIS DISCHARGE FROM THE MILITARY, SCHULZ RETURNED TO HIS FATHER'S APARTMENT IN ST. PAUL.
HE STILL WANTED TO BE A CARTOONIST AND SO BEGAN TO SEND OUT SAMPLES WHILE TAKING TWO ART-RELATED JOBS.
HELLO! HERE'S YESTERDAY'S SCRIPT.
SCHULZ, 23 YEARS OLD
THANK YOU! HERE'S THE NEXT BATCH.
ONE WAS LETTERING BIBLE STORIES FOR 'TOPIX' COMICS, A CATHOLIC PUBLICATION.
RSTL
I CAN'T READ IT...
IS THIS SPANISH?
YES. IT DOESN'T MATTER THAT YOU CAN'T READ IT. ALL YOU HAVE TO DO IS COPY THE DRAFT TEXT.

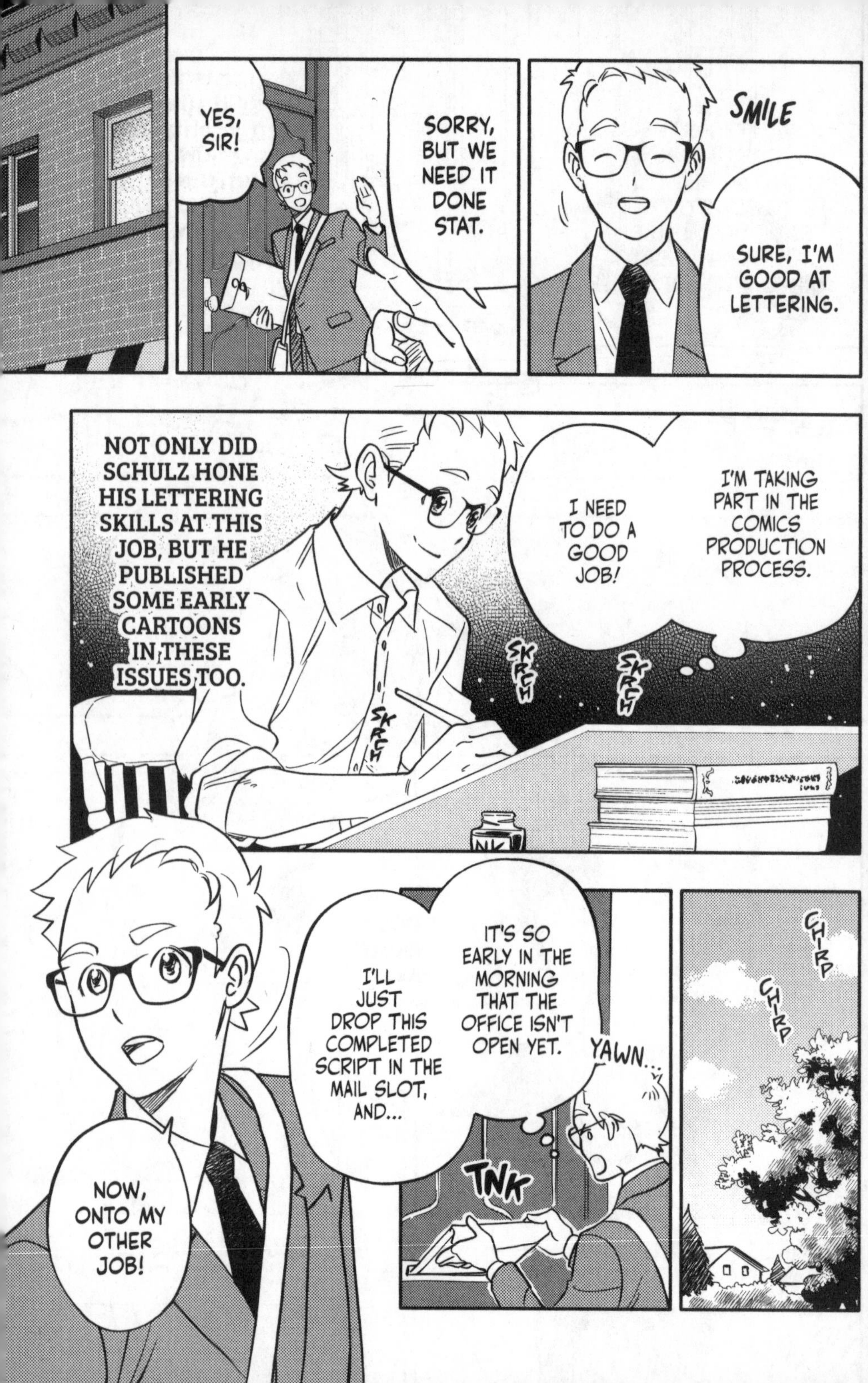
SMILE
SURE, I'M GOOD AT LETTERING.
SORRY, BUT WE NEED IT DONE STAT.
YES, SIR!
I'M TAKING PART IN THE COMICS PRODUCTION PROCESS.
I NEED TO DO A GOOD JOB!
NOT ONLY DID SCHULZ HONE HIS LETTERING SKILLS AT THIS JOB, BUT HE PUBLISHED SOME EARLY CARTOONS IN THESE ISSUES TOO.
SKRCH
SKRCH
SKRCH
CHIRP
CHIRP
IT'S SO EARLY IN THE MORNING THAT THE OFFICE ISN'T OPEN YET.
I'LL JUST DROP THIS COMPLETED SCRIPT IN THE MAIL SLOT, AND...
YAWN...
TNK
NOW, ONTO MY OTHER JOB!

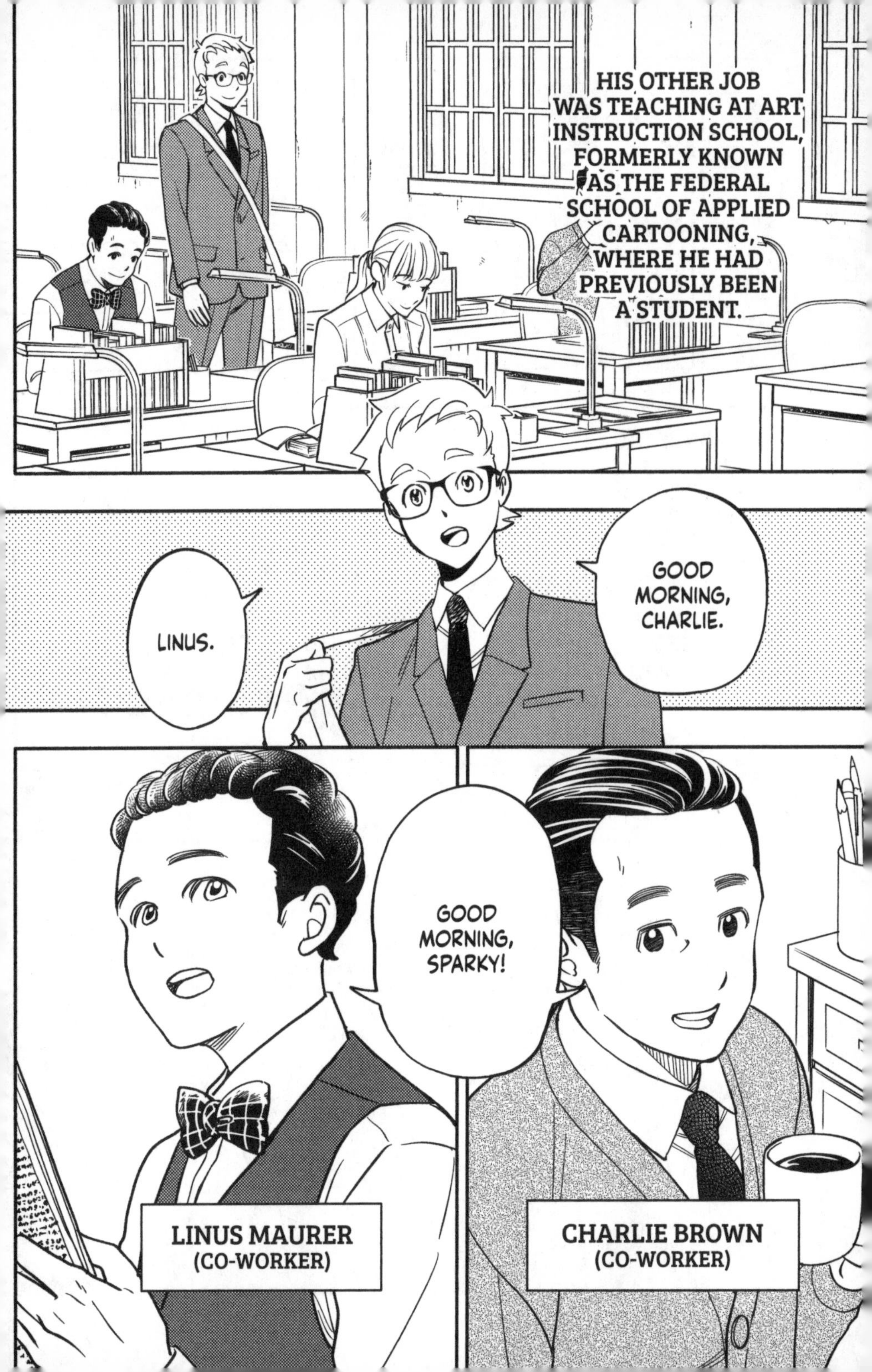
HIS OTHER JOB WAS TEACHING AT ART INSTRUCTION SCHOOL, FORMERLY KNOWN AS THE FEDERAL SCHOOL OF APPLIED CARTOONING, WHERE HE HAD PREVIOUSLY BEEN A STUDENT.
GOOD MORNING, CHARLIE.
LINUS.
GOOD MORNING, SPARKY!
CHARLIE BROWN (CO-WORKER)
LINUS MAURER (CO-WORKER)

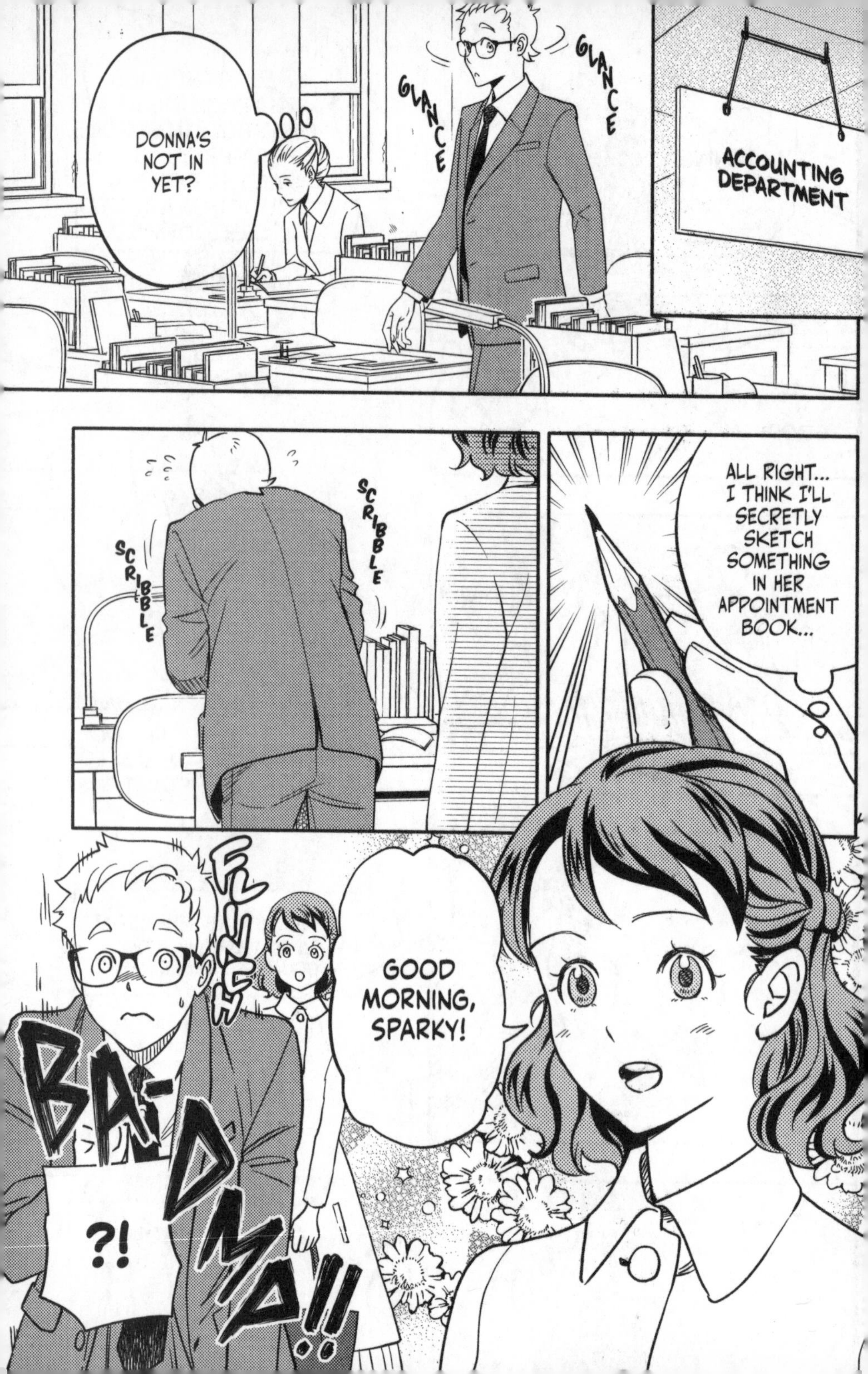

ACCOUNTING DEPARTMENT
GLANCE
GLANCE
DONNA'S NOT IN YET?
ALL RIGHT... I THINK I'LL SECRETLY SKETCH SOMETHING IN HER APPOINTMENT BOOK...
SCRIBBLE
SCRIBBLE
GOOD MORNING, SPARKY!
FLINCH
BA-DMP!!
?!

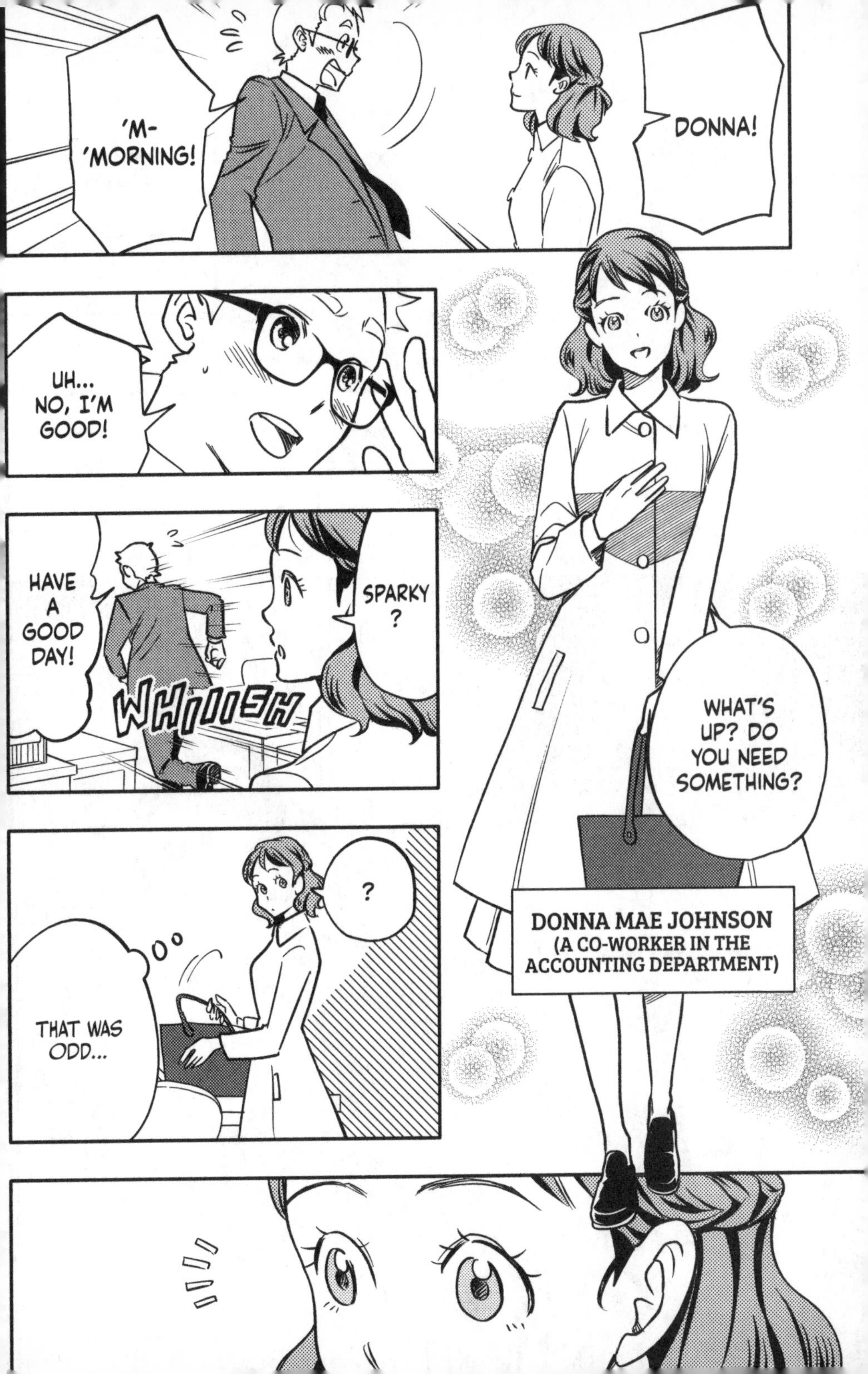
DONNA!
'M-
'MORNING!
WHAT'S UP? DO YOU NEED SOMETHING?
DONNA MAE JOHNSON (A CO-WORKER IN THE ACCOUNTING DEPARTMENT)
UH... NO, I'M GOOD!
SPARKY ?
HAVE A GOOD DAY!
WHIIISH
?
THAT WAS ODD...

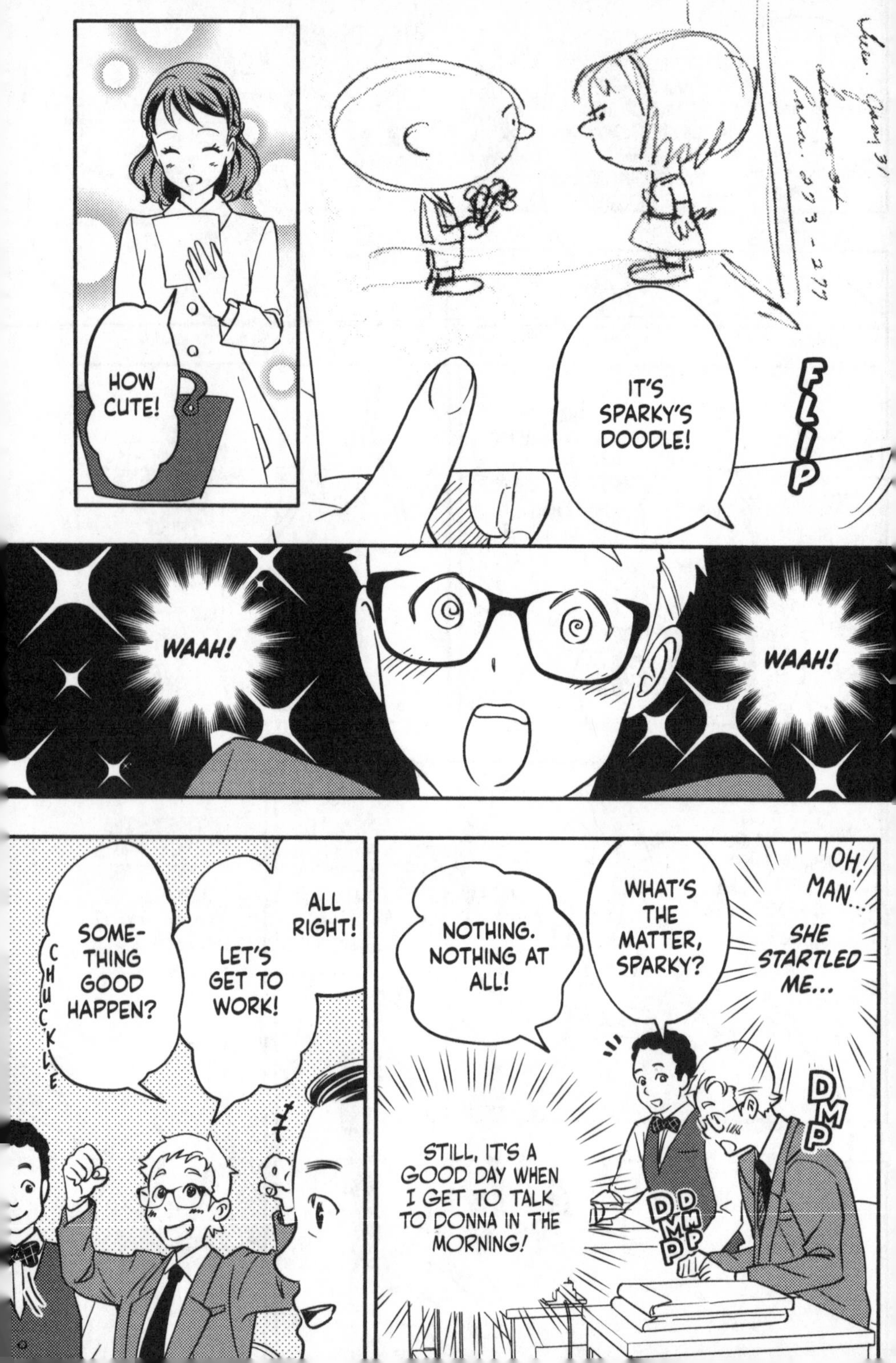
FLIP
IT'S SPARKY'S DOODLE!
HOW CUTE!
WAAH!
WAAH!
OH, MAN... SHE STARTLED ME...
WHAT'S THE MATTER, SPARKY?
NOTHING. NOTHING AT ALL!
DMP
DMP DMP
STILL, IT'S A GOOD DAY WHEN I GET TO TALK TO DONNA IN THE MORNING!
ALL RIGHT!
LET'S GET TO WORK!
SOME-THING GOOD HAPPEN?
CHUCKLE

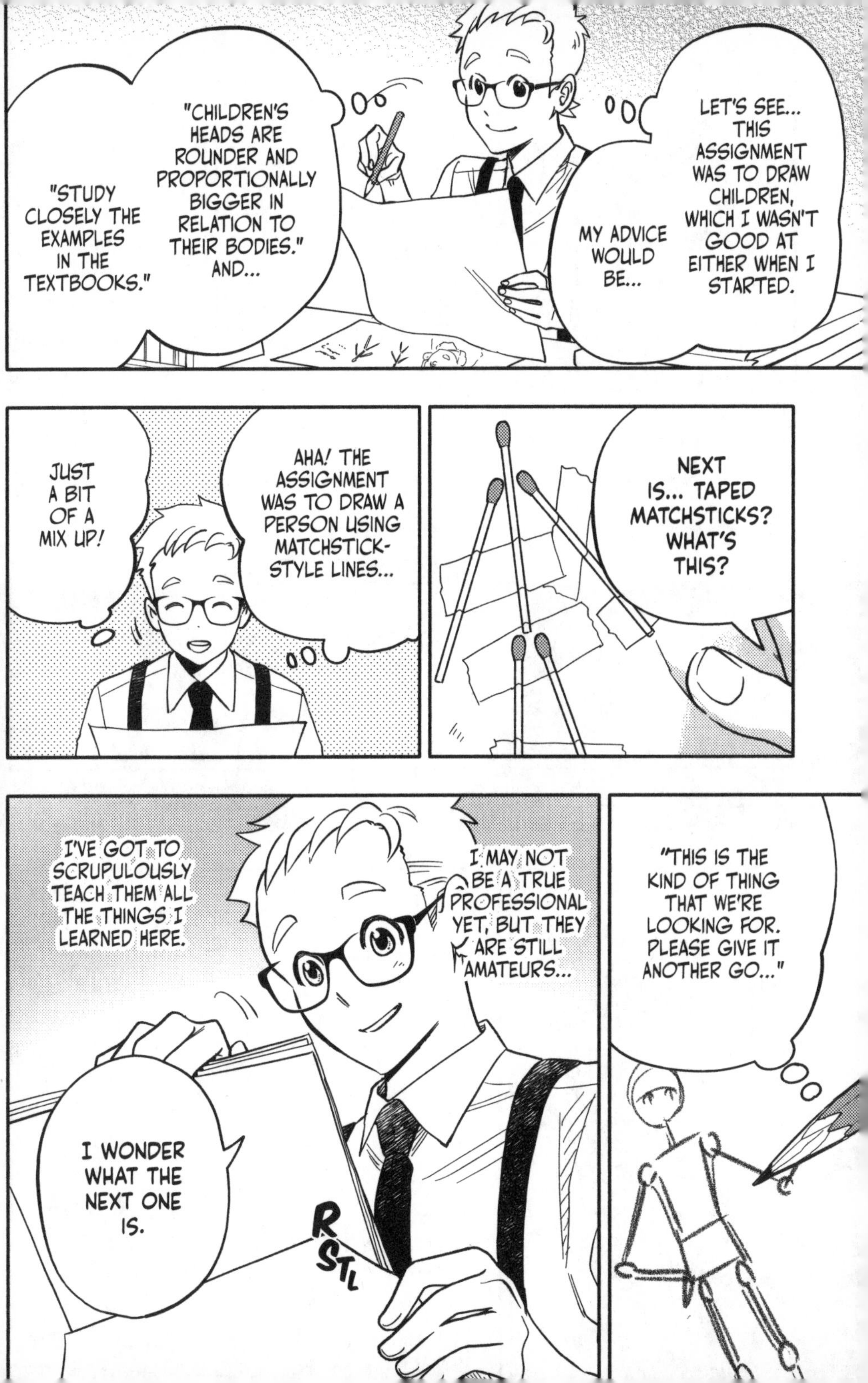
LET'S SEE... THIS ASSIGNMENT WAS TO DRAW CHILDREN, WHICH I WASN'T GOOD AT EITHER WHEN I STARTED.
MY ADVICE WOULD BE...
"CHILDREN'S HEADS ARE ROUNDER AND PROPORTIONALLY BIGGER IN RELATION TO THEIR BODIES." AND...
"STUDY CLOSELY THE EXAMPLES IN THE TEXTBOOKS."
NEXT IS... TAPED MATCHSTICKS? WHAT'S THIS?
AHA! THE ASSIGNMENT WAS TO DRAW A PERSON USING MATCHSTICK-STYLE LINES...
JUST A BIT OF A MIX UP!
"THIS IS THE KIND OF THING THAT WE'RE LOOKING FOR. PLEASE GIVE IT ANOTHER GO..."
I MAY NOT BE A TRUE PROFESSIONAL YET, BUT THEY ARE STILL AMATEURS...
I'VE GOT TO SCRUPULOUSLY TEACH THEM ALL THE THINGS I LEARNED HERE.
I WONDER WHAT THE NEXT ONE IS.
RSTL

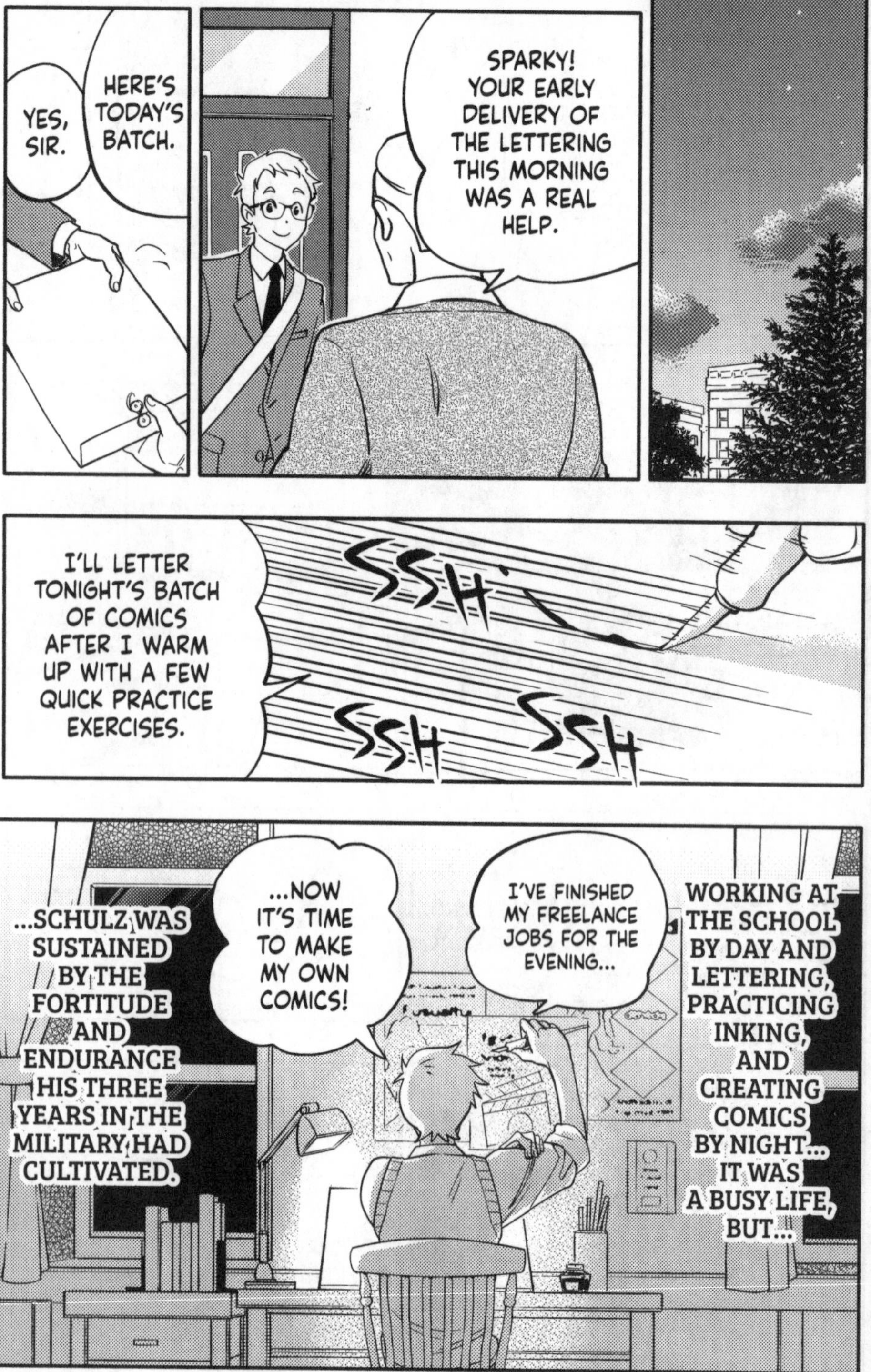
SPARKY! YOUR EARLY DELIVERY OF THE LETTERING THIS MORNING WAS A REAL HELP.
HERE'S TODAY'S BATCH.
YES, SIR.
SSH
I'LL LETTER TONIGHT'S BATCH OF COMICS AFTER I WARM UP WITH A FEW QUICK PRACTICE EXERCISES.
SSH
SSH
WORKING AT THE SCHOOL BY DAY AND LETTERING, PRACTICING INKING, AND CREATING COMICS BY NIGHT... IT WAS A BUSY LIFE, BUT...
I'VE FINISHED MY FREELANCE JOBS FOR THE EVENING...
...NOW IT'S TIME TO MAKE MY OWN COMICS!
...SCHULZ WAS SUSTAINED BY THE FORTITUDE AND ENDURANCE HIS THREE YEARS IN THE MILITARY HAD CULTIVATED.

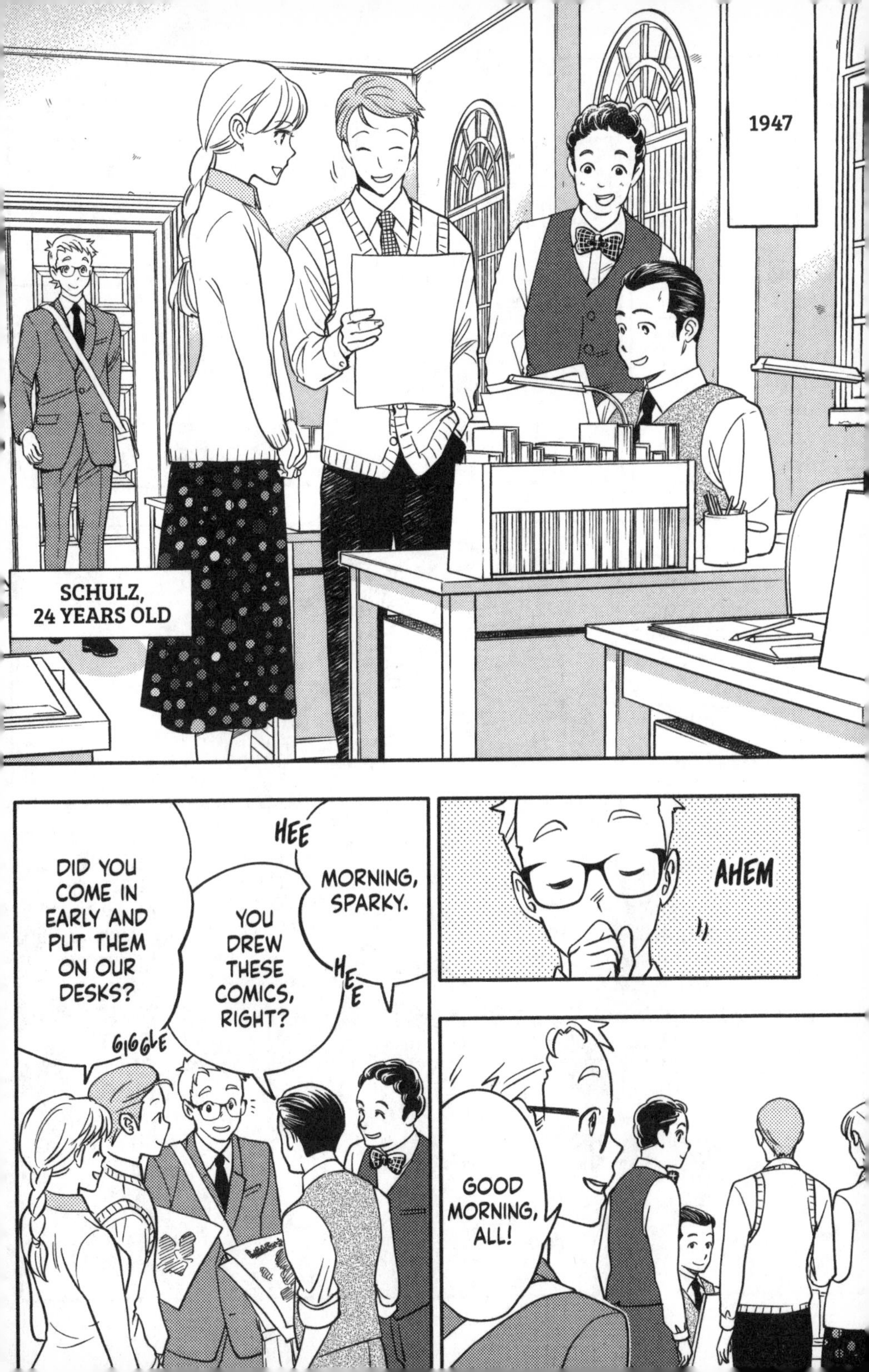
1947
SCHULZ, 24 YEARS OLD
AHEM
GOOD MORNING, ALL!
HEE
MORNING, SPARKY.
HEE
YOU DREW THESE COMICS, RIGHT?
DID YOU COME IN EARLY AND PUT THEM ON OUR DESKS?
GIGGLE

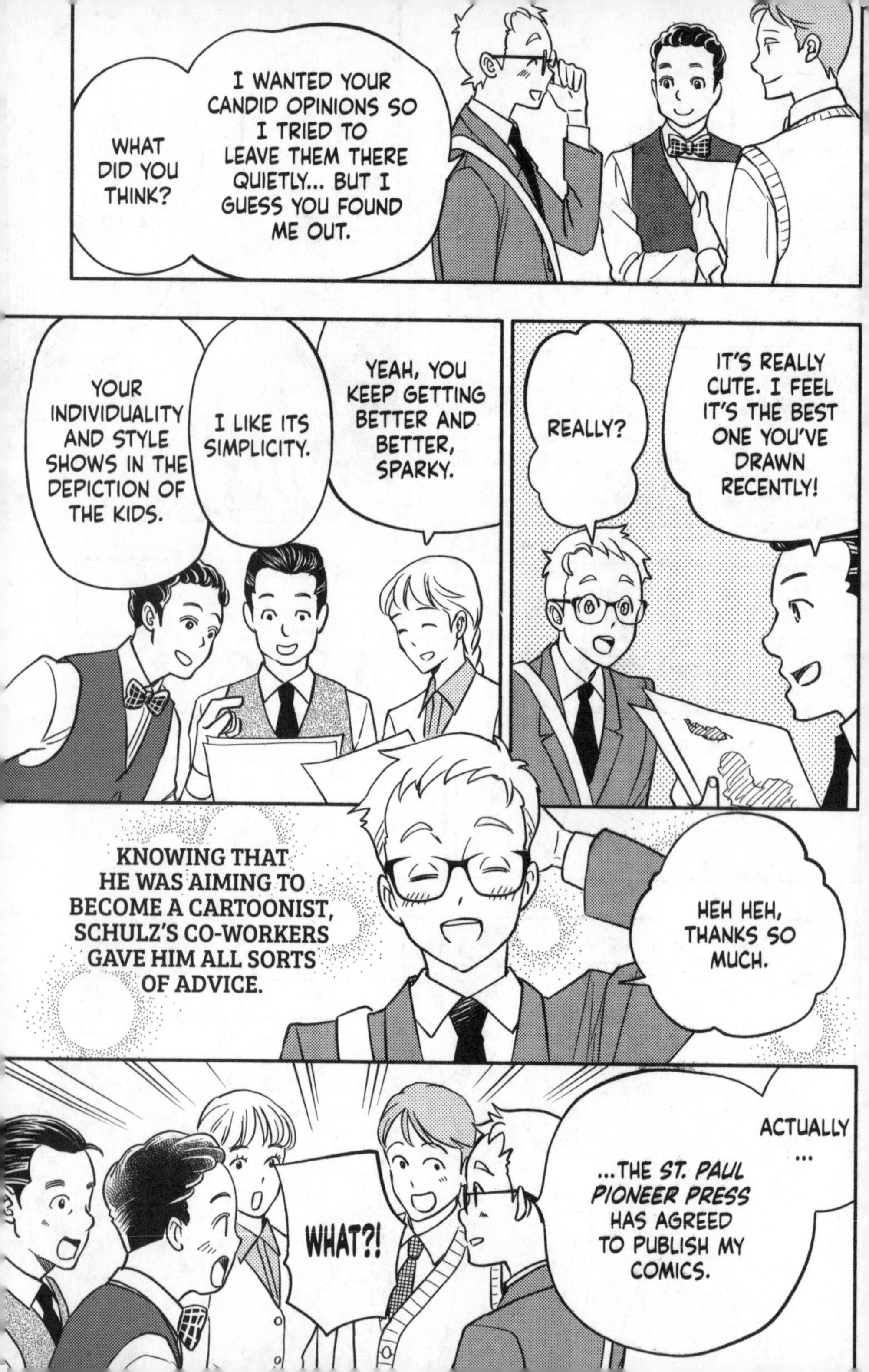
I WANTED YOUR CANDID OPINIONS SO I TRIED TO LEAVE THEM THERE QUIETLY... BUT I GUESS YOU FOUND ME OUT.
WHAT DID YOU THINK?
IT'S REALLY CUTE. I FEEL IT'S THE BEST ONE YOU'VE DRAWN RECENTLY!
REALLY?
YEAH, YOU KEEP GETTING BETTER AND BETTER, SPARKY.
I LIKE ITS SIMPLICITY.
YOUR INDIVIDUALITY AND STYLE SHOWS IN THE DEPICTION OF THE KIDS.
HEH HEH, THANKS SO MUCH.
KNOWING THAT HE WAS AIMING TO BECOME A CARTOONIST, SCHULZ'S CO-WORKERS GAVE HIM ALL SORTS OF ADVICE.
ACTUALLY ...
...THE *ST. PAUL PIONEER PRESS* HAS AGREED TO PUBLISH MY COMICS.
WHAT?!

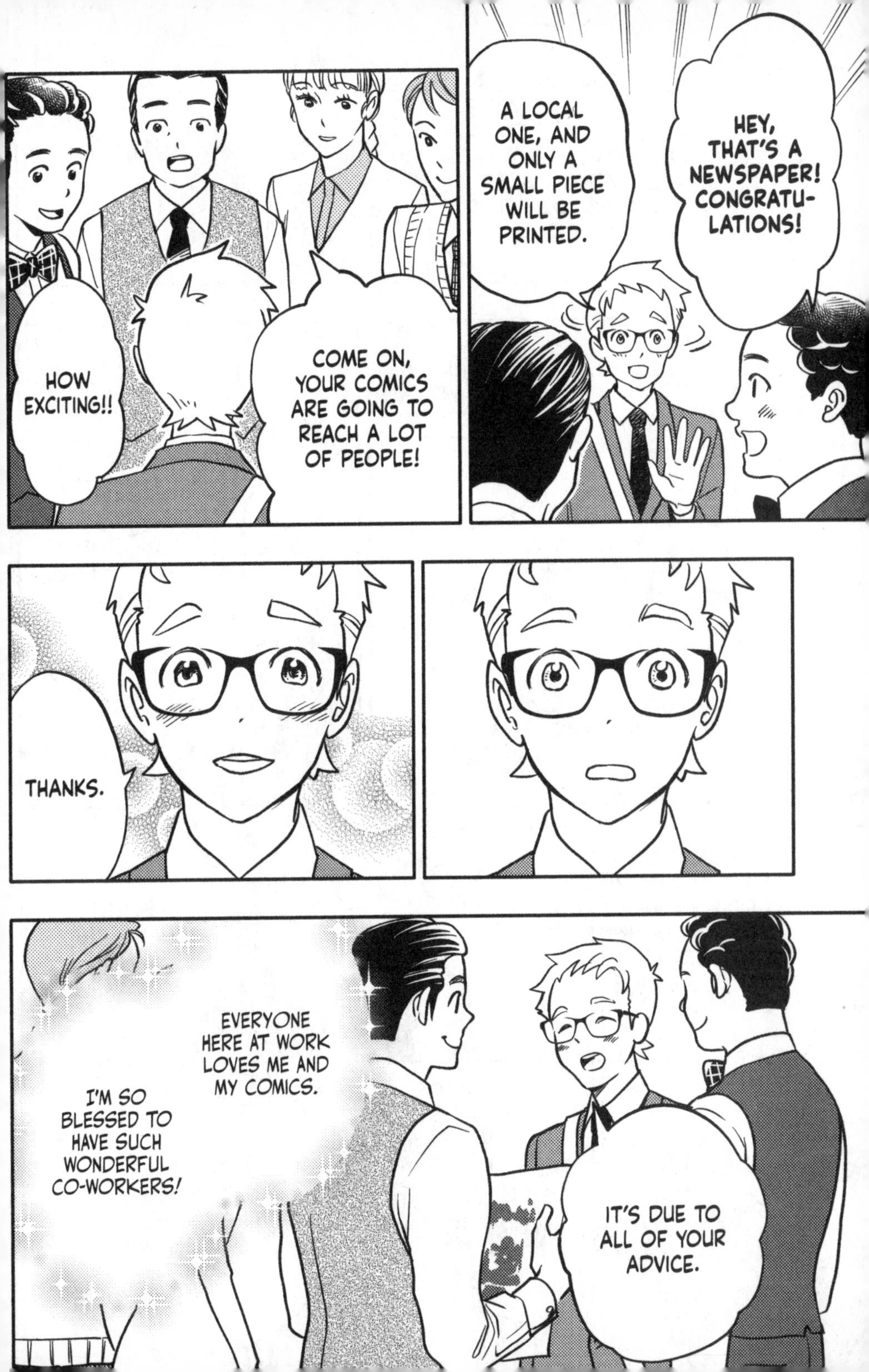
HEY, THAT'S A NEWSPAPER! CONGRATU-LATIONS!
A LOCAL ONE, AND ONLY A SMALL PIECE WILL BE PRINTED.
COME ON, YOUR COMICS ARE GOING TO REACH A LOT OF PEOPLE!
HOW EXCITING!!
THANKS.
IT'S DUE TO ALL OF YOUR ADVICE.
EVERYONE HERE AT WORK LOVES ME AND MY COMICS.
I'M SO BLESSED TO HAVE SUCH WONDERFUL CO-WORKERS!

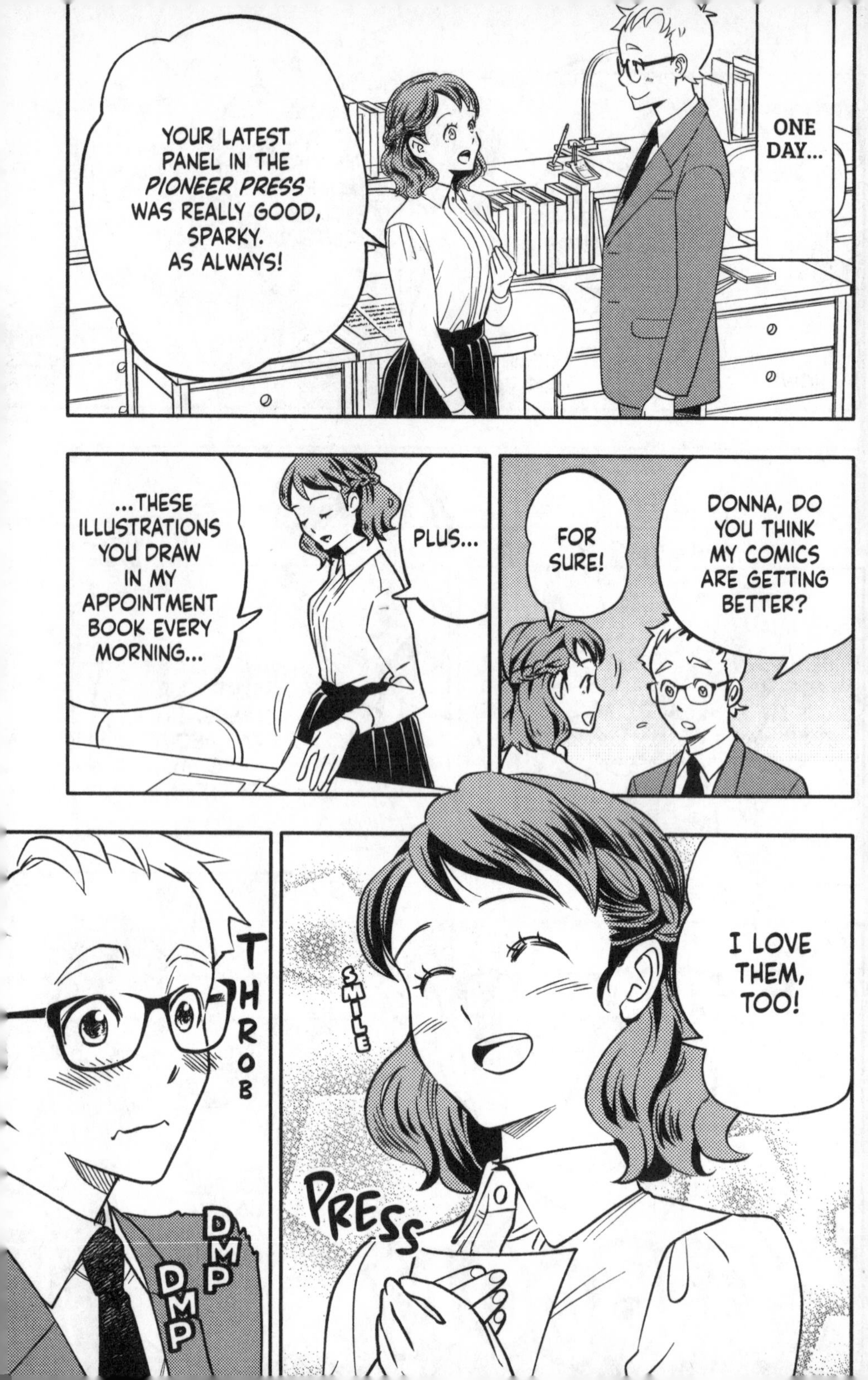
ONE DAY...
YOUR LATEST PANEL IN THE *PIONEER PRESS* WAS REALLY GOOD, SPARKY. AS ALWAYS!
DONNA, DO YOU THINK MY COMICS ARE GETTING BETTER?
FOR SURE!
PLUS...
...THESE ILLUSTRATIONS YOU DRAW IN MY APPOINTMENT BOOK EVERY MORNING...
I LOVE THEM, TOO!
SMILE
PRESS
THROB
DMP
DMP

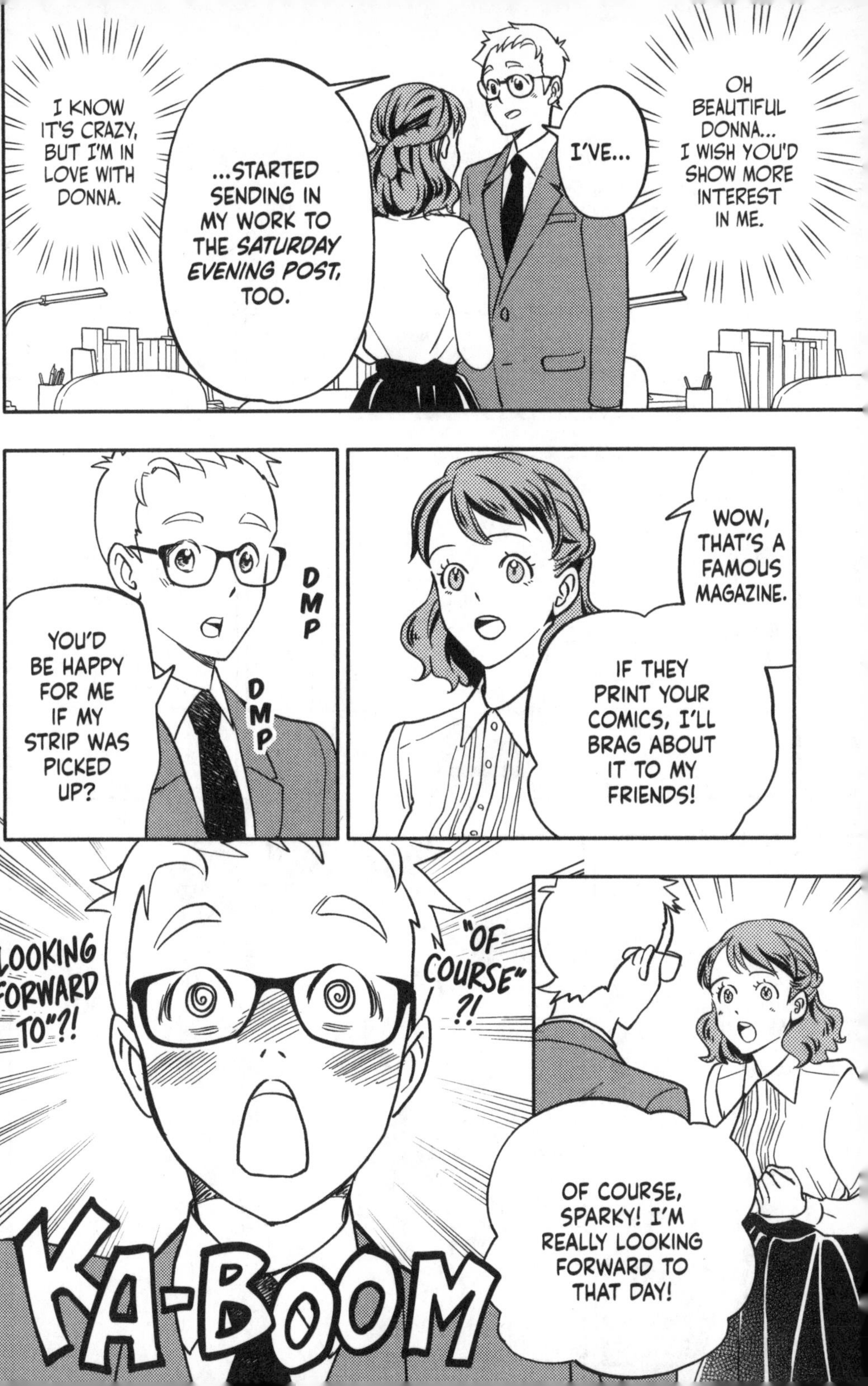
OH BEAUTIFUL DONNA... I WISH YOU'D SHOW MORE INTEREST IN ME.
I'VE...
...STARTED SENDING IN MY WORK TO THE *SATURDAY EVENING POST,* TOO.
I KNOW IT'S CRAZY, BUT I'M IN LOVE WITH DONNA.
WOW, THAT'S A FAMOUS MAGAZINE.
IF THEY PRINT YOUR COMICS, I'LL BRAG ABOUT IT TO MY FRIENDS!
DMP
DMP
YOU'D BE HAPPY FOR ME IF MY STRIP WAS PICKED UP?
OF COURSE, SPARKY! I'M REALLY LOOKING FORWARD TO THAT DAY!
"OF COURSE"?!
LOOKING FORWARD TO"?!
KA-BOOM

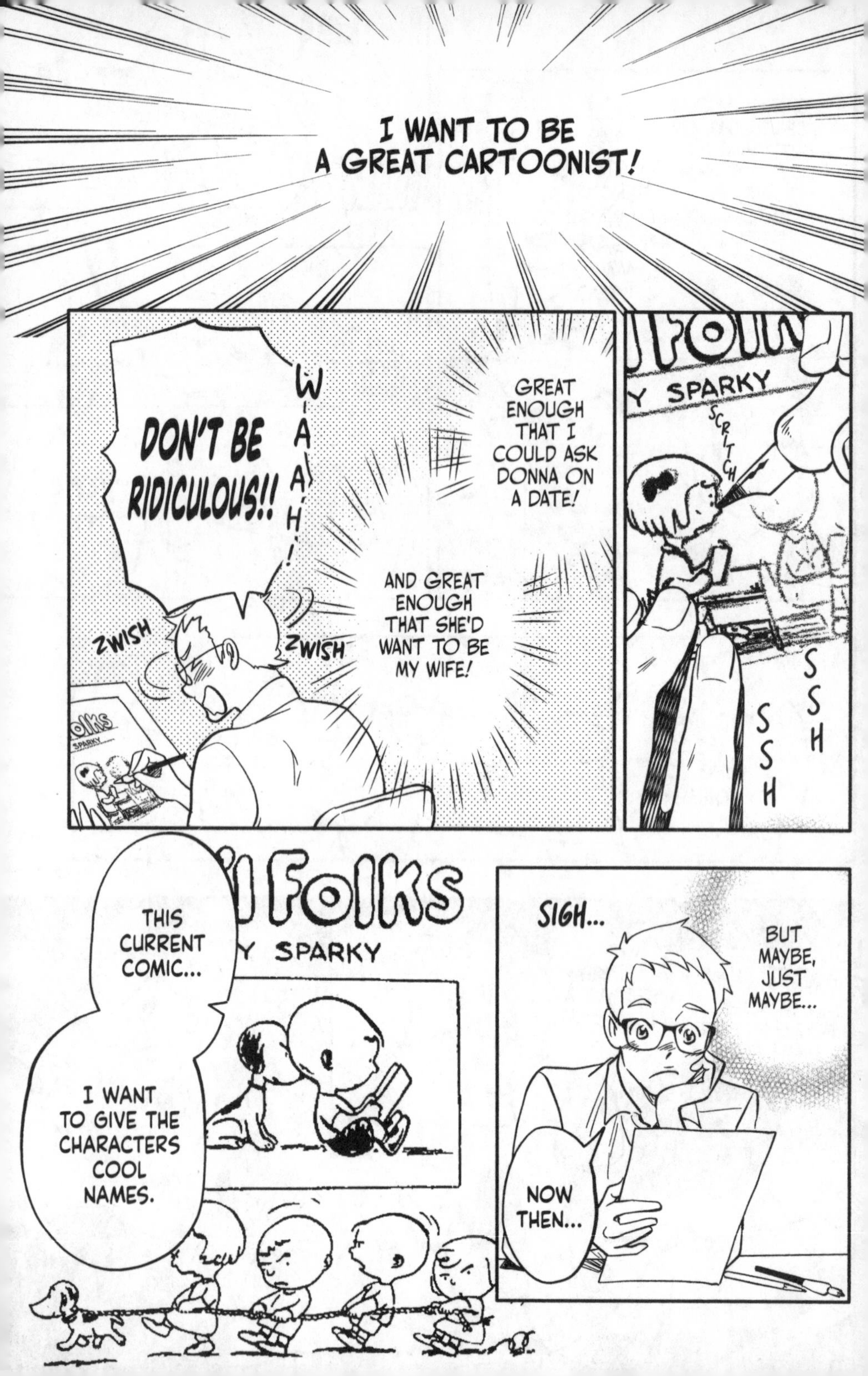
I WANT TO BE A GREAT CARTOONIST!
SPARKY
SCRITCH
SSH SSH
GREAT ENOUGH THAT I COULD ASK DONNA ON A DATE!
WAAAH!
DON'T BE RIDICULOUS!!
AND GREAT ENOUGH THAT SHE'D WANT TO BE MY WIFE!
ZWISH
ZWISH
SIGH...
BUT MAYBE, JUST MAYBE...
NOW THEN...
SPARKY
THIS CURRENT COMIC...
I WANT TO GIVE THE CHARACTERS COOL NAMES.

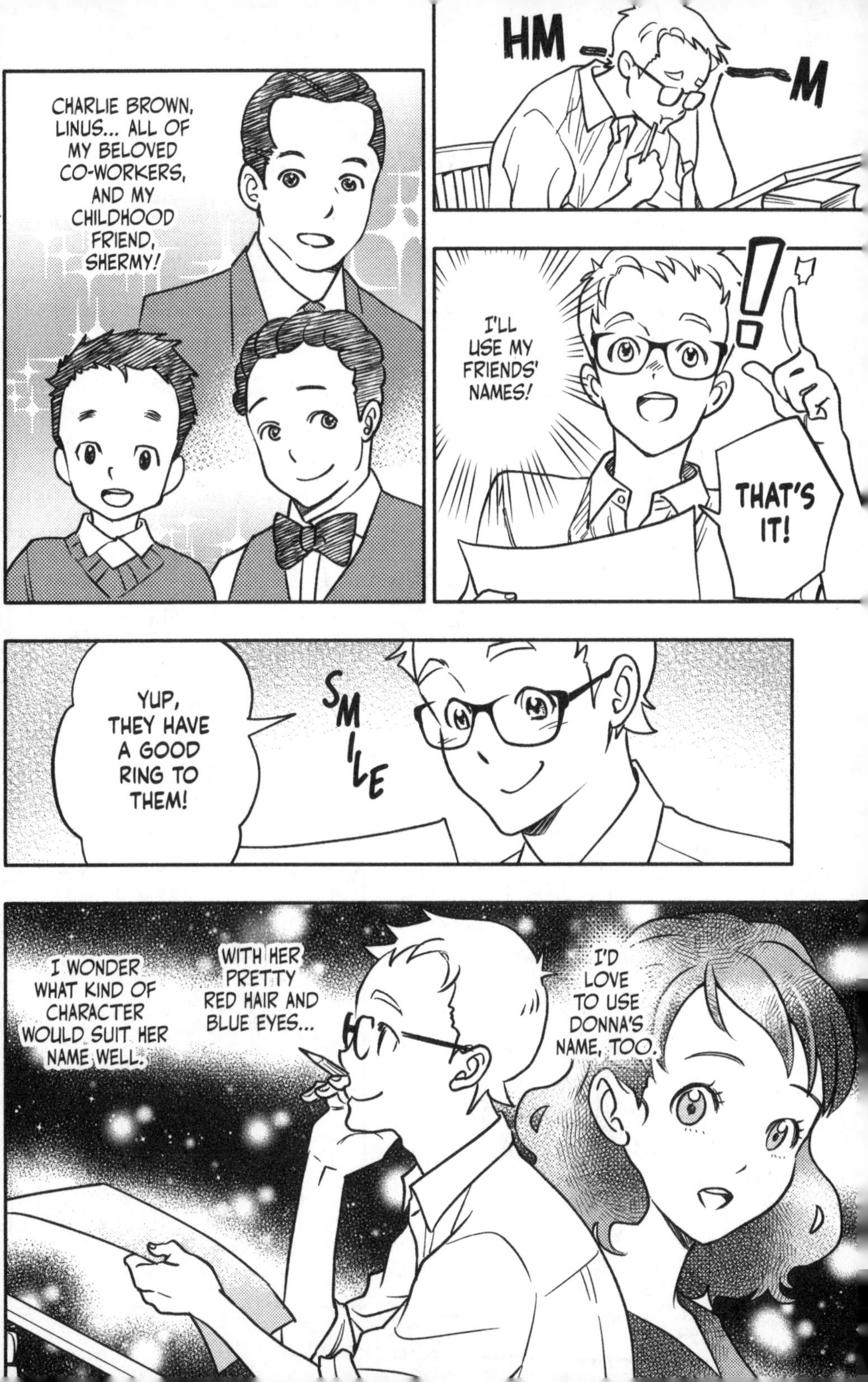
HM--M
THAT'S IT!
I'LL USE MY FRIENDS' NAMES!
CHARLIE BROWN, LINUS... ALL OF MY BELOVED CO-WORKERS, AND MY CHILDHOOD FRIEND, SHERMY!
SMILE
YUP, THEY HAVE A GOOD RING TO THEM!
I'D LOVE TO USE DONNA'S NAME, TOO.
WITH HER PRETTY RED HAIR AND BLUE EYES...
I WONDER WHAT KIND OF CHARACTER WOULD SUIT HER NAME WELL.

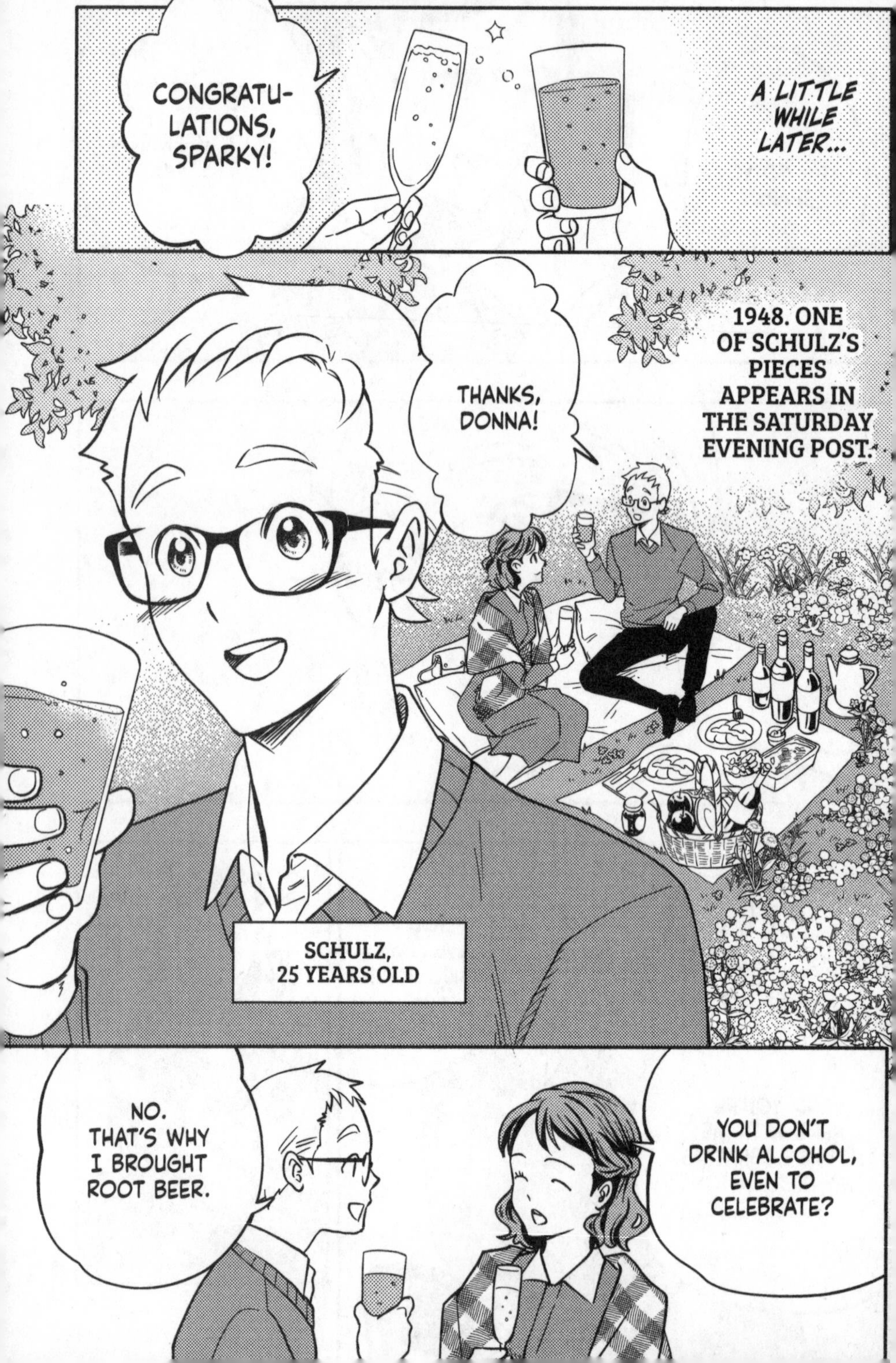
A LITTLE WHILE LATER...
CONGRATU-LATIONS, SPARKY!
1948. ONE OF SCHULZ'S PIECES APPEARS IN THE SATURDAY EVENING POST.
THANKS, DONNA!
SCHULZ, 25 YEARS OLD
YOU DON'T DRINK ALCOHOL, EVEN TO CELEBRATE?
NO. THAT'S WHY I BROUGHT ROOT BEER.

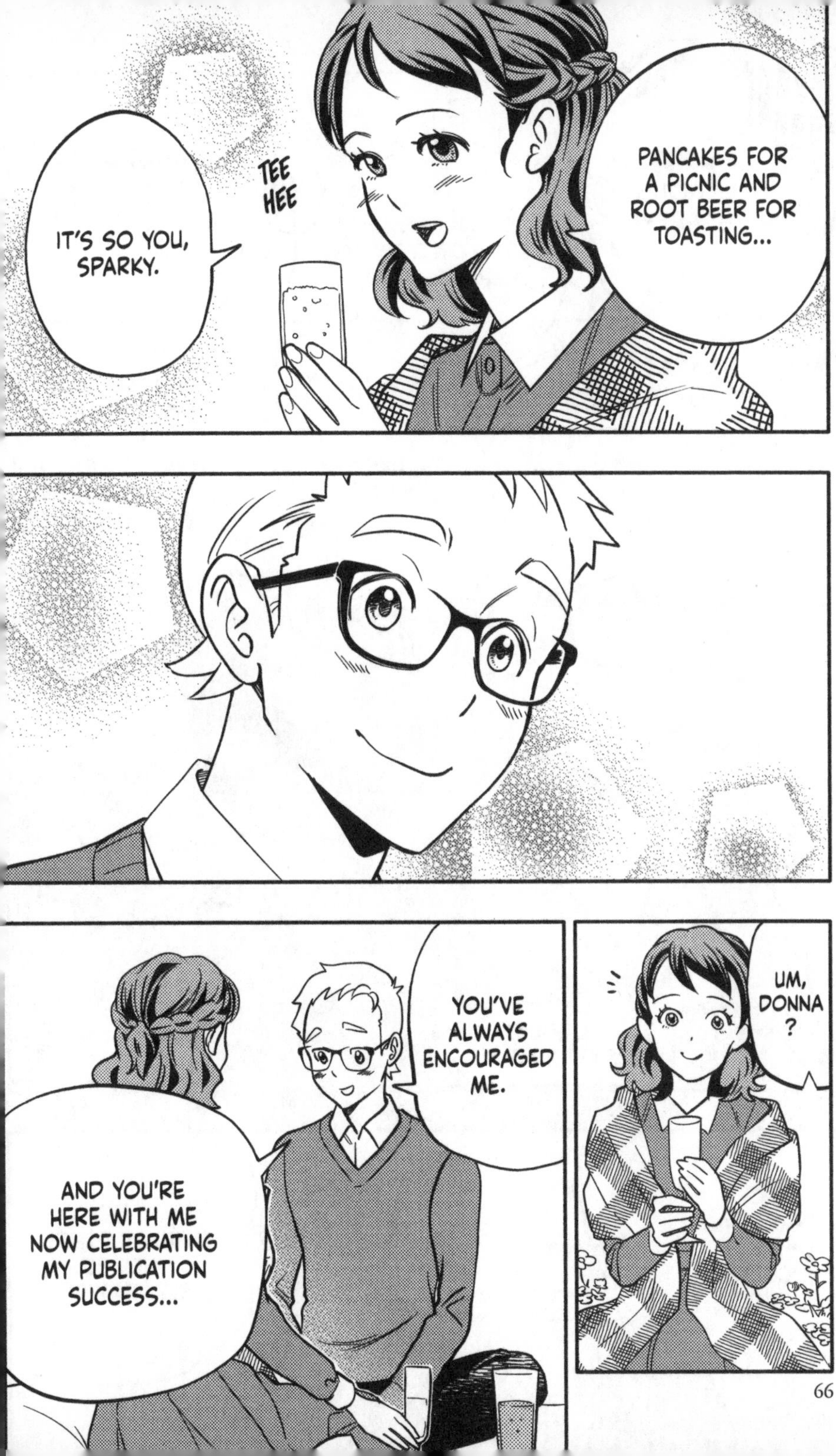
PANCAKES FOR A PICNIC AND ROOT BEER FOR TOASTING...
TEE HEE
IT'S SO YOU, SPARKY.
UM, DONNA ?
YOU'VE ALWAYS ENCOURAGED ME.
AND YOU'RE HERE WITH ME NOW CELEBRATING MY PUBLICATION SUCCESS...

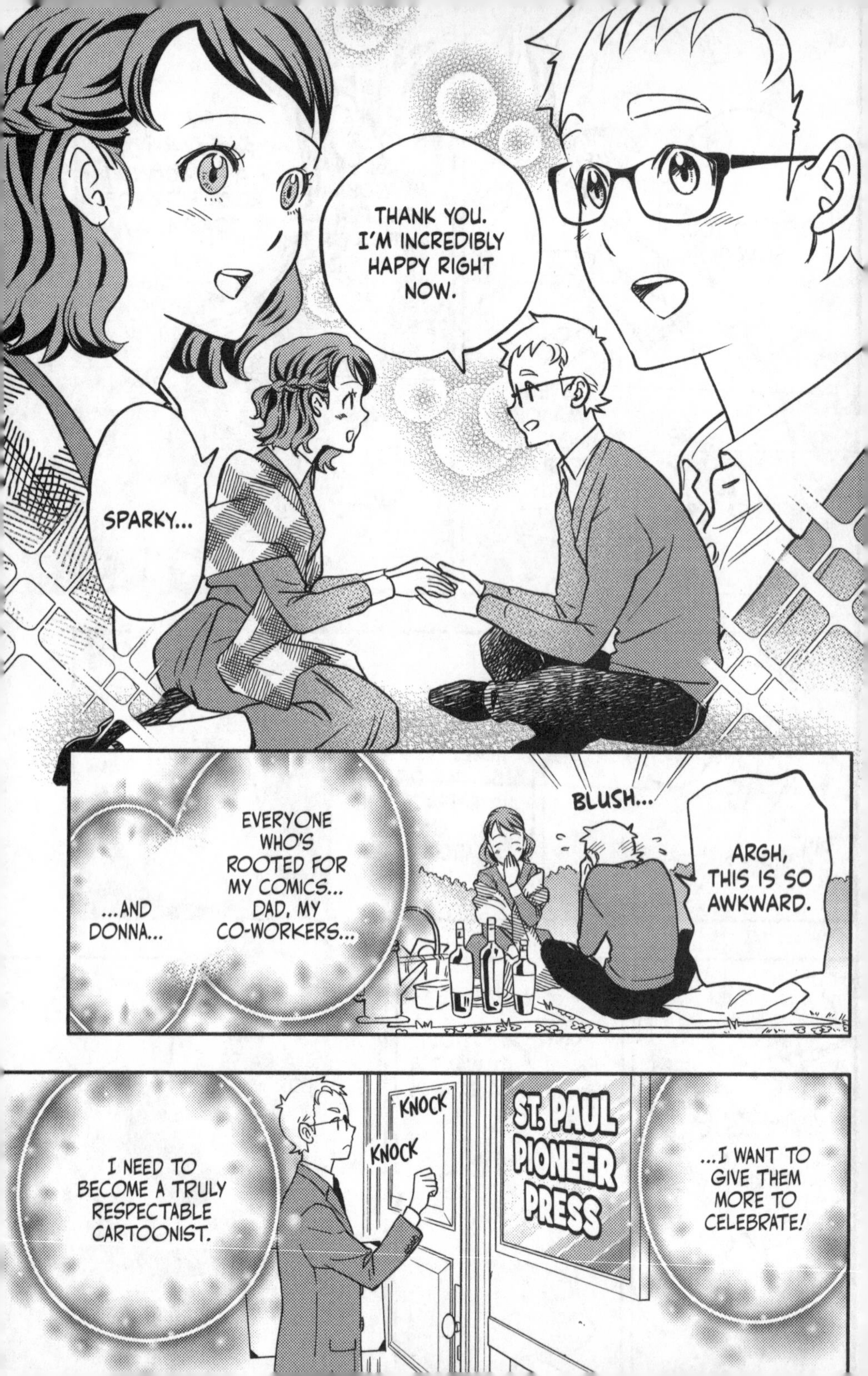
THANK YOU. I'M INCREDIBLY HAPPY RIGHT NOW.
SPARKY...
ARGH, THIS IS SO AWKWARD.
BLUSH...
EVERYONE WHO'S ROOTED FOR MY COMICS... DAD, MY CO-WORKERS...
...AND DONNA...
...I WANT TO GIVE THEM MORE TO CELEBRATE!
ST. PAUL PIONEER PRESS
KNOCK
KNOCK
I NEED TO BECOME A TRULY RESPECTABLE CARTOONIST.

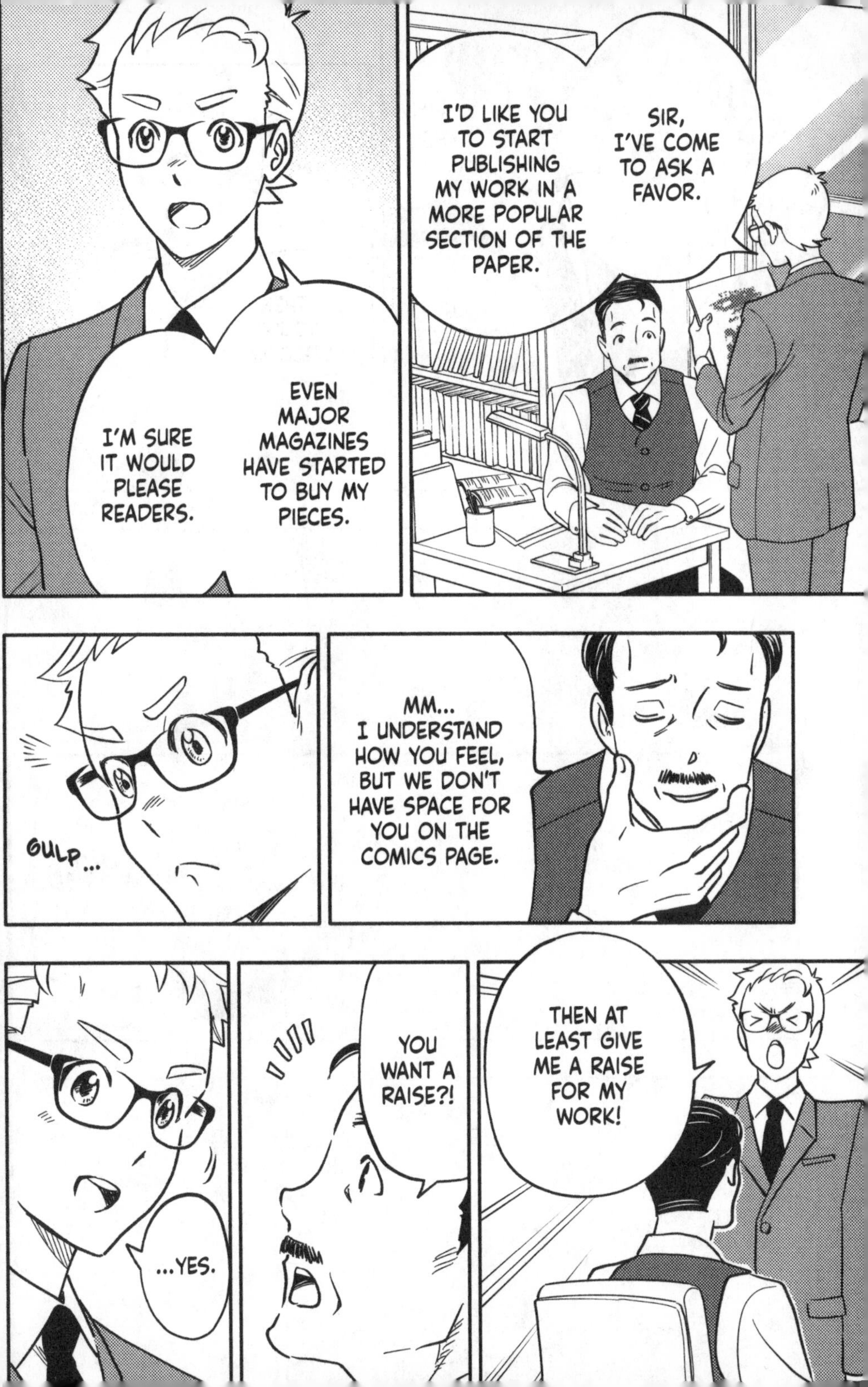
SIR, I'VE COME TO ASK A FAVOR.
I'D LIKE YOU TO START PUBLISHING MY WORK IN A MORE POPULAR SECTION OF THE PAPER.
EVEN MAJOR MAGAZINES HAVE STARTED TO BUY MY PIECES.
I'M SURE IT WOULD PLEASE READERS.
MM... I UNDERSTAND HOW YOU FEEL, BUT WE DON'T HAVE SPACE FOR YOU ON THE COMICS PAGE.
GULP...
THEN AT LEAST GIVE ME A RAISE FOR MY WORK!
YOU WANT A RAISE?!
...YES.

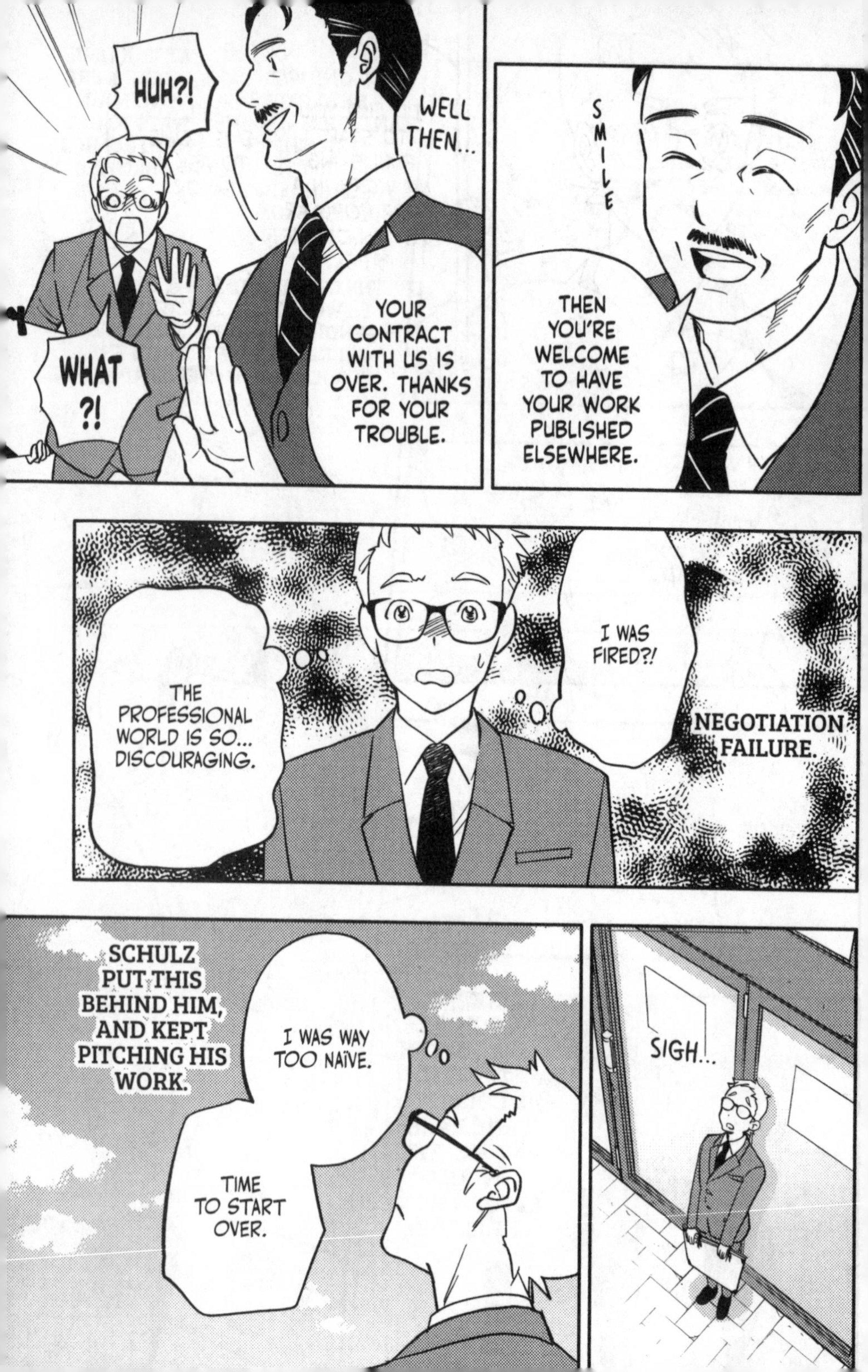
HUH?!
WELL THEN...
WHAT?!
YOUR CONTRACT WITH US IS OVER. THANKS FOR YOUR TROUBLE.
SMILE
THEN YOU'RE WELCOME TO HAVE YOUR WORK PUBLISHED ELSEWHERE.
THE PROFESSIONAL WORLD IS SO... DISCOURAGING.
I WAS FIRED?!
NEGOTIATION FAILURE.
SCHULZ PUT THIS BEHIND HIM, AND KEPT PITCHING HIS WORK.
I WAS WAY TOO NAÏVE.
TIME TO START OVER.
SIGH...

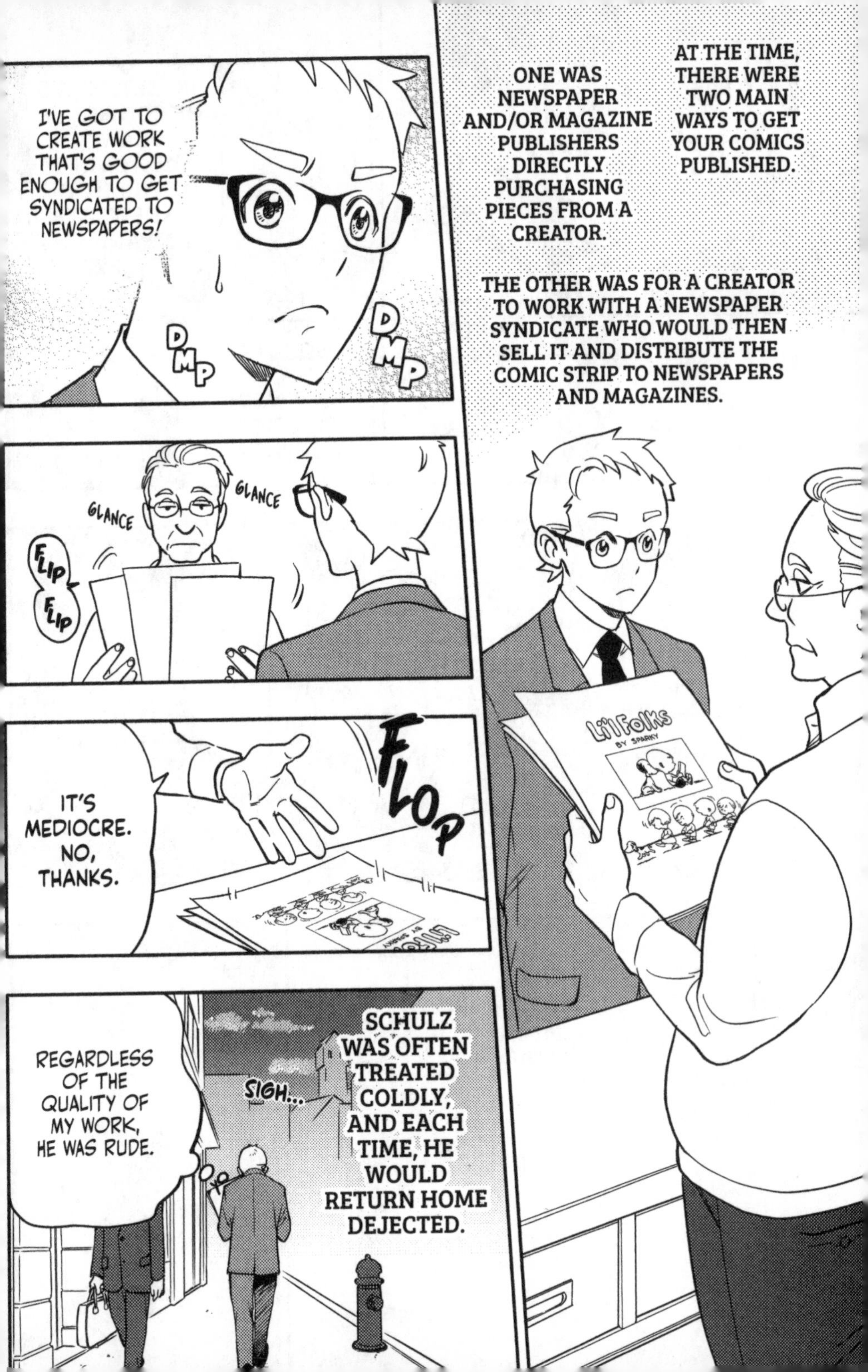
AT THE TIME, THERE WERE TWO MAIN WAYS TO GET YOUR COMICS PUBLISHED.
ONE WAS NEWSPAPER AND/OR MAGAZINE PUBLISHERS DIRECTLY PURCHASING PIECES FROM A CREATOR.
THE OTHER WAS FOR A CREATOR TO WORK WITH A NEWSPAPER SYNDICATE WHO WOULD THEN SELL IT AND DISTRIBUTE THE COMIC STRIP TO NEWSPAPERS AND MAGAZINES.
Li'l Folks
BY SPARKY
I'VE GOT TO CREATE WORK THAT'S GOOD ENOUGH TO GET SYNDICATED TO NEWSPAPERS!
DMP
DMP
GLANCE
GLANCE
FLIP
FLIP
FLOP
IT'S MEDIOCRE. NO, THANKS.
SCHULZ WAS OFTEN TREATED COLDLY, AND EACH TIME, HE WOULD RETURN HOME DEJECTED.
SIGH...
REGARDLESS OF THE QUALITY OF MY WORK, HE WAS RUDE.

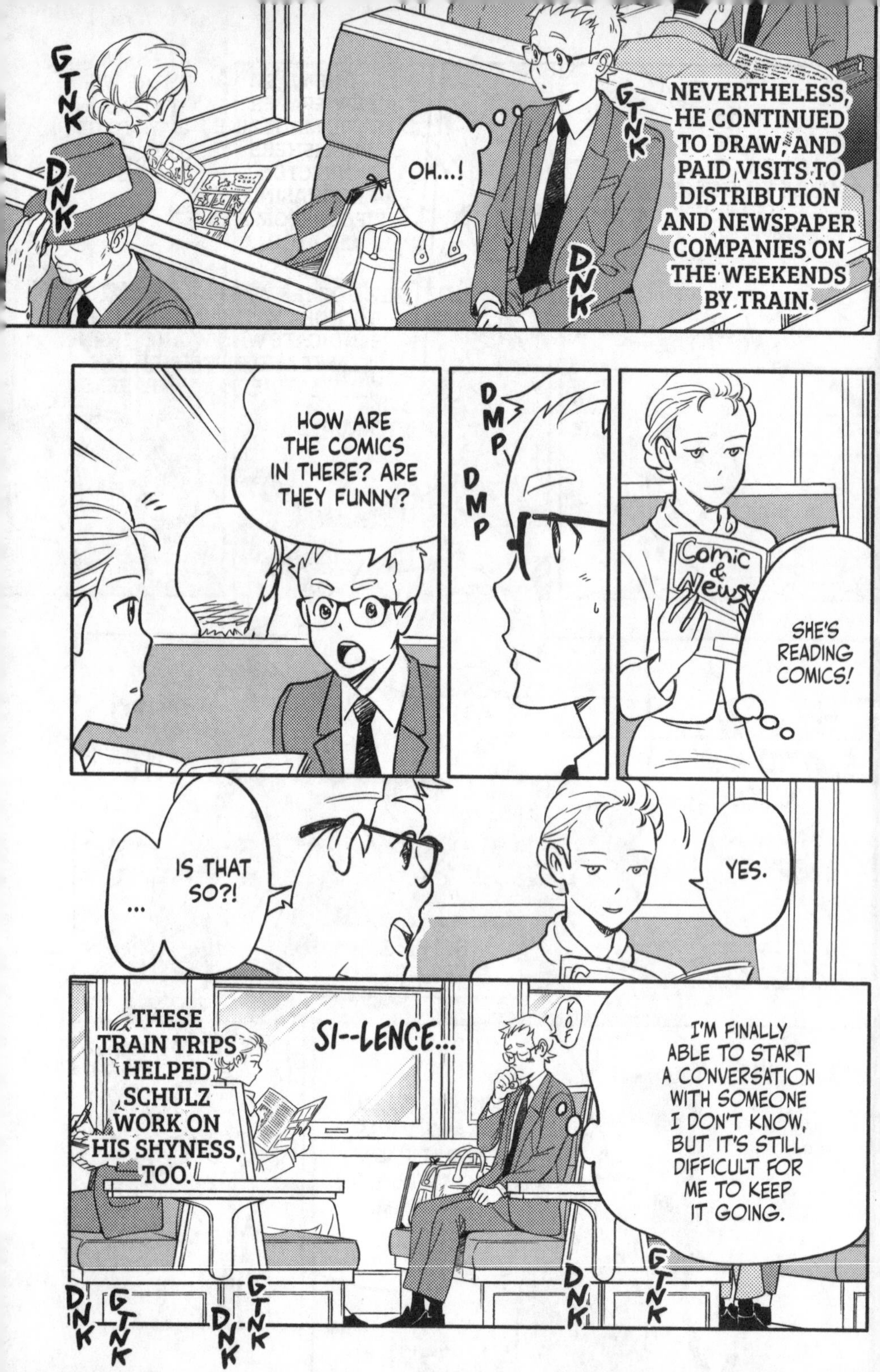
NEVERTHELESS, HE CONTINUED TO DRAW, AND PAID VISITS TO DISTRIBUTION AND NEWSPAPER COMPANIES ON THE WEEKENDS BY TRAIN.
GTNK
DNK
OH...!
GTNK
DNK
SHE'S READING COMICS!
Comic & News
DMP
DMP
HOW ARE THE COMICS IN THERE? ARE THEY FUNNY?
YES.
IS THAT SO?!
...
I'M FINALLY ABLE TO START A CONVERSATION WITH SOMEONE I DON'T KNOW, BUT IT'S STILL DIFFICULT FOR ME TO KEEP IT GOING.
KOF
SI--LENCE...
THESE TRAIN TRIPS HELPED SCHULZ WORK ON HIS SHYNESS, TOO.
GTNK
DNK
GTNK
DNK
GTNK
DNK

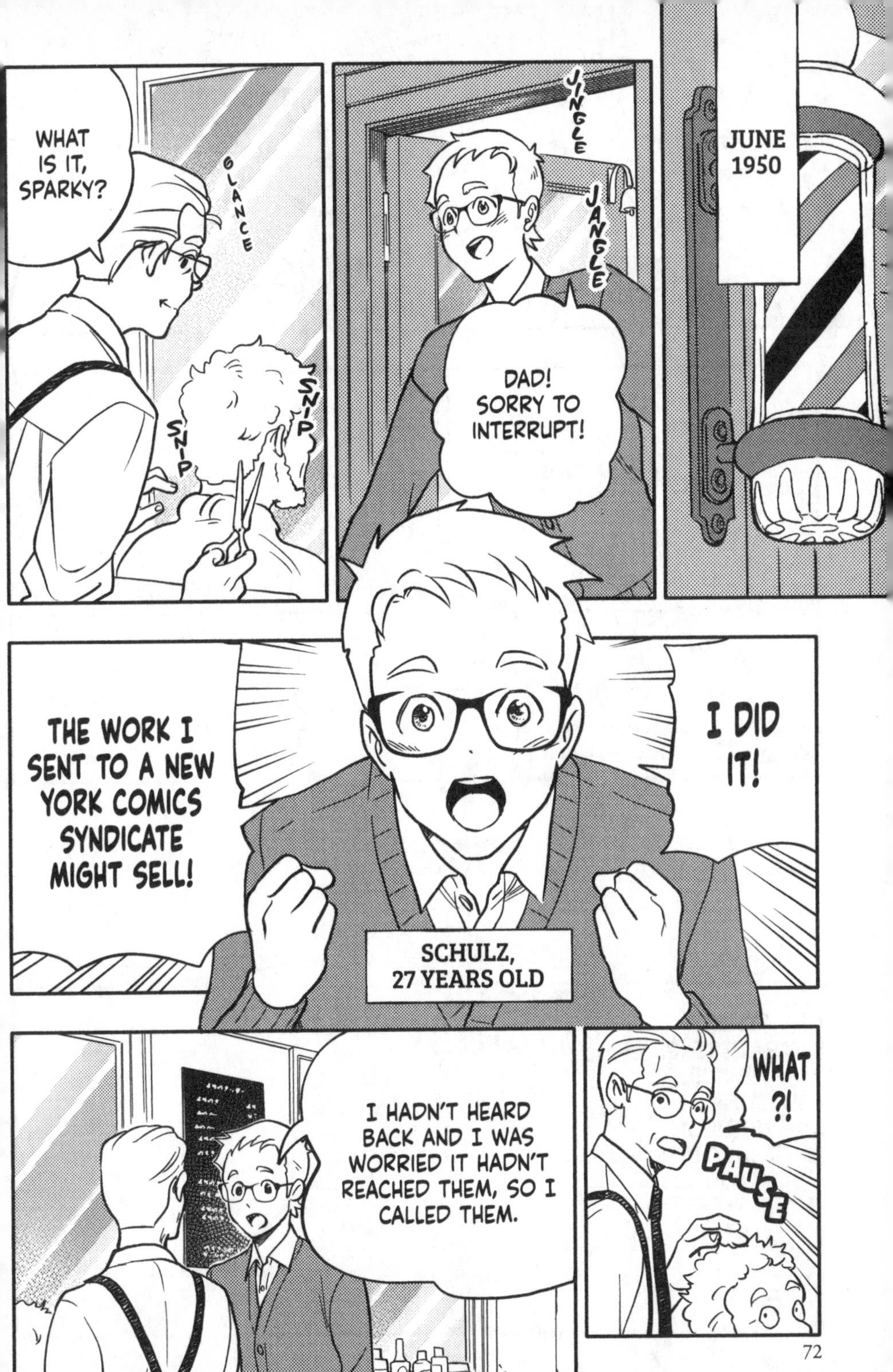
JUNE 1950
JINGLE
JANGLE
DAD! SORRY TO INTERRUPT!
GLANCE
WHAT IS IT, SPARKY?
SNIP
SNIP
I DID IT!
THE WORK I SENT TO A NEW YORK COMICS SYNDICATE MIGHT SELL!
SCHULZ, 27 YEARS OLD
WHAT ?!
PAUSE
I HADN'T HEARD BACK AND I WAS WORRIED IT HADN'T REACHED THEM, SO I CALLED THEM.

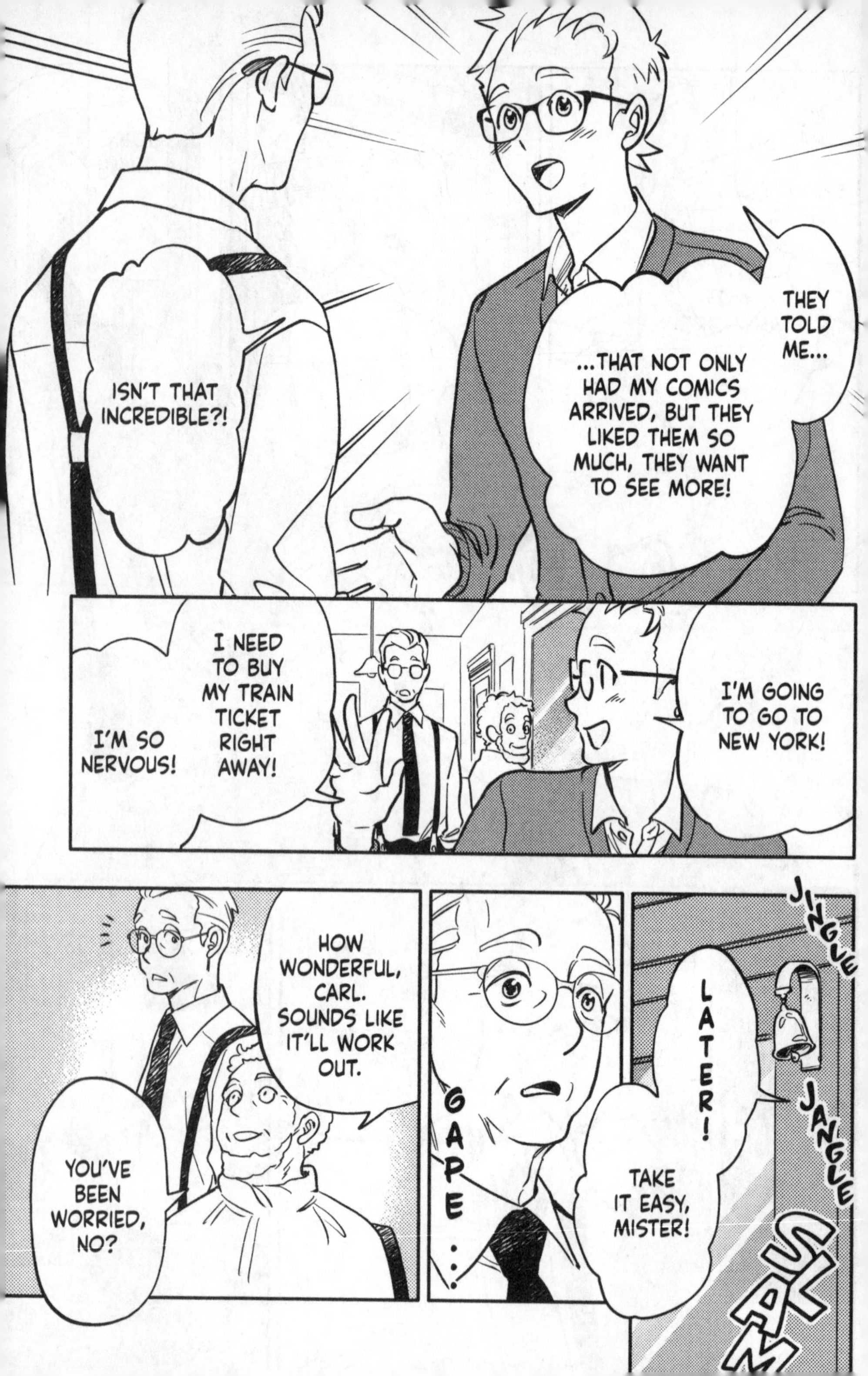
THEY TOLD ME...
...THAT NOT ONLY HAD MY COMICS ARRIVED, BUT THEY LIKED THEM SO MUCH, THEY WANT TO SEE MORE!
ISN'T THAT INCREDIBLE?!
I'M GOING TO GO TO NEW YORK!
I NEED TO BUY MY TRAIN TICKET RIGHT AWAY!
I'M SO NERVOUS!
JINGLE
LATER!
JANGLE
TAKE IT EASY, MISTER!
SLAM
GAPE...
HOW WONDERFUL, CARL. SOUNDS LIKE IT'LL WORK OUT.
YOU'VE BEEN WORRIED, NO?

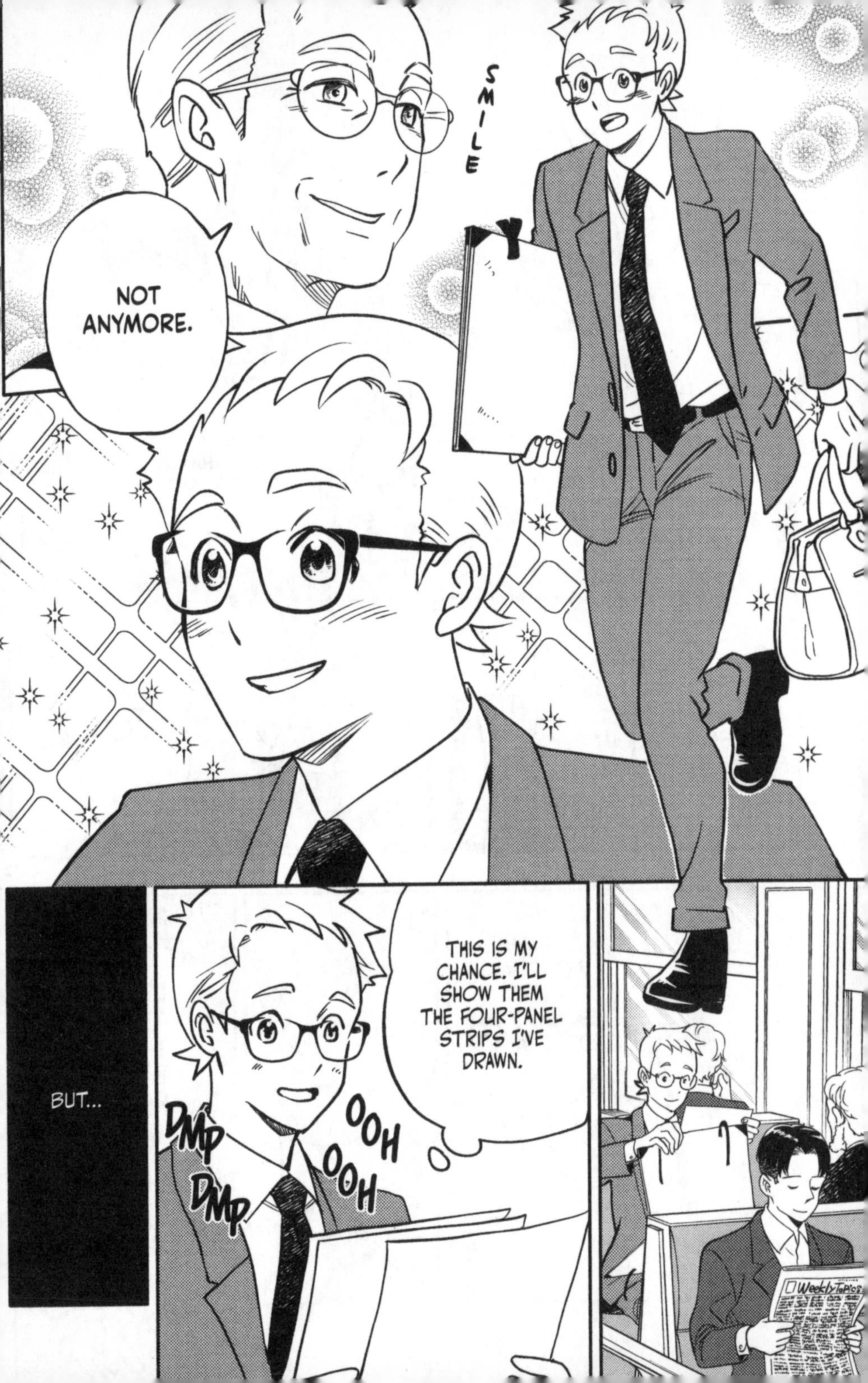
SMILE
NOT ANYMORE.
Weekly Topics
THIS IS MY CHANCE. I'LL SHOW THEM THE FOUR-PANEL STRIPS I'VE DRAWN.
OOH OOH
DMP DMP
BUT...

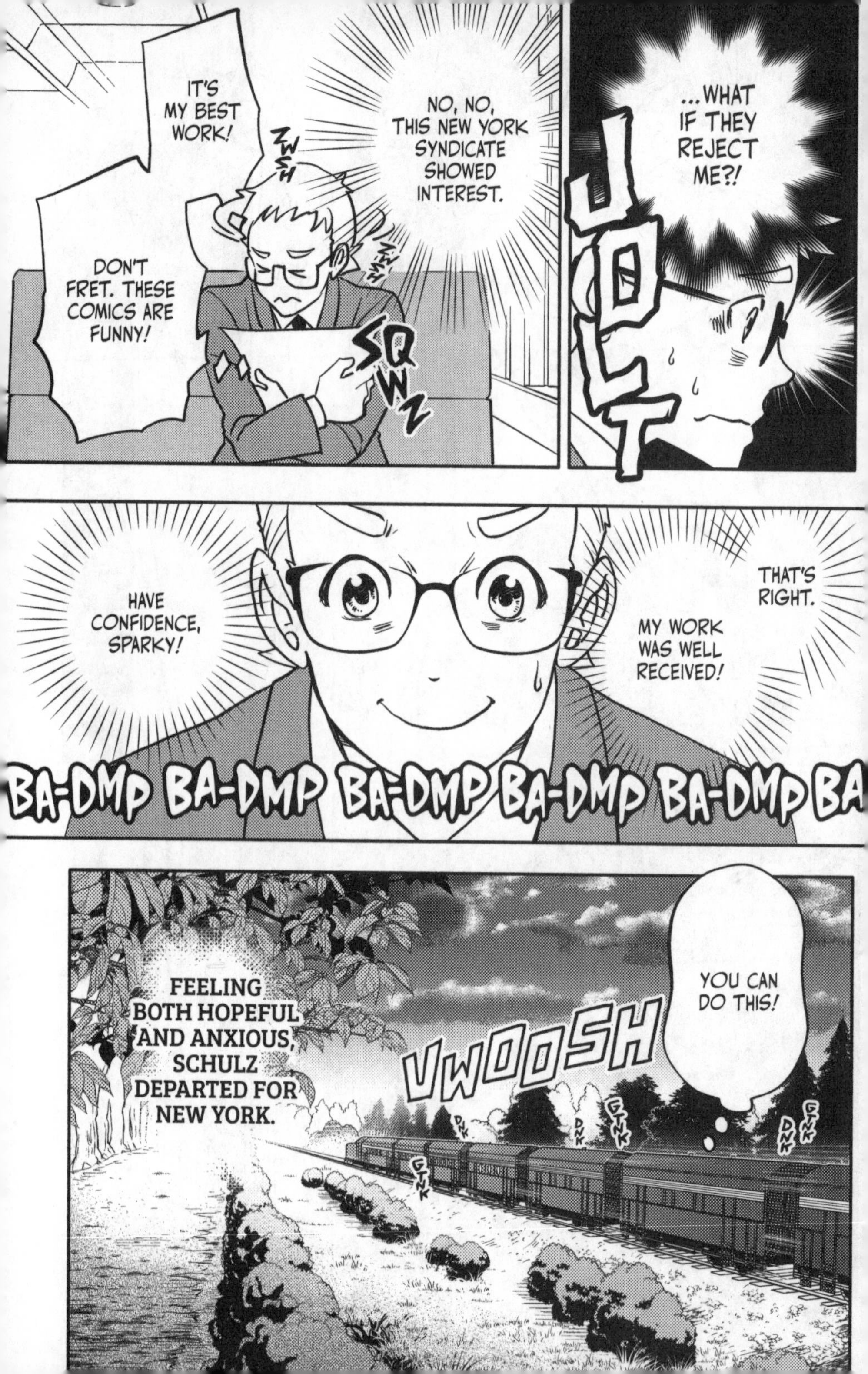
...WHAT IF THEY REJECT ME?!
JOLT
NO, NO, THIS NEW YORK SYNDICATE SHOWED INTEREST.
IT'S MY BEST WORK!
ZWSH
ZWSH
DON'T FRET. THESE COMICS ARE FUNNY!
SQWZ
THAT'S RIGHT.
MY WORK WAS WELL RECEIVED!
HAVE CONFIDENCE, SPARKY!
BA-DMP BA-DMP BA-DMP BA-DMP BA-DMP BA
YOU CAN DO THIS!
GTNK
DNK
GTNK
DNK
UWOOSH
DNK
GTNK
FEELING BOTH HOPEFUL AND ANXIOUS, SCHULZ DEPARTED FOR NEW YORK.

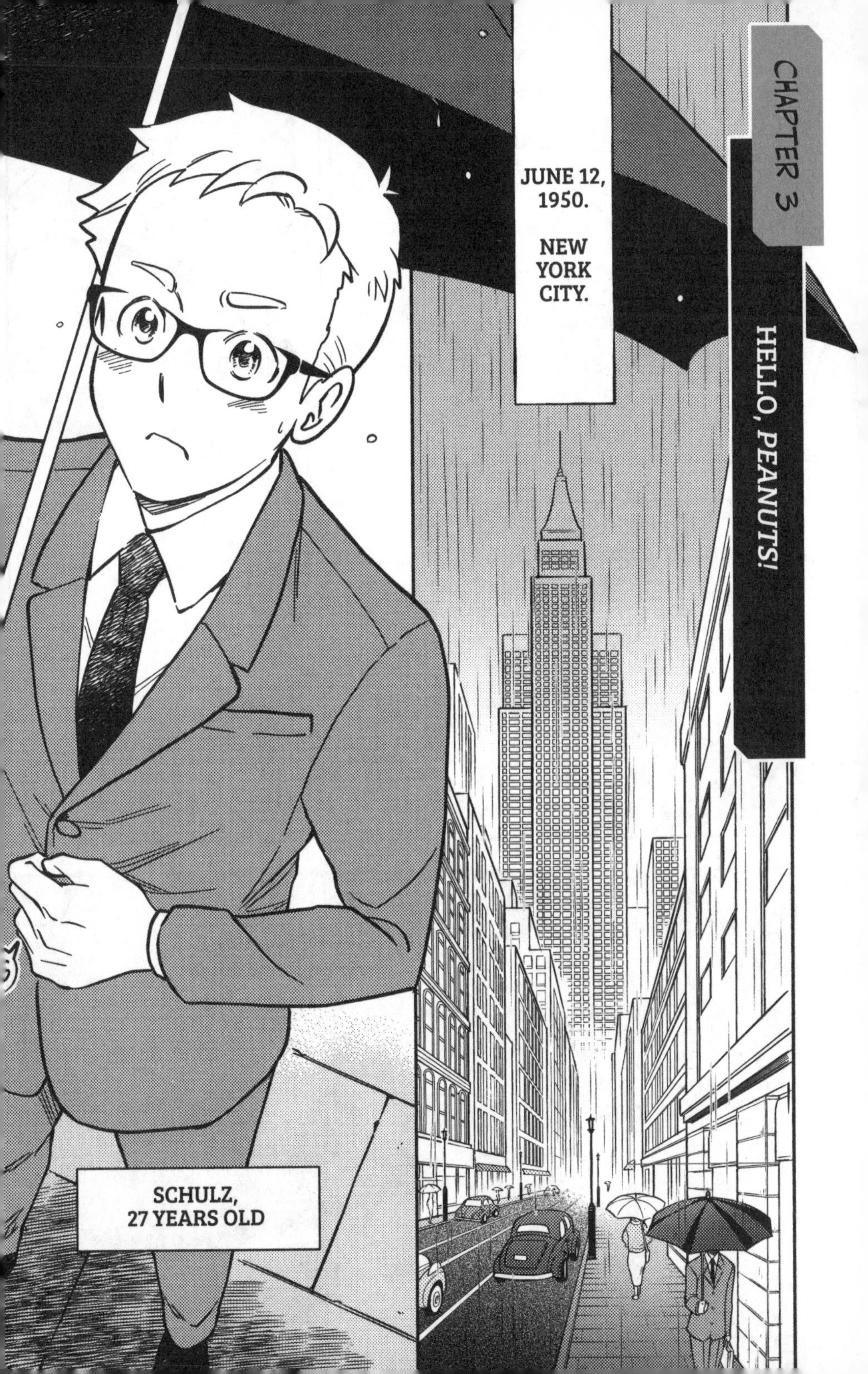
CHAPTER 3
HELLO, PEANUTS!
JUNE 12, 1950.
NEW YORK CITY.
SCHULZ, 27 YEARS OLD

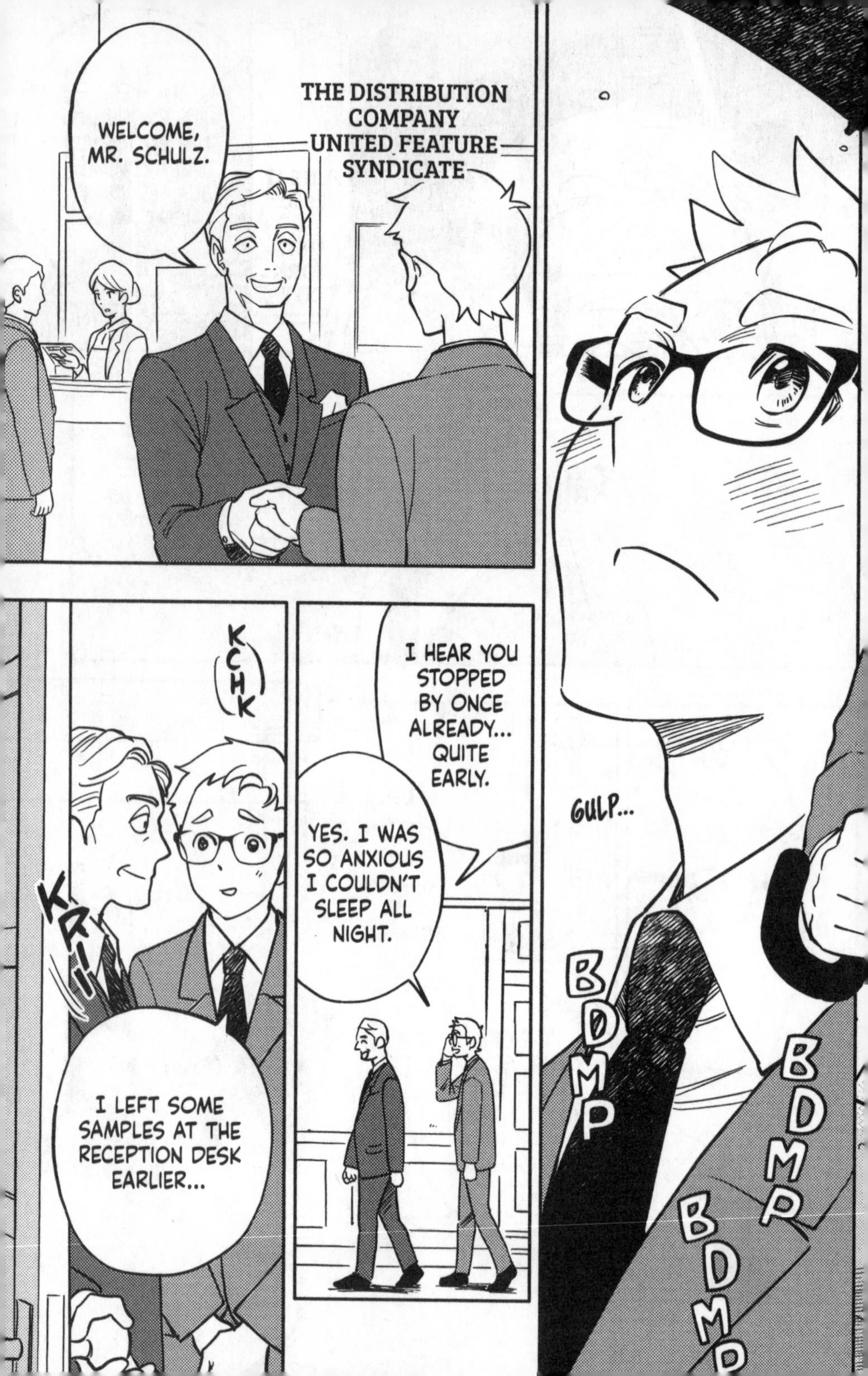
GULP...
BDMP
BDMP
BDMP
BDMP
THE DISTRIBUTION COMPANY UNITED FEATURE SYNDICATE
WELCOME, MR. SCHULZ.
I HEAR YOU STOPPED BY ONCE ALREADY... QUITE EARLY.
YES. I WAS SO ANXIOUS I COULDN'T SLEEP ALL NIGHT.
KCHK
KRII
I LEFT SOME SAMPLES AT THE RECEPTION DESK EARLIER...

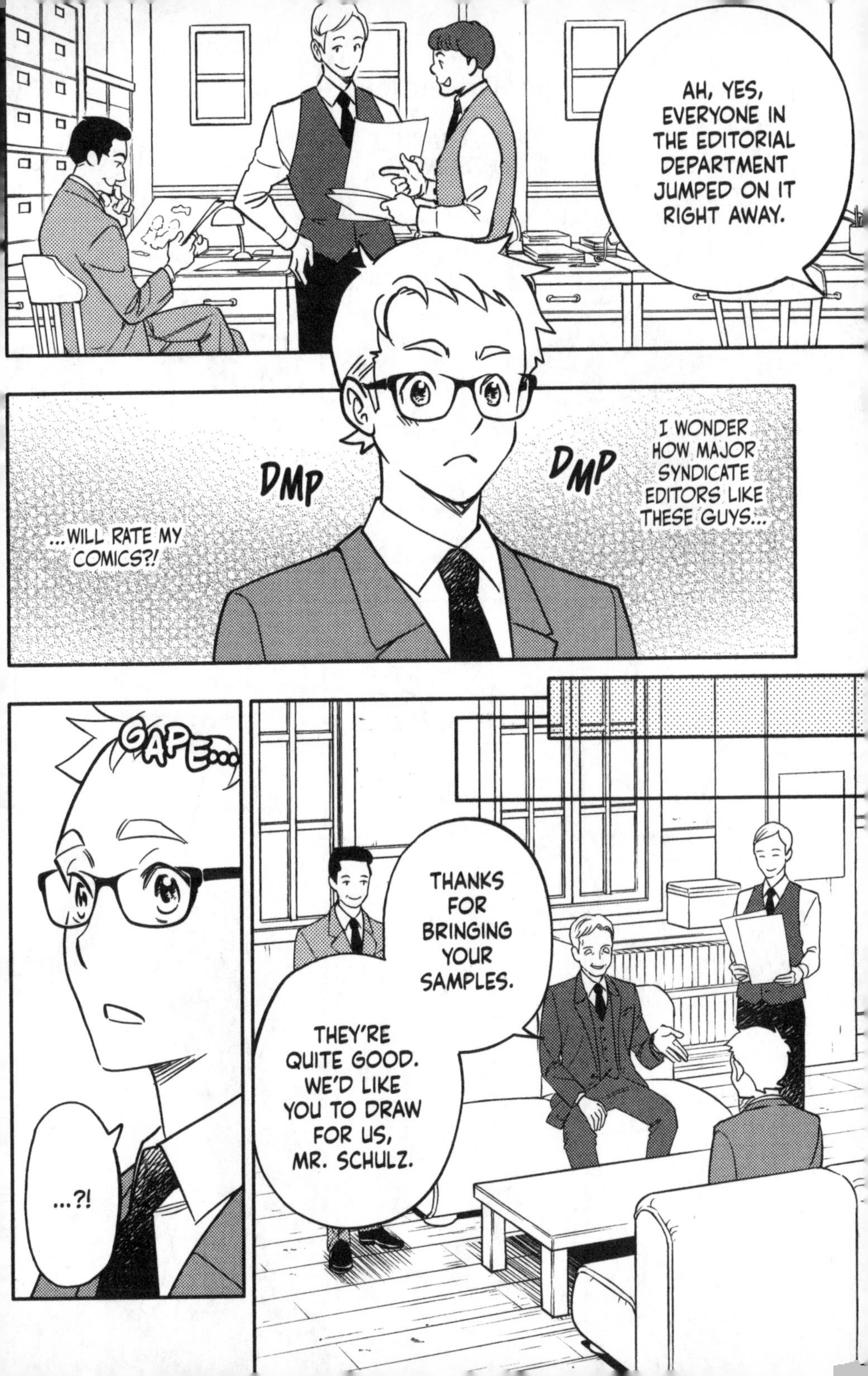
AH, YES, EVERYONE IN THE EDITORIAL DEPARTMENT JUMPED ON IT RIGHT AWAY.
I WONDER HOW MAJOR SYNDICATE EDITORS LIKE THESE GUYS...
DMP
DMP
...WILL RATE MY COMICS?!
THANKS FOR BRINGING YOUR SAMPLES.
THEY'RE QUITE GOOD. WE'D LIKE YOU TO DRAW FOR US, MR. SCHULZ.
GAPE...
...?!

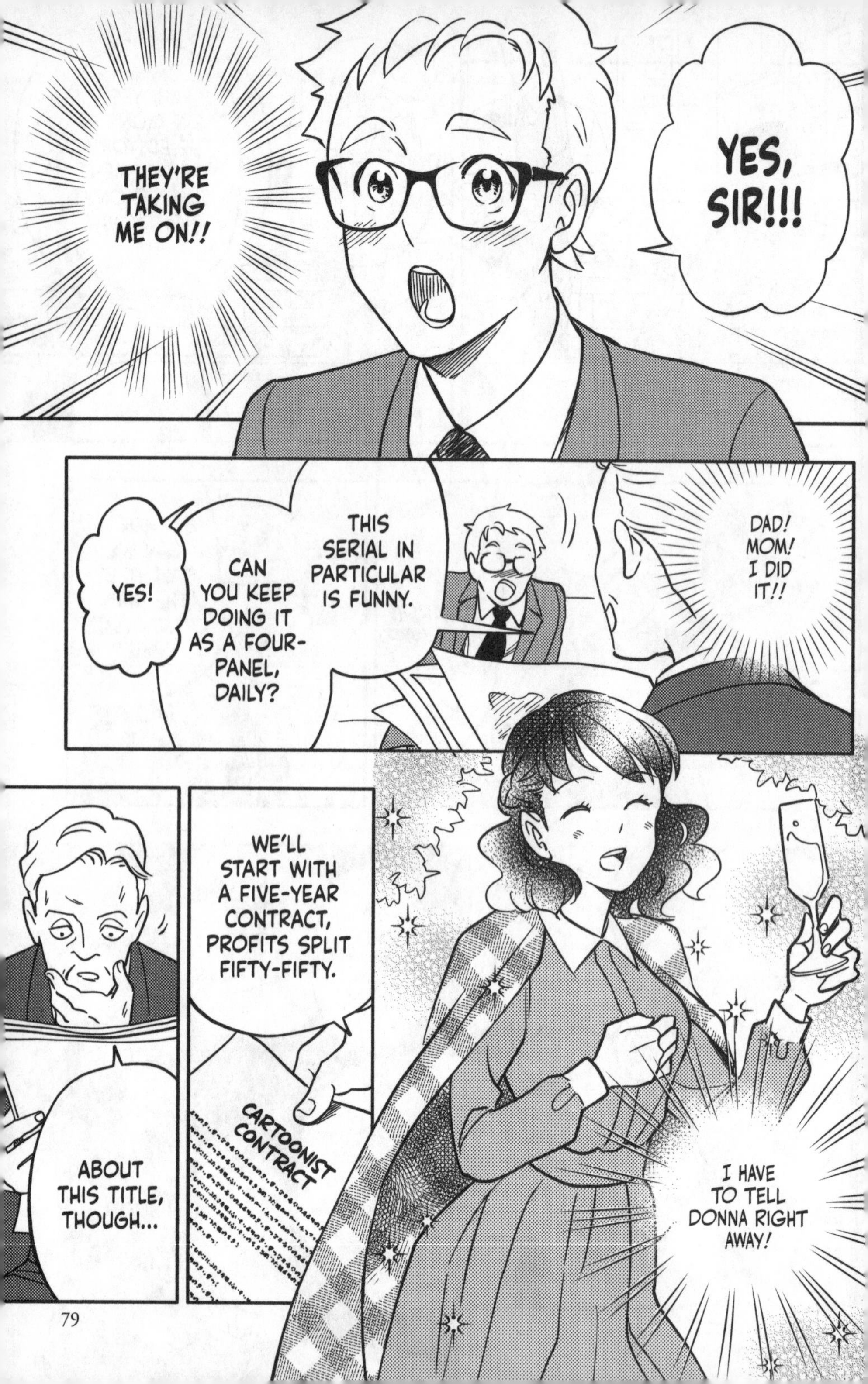
YES, SIR!!!
THEY'RE TAKING ME ON!!
DAD! MOM! I DID IT!!
THIS SERIAL IN PARTICULAR IS FUNNY.
CAN YOU KEEP DOING IT AS A FOUR-PANEL, DAILY?
YES!
I HAVE TO TELL DONNA RIGHT AWAY!
WE'LL START WITH A FIVE-YEAR CONTRACT, PROFITS SPLIT FIFTY-FIFTY.
CARTOONIST CONTRACT
ABOUT THIS TITLE, THOUGH...

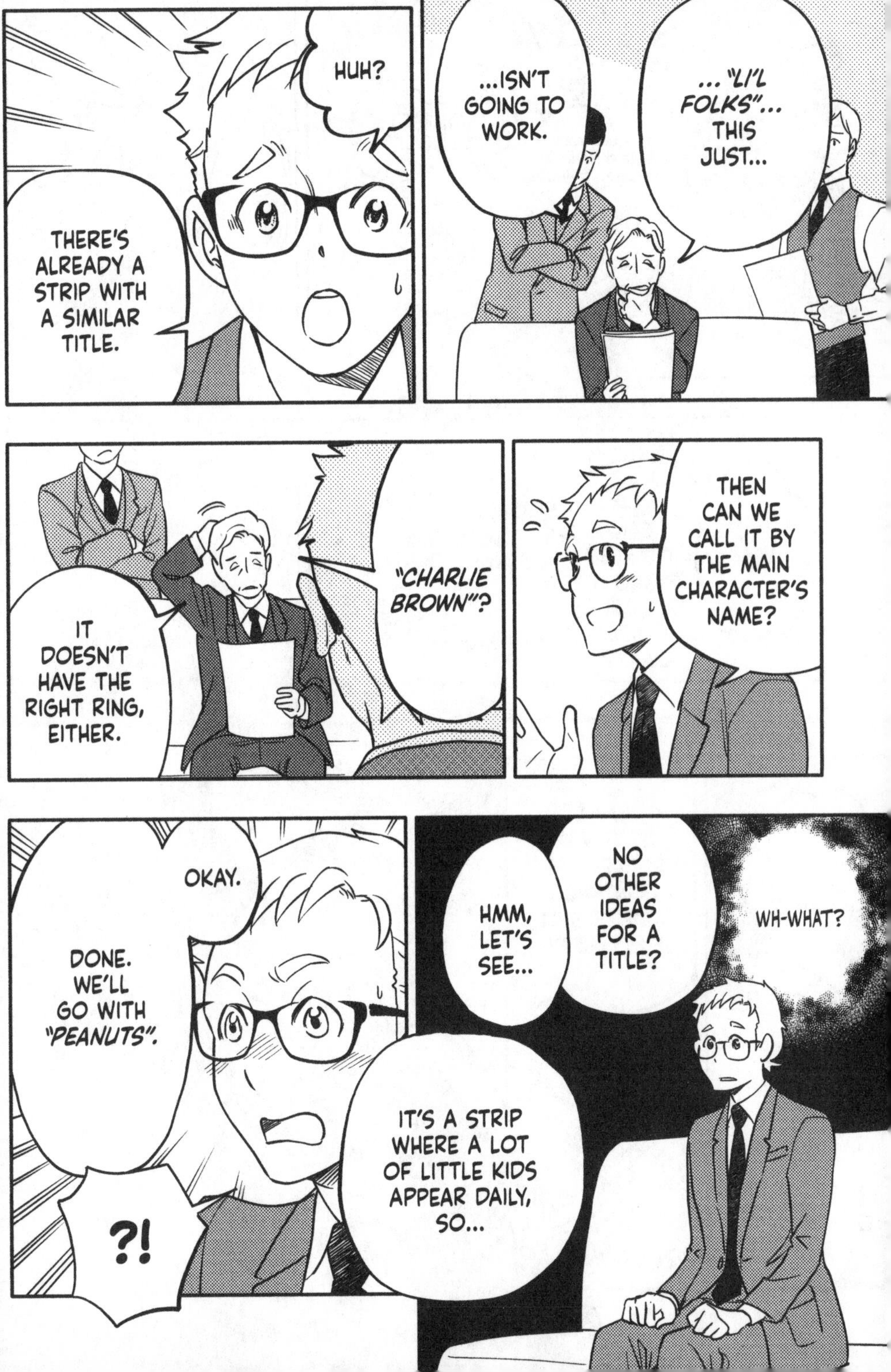
…"LI'L FOLKS"… THIS JUST…
…ISN'T GOING TO WORK.
HUH?
THERE'S ALREADY A STRIP WITH A SIMILAR TITLE.
THEN CAN WE CALL IT BY THE MAIN CHARACTER'S NAME?
"CHARLIE BROWN"?
IT DOESN'T HAVE THE RIGHT RING, EITHER.
WH-WHAT?
NO OTHER IDEAS FOR A TITLE?
HMM, LET'S SEE…
IT'S A STRIP WHERE A LOT OF LITTLE KIDS APPEAR DAILY, SO…
OKAY.
DONE. WE'LL GO WITH "PEANUTS".
?!

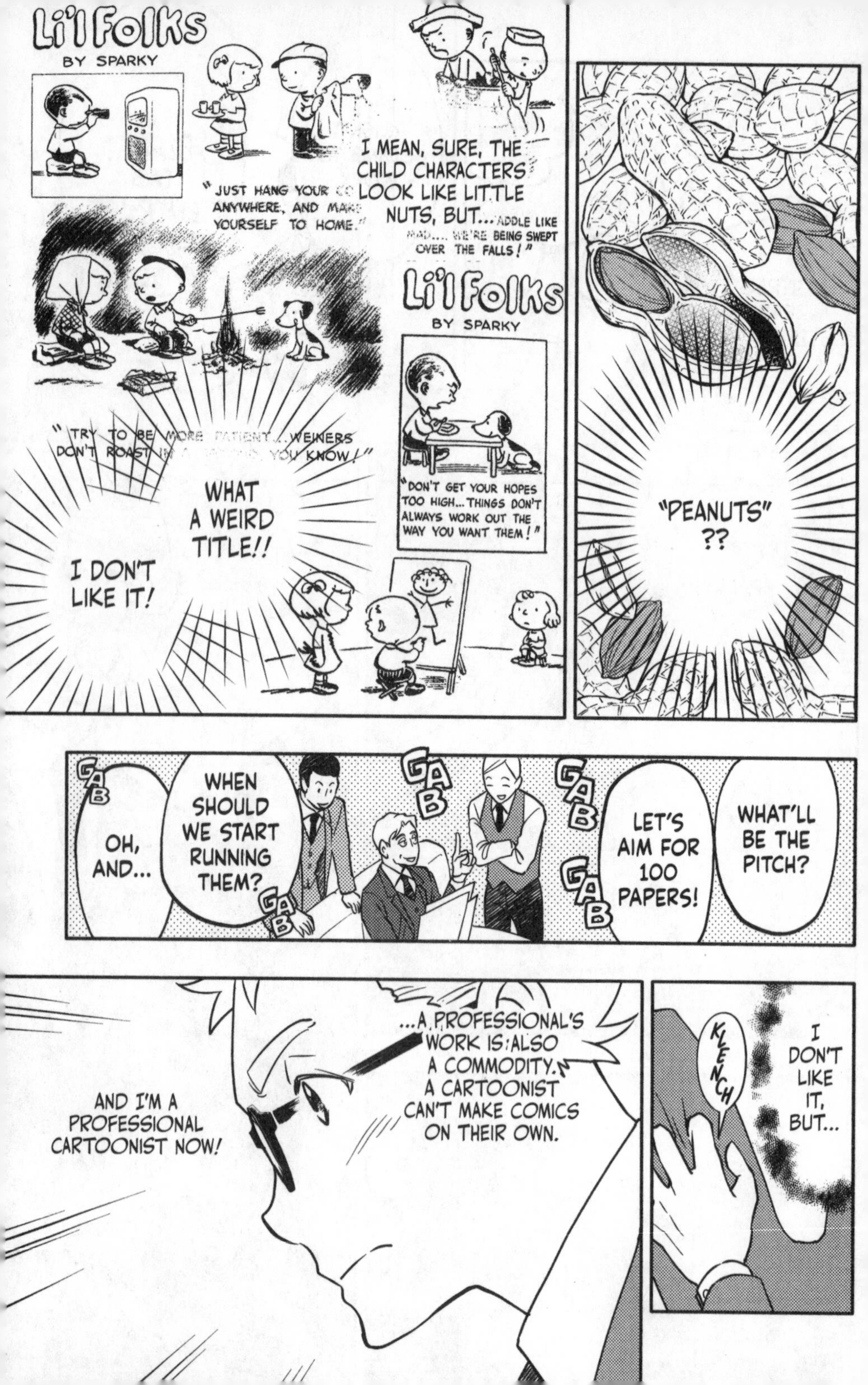
"PEANUTS" ??
LI'L FOLKS BY SPARKY
I MEAN, SURE, THE CHILD CHARACTERS LOOK LIKE LITTLE NUTS, BUT...
"DON'T GET YOUR HOPES TOO HIGH... THINGS DON'T ALWAYS WORK OUT THE WAY YOU WANT THEM!"
WHAT A WEIRD TITLE!!
I DON'T LIKE IT!
WHAT'LL BE THE PITCH?
LET'S AIM FOR 100 PAPERS!
GAB
GAB
GAB
WHEN SHOULD WE START RUNNING THEM?
GAB
OH, AND...
KLENCH
I DON'T LIKE IT, BUT...
...A PROFESSIONAL'S WORK IS ALSO A COMMODITY. A CARTOONIST CAN'T MAKE COMICS ON THEIR OWN.
AND I'M A PROFESSIONAL CARTOONIST NOW!

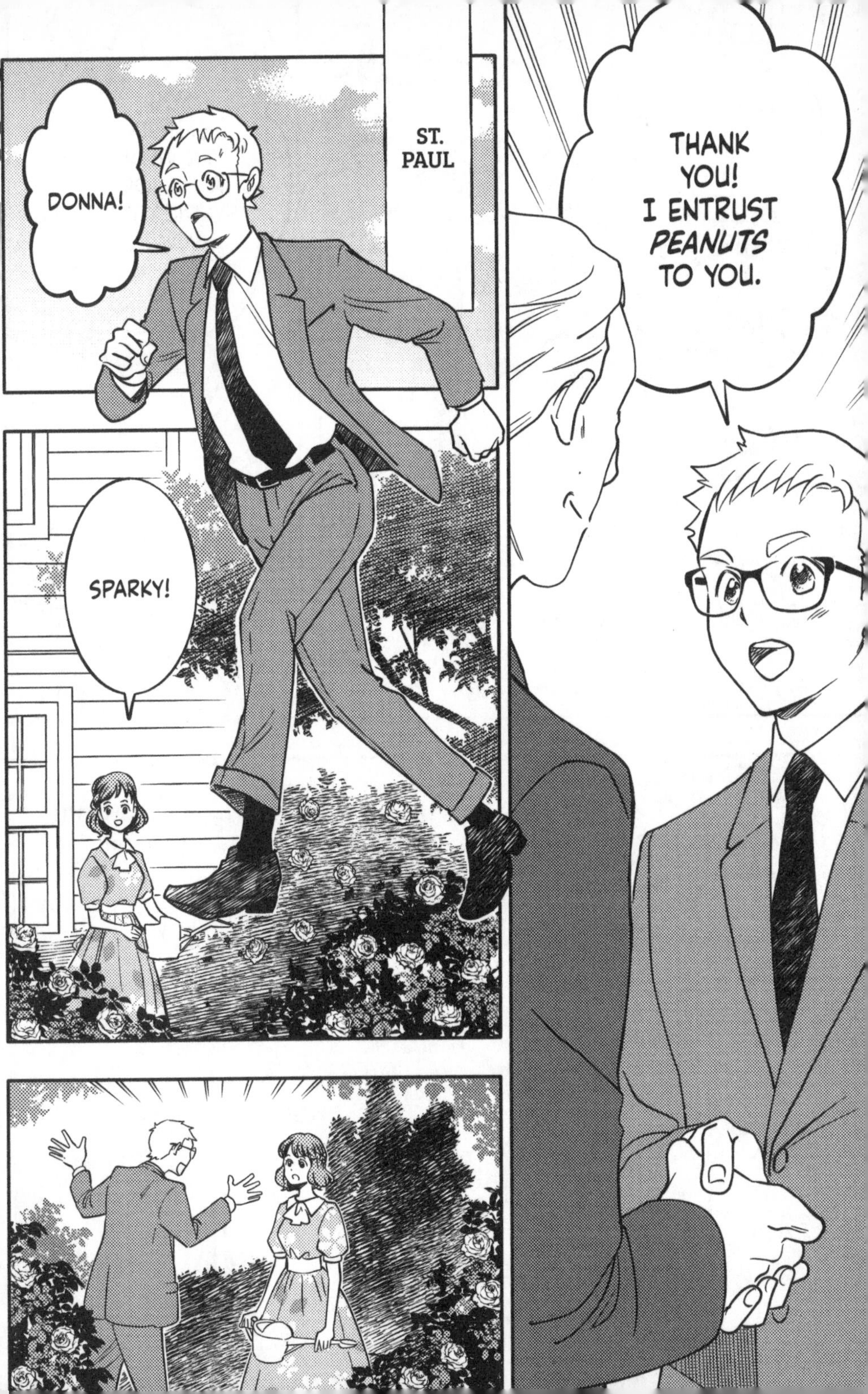
THANK YOU! I ENTRUST *PEANUTS* TO YOU.
ST. PAUL
DONNA!
SPARKY!

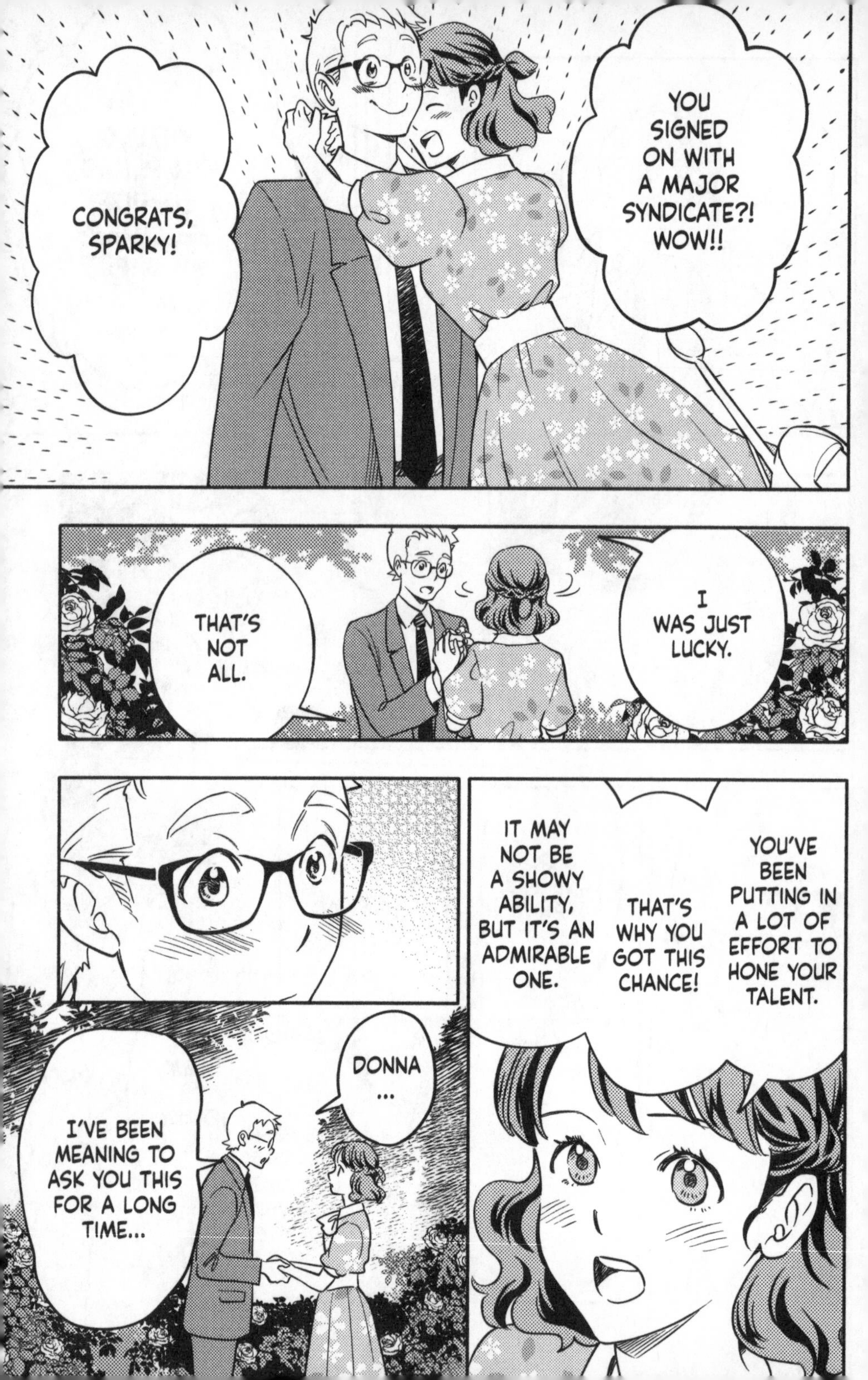
YOU SIGNED ON WITH A MAJOR SYNDICATE?! WOW!!
CONGRATS, SPARKY!
I WAS JUST LUCKY.
THAT'S NOT ALL.
YOU'VE BEEN PUTTING IN A LOT OF EFFORT TO HONE YOUR TALENT.
THAT'S WHY YOU GOT THIS CHANCE!
IT MAY NOT BE A SHOWY ABILITY, BUT IT'S AN ADMIRABLE ONE.
DONNA ...
I'VE BEEN MEANING TO ASK YOU THIS FOR A LONG TIME...

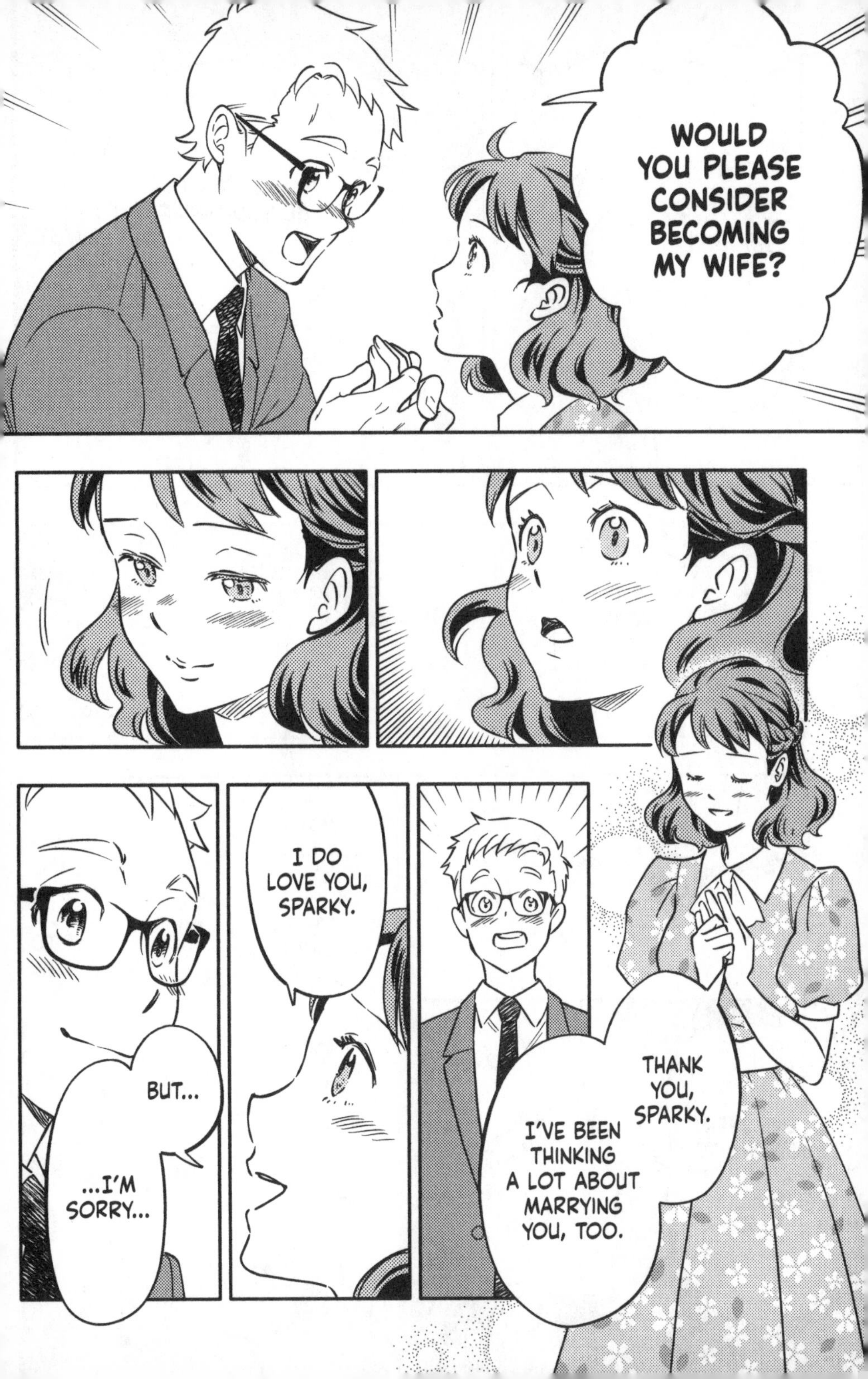
WOULD YOU PLEASE CONSIDER BECOMING MY WIFE?
THANK YOU, SPARKY.
I'VE BEEN THINKING A LOT ABOUT MARRYING YOU, TOO.
I DO LOVE YOU, SPARKY.
BUT...
...I'M SORRY...

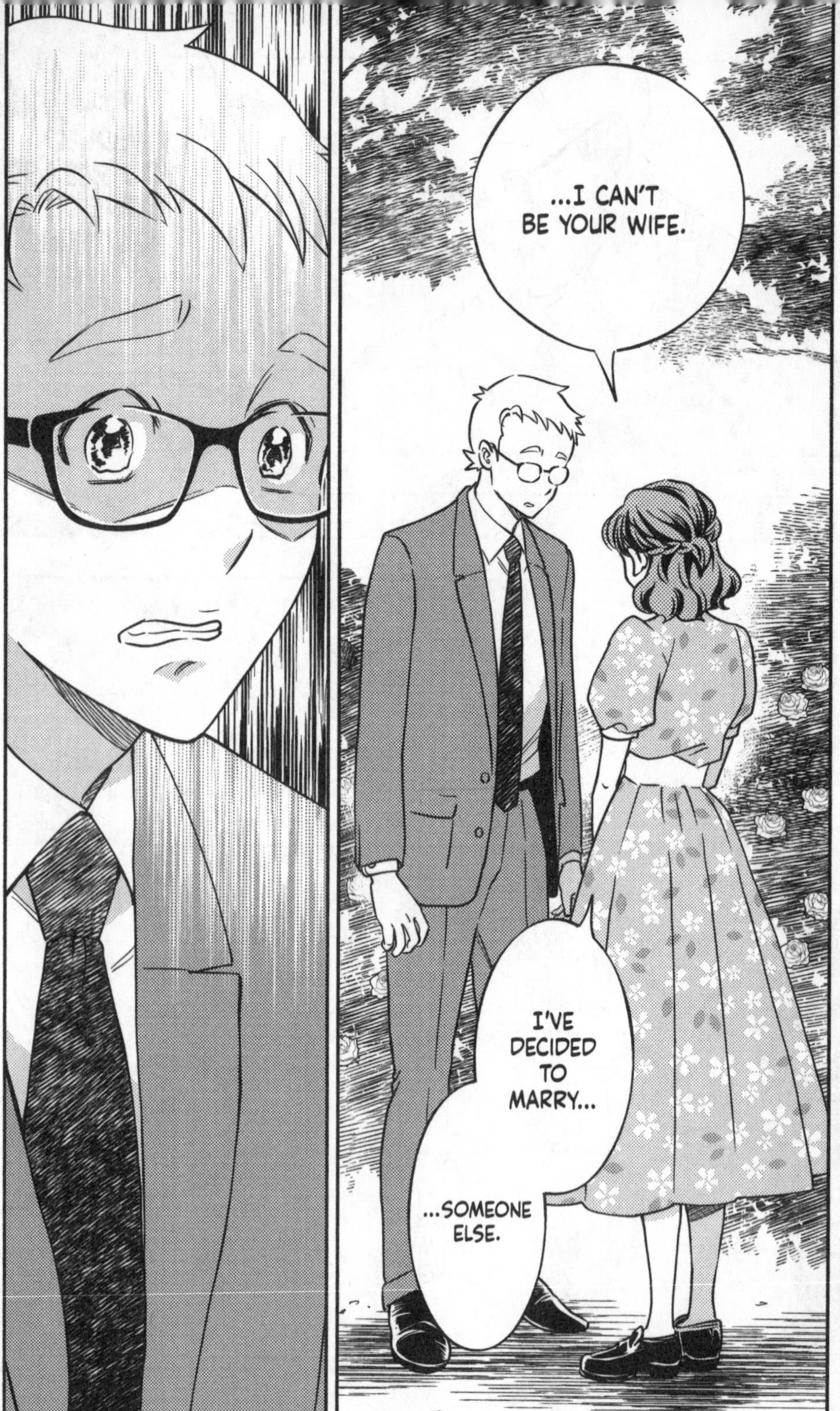
...I CAN'T BE YOUR WIFE.
I'VE DECIDED TO MARRY...
...SOMEONE ELSE.

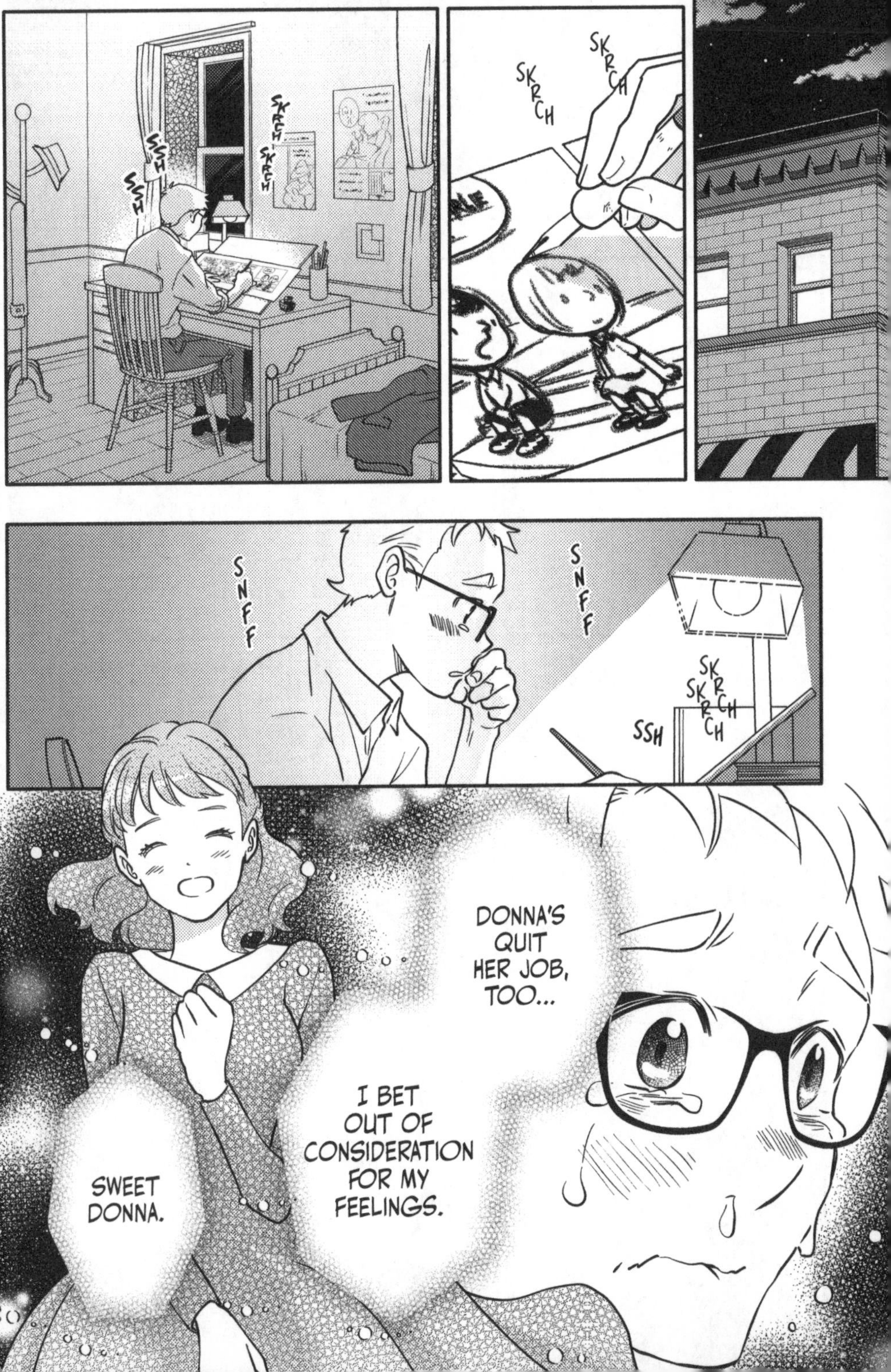
SKRCH
SKRCH
SSH
SSH
SKRCH
SKRCH
SNFF
SNFF
SKRCH
SKRCH
SSH
DONNA'S QUIT HER JOB, TOO...
I BET OUT OF CONSIDERATION FOR MY FEELINGS.
SWEET DONNA.

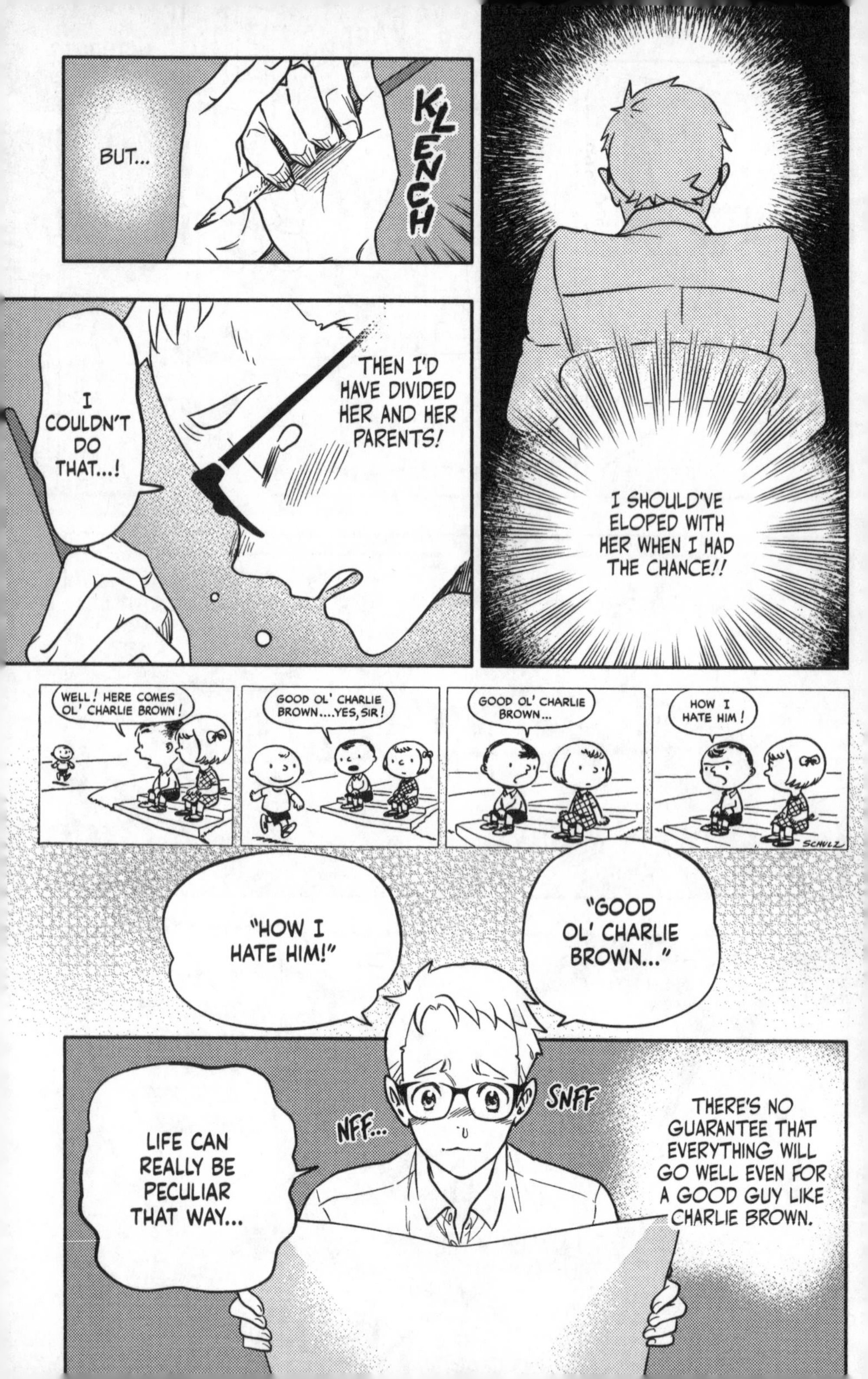
I SHOULD'VE ELOPED WITH HER WHEN I HAD THE CHANCE!!
BUT...
KLENCH
THEN I'D HAVE DIVIDED HER AND HER PARENTS!
I COULDN'T DO THAT...!
WELL! HERE COMES OL' CHARLIE BROWN!
GOOD OL' CHARLIE BROWN....YES, SIR!
GOOD OL' CHARLIE BROWN...
HOW I HATE HIM!
SCHULZ
"GOOD OL' CHARLIE BROWN..."
"HOW I HATE HIM!"
THERE'S NO GUARANTEE THAT EVERYTHING WILL GO WELL EVEN FOR A GOOD GUY LIKE CHARLIE BROWN.
SNFF
NFF...
LIFE CAN REALLY BE PECULIAR THAT WAY...

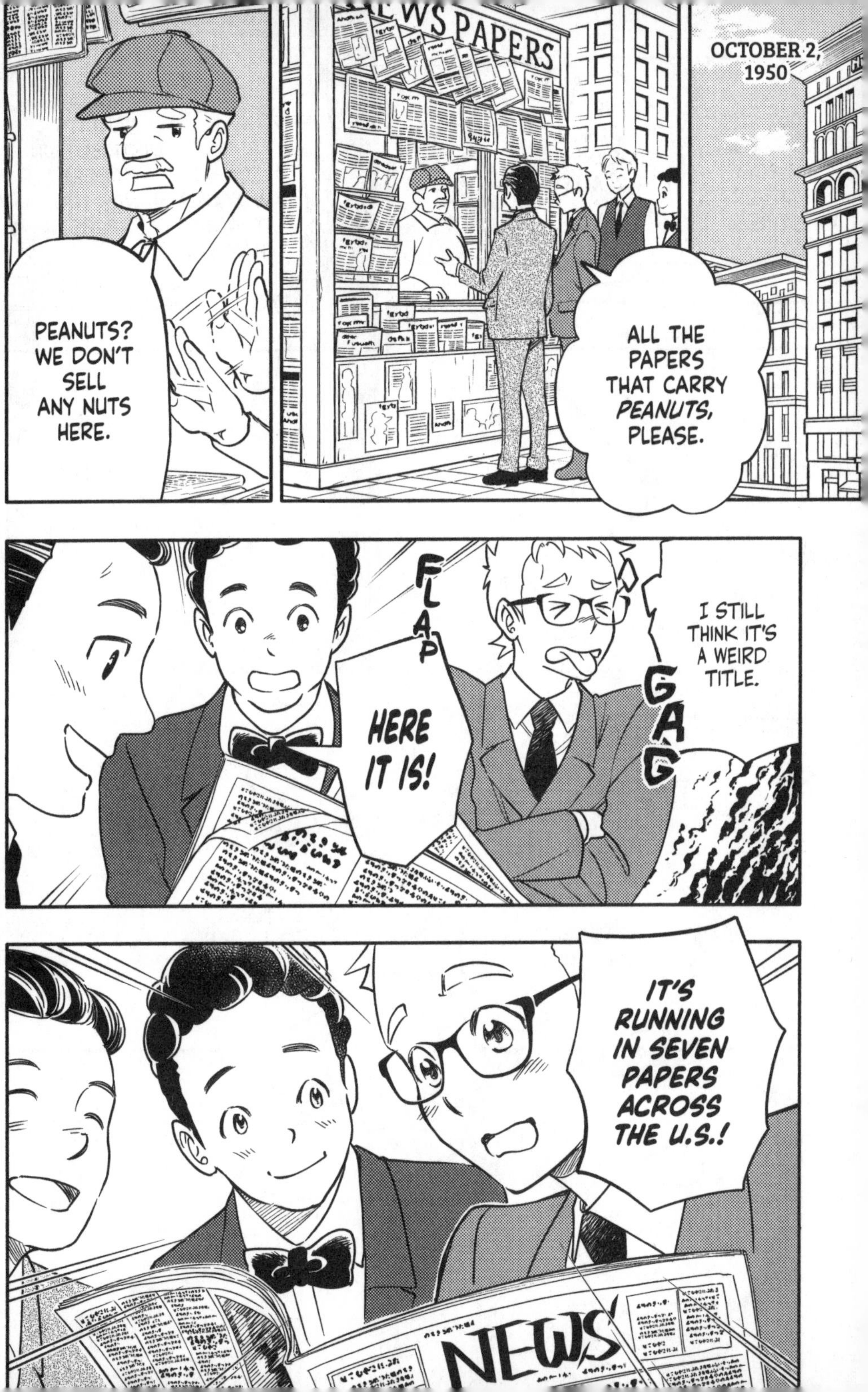

WS PAPERS
OCTOBER 2, 1950
ALL THE PAPERS THAT CARRY *PEANUTS*, PLEASE.
PEANUTS? WE DON'T SELL ANY NUTS HERE.
I STILL THINK IT'S A WEIRD TITLE.
GAG
FLAP
HERE IT IS!
IT'S RUNNING IN SEVEN PAPERS ACROSS THE U.S.!
NEWS

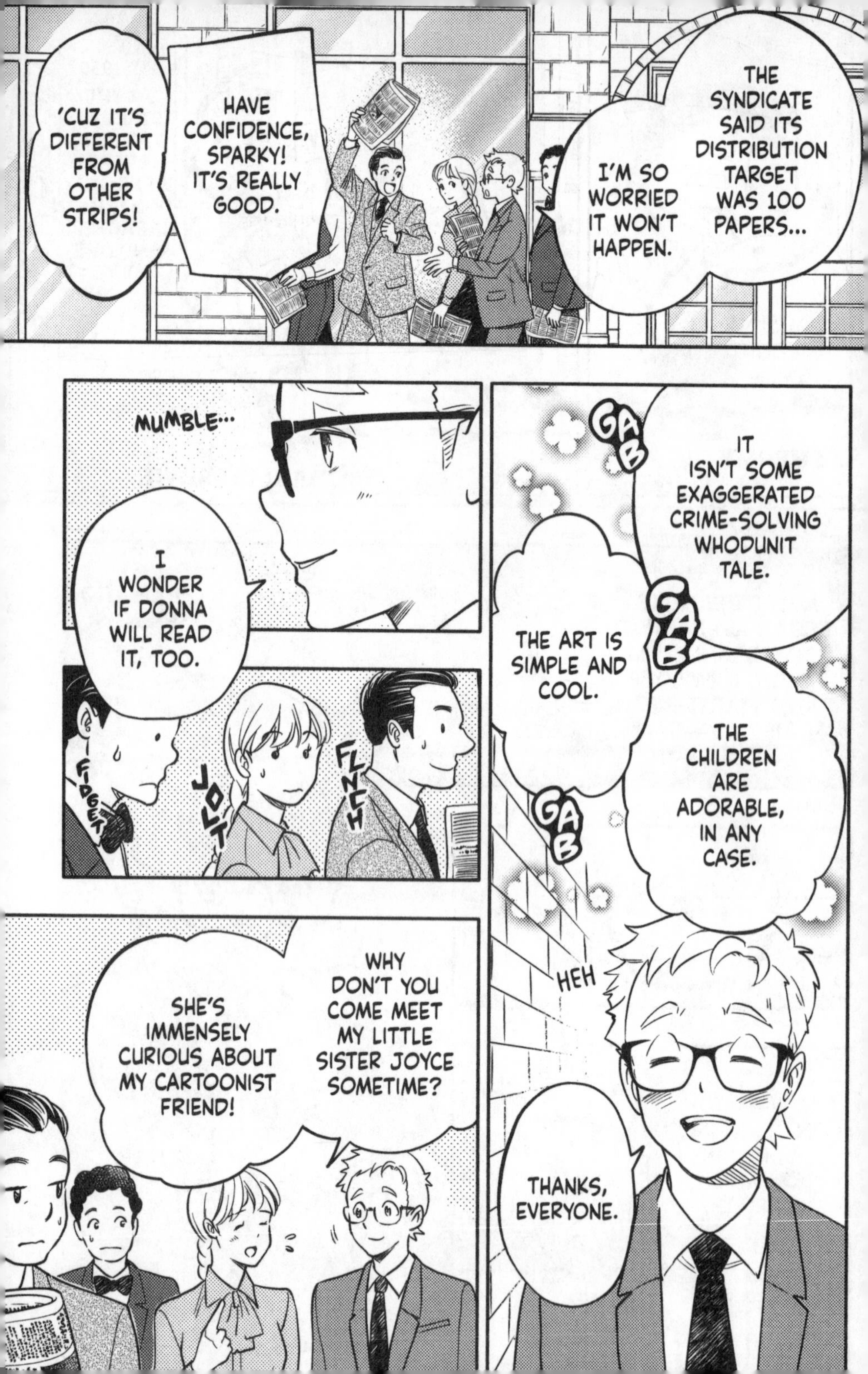
THE SYNDICATE SAID ITS DISTRIBUTION TARGET WAS 100 PAPERS...
I'M SO WORRIED IT WON'T HAPPEN.
HAVE CONFIDENCE, SPARKY! IT'S REALLY GOOD.
'CUZ IT'S DIFFERENT FROM OTHER STRIPS!
GAB GAB
IT ISN'T SOME EXAGGERATED CRIME-SOLVING WHODUNIT TALE.
GAB GAB
THE ART IS SIMPLE AND COOL.
GAB GAB
THE CHILDREN ARE ADORABLE, IN ANY CASE.
HEH
THANKS, EVERYONE.
MUMBLE...
I WONDER IF DONNA WILL READ IT, TOO.
FLINCH
JOLT
FIDGET
WHY DON'T YOU COME MEET MY LITTLE SISTER JOYCE SOMETIME?
SHE'S IMMENSELY CURIOUS ABOUT MY CARTOONIST FRIEND!

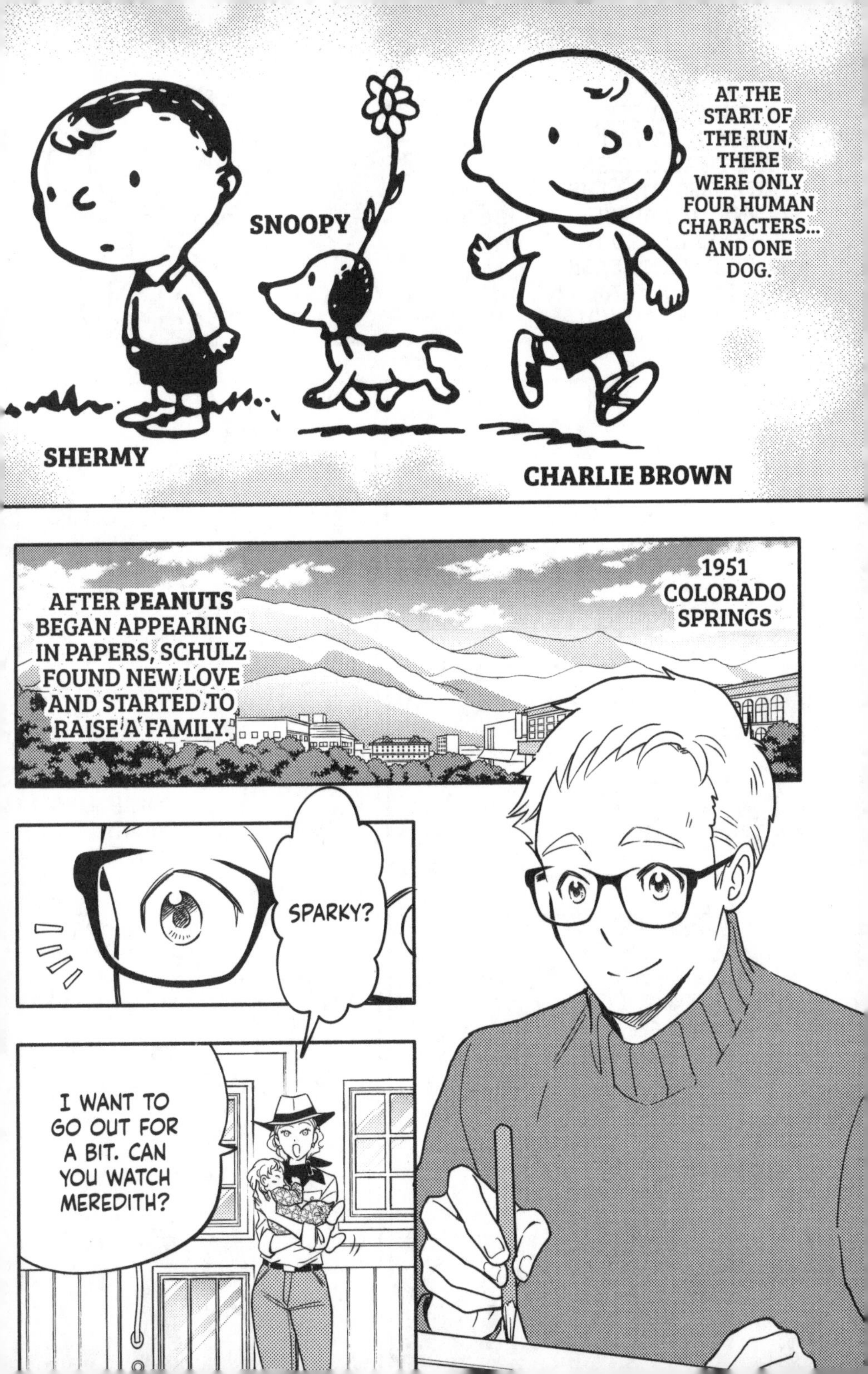
AT THE START OF THE RUN, THERE WERE ONLY FOUR HUMAN CHARACTERS... AND ONE DOG.
CHARLIE BROWN
SNOOPY
SHERMY
1951 COLORADO SPRINGS
AFTER PEANUTS BEGAN APPEARING IN PAPERS, SCHULZ FOUND NEW LOVE AND STARTED TO RAISE A FAMILY.
SPARKY?
I WANT TO GO OUT FOR A BIT. CAN YOU WATCH MEREDITH?

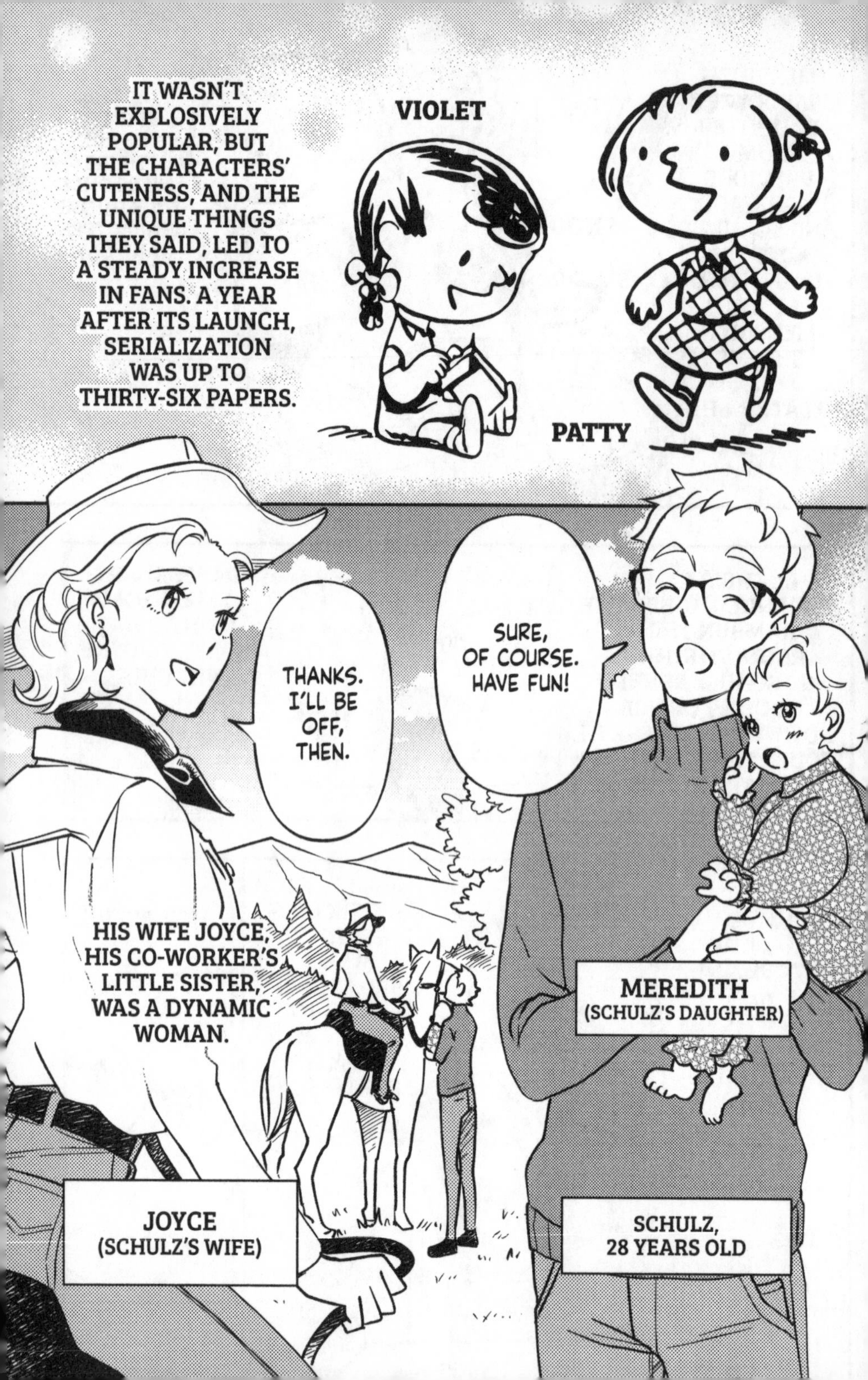

IT WASN'T EXPLOSIVELY POPULAR, BUT THE CHARACTERS' CUTENESS, AND THE UNIQUE THINGS THEY SAID, LED TO A STEADY INCREASE IN FANS. A YEAR AFTER ITS LAUNCH, SERIALIZATION WAS UP TO THIRTY-SIX PAPERS.
VIOLET
PATTY
SURE, OF COURSE. HAVE FUN!
THANKS. I'LL BE OFF, THEN.
MEREDITH (SCHULZ'S DAUGHTER)
HIS WIFE JOYCE, HIS CO-WORKER'S LITTLE SISTER, WAS A DYNAMIC WOMAN.
SCHULZ, 28 YEARS OLD
JOYCE (SCHULZ'S WIFE)

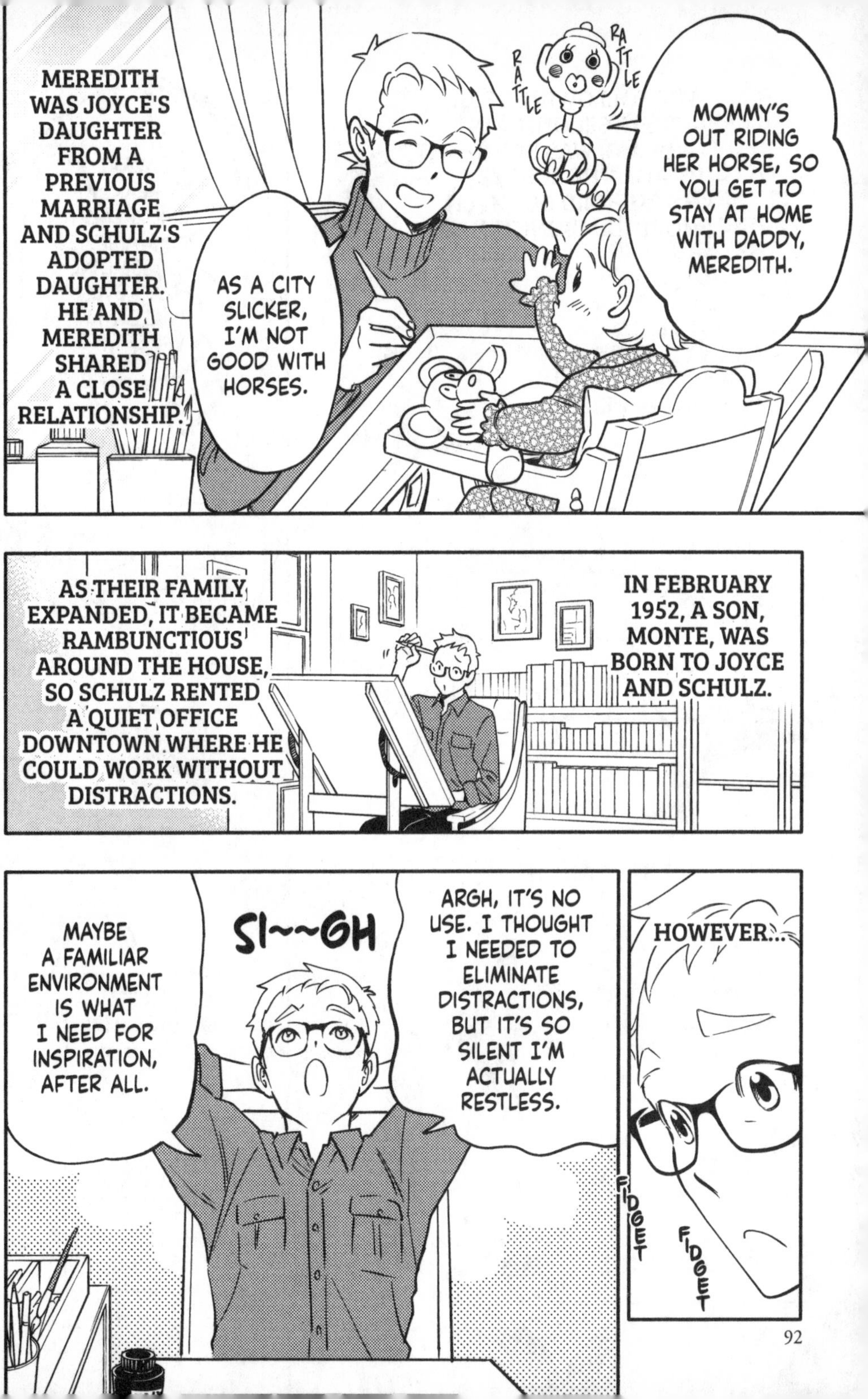
RATTLE
RATTLE
MOMMY'S OUT RIDING HER HORSE, SO YOU GET TO STAY AT HOME WITH DADDY, MEREDITH.
MEREDITH WAS JOYCE'S DAUGHTER FROM A PREVIOUS MARRIAGE AND SCHULZ'S ADOPTED DAUGHTER. HE AND MEREDITH SHARED A CLOSE RELATIONSHIP.
AS A CITY SLICKER, I'M NOT GOOD WITH HORSES.
IN FEBRUARY 1952, A SON, MONTE, WAS BORN TO JOYCE AND SCHULZ.
AS THEIR FAMILY EXPANDED, IT BECAME RAMBUNCTIOUS AROUND THE HOUSE, SO SCHULZ RENTED A QUIET OFFICE DOWNTOWN WHERE HE COULD WORK WITHOUT DISTRACTIONS.
HOWEVER...
FIDGET
FIDGET
ARGH, IT'S NO USE. I THOUGHT I NEEDED TO ELIMINATE DISTRACTIONS, BUT IT'S SO SILENT I'M ACTUALLY RESTLESS.
SI~~GH
MAYBE A FAMILIAR ENVIRONMENT IS WHAT I NEED FOR INSPIRATION, AFTER ALL.

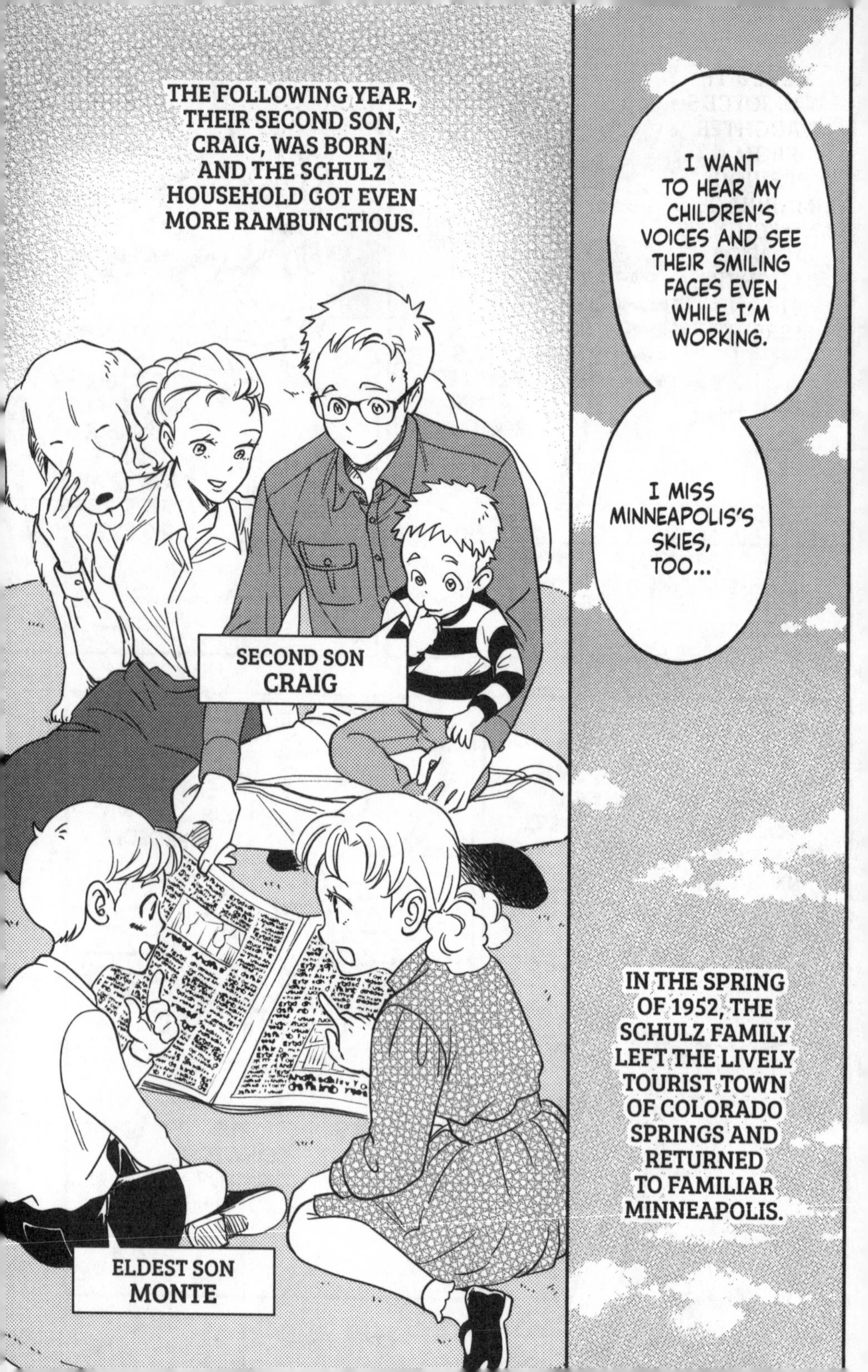
I WANT TO HEAR MY CHILDREN'S VOICES AND SEE THEIR SMILING FACES EVEN WHILE I'M WORKING.
I MISS MINNEAPOLIS'S SKIES, TOO...
IN THE SPRING OF 1952, THE SCHULZ FAMILY LEFT THE LIVELY TOURIST TOWN OF COLORADO SPRINGS AND RETURNED TO FAMILIAR MINNEAPOLIS.
THE FOLLOWING YEAR, THEIR SECOND SON, CRAIG, WAS BORN, AND THE SCHULZ HOUSEHOLD GOT EVEN MORE RAMBUNCTIOUS.
SECOND SON CRAIG
ELDEST SON MONTE

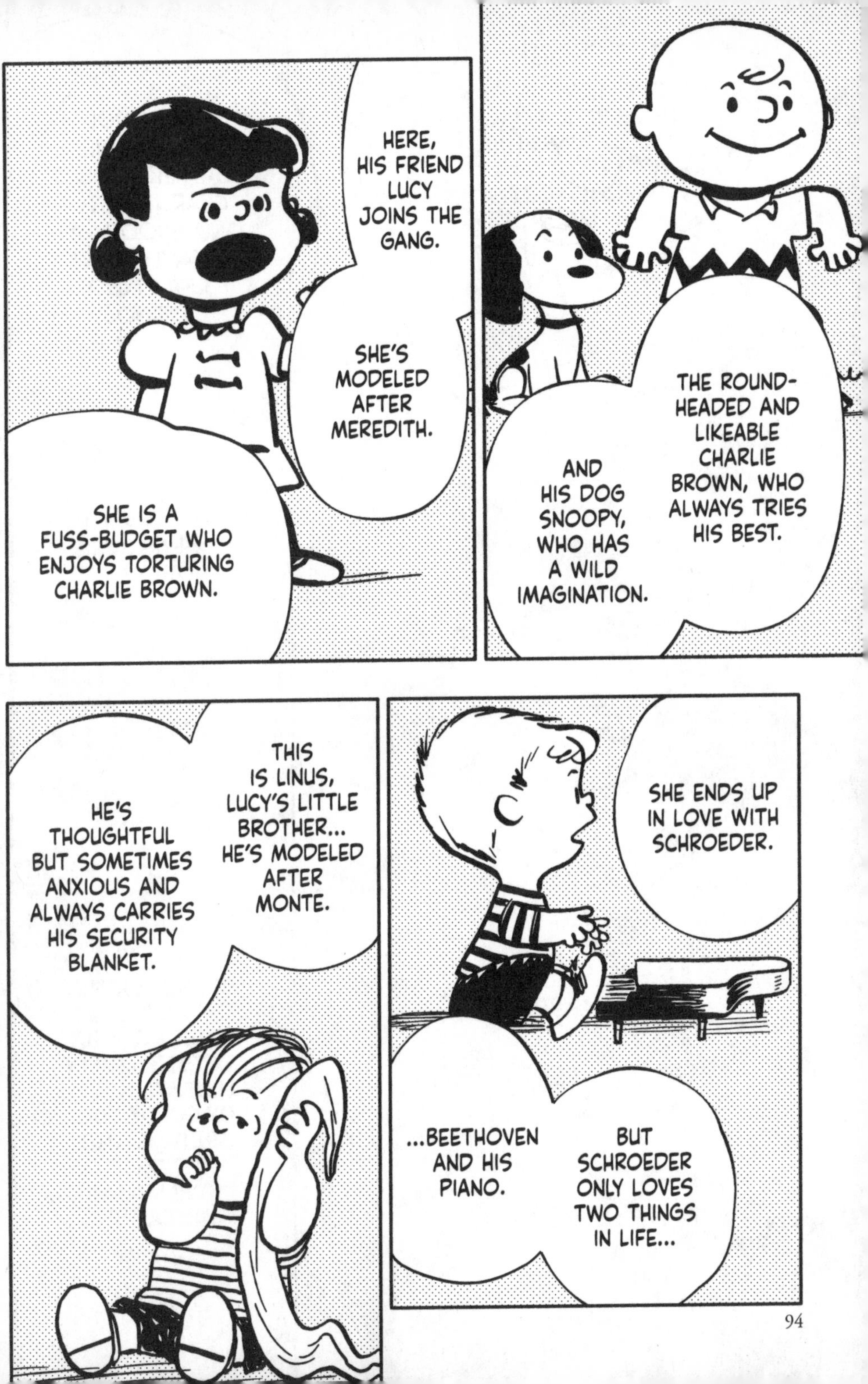
THE ROUND-HEADED AND LIKEABLE CHARLIE BROWN, WHO ALWAYS TRIES HIS BEST.
AND HIS DOG SNOOPY, WHO HAS A WILD IMAGINATION.
HERE, HIS FRIEND LUCY JOINS THE GANG.
SHE'S MODELED AFTER MEREDITH.
SHE IS A FUSS-BUDGET WHO ENJOYS TORTURING CHARLIE BROWN.
SHE ENDS UP IN LOVE WITH SCHROEDER.
BUT SCHROEDER ONLY LOVES TWO THINGS IN LIFE...
...BEETHOVEN AND HIS PIANO.
THIS IS LINUS, LUCY'S LITTLE BROTHER... HE'S MODELED AFTER MONTE.
HE'S THOUGHTFUL BUT SOMETIMES ANXIOUS AND ALWAYS CARRIES HIS SECURITY BLANKET.

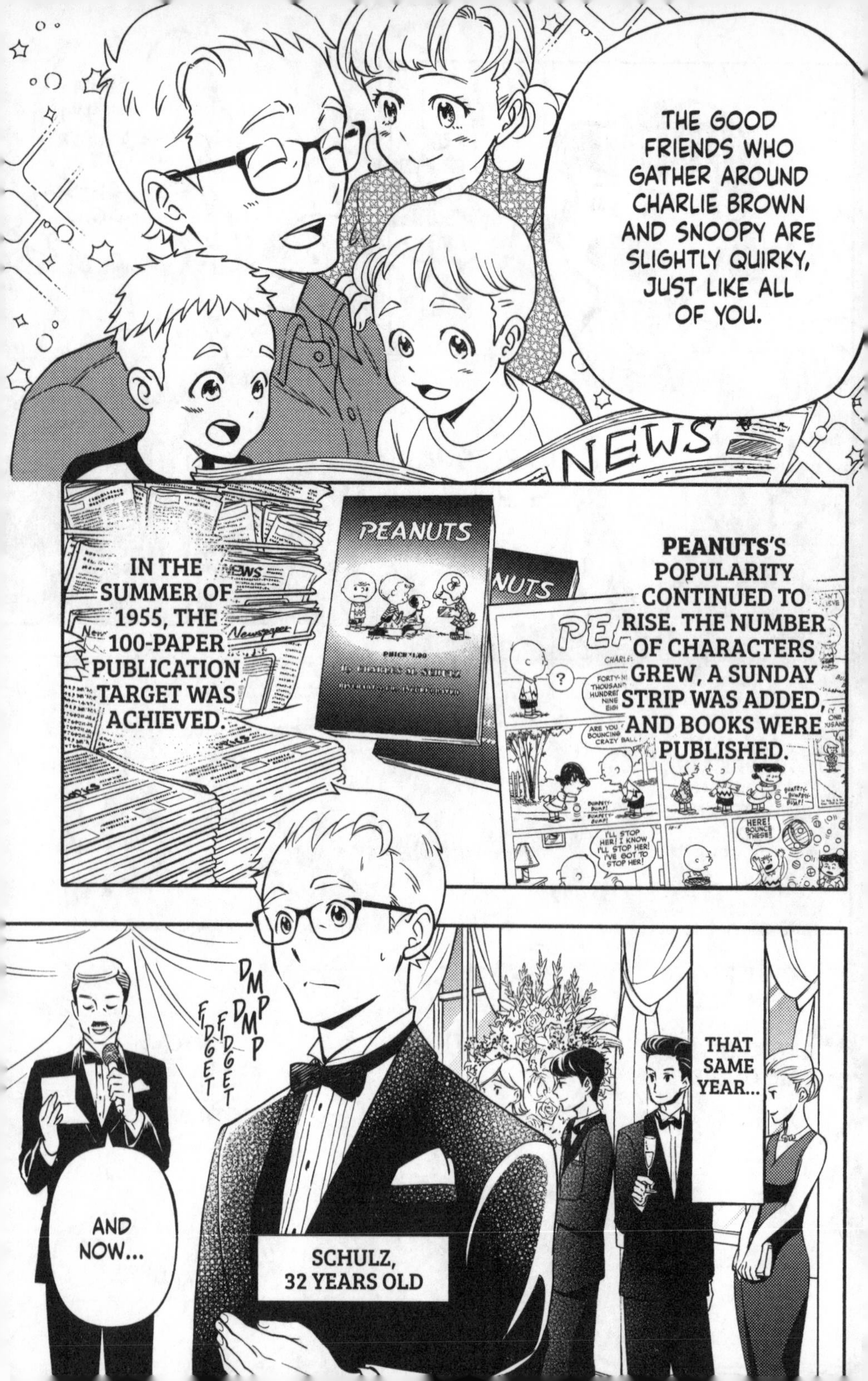
THE GOOD FRIENDS WHO GATHER AROUND CHARLIE BROWN AND SNOOPY ARE SLIGHTLY QUIRKY, JUST LIKE ALL OF YOU.
NEWS
PEANUTS'S POPULARITY CONTINUED TO RISE. THE NUMBER OF CHARACTERS GREW, A SUNDAY STRIP WAS ADDED, AND BOOKS WERE PUBLISHED.
HERE! BOUNCE THESE!
I'LL STOP HER! I KNOW I'LL STOP HER! I'VE GOT TO STOP HER!
PEANUTS
IN THE SUMMER OF 1955, THE 100-PAPER PUBLICATION TARGET WAS ACHIEVED.
THAT SAME YEAR...
DMP DMP
FIDGET FIDGET
SCHULZ, 32 YEARS OLD
AND NOW...

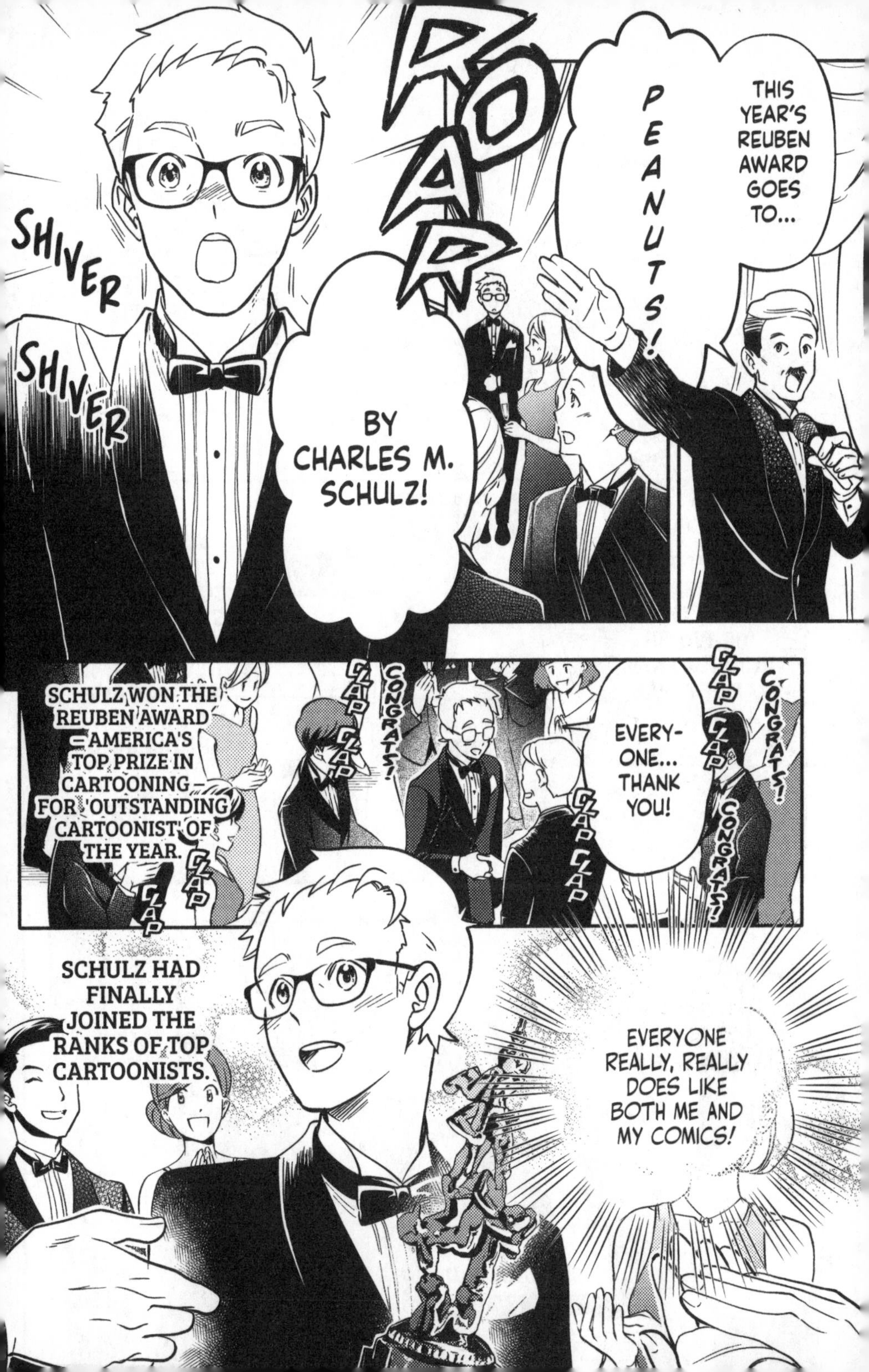
THIS YEAR'S REUBEN AWARD GOES TO...
PEANUTS!
ROAR
BY CHARLES M. SCHULZ!
SHIVER
SHIVER
CONGRATS!
CLAP CLAP
CONGRATS!
CONGRATS!
EVERY-ONE... THANK YOU!
CLAP CLAP
CONGRATS!
CLAP CLAP
SCHULZ WON THE REUBEN AWARD – AMERICA'S TOP PRIZE IN CARTOONING – FOR 'OUTSTANDING CARTOONIST' OF THE YEAR.
CLAP
CLAP
EVERYONE REALLY, REALLY DOES LIKE BOTH ME AND MY COMICS!
SCHULZ HAD FINALLY JOINED THE RANKS OF TOP CARTOONISTS.

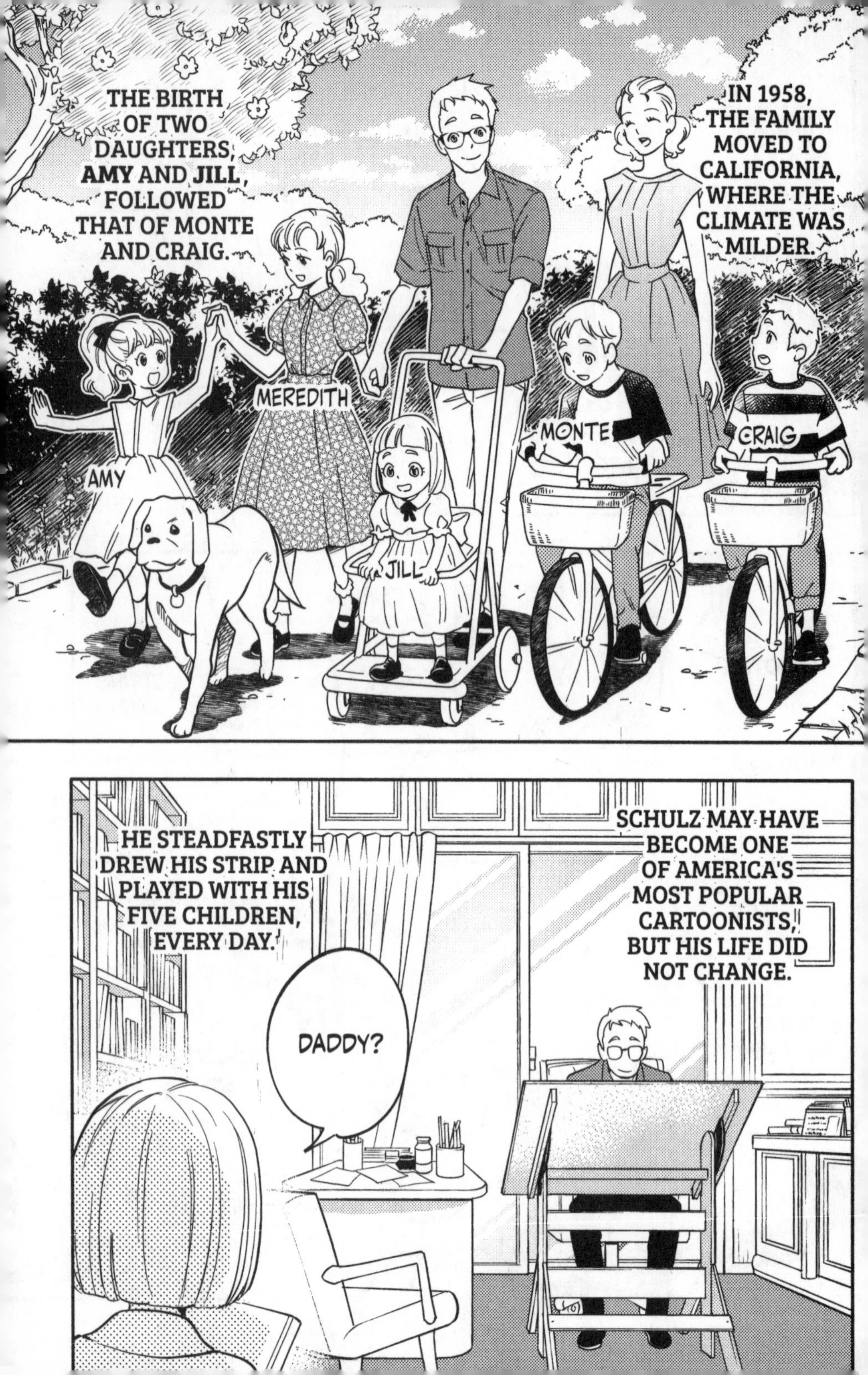
IN 1958, THE FAMILY MOVED TO CALIFORNIA, WHERE THE CLIMATE WAS MILDER.
THE BIRTH OF TWO DAUGHTERS, **AMY AND JILL**, FOLLOWED THAT OF MONTE AND CRAIG.
CRAIG
MONTE
JILL
MEREDITH
AMY
SCHULZ MAY HAVE BECOME ONE OF AMERICA'S MOST POPULAR CARTOONISTS, BUT HIS LIFE DID NOT CHANGE.
HE STEADFASTLY DREW HIS STRIP AND PLAYED WITH HIS FIVE CHILDREN, EVERY DAY.
DADDY?

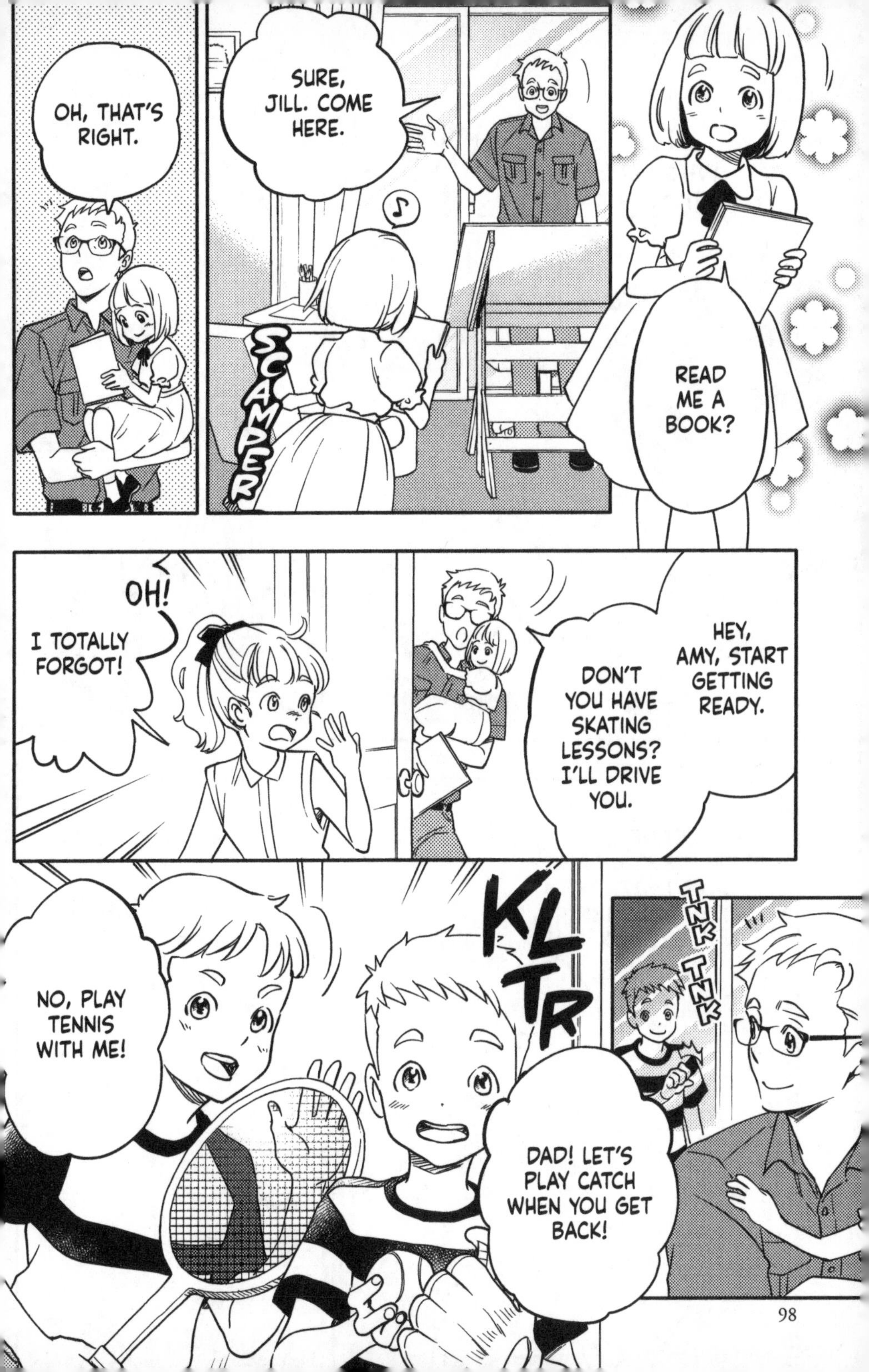
READ ME A BOOK?
SURE, JILL. COME HERE.
♪
SCAMPER
OH, THAT'S RIGHT.
HEY, AMY, START GETTING READY.
DON'T YOU HAVE SKATING LESSONS? I'LL DRIVE YOU.
OH!
I TOTALLY FORGOT!
TNK TNK
DAD! LET'S PLAY CATCH WHEN YOU GET BACK!
KLTR
NO, PLAY TENNIS WITH ME!

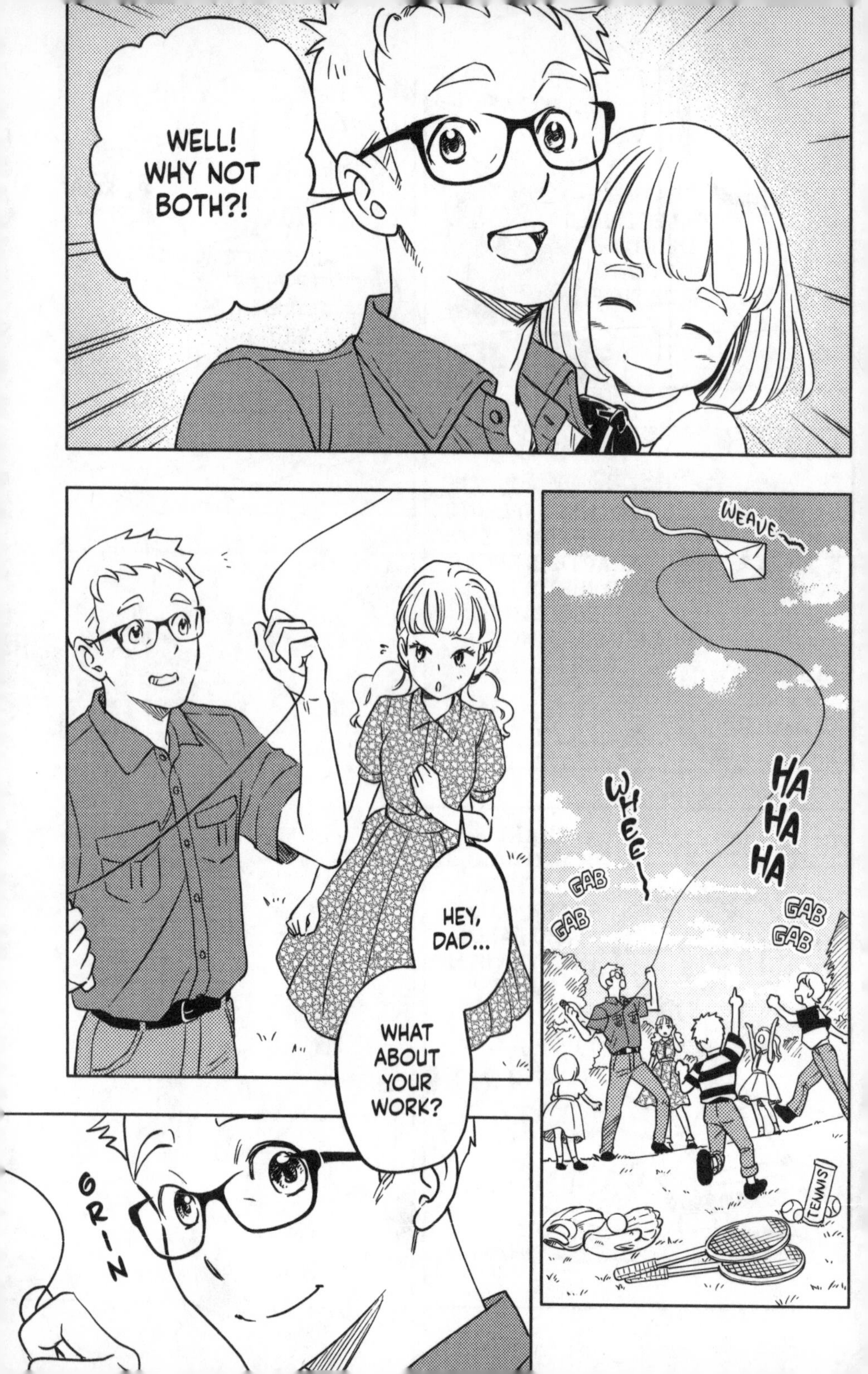
WELL! WHY NOT BOTH?!
WEAVE~
HA HA HA
WHEE~
GAB GAB
GAB GAB
TENNIS
HEY, DAD...
WHAT ABOUT YOUR WORK?
GRIN

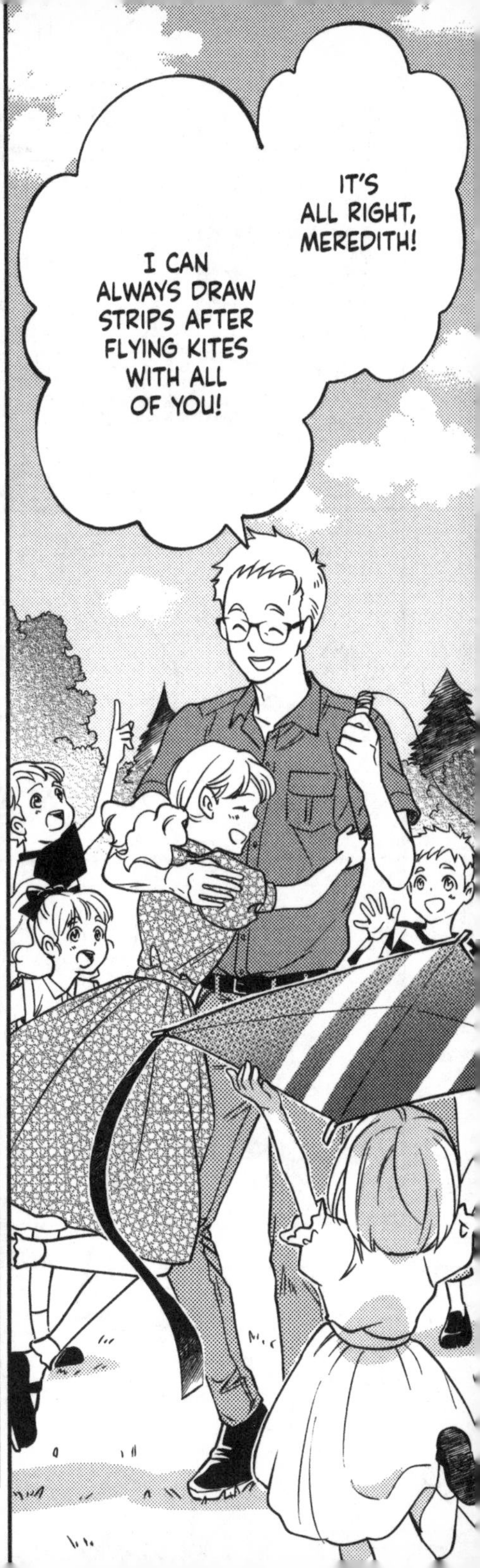
IT'S ALL RIGHT, MEREDITH!
I CAN ALWAYS DRAW STRIPS AFTER FLYING KITES WITH ALL OF YOU!

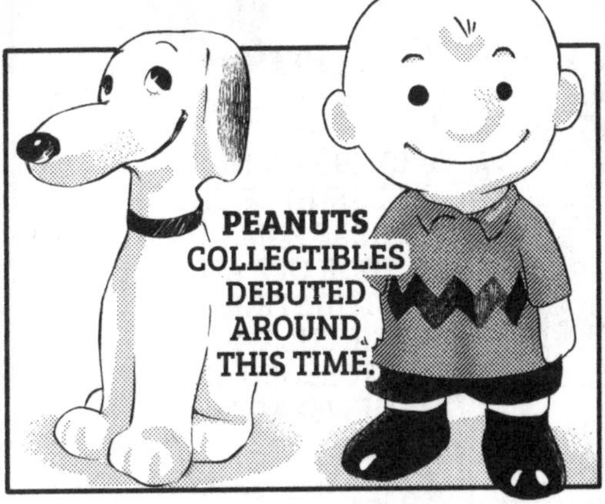
PEANUTS COLLECTIBLES DEBUTED AROUND THIS TIME.

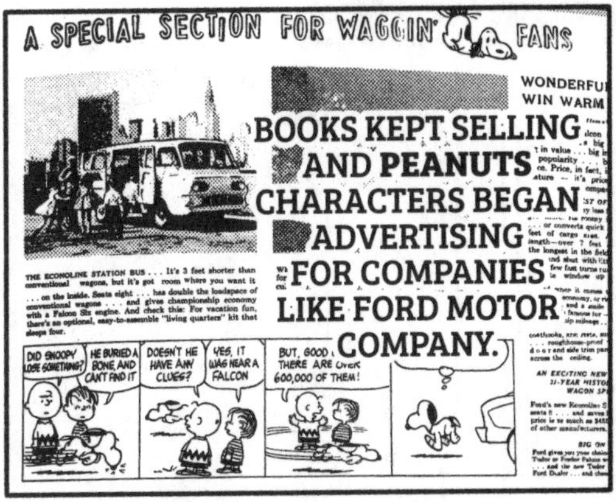
A SPECIAL SECTION FOR WAGGIN' FANS
BOOKS KEPT SELLING AND **PEANUTS** CHARACTERS BEGAN ADVERTISING FOR COMPANIES LIKE FORD MOTOR COMPANY.
THE ECONOLINE STATION BUS . . . It's 3 feet shorter than conventional wagons, but it's got room where you want it . . . on the inside. Seats eight . . . has double the loadspace of conventional wagons . . . and gives championship economy with a Falcon Six engine. And check this: For vacation fun, there's an optional, easy-to-assemble "living quarters" kit that sleeps four.
DID SNOOPY LOSE SOMETHING?
HE BURIED A BONE, AND CAN'T FIND IT
DOESN'T HE HAVE ANY CLUES?
YES, IT WAS NEAR A FALCON

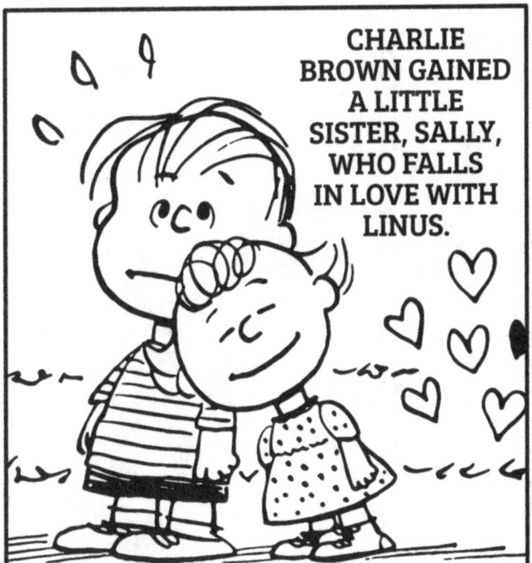
CHARLIE BROWN GAINED A LITTLE SISTER, SALLY, WHO FALLS IN LOVE WITH LINUS.

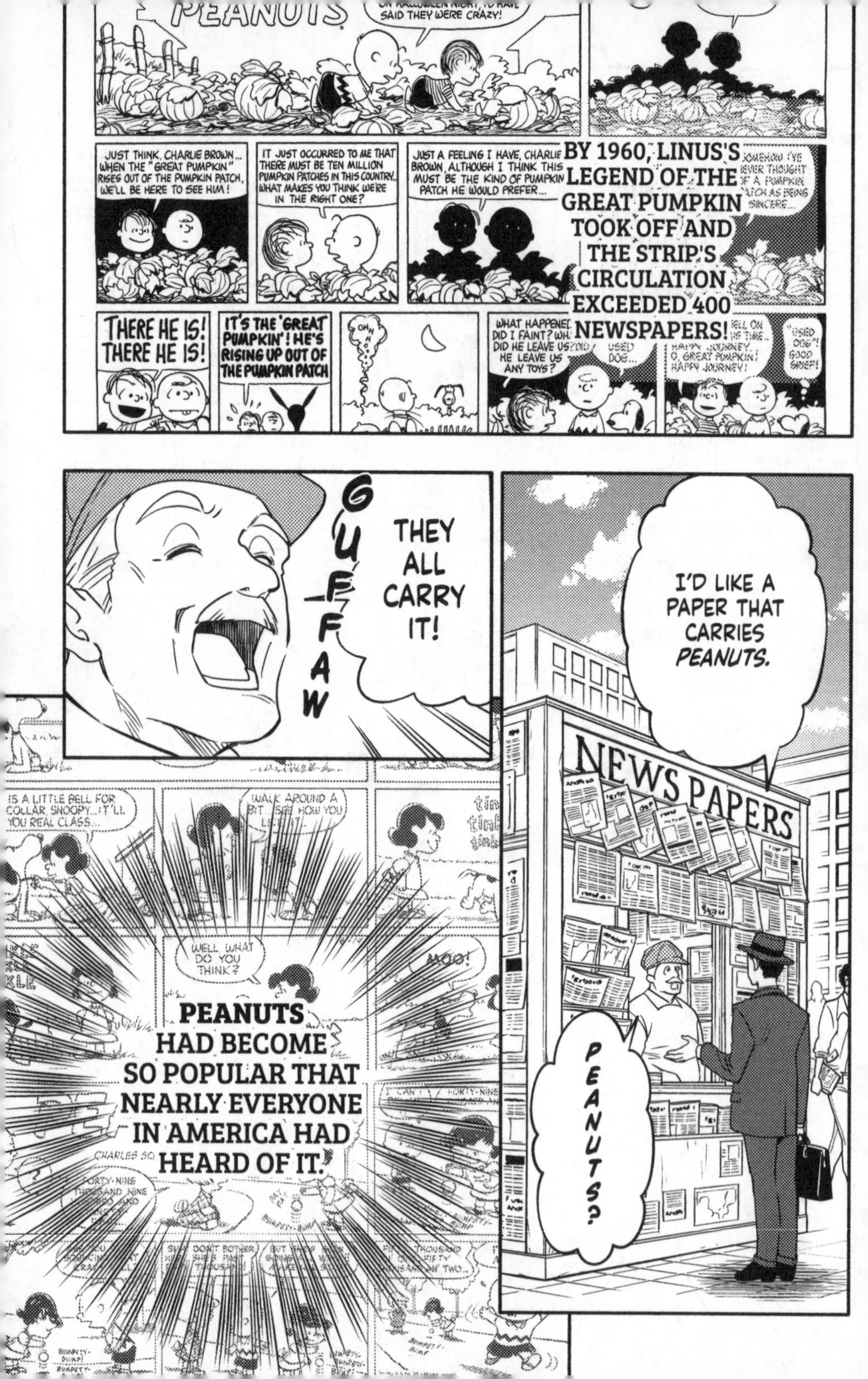

PEANUTS
SAID THEY WERE CRAZY!
JUST THINK, CHARLIE BROWN... WHEN THE "GREAT PUMPKIN" RISES OUT OF THE PUMPKIN PATCH, WE'LL BE HERE TO SEE HIM!
IT JUST OCCURRED TO ME THAT THERE MUST BE TEN MILLION PUMPKIN PATCHES IN THIS COUNTRY.. WHAT MAKES YOU THINK WE'RE IN THE RIGHT ONE?
JUST A FEELING I HAVE, CHARLIE BROWN, ALTHOUGH I THINK THIS MUST BE THE KIND OF PUMPKIN PATCH HE WOULD PREFER...
BY 1960, LINUS'S LEGEND OF THE GREAT PUMPKIN TOOK OFF AND THE STRIP'S CIRCULATION EXCEEDED 400 NEWSPAPERS!
THERE HE IS! THERE HE IS!
IT'S THE 'GREAT PUMPKIN'! HE'S RISING UP OUT OF THE PUMPKIN PATCH
HAPPY JOURNEY, O, GREAT PUMPKIN! HAPPY JOURNEY!
"USED DOG"! GOOD GRIEF!
NEWS PAPERS
I'D LIKE A PAPER THAT CARRIES *PEANUTS.*
PEANUTS?
GUFFAW
THEY ALL CARRY IT!
WALK AROUND A BIT... SEE HOW YOU LIKE IT...
WELL, WHAT DO YOU THINK?
MOO!
PEANUTS HAD BECOME SO POPULAR THAT NEARLY EVERYONE IN AMERICA HAD HEARD OF IT.

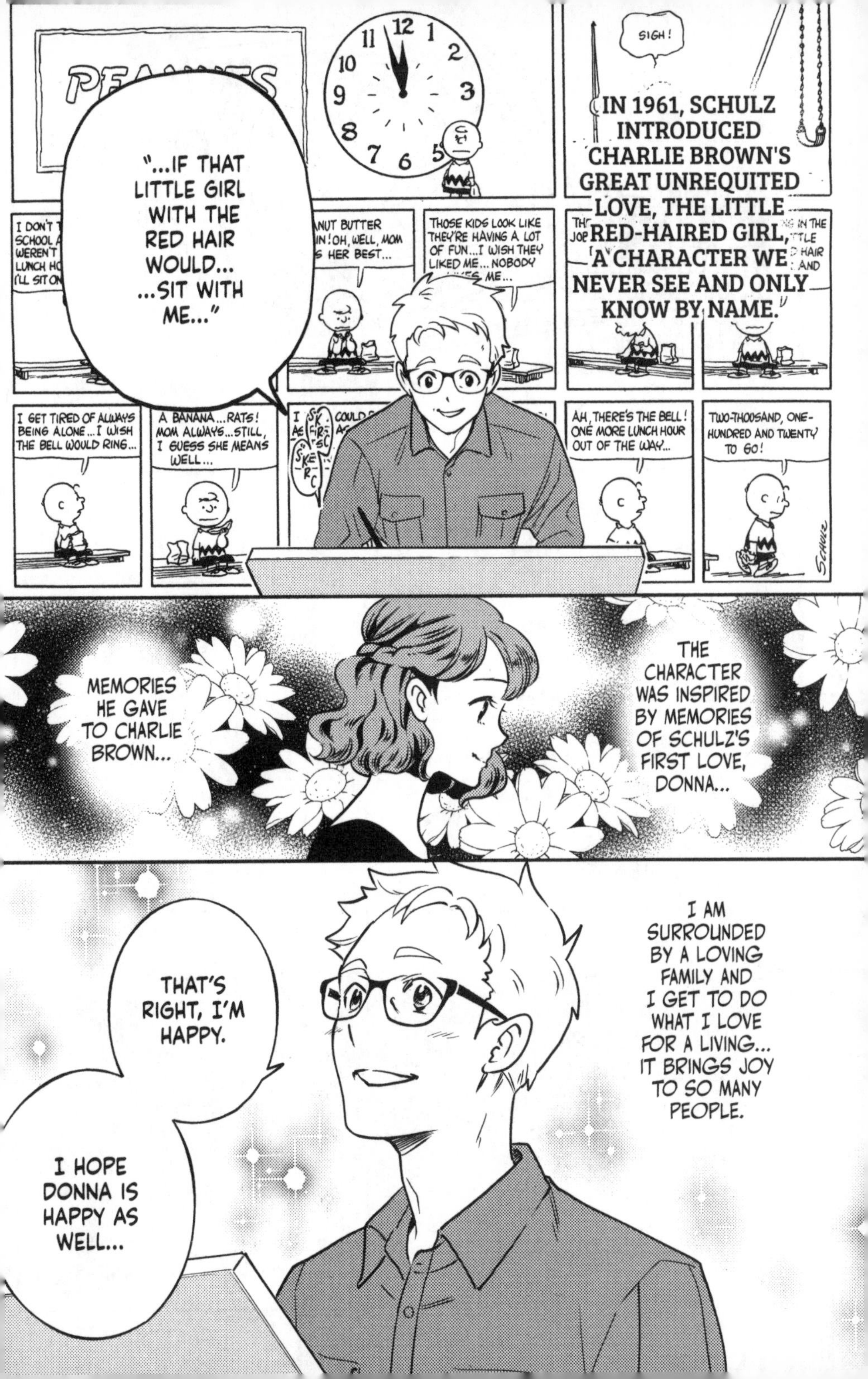
SIGH!
IN 1961, SCHULZ INTRODUCED CHARLIE BROWN'S GREAT UNREQUITED LOVE, THE LITTLE RED-HAIRED GIRL, A CHARACTER WE NEVER SEE AND ONLY KNOW BY NAME.
"...IF THAT LITTLE GIRL WITH THE RED HAIR WOULD... ...SIT WITH ME..."
TWO-THOUSAND, ONE-HUNDRED AND TWENTY TO GO!
AH, THERE'S THE BELL! ONE MORE LUNCH HOUR OUT OF THE WAY...
A BANANA...RATS! MOM ALWAYS...STILL, I GUESS SHE MEANS WELL...
I GET TIRED OF ALWAYS BEING ALONE...I WISH THE BELL WOULD RING...
SCHULZ
THE CHARACTER WAS INSPIRED BY MEMORIES OF SCHULZ'S FIRST LOVE, DONNA...
MEMORIES HE GAVE TO CHARLIE BROWN...
I AM SURROUNDED BY A LOVING FAMILY AND I GET TO DO WHAT I LOVE FOR A LIVING... IT BRINGS JOY TO SO MANY PEOPLE.
THAT'S RIGHT, I'M HAPPY.
I HOPE DONNA IS HAPPY AS WELL...

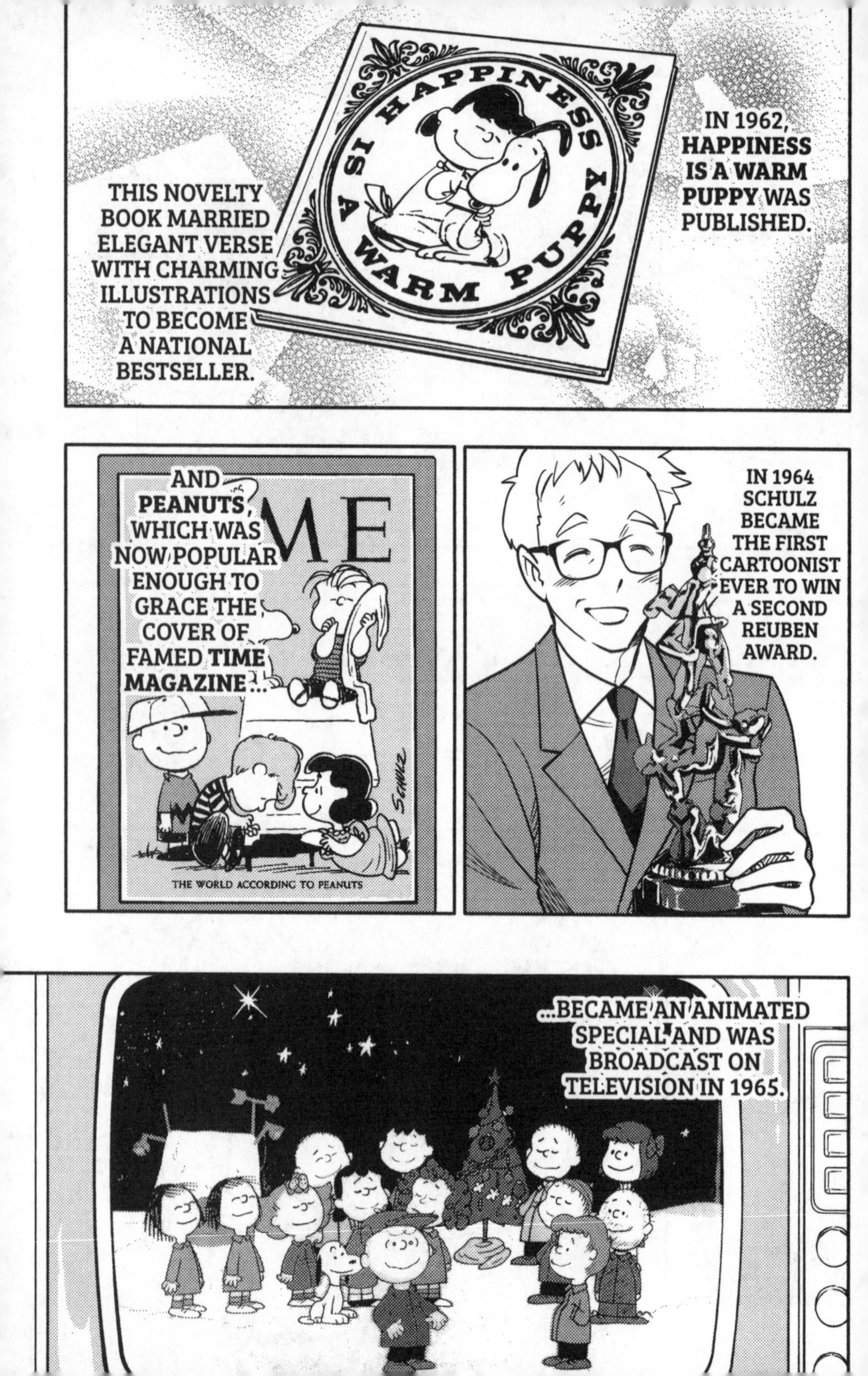
IN 1962, HAPPINESS IS A WARM PUPPY WAS PUBLISHED.
HAPPINESS IS A WARM PUPPY
THIS NOVELTY BOOK MARRIED ELEGANT VERSE WITH CHARMING ILLUSTRATIONS TO BECOME A NATIONAL BESTSELLER.
IN 1964 SCHULZ BECAME THE FIRST CARTOONIST EVER TO WIN A SECOND REUBEN AWARD.
AND PEANUTS, WHICH WAS NOW POPULAR ENOUGH TO GRACE THE COVER OF FAMED TIME MAGAZINE...
ME
SCHULZ
THE WORLD ACCORDING TO PEANUTS
...BECAME AN ANIMATED SPECIAL AND WAS BROADCAST ON TELEVISION IN 1965.

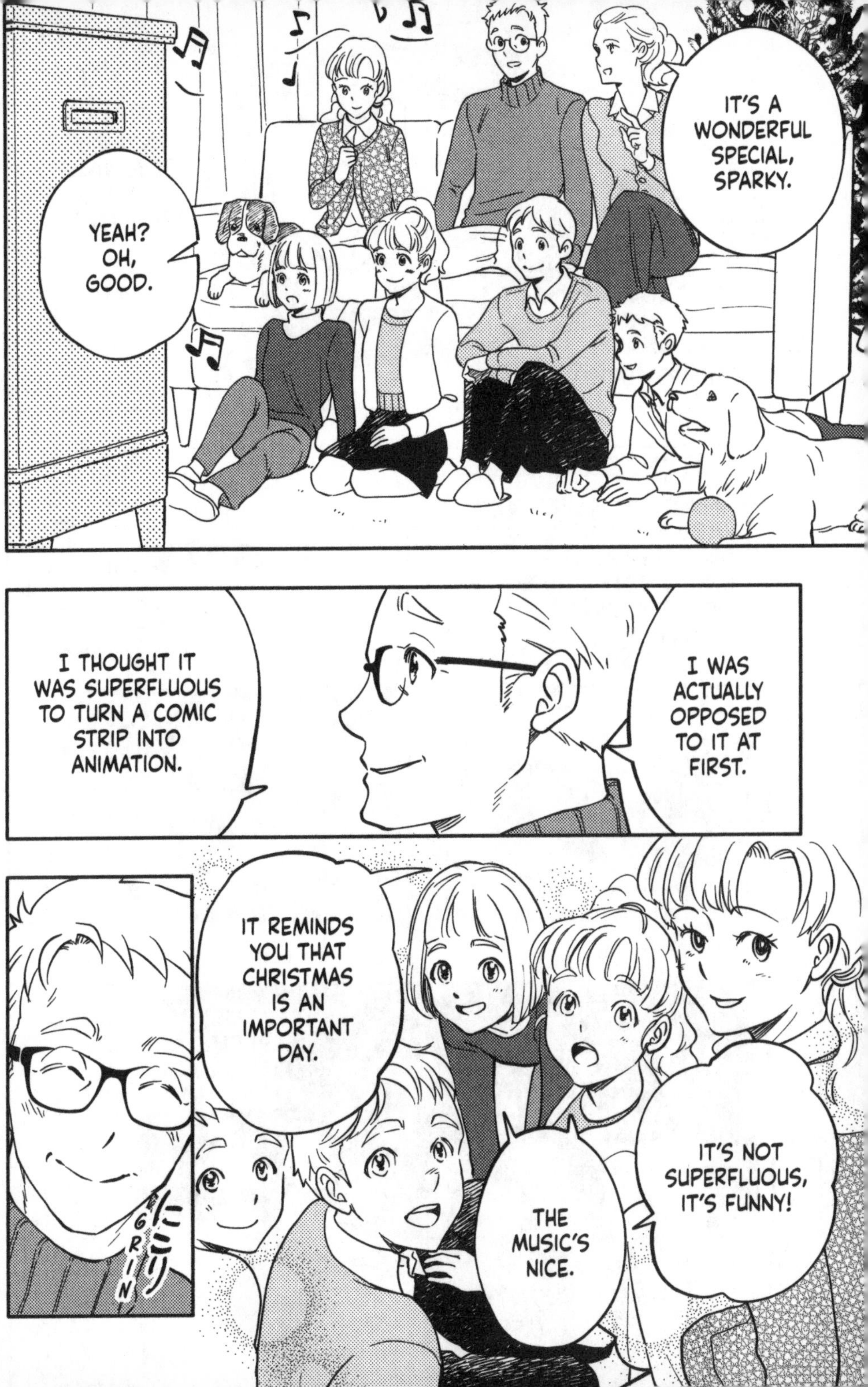
IT'S A WONDERFUL SPECIAL, SPARKY.
YEAH? OH, GOOD.
I WAS ACTUALLY OPPOSED TO IT AT FIRST.
I THOUGHT IT WAS SUPERFLUOUS TO TURN A COMIC STRIP INTO ANIMATION.
IT'S NOT SUPERFLUOUS, IT'S FUNNY!
THE MUSIC'S NICE.
IT REMINDS YOU THAT CHRISTMAS IS AN IMPORTANT DAY.
にこり
GRIN

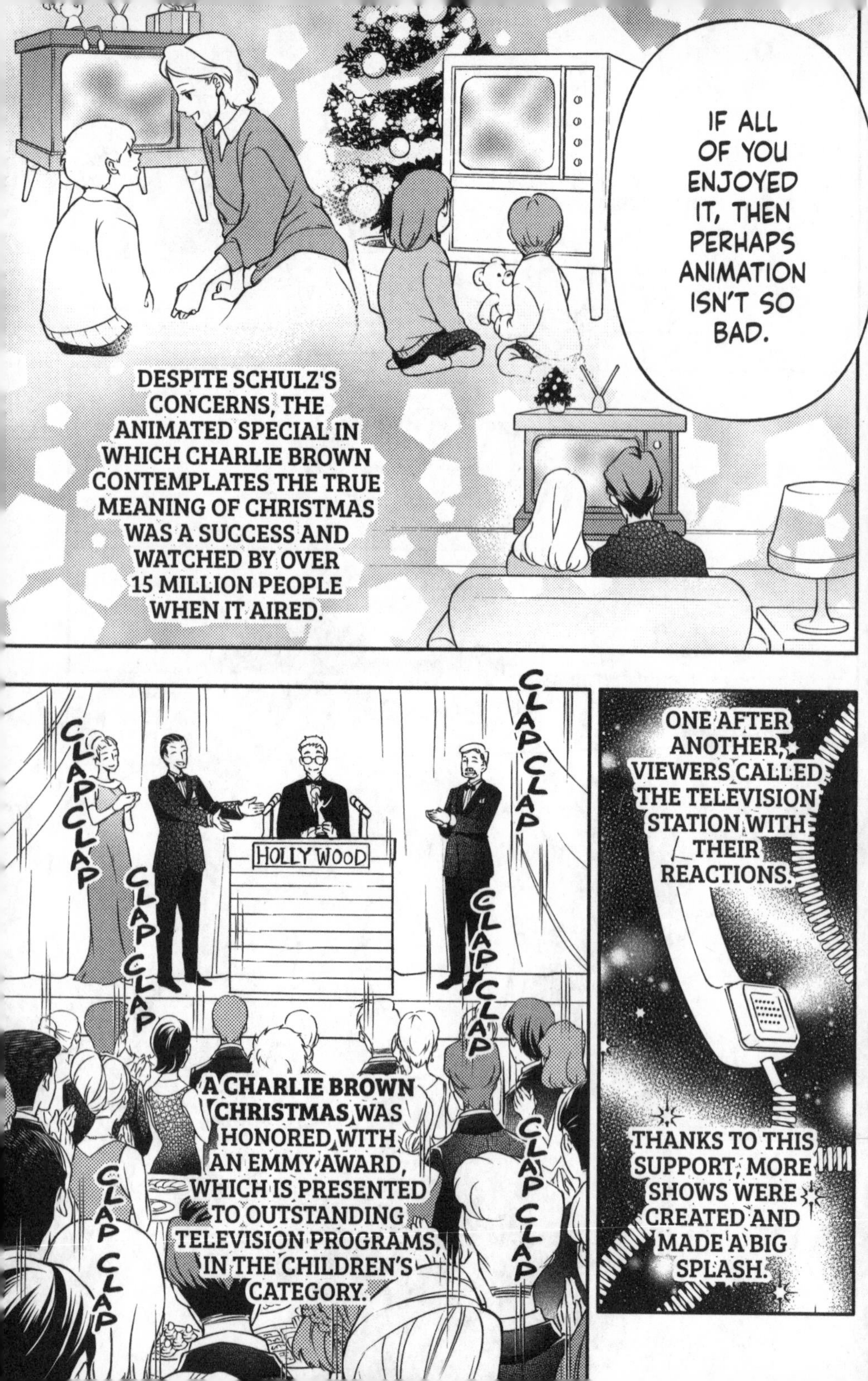
IF ALL OF YOU ENJOYED IT, THEN PERHAPS ANIMATION ISN'T SO BAD.
DESPITE SCHULZ'S CONCERNS, THE ANIMATED SPECIAL IN WHICH CHARLIE BROWN CONTEMPLATES THE TRUE MEANING OF CHRISTMAS WAS A SUCCESS AND WATCHED BY OVER 15 MILLION PEOPLE WHEN IT AIRED.
ONE AFTER ANOTHER, VIEWERS CALLED THE TELEVISION STATION WITH THEIR REACTIONS.
THANKS TO THIS SUPPORT, MORE SHOWS WERE CREATED AND MADE A BIG SPLASH.
CLAP CLAP
CLAP CLAP
HOLLYWOOD
CLAP CLAP
CLAP CLAP
CLAP CLAP
A CHARLIE BROWN CHRISTMAS WAS HONORED WITH AN EMMY AWARD, WHICH IS PRESENTED TO OUTSTANDING TELEVISION PROGRAMS, IN THE CHILDREN'S CATEGORY.
CLAP CLAP

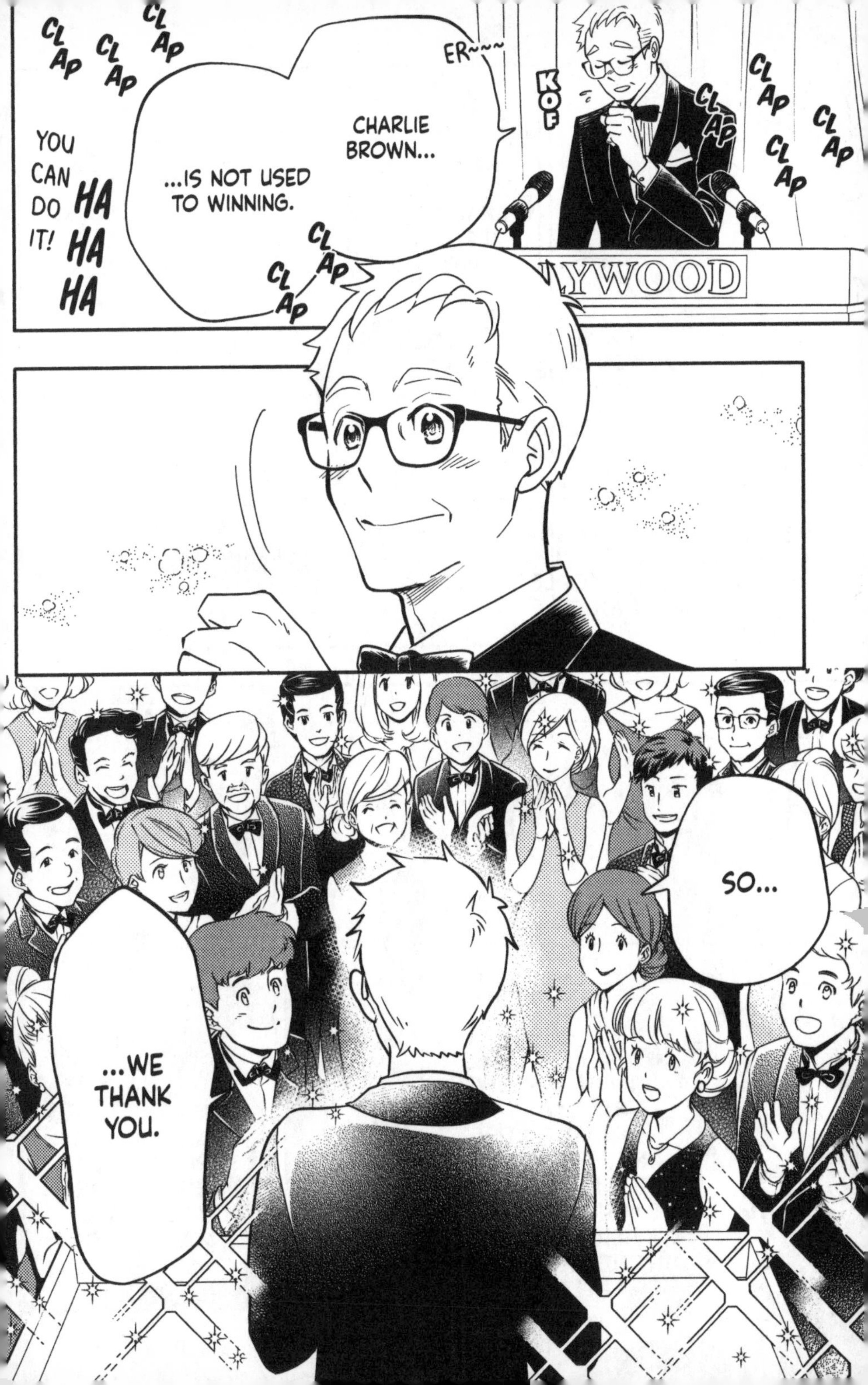
CLAP CLAP CLAP CLAP
KOF
ER~~~
CHARLIE BROWN...
...IS NOT USED TO WINNING.
CLAP CLAP
YOU CAN DO IT!
HA HA HA
CLAP CLAP CLAP
SO...
...WE THANK YOU.

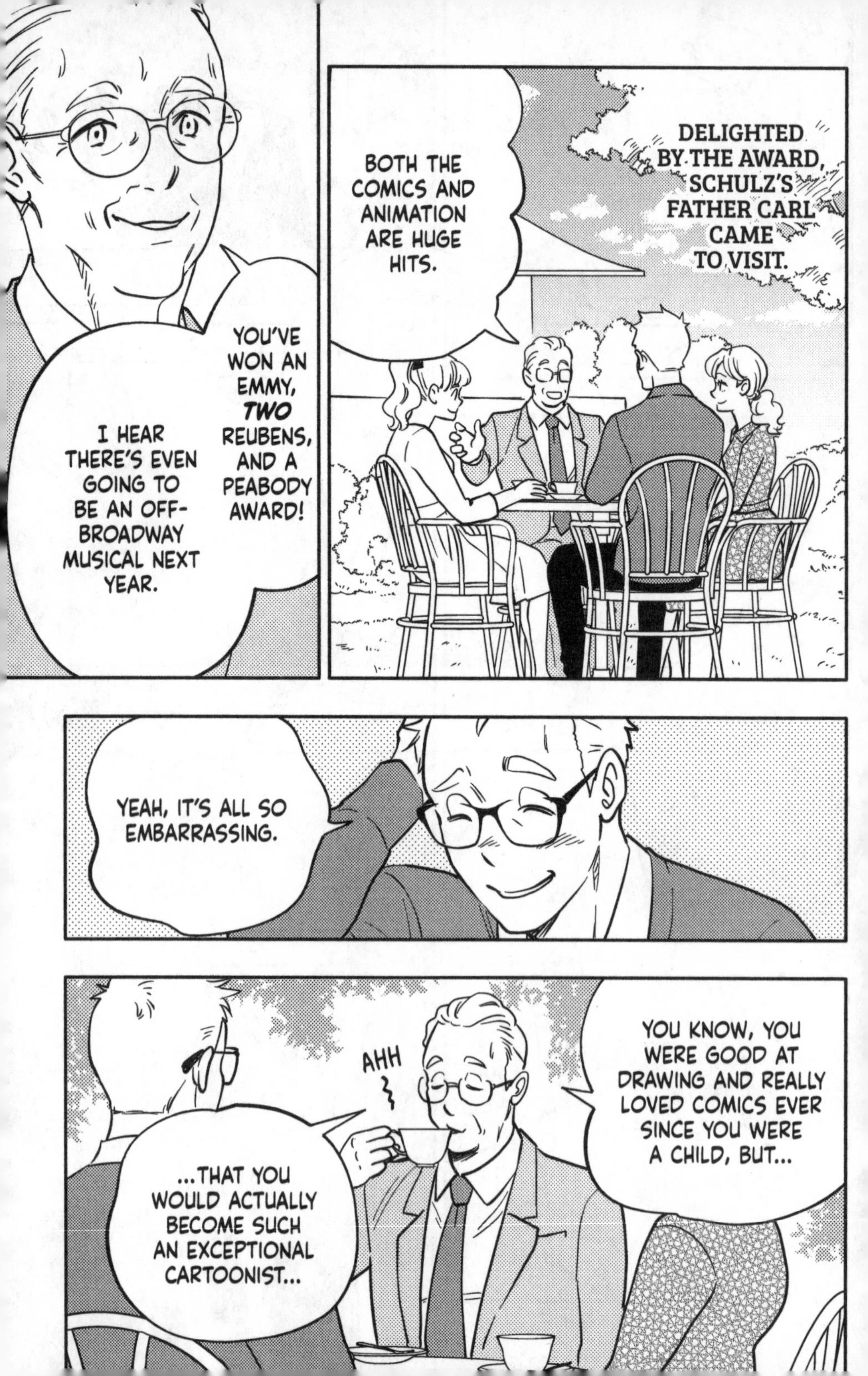
DELIGHTED BY THE AWARD, SCHULZ'S FATHER CARL CAME TO VISIT.
BOTH THE COMICS AND ANIMATION ARE HUGE HITS.
YOU'VE WON AN EMMY, *TWO* REUBENS, AND A PEABODY AWARD!
I HEAR THERE'S EVEN GOING TO BE AN OFF-BROADWAY MUSICAL NEXT YEAR.
YEAH, IT'S ALL SO EMBARRASSING.
YOU KNOW, YOU WERE GOOD AT DRAWING AND REALLY LOVED COMICS EVER SINCE YOU WERE A CHILD, BUT...
AHH
...THAT YOU WOULD ACTUALLY BECOME SUCH AN EXCEPTIONAL CARTOONIST...

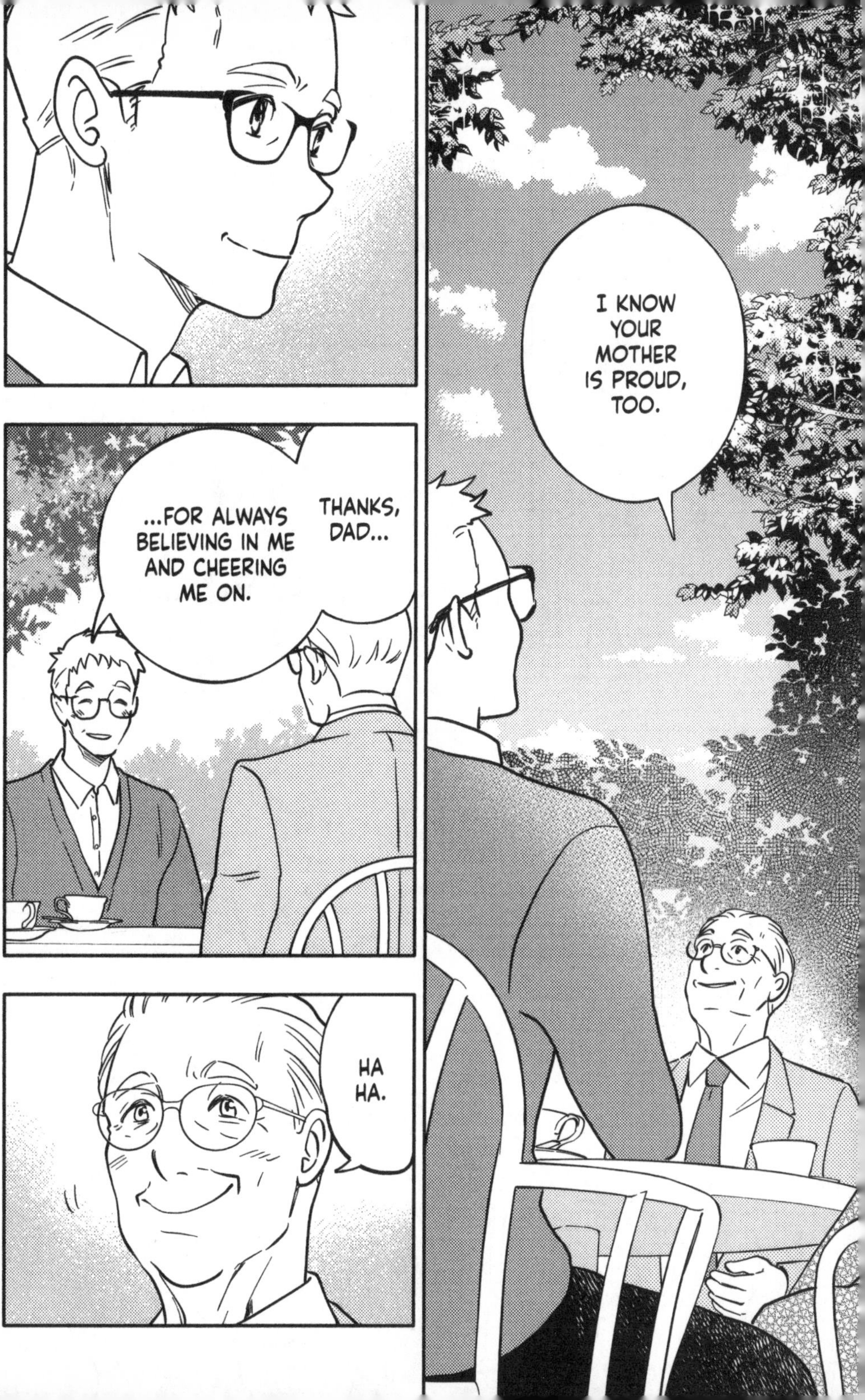
I KNOW YOUR MOTHER IS PROUD, TOO.
THANKS, DAD...
...FOR ALWAYS BELIEVING IN ME AND CHEERING ME ON.
HA HA.

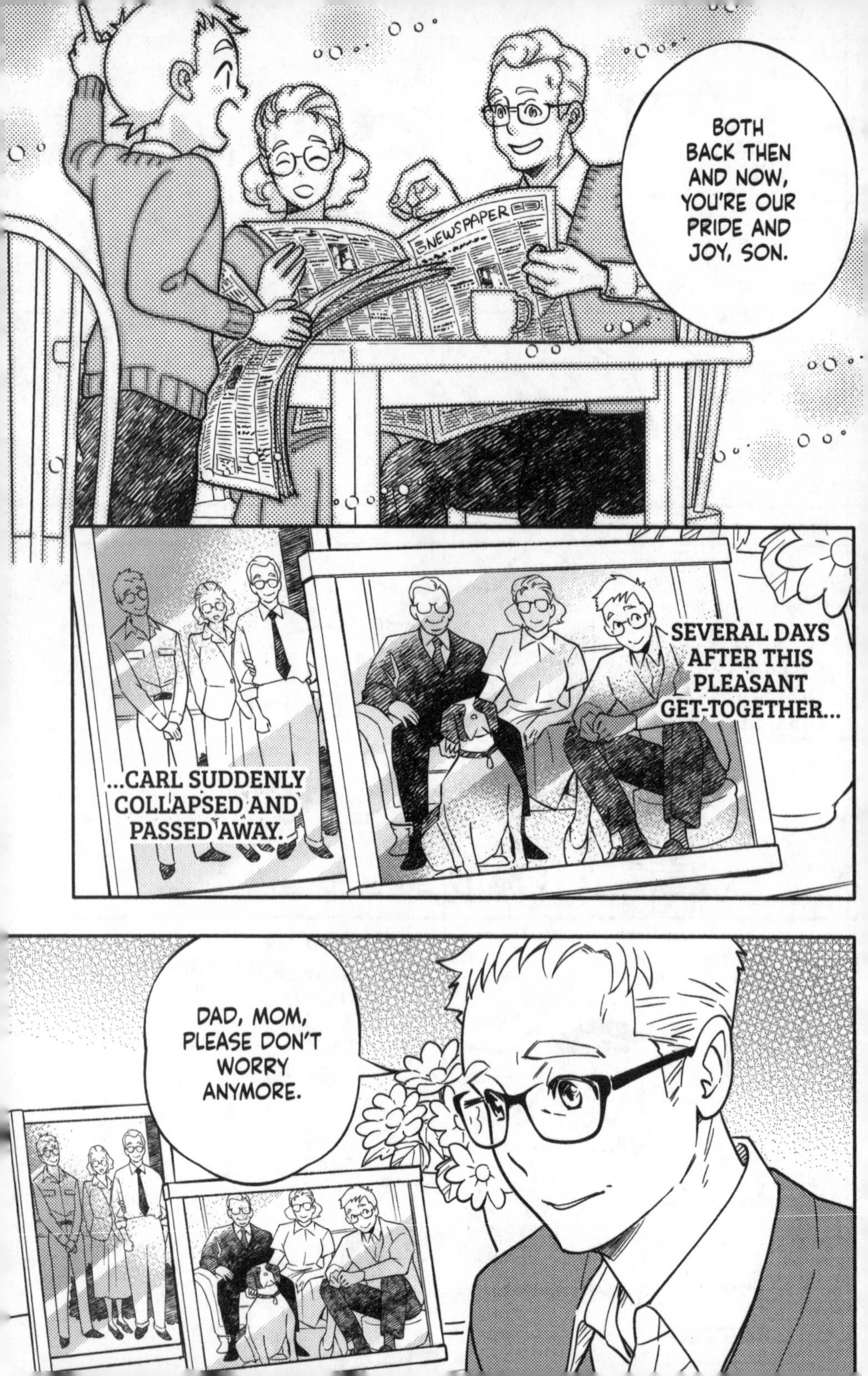
BOTH BACK THEN AND NOW, YOU'RE OUR PRIDE AND JOY, SON.
NEWSPAPER
SEVERAL DAYS AFTER THIS PLEASANT GET-TOGETHER...
...CARL SUDDENLY COLLAPSED AND PASSED AWAY.
DAD, MOM, PLEASE DON'T WORRY ANYMORE.

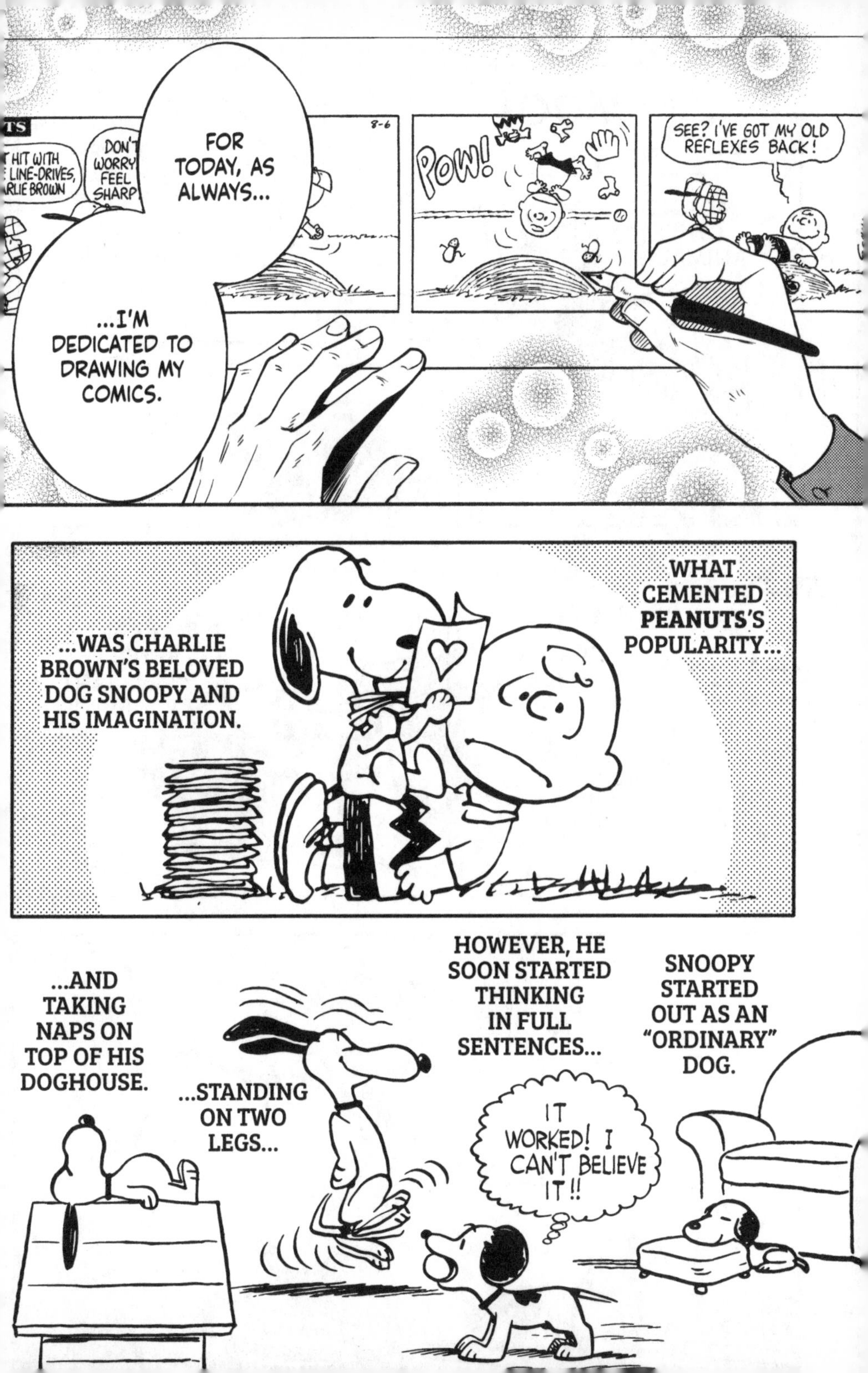
FOR TODAY, AS ALWAYS...
...I'M DEDICATED TO DRAWING MY COMICS.
SEE? I'VE GOT MY OLD REFLEXES BACK!
POW!
8-6
DON'T WORRY FEEL SHARP
WHAT CEMENTED PEANUTS'S POPULARITY...
...WAS CHARLIE BROWN'S BELOVED DOG SNOOPY AND HIS IMAGINATION.
SNOOPY STARTED OUT AS AN "ORDINARY" DOG.
HOWEVER, HE SOON STARTED THINKING IN FULL SENTENCES...
IT WORKED! I CAN'T BELIEVE IT!!
...STANDING ON TWO LEGS...
...AND TAKING NAPS ON TOP OF HIS DOGHOUSE.

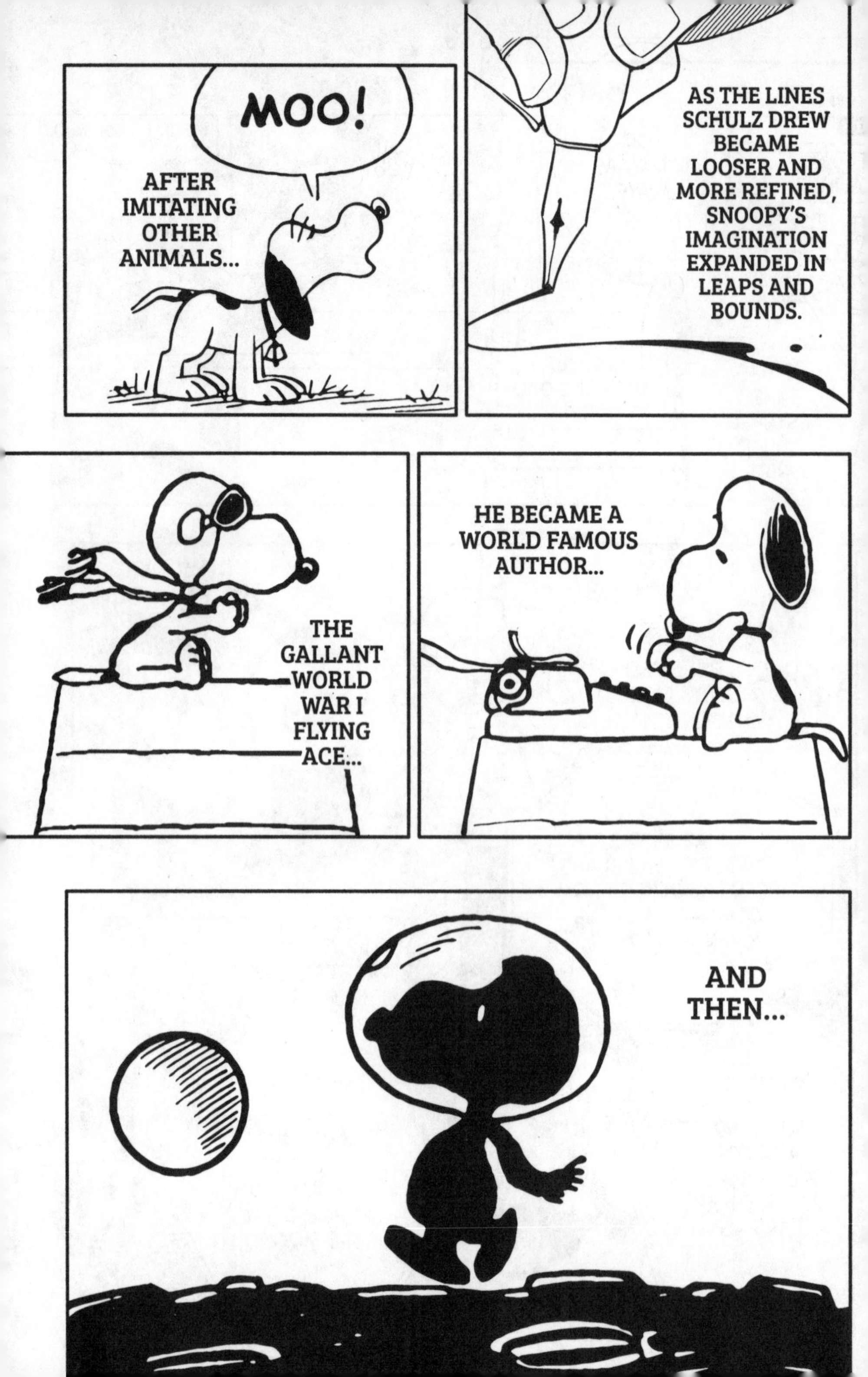
AS THE LINES SCHULZ DREW BECAME LOOSER AND MORE REFINED, SNOOPY'S IMAGINATION EXPANDED IN LEAPS AND BOUNDS.
MOO!
AFTER IMITATING OTHER ANIMALS...
HE BECAME A WORLD FAMOUS AUTHOR...
THE GALLANT WORLD WAR I FLYING ACE...
AND THEN...

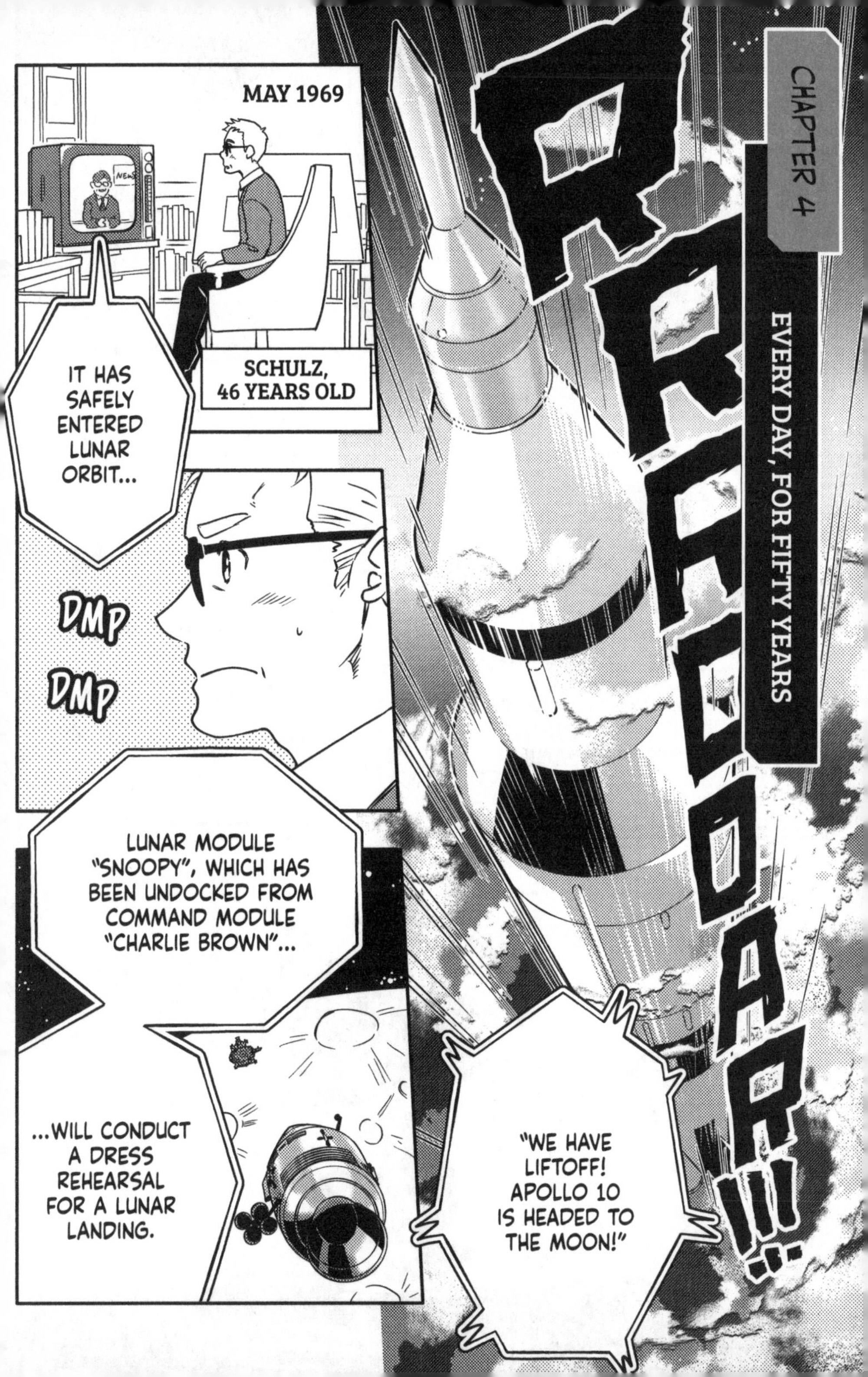
CHAPTER 4
EVERY DAY, FOR FIFTY YEARS
RRROOOOAAR!!!
"WE HAVE LIFTOFF! APOLLO 10 IS HEADED TO THE MOON!"
MAY 1969
SCHULZ, 46 YEARS OLD
IT HAS SAFELY ENTERED LUNAR ORBIT...
DMP
DMP
LUNAR MODULE "SNOOPY", WHICH HAS BEEN UNDOCKED FROM COMMAND MODULE "CHARLIE BROWN"...
...WILL CONDUCT A DRESS REHEARSAL FOR A LUNAR LANDING.

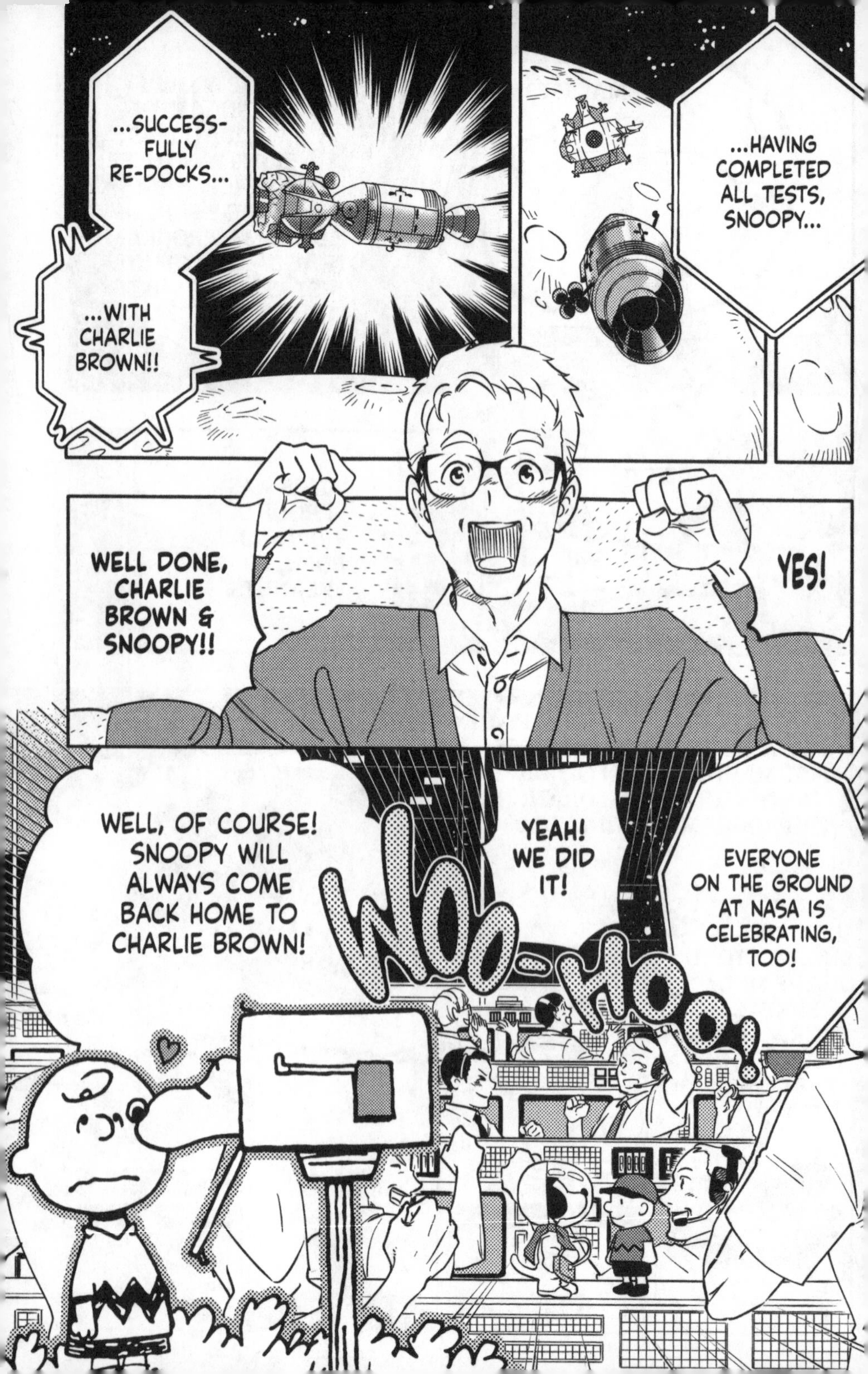
...HAVING COMPLETED ALL TESTS, SNOOPY...
...SUCCESS-FULLY RE-DOCKS...
...WITH CHARLIE BROWN!!
YES!
WELL DONE, CHARLIE BROWN & SNOOPY!!
EVERYONE ON THE GROUND AT NASA IS CELEBRATING, TOO!
YEAH! WE DID IT!
WOO-HOO!
WELL, OF COURSE! SNOOPY WILL ALWAYS COME BACK HOME TO CHARLIE BROWN!

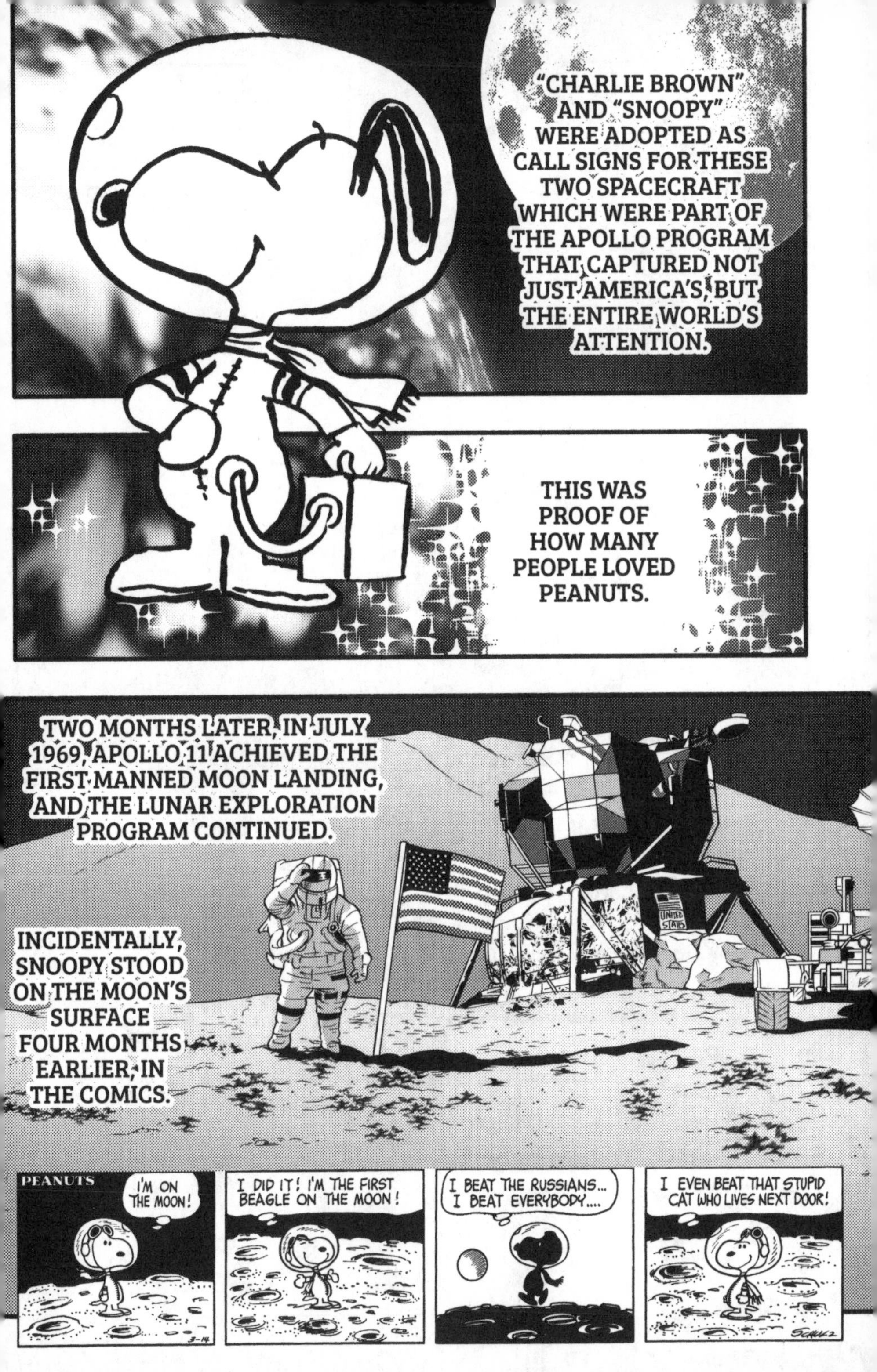
"CHARLIE BROWN" AND "SNOOPY" WERE ADOPTED AS CALL SIGNS FOR THESE TWO SPACECRAFT WHICH WERE PART OF THE APOLLO PROGRAM THAT CAPTURED NOT JUST AMERICA'S, BUT THE ENTIRE WORLD'S ATTENTION.
THIS WAS PROOF OF HOW MANY PEOPLE LOVED PEANUTS.
TWO MONTHS LATER, IN JULY 1969, APOLLO 11 ACHIEVED THE FIRST MANNED MOON LANDING, AND THE LUNAR EXPLORATION PROGRAM CONTINUED.
UNITED STATES
INCIDENTALLY, SNOOPY STOOD ON THE MOON'S SURFACE FOUR MONTHS EARLIER, IN THE COMICS.
PEANUTS
I'M ON THE MOON!
I DID IT! I'M THE FIRST BEAGLE ON THE MOON!
I BEAT THE RUSSIANS... I BEAT EVERYBODY....
I EVEN BEAT THAT STUPID CAT WHO LIVES NEXT DOOR!
3-14
SCHULZ

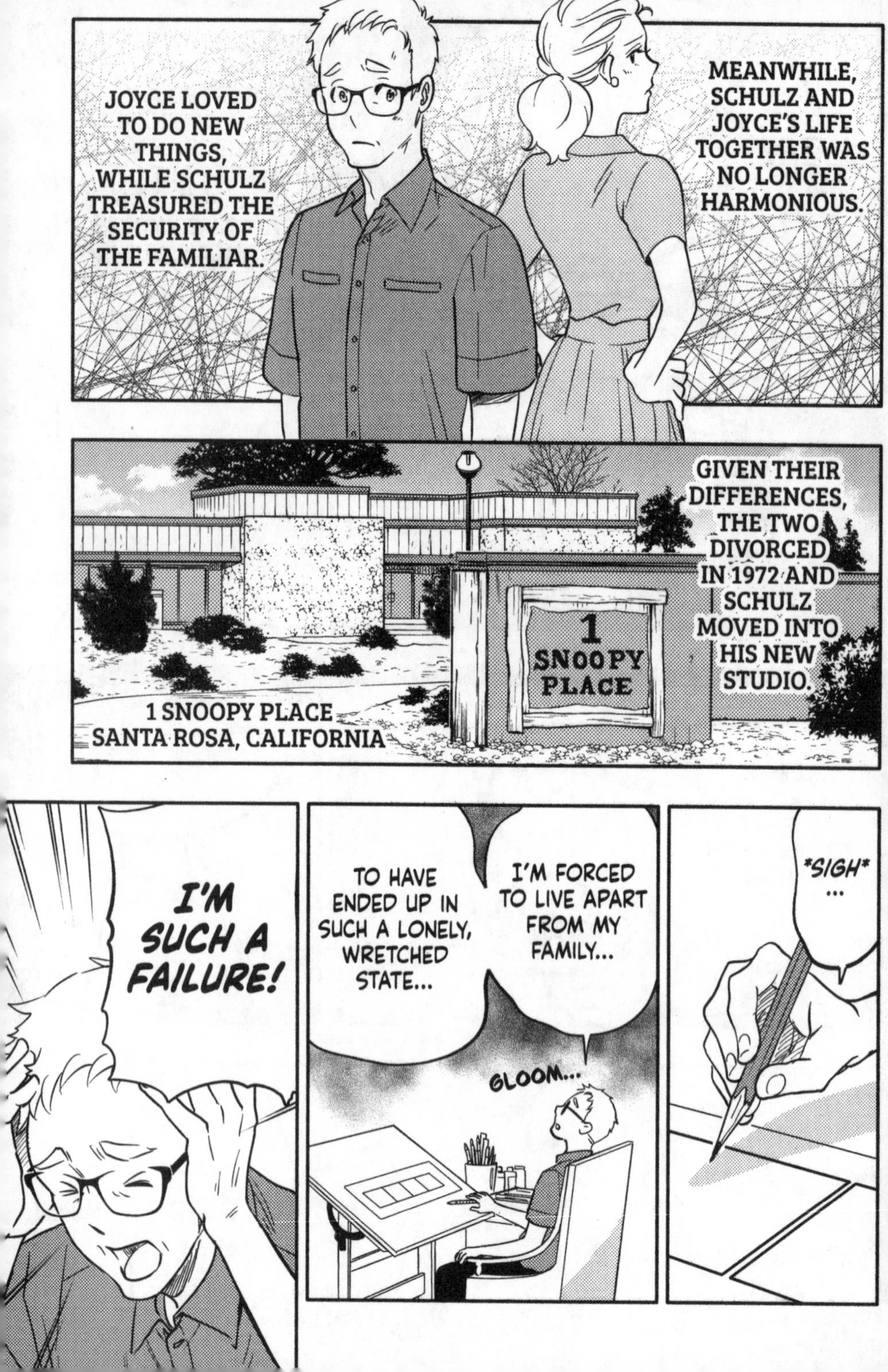
MEANWHILE, SCHULZ AND JOYCE'S LIFE TOGETHER WAS NO LONGER HARMONIOUS.
JOYCE LOVED TO DO NEW THINGS, WHILE SCHULZ TREASURED THE SECURITY OF THE FAMILIAR.
GIVEN THEIR DIFFERENCES, THE TWO DIVORCED IN 1972 AND SCHULZ MOVED INTO HIS NEW STUDIO.
1 SNOOPY PLACE
1 SNOOPY PLACE SANTA ROSA, CALIFORNIA
SIGH ...
I'M FORCED TO LIVE APART FROM MY FAMILY...
TO HAVE ENDED UP IN SUCH A LONELY, WRETCHED STATE...
GLOOM...
I'M SUCH A FAILURE!

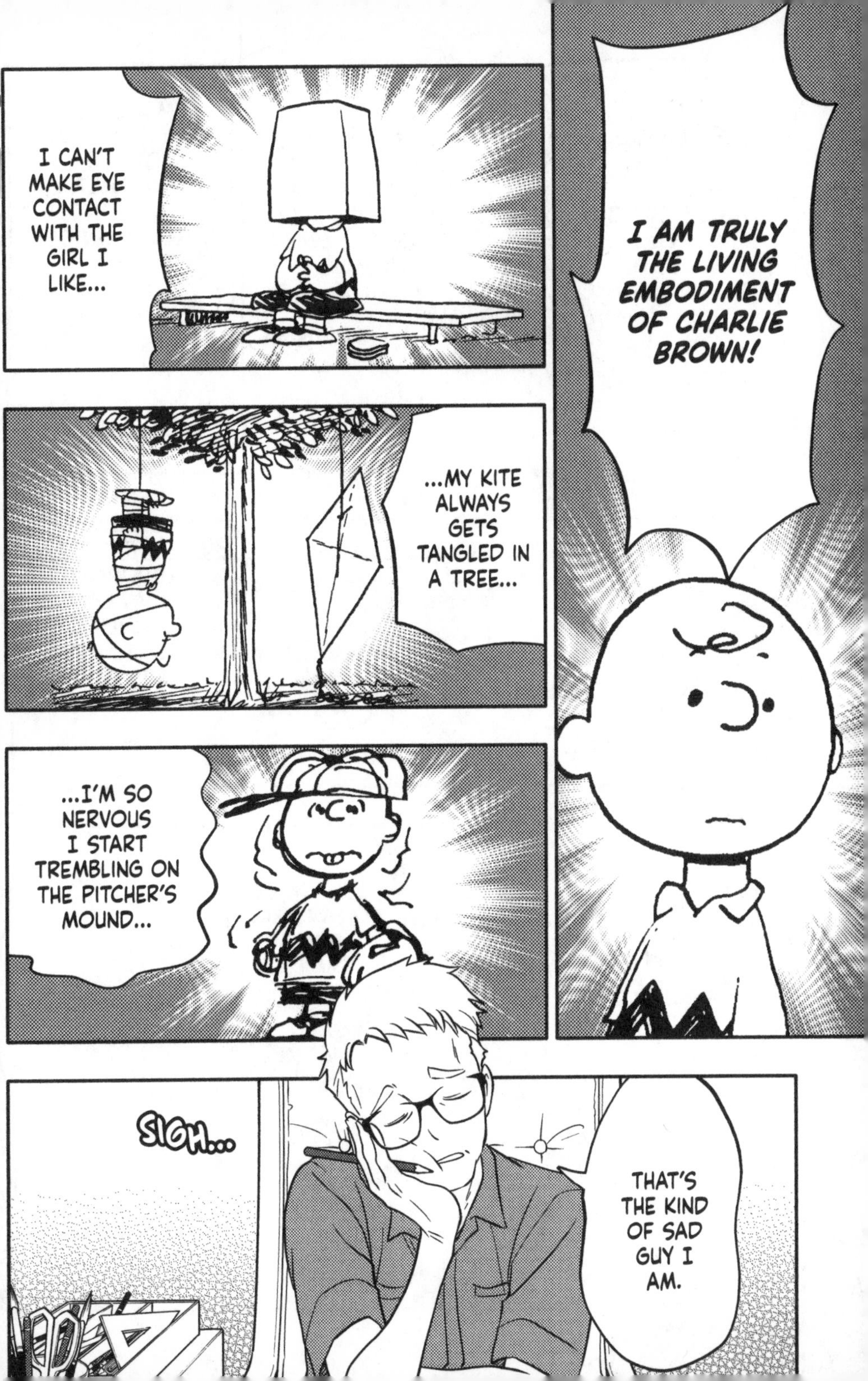
I AM TRULY THE LIVING EMBODIMENT OF CHARLIE BROWN!
I CAN'T MAKE EYE CONTACT WITH THE GIRL I LIKE...
...MY KITE ALWAYS GETS TANGLED IN A TREE...
...I'M SO NERVOUS I START TREMBLING ON THE PITCHER'S MOUND...
THAT'S THE KIND OF SAD GUY I AM.
SIGH...

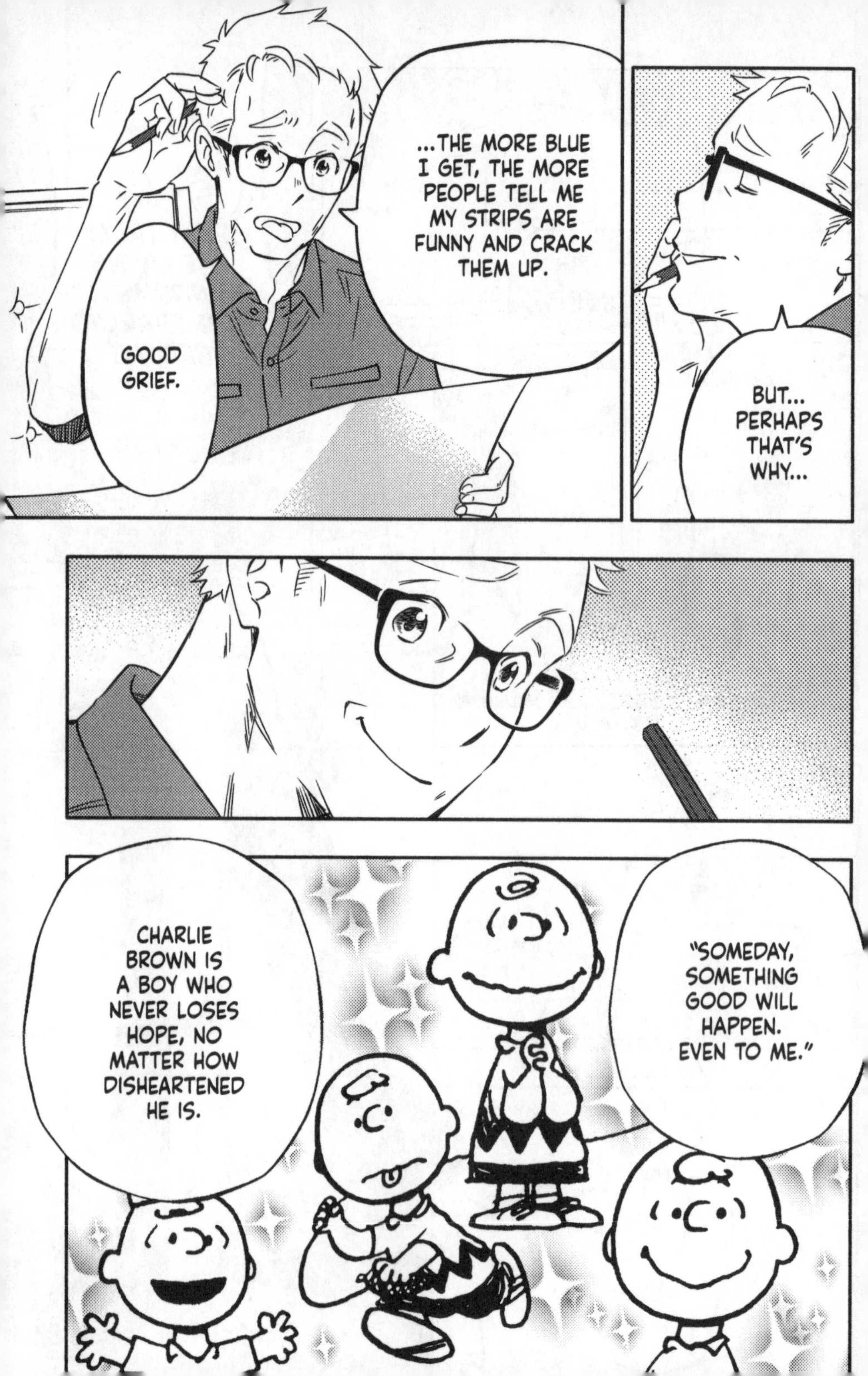
BUT... PERHAPS THAT'S WHY...
...THE MORE BLUE I GET, THE MORE PEOPLE TELL ME MY STRIPS ARE FUNNY AND CRACK THEM UP.
GOOD GRIEF.
"SOMEDAY, SOMETHING GOOD WILL HAPPEN. EVEN TO ME."
CHARLIE BROWN IS A BOY WHO NEVER LOSES HOPE, NO MATTER HOW DISHEARTENED HE IS.

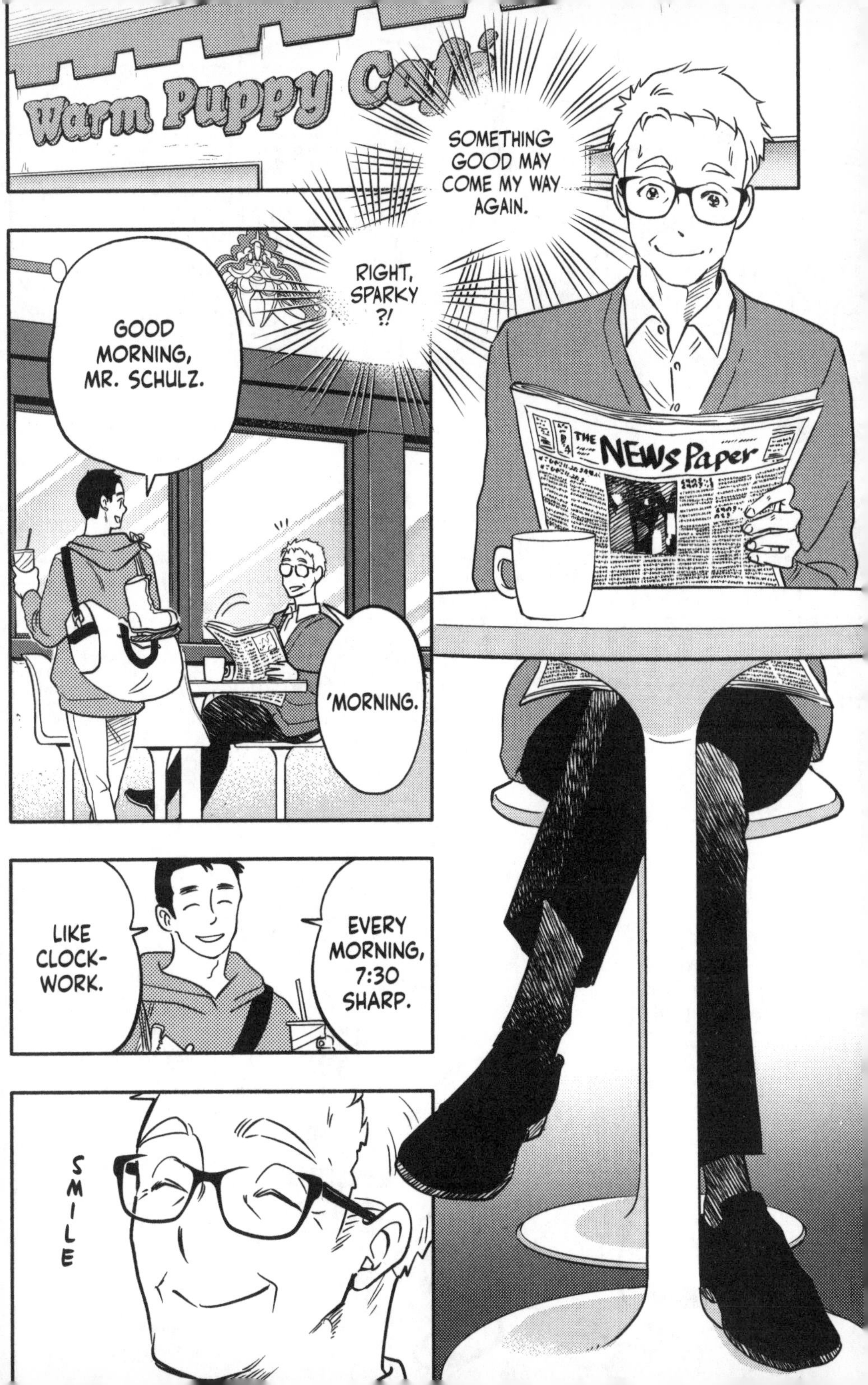
SOMETHING GOOD MAY COME MY WAY AGAIN.
RIGHT, SPARKY?!
THE NEWS Paper
Warm Puppy Caf
GOOD MORNING, MR. SCHULZ.
'MORNING.
EVERY MORNING, 7:30 SHARP.
LIKE CLOCK-WORK.
SMILE

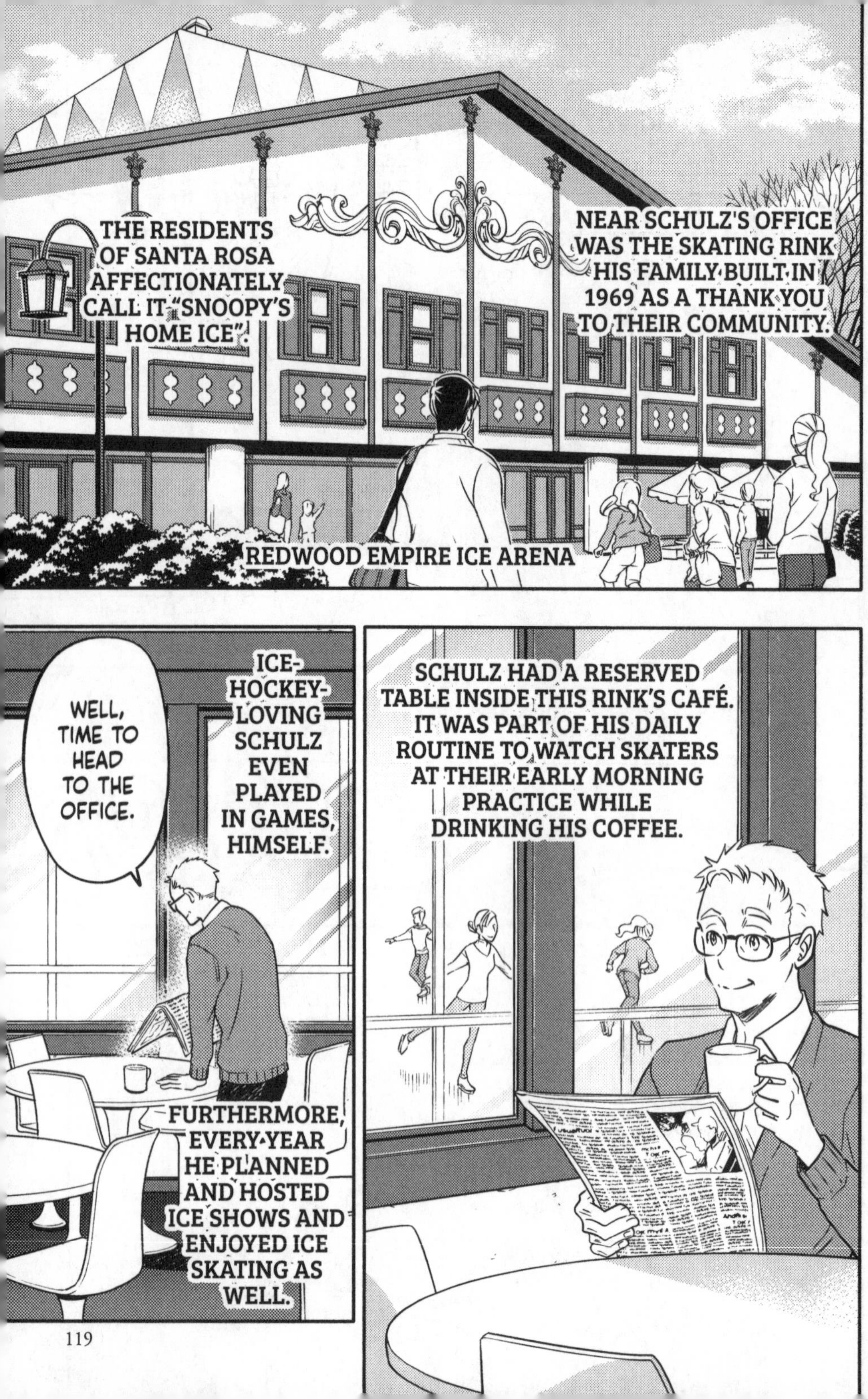
NEAR SCHULZ'S OFFICE WAS THE SKATING RINK HIS FAMILY BUILT IN 1969 AS A THANK YOU TO THEIR COMMUNITY.
THE RESIDENTS OF SANTA ROSA AFFECTIONATELY CALL IT "SNOOPY'S HOME ICE".
REDWOOD EMPIRE ICE ARENA
SCHULZ HAD A RESERVED TABLE INSIDE THIS RINK'S CAFÉ. IT WAS PART OF HIS DAILY ROUTINE TO WATCH SKATERS AT THEIR EARLY MORNING PRACTICE WHILE DRINKING HIS COFFEE.
ICE-HOCKEY-LOVING SCHULZ EVEN PLAYED IN GAMES, HIMSELF.
WELL, TIME TO HEAD TO THE OFFICE.
FURTHERMORE, EVERY YEAR HE PLANNED AND HOSTED ICE SHOWS AND ENJOYED ICE SKATING AS WELL.

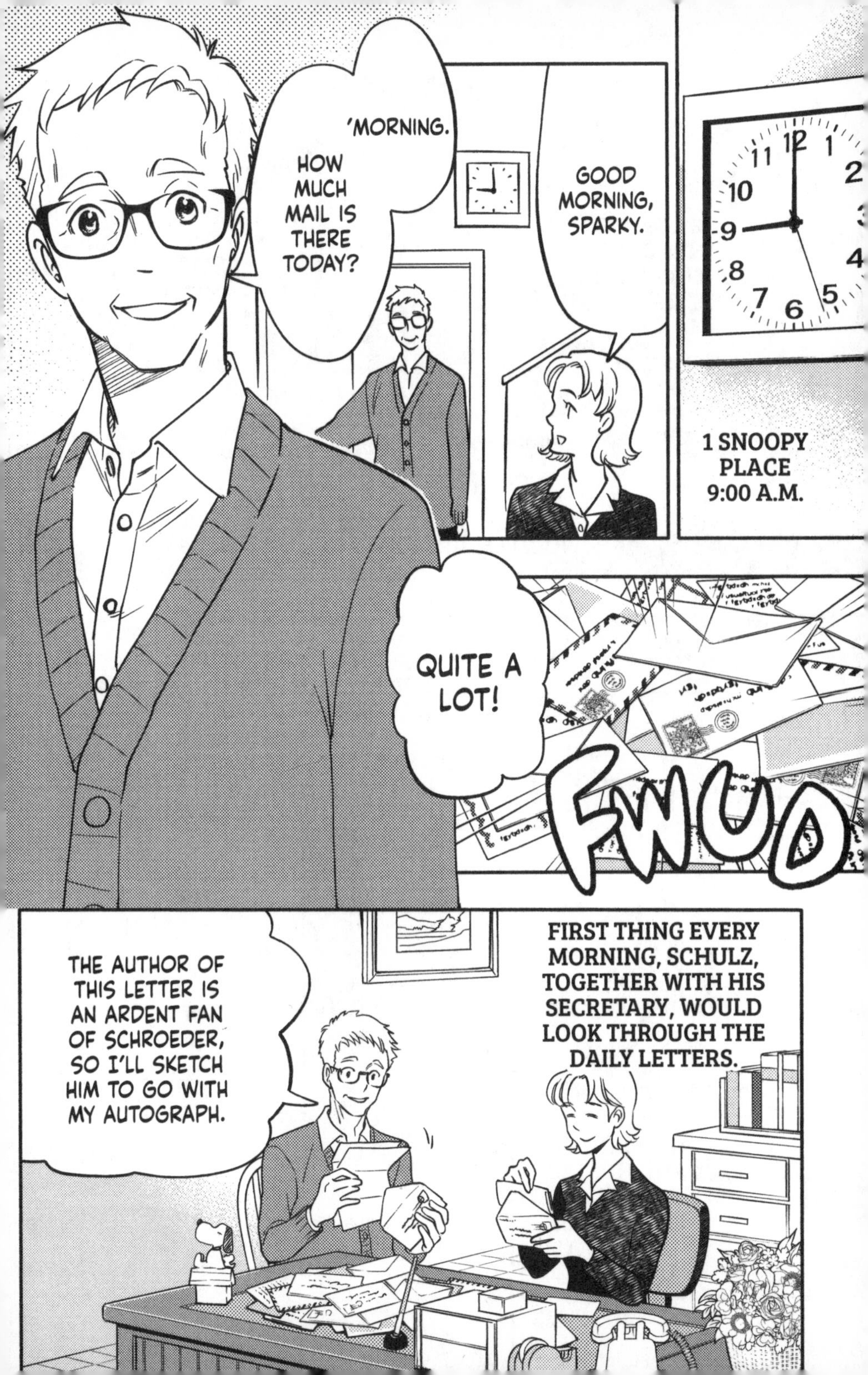
1 SNOOPY PLACE 9:00 A.M.
GOOD MORNING, SPARKY.
QUITE A LOT!
FWUD
'MORNING.
HOW MUCH MAIL IS THERE TODAY?
FIRST THING EVERY MORNING, SCHULZ, TOGETHER WITH HIS SECRETARY, WOULD LOOK THROUGH THE DAILY LETTERS.
THE AUTHOR OF THIS LETTER IS AN ARDENT FAN OF SCHROEDER, SO I'LL SKETCH HIM TO GO WITH MY AUTOGRAPH.

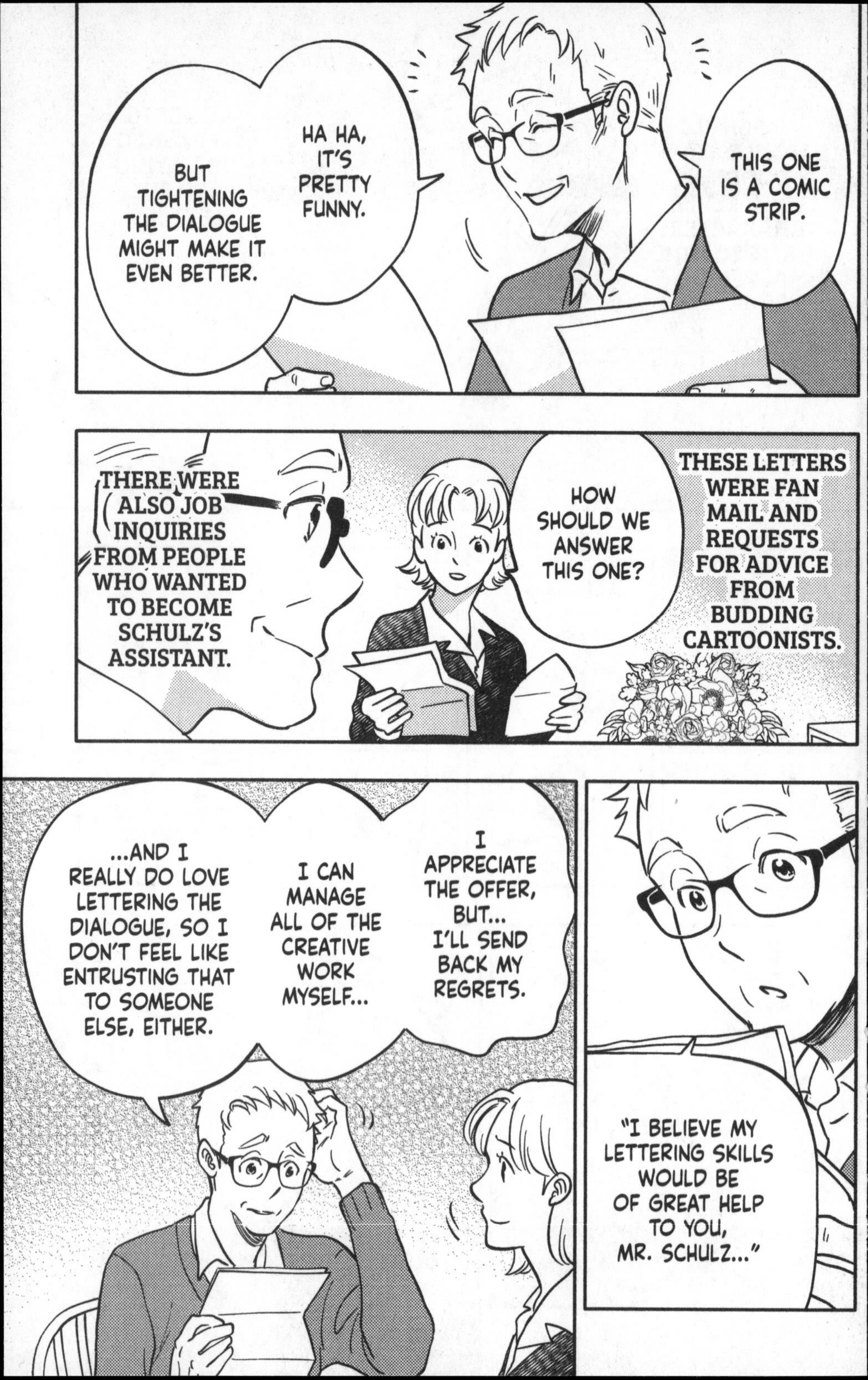

THIS ONE IS A COMIC STRIP.
HA HA, IT'S PRETTY FUNNY.
BUT TIGHTENING THE DIALOGUE MIGHT MAKE IT EVEN BETTER.
THESE LETTERS WERE FAN MAIL AND REQUESTS FOR ADVICE FROM BUDDING CARTOONISTS.
HOW SHOULD WE ANSWER THIS ONE?
THERE WERE ALSO JOB INQUIRIES FROM PEOPLE WHO WANTED TO BECOME SCHULZ'S ASSISTANT.
"I BELIEVE MY LETTERING SKILLS WOULD BE OF GREAT HELP TO YOU, MR. SCHULZ..."
I APPRECIATE THE OFFER, BUT... I'LL SEND BACK MY REGRETS.
I CAN MANAGE ALL OF THE CREATIVE WORK MYSELF...
...AND I REALLY DO LOVE LETTERING THE DIALOGUE, SO I DON'T FEEL LIKE ENTRUSTING THAT TO SOMEONE ELSE, EITHER.

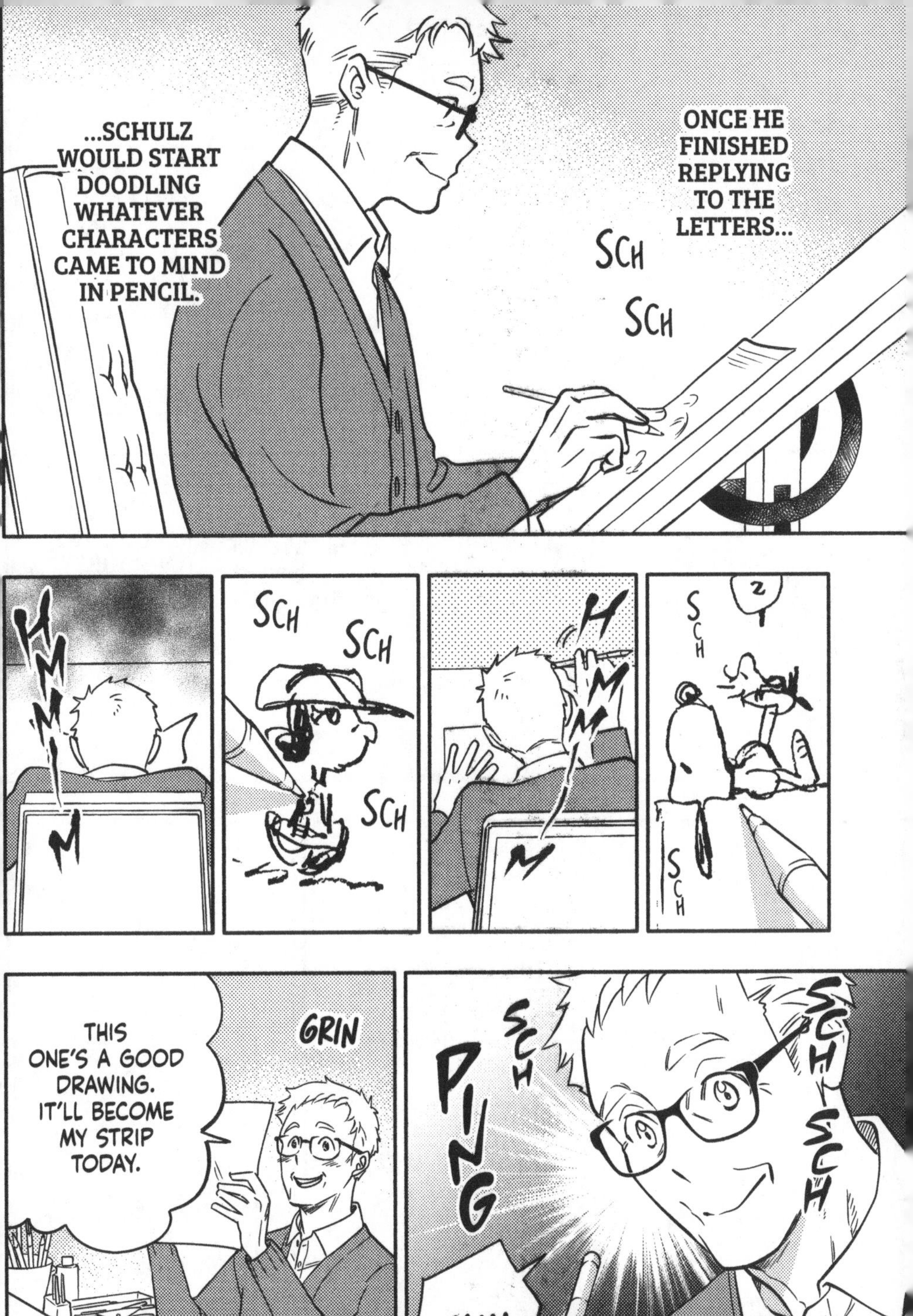

ONCE HE FINISHED REPLYING TO THE LETTERS...
...SCHULZ WOULD START DOODLING WHATEVER CHARACTERS CAME TO MIND IN PENCIL.
SCH
SCH
SCH
SCH
HMMM
SCH
SCH
SCH
HMMMM
SCH-SCH
SCH
PING
MM!
GRIN
THIS ONE'S A GOOD DRAWING. IT'LL BECOME MY STRIP TODAY.

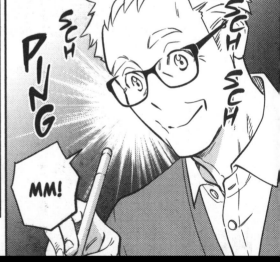

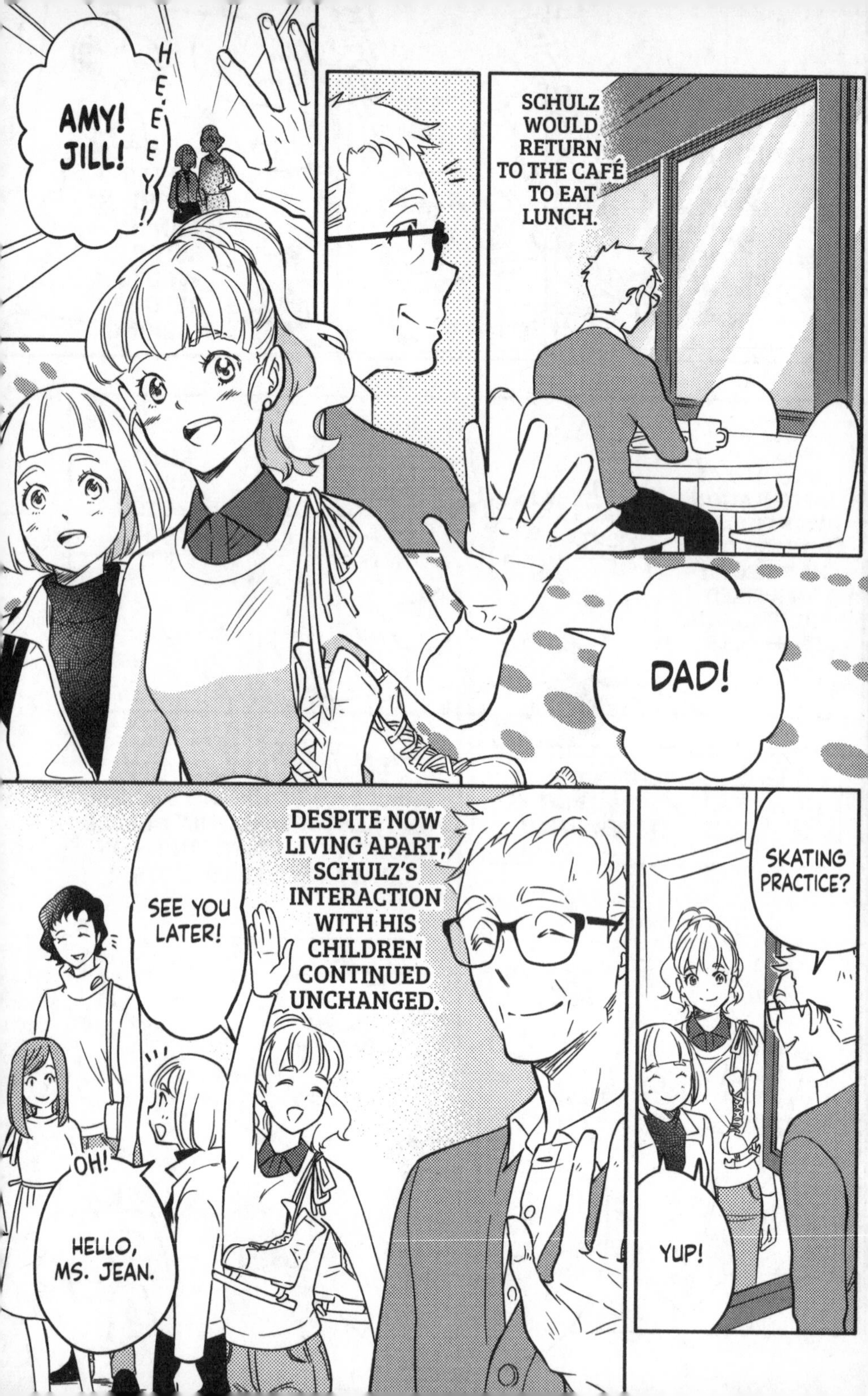
SCHULZ WOULD RETURN TO THE CAFÉ TO EAT LUNCH.
AMY! JILL!
HE-E-E-E-Y!!
DAD!
SKATING PRACTICE?
YUP!
DESPITE NOW LIVING APART, SCHULZ'S INTERACTION WITH HIS CHILDREN CONTINUED UNCHANGED.
SEE YOU LATER!
OH!
HELLO, MS. JEAN.

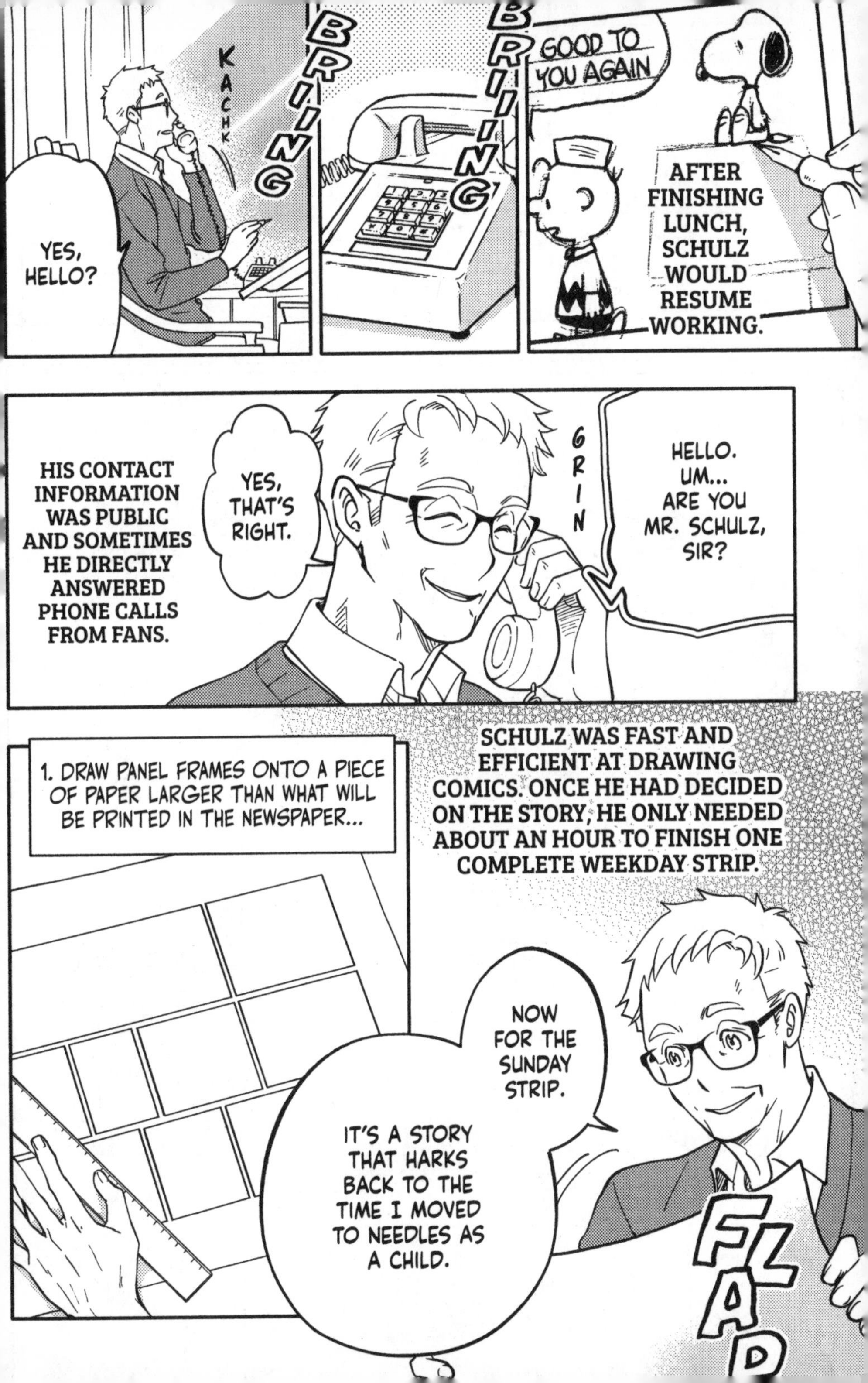
GOOD TO YOU AGAIN
AFTER FINISHING LUNCH, SCHULZ WOULD RESUME WORKING.
BRIIING
BRIIING
KACHK
YES, HELLO?
HELLO. UM... ARE YOU MR. SCHULZ, SIR?
GRIN
YES, THAT'S RIGHT.
HIS CONTACT INFORMATION WAS PUBLIC AND SOMETIMES HE DIRECTLY ANSWERED PHONE CALLS FROM FANS.
SCHULZ WAS FAST AND EFFICIENT AT DRAWING COMICS. ONCE HE HAD DECIDED ON THE STORY, HE ONLY NEEDED ABOUT AN HOUR TO FINISH ONE COMPLETE WEEKDAY STRIP.
NOW FOR THE SUNDAY STRIP.
IT'S A STORY THAT HARKS BACK TO THE TIME I MOVED TO NEEDLES AS A CHILD.
FLAD
1. DRAW PANEL FRAMES ONTO A PIECE OF PAPER LARGER THAN WHAT WILL BE PRINTED IN THE NEWSPAPER...

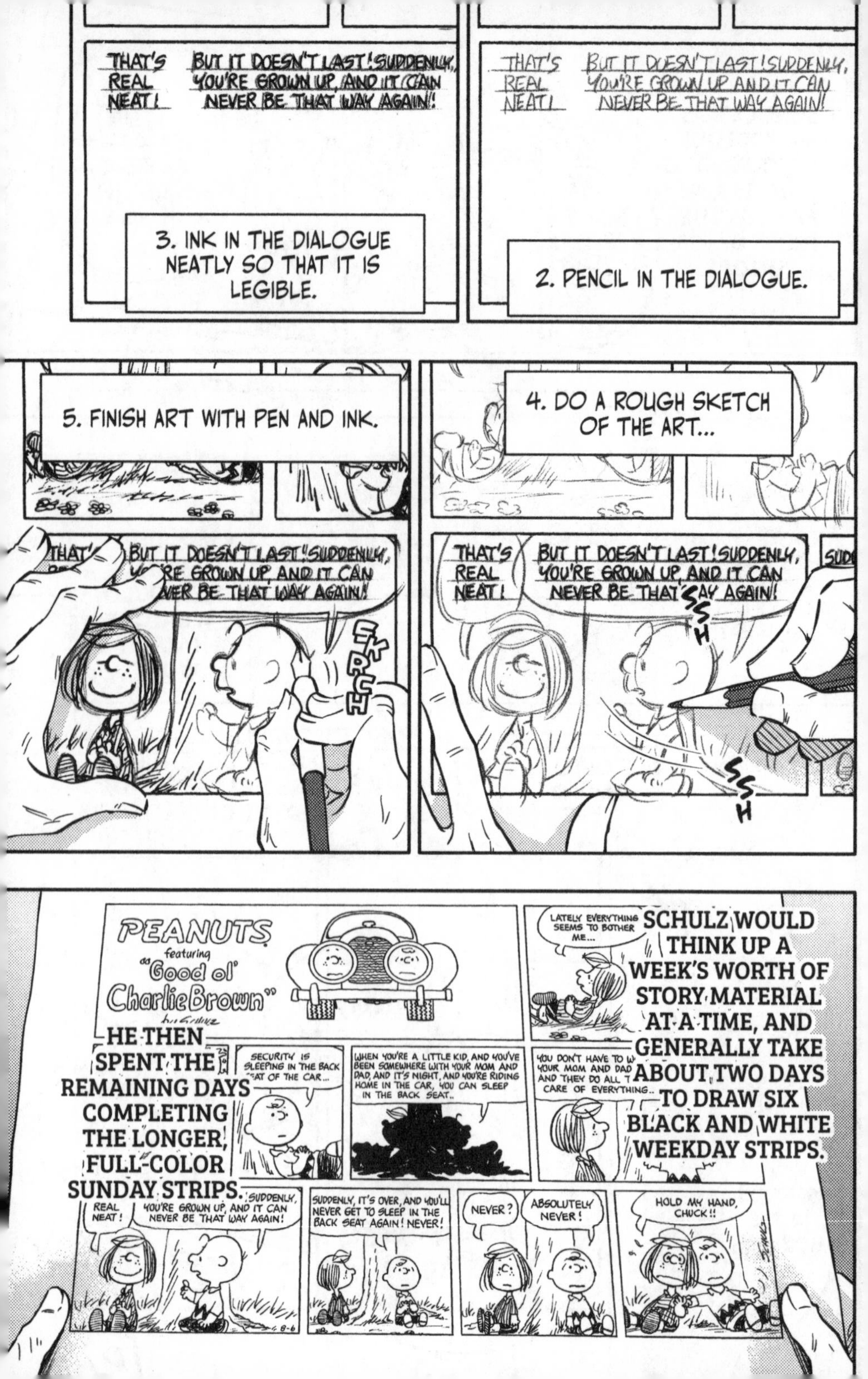
THAT'S REAL NEAT!
BUT IT DOESN'T LAST! SUDDENLY, YOU'RE GROWN UP AND IT CAN NEVER BE THAT WAY AGAIN!
2. PENCIL IN THE DIALOGUE.
THAT'S REAL NEAT!
BUT IT DOESN'T LAST! SUDDENLY, YOU'RE GROWN UP, AND IT CAN NEVER BE THAT WAY AGAIN!
3. INK IN THE DIALOGUE NEATLY SO THAT IT IS LEGIBLE.
4. DO A ROUGH SKETCH OF THE ART...
THAT'S REAL NEAT!
BUT IT DOESN'T LAST! SUDDENLY, YOU'RE GROWN UP, AND IT CAN NEVER BE THAT WAY AGAIN!
SSH
SSH
5. FINISH ART WITH PEN AND INK.
BUT IT DOESN'T LAST! SUDDENLY, YOU'RE GROWN UP, AND IT CAN NEVER BE THAT WAY AGAIN!
SKRCH
SCHULZ WOULD THINK UP A WEEK'S WORTH OF STORY MATERIAL AT A TIME, AND GENERALLY TAKE ABOUT TWO DAYS TO DRAW SIX BLACK AND WHITE WEEKDAY STRIPS.
HE THEN SPENT THE REMAINING DAYS COMPLETING THE LONGER, FULL-COLOR SUNDAY STRIPS.
PEANUTS
featuring "Good ol' CharlieBrown"
LATELY EVERYTHING SEEMS TO BOTHER ME...
SECURITY IS SLEEPING IN THE BACK SEAT OF THE CAR...
WHEN YOU'RE A LITTLE KID, AND YOU'VE BEEN SOMEWHERE WITH YOUR MOM AND DAD, AND IT'S NIGHT, AND YOU'RE RIDING HOME IN THE CAR, YOU CAN SLEEP IN THE BACK SEAT..
YOU DON'T HAVE TO W YOUR MOM AND DAD AND THEY DO ALL T CARE OF EVERYTHING..
REAL NEAT!
SUDDENLY, YOU'RE GROWN UP, AND IT CAN NEVER BE THAT WAY AGAIN!
SUDDENLY, IT'S OVER, AND YOU'LL NEVER GET TO SLEEP IN THE BACK SEAT AGAIN! NEVER!
NEVER?
ABSOLUTELY NEVER!
HOLD MY HAND, CHUCK!!

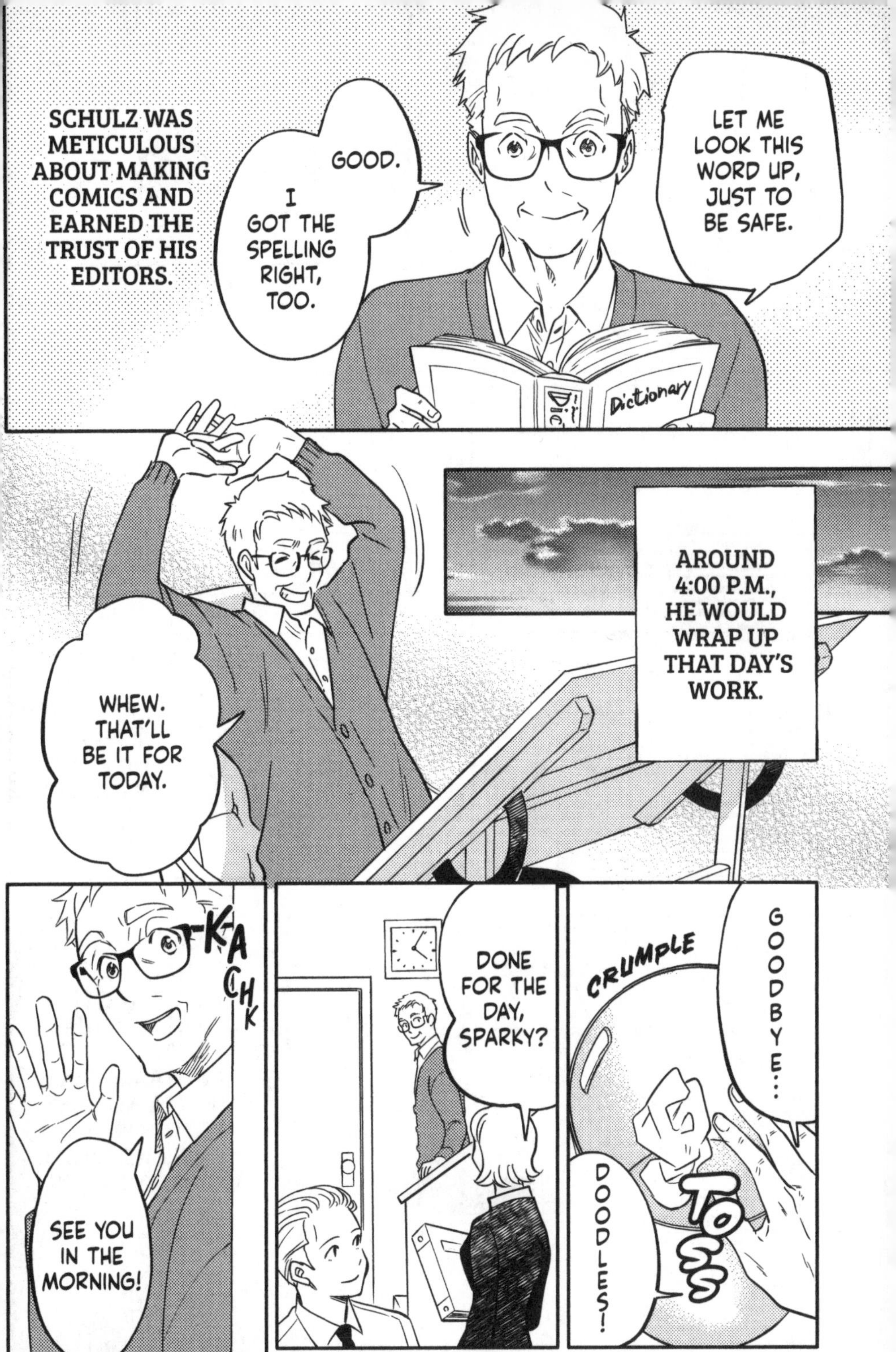
LET ME LOOK THIS WORD UP, JUST TO BE SAFE.
GOOD. I GOT THE SPELLING RIGHT, TOO.
SCHULZ WAS METICULOUS ABOUT MAKING COMICS AND EARNED THE TRUST OF HIS EDITORS.
Dictionary
AROUND 4:00 P.M., HE WOULD WRAP UP THAT DAY'S WORK.
WHEW. THAT'LL BE IT FOR TODAY.
CRUMPLE
GOODBYE...
TOSS
DOODLES!
DONE FOR THE DAY, SPARKY?
KACHK
SEE YOU IN THE MORNING!

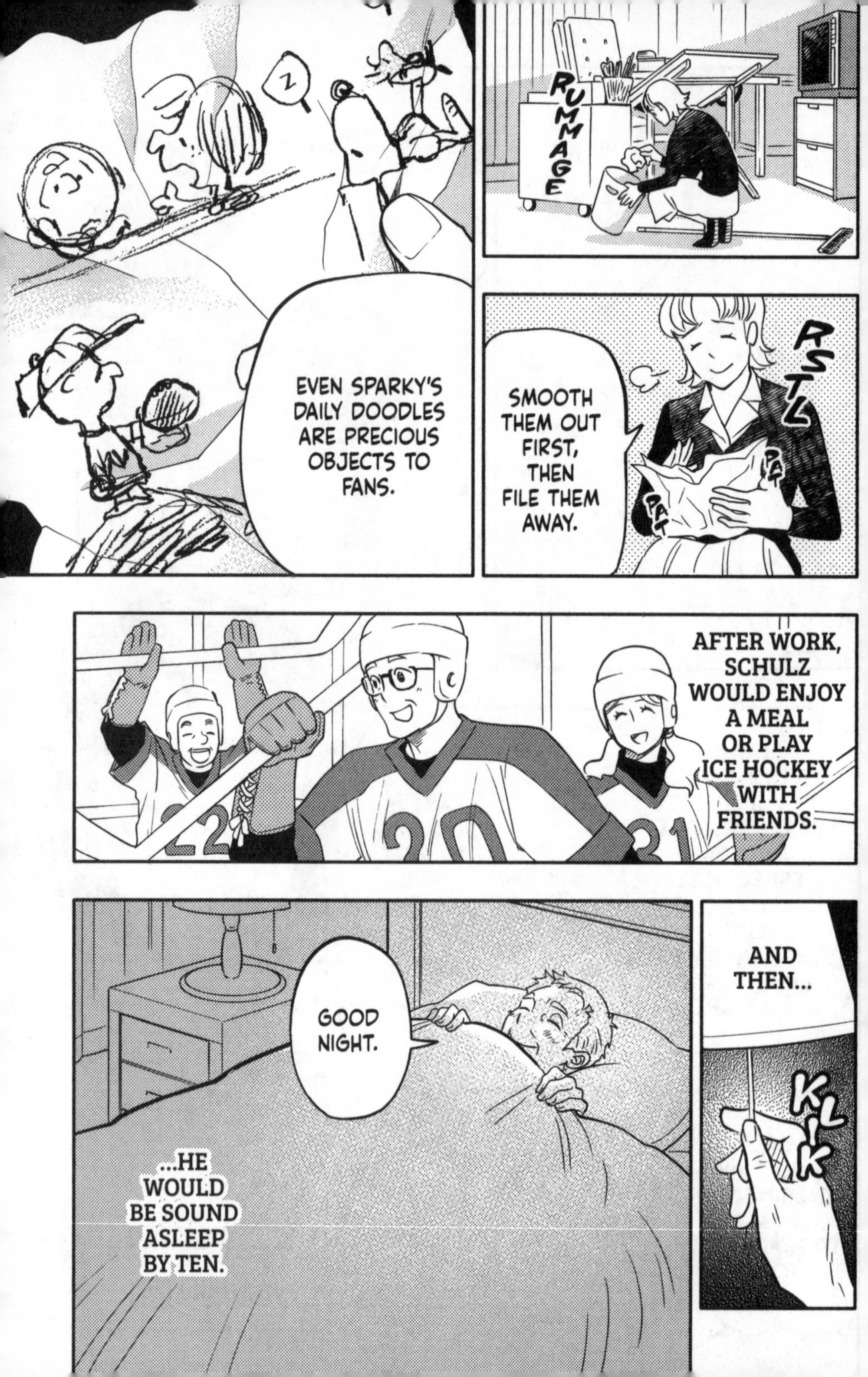
RUMMAGE
SMOOTH THEM OUT FIRST, THEN FILE THEM AWAY.
RSTL
PAT
PAT
EVEN SPARKY'S DAILY DOODLES ARE PRECIOUS OBJECTS TO FANS.
AFTER WORK, SCHULZ WOULD ENJOY A MEAL OR PLAY ICE HOCKEY WITH FRIENDS.
AND THEN...
KLIK
GOOD NIGHT.
...HE WOULD BE SOUND ASLEEP BY TEN.

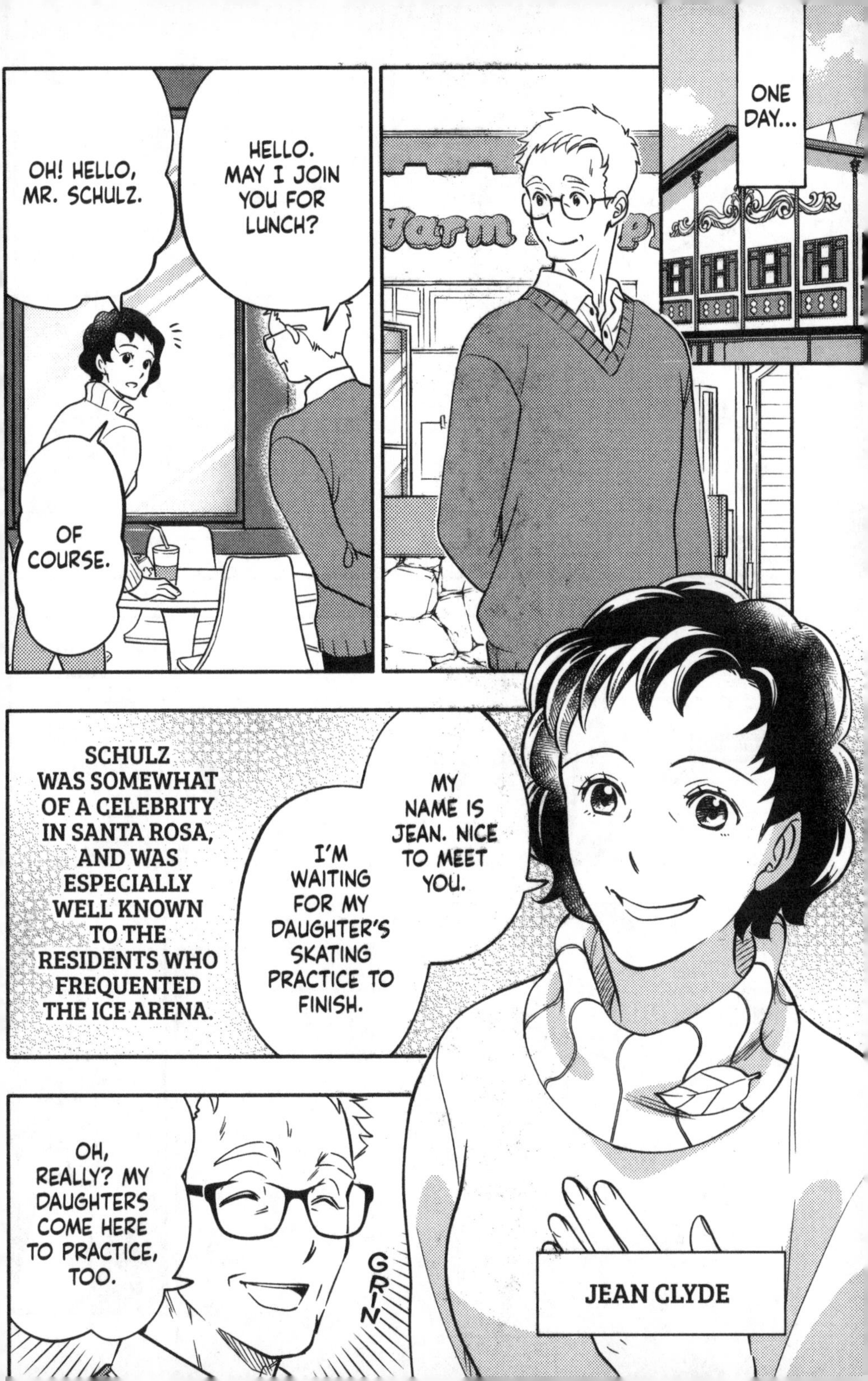
ONE DAY...
HELLO. MAY I JOIN YOU FOR LUNCH?
OH! HELLO, MR. SCHULZ.
OF COURSE.
MY NAME IS JEAN. NICE TO MEET YOU.
I'M WAITING FOR MY DAUGHTER'S SKATING PRACTICE TO FINISH.
SCHULZ WAS SOMEWHAT OF A CELEBRITY IN SANTA ROSA, AND WAS ESPECIALLY WELL KNOWN TO THE RESIDENTS WHO FREQUENTED THE ICE ARENA.
JEAN CLYDE
OH, REALLY? MY DAUGHTERS COME HERE TO PRACTICE, TOO.
GRIN

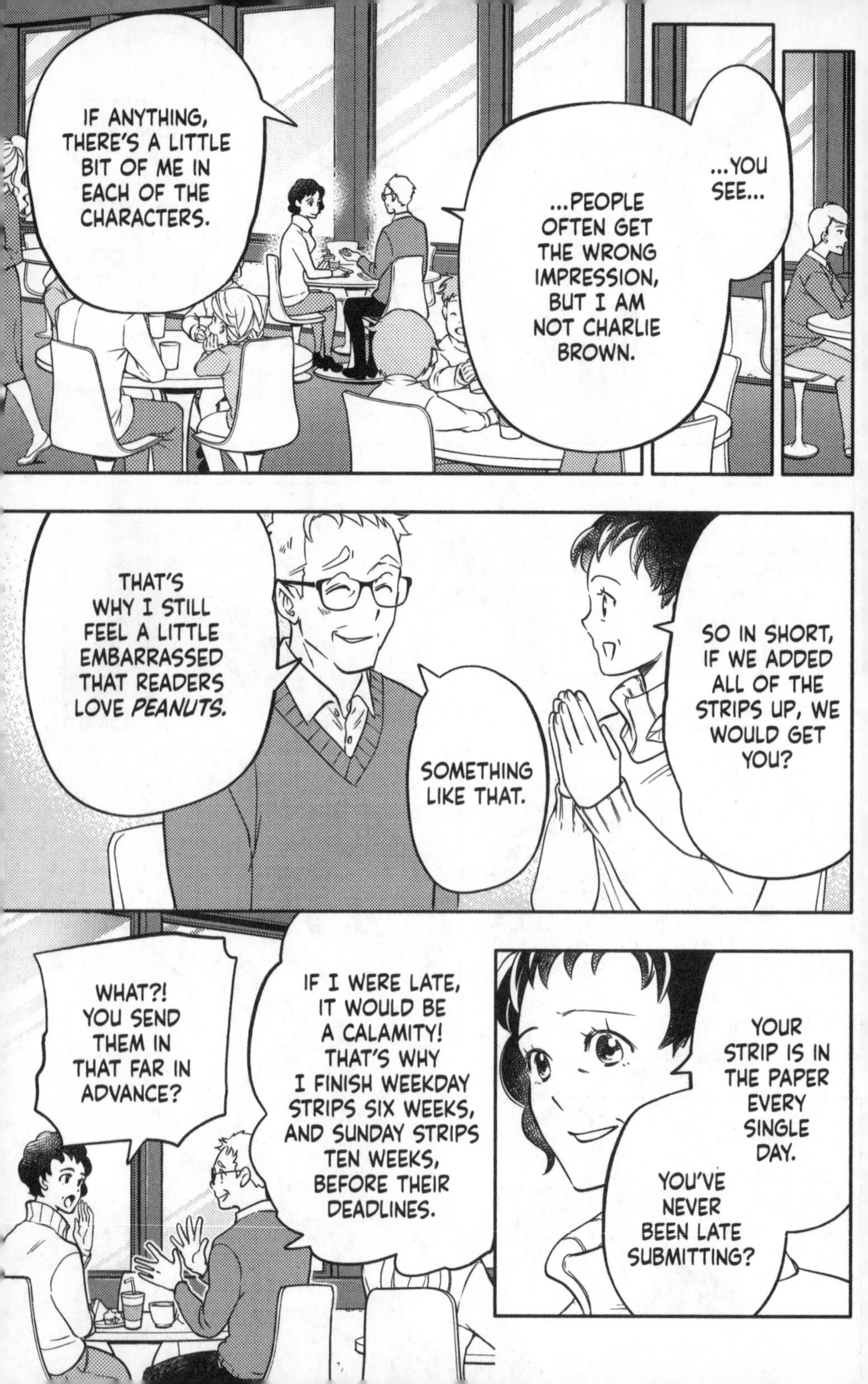
...YOU SEE...
...PEOPLE OFTEN GET THE WRONG IMPRESSION, BUT I AM NOT CHARLIE BROWN.
IF ANYTHING, THERE'S A LITTLE BIT OF ME IN EACH OF THE CHARACTERS.
SO IN SHORT, IF WE ADDED ALL OF THE STRIPS UP, WE WOULD GET YOU?
SOMETHING LIKE THAT.
THAT'S WHY I STILL FEEL A LITTLE EMBARRASSED THAT READERS LOVE *PEANUTS*.
YOUR STRIP IS IN THE PAPER EVERY SINGLE DAY.
YOU'VE NEVER BEEN LATE SUBMITTING?
IF I WERE LATE, IT WOULD BE A CALAMITY! THAT'S WHY I FINISH WEEKDAY STRIPS SIX WEEKS, AND SUNDAY STRIPS TEN WEEKS, BEFORE THEIR DEADLINES.
WHAT?! YOU SEND THEM IN THAT FAR IN ADVANCE?

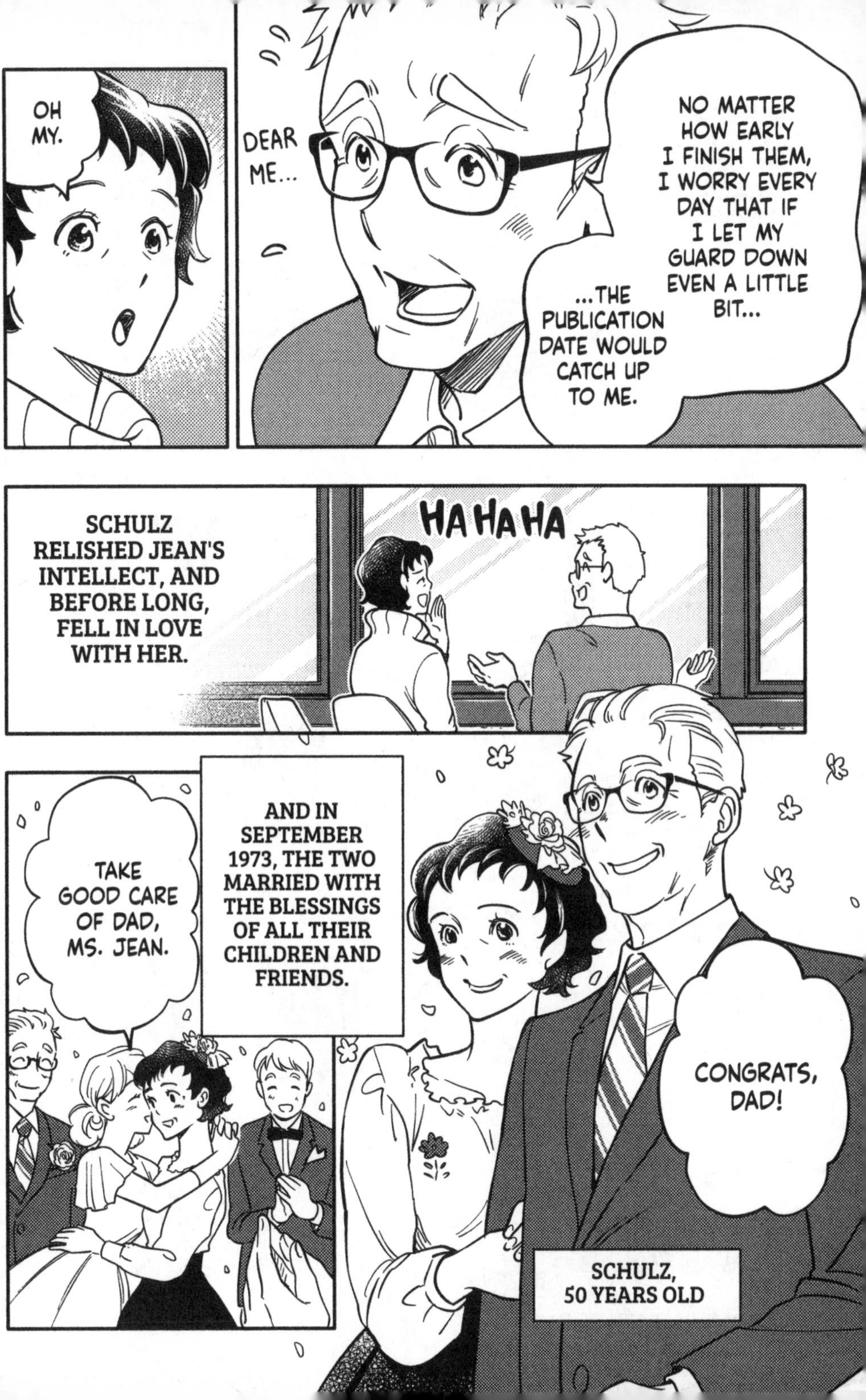
NO MATTER HOW EARLY I FINISH THEM, I WORRY EVERY DAY THAT IF I LET MY GUARD DOWN EVEN A LITTLE BIT...
...THE PUBLICATION DATE WOULD CATCH UP TO ME.
DEAR ME...
OH MY.
HA HA HA
SCHULZ RELISHED JEAN'S INTELLECT, AND BEFORE LONG, FELL IN LOVE WITH HER.
AND IN SEPTEMBER 1973, THE TWO MARRIED WITH THE BLESSINGS OF ALL THEIR CHILDREN AND FRIENDS.
CONGRATS, DAD!
SCHULZ, 50 YEARS OLD
TAKE GOOD CARE OF DAD, MS. JEAN.

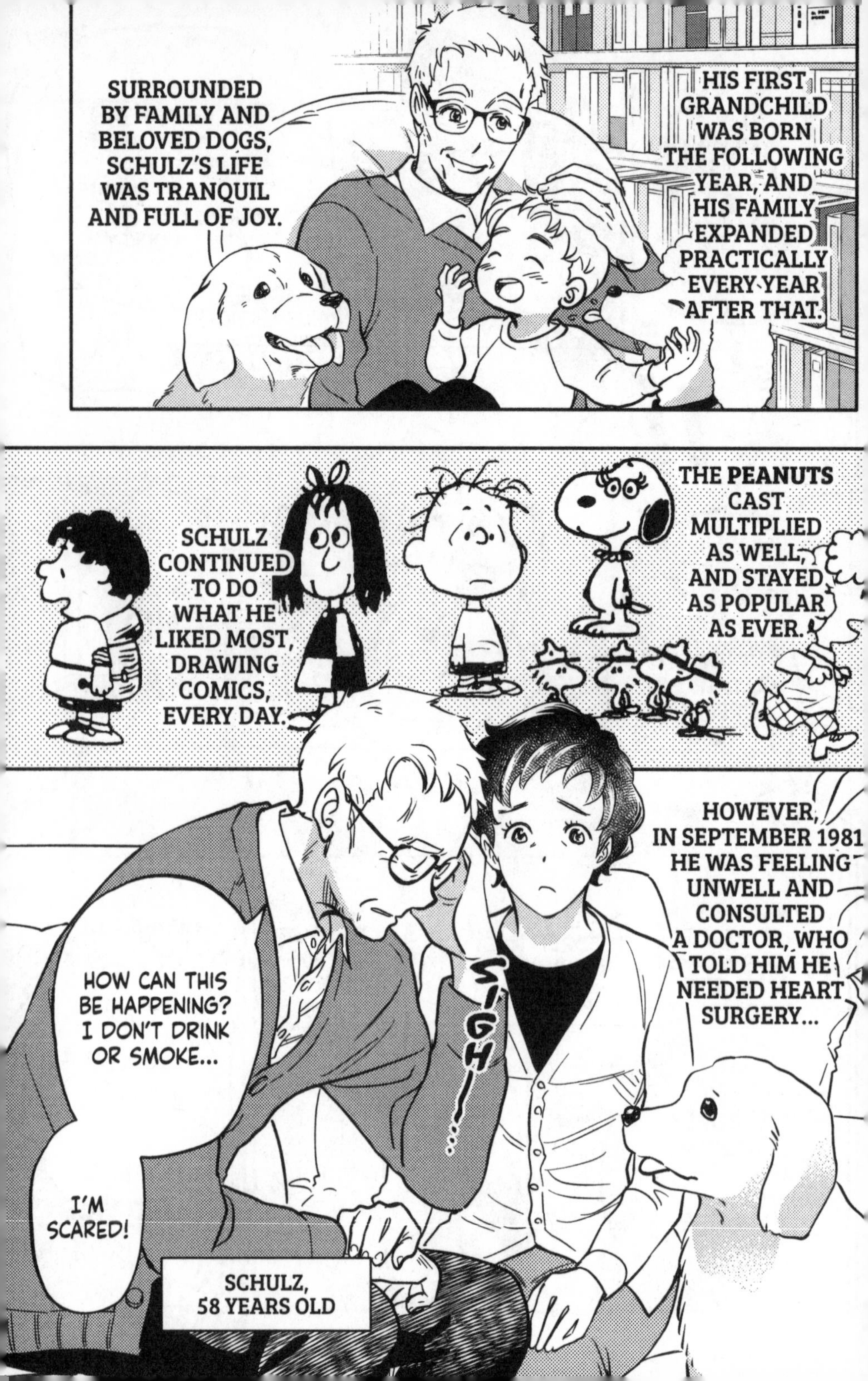
HIS FIRST GRANDCHILD WAS BORN THE FOLLOWING YEAR, AND HIS FAMILY EXPANDED PRACTICALLY EVERY YEAR AFTER THAT.
SURROUNDED BY FAMILY AND BELOVED DOGS, SCHULZ'S LIFE WAS TRANQUIL AND FULL OF JOY.
THE **PEANUTS** CAST MULTIPLIED AS WELL, AND STAYED AS POPULAR AS EVER.
SCHULZ CONTINUED TO DO WHAT HE LIKED MOST, DRAWING COMICS, EVERY DAY.
HOWEVER, IN SEPTEMBER 1981 HE WAS FEELING UNWELL AND CONSULTED A DOCTOR, WHO TOLD HIM HE NEEDED HEART SURGERY...
SIGH...
HOW CAN THIS BE HAPPENING? I DON'T DRINK OR SMOKE...
I'M SCARED!
SCHULZ, 58 YEARS OLD

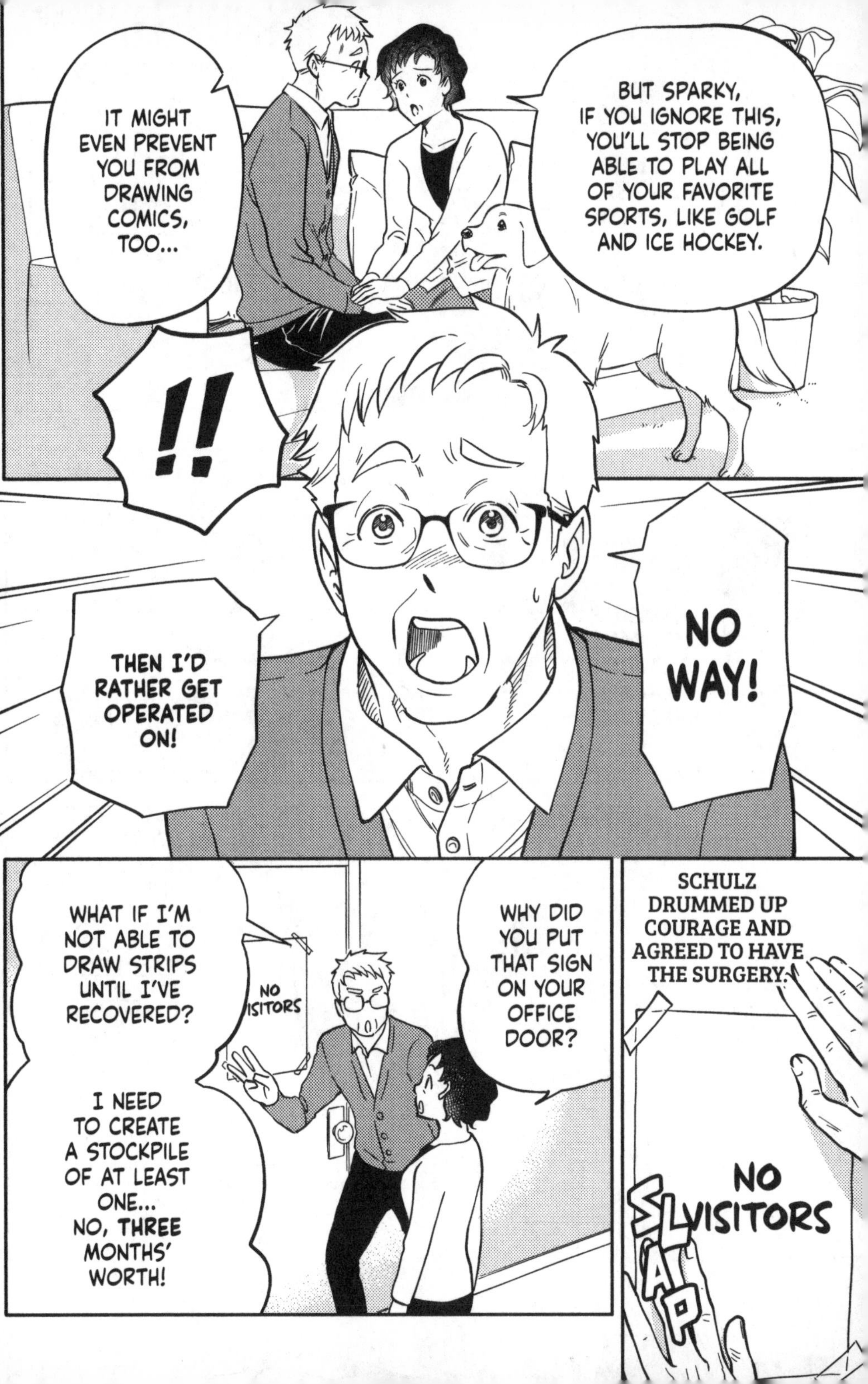
BUT SPARKY, IF YOU IGNORE THIS, YOU'LL STOP BEING ABLE TO PLAY ALL OF YOUR FAVORITE SPORTS, LIKE GOLF AND ICE HOCKEY.
IT MIGHT EVEN PREVENT YOU FROM DRAWING COMICS, TOO...
!!
NO WAY!
THEN I'D RATHER GET OPERATED ON!
SCHULZ DRUMMED UP COURAGE AND AGREED TO HAVE THE SURGERY.
NO VISITORS
SLAP
WHY DID YOU PUT THAT SIGN ON YOUR OFFICE DOOR?
WHAT IF I'M NOT ABLE TO DRAW STRIPS UNTIL I'VE RECOVERED?
NO VISITORS
I NEED TO CREATE A STOCKPILE OF AT LEAST ONE... NO, THREE MONTHS' WORTH!

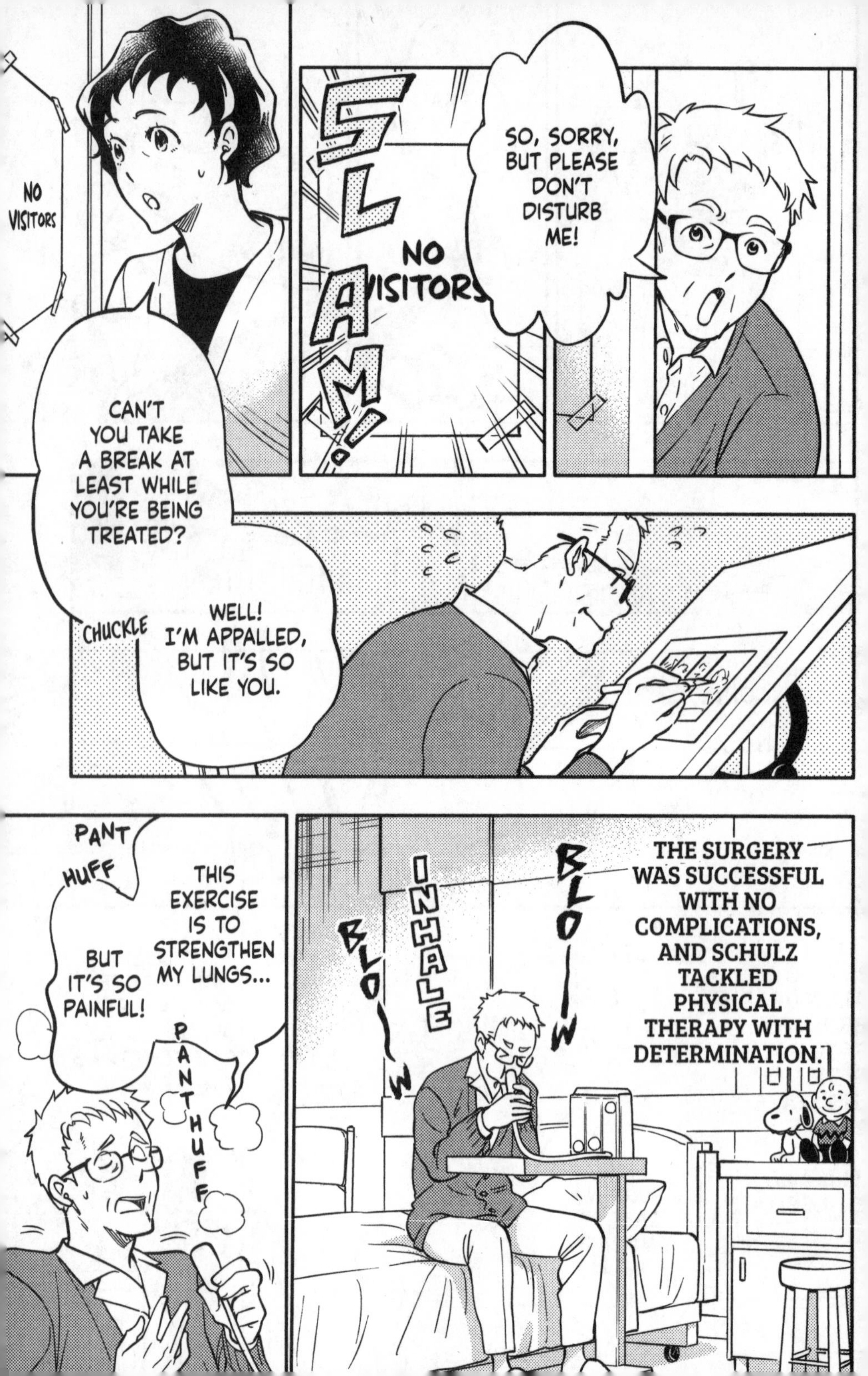
SO, SORRY, BUT PLEASE DON'T DISTURB ME!
SLAM!
NO VISITORS
NO VISITORS
CAN'T YOU TAKE A BREAK AT LEAST WHILE YOU'RE BEING TREATED?
WELL! I'M APPALLED, BUT IT'S SO LIKE YOU.
CHUCKLE
THE SURGERY WAS SUCCESSFUL WITH NO COMPLICATIONS, AND SCHULZ TACKLED PHYSICAL THERAPY WITH DETERMINATION.
BLOW
INHALE
BLOW
PANT
HUFF
THIS EXERCISE IS TO STRENGTHEN MY LUNGS...
BUT IT'S SO PAINFUL!
PANT HUFF

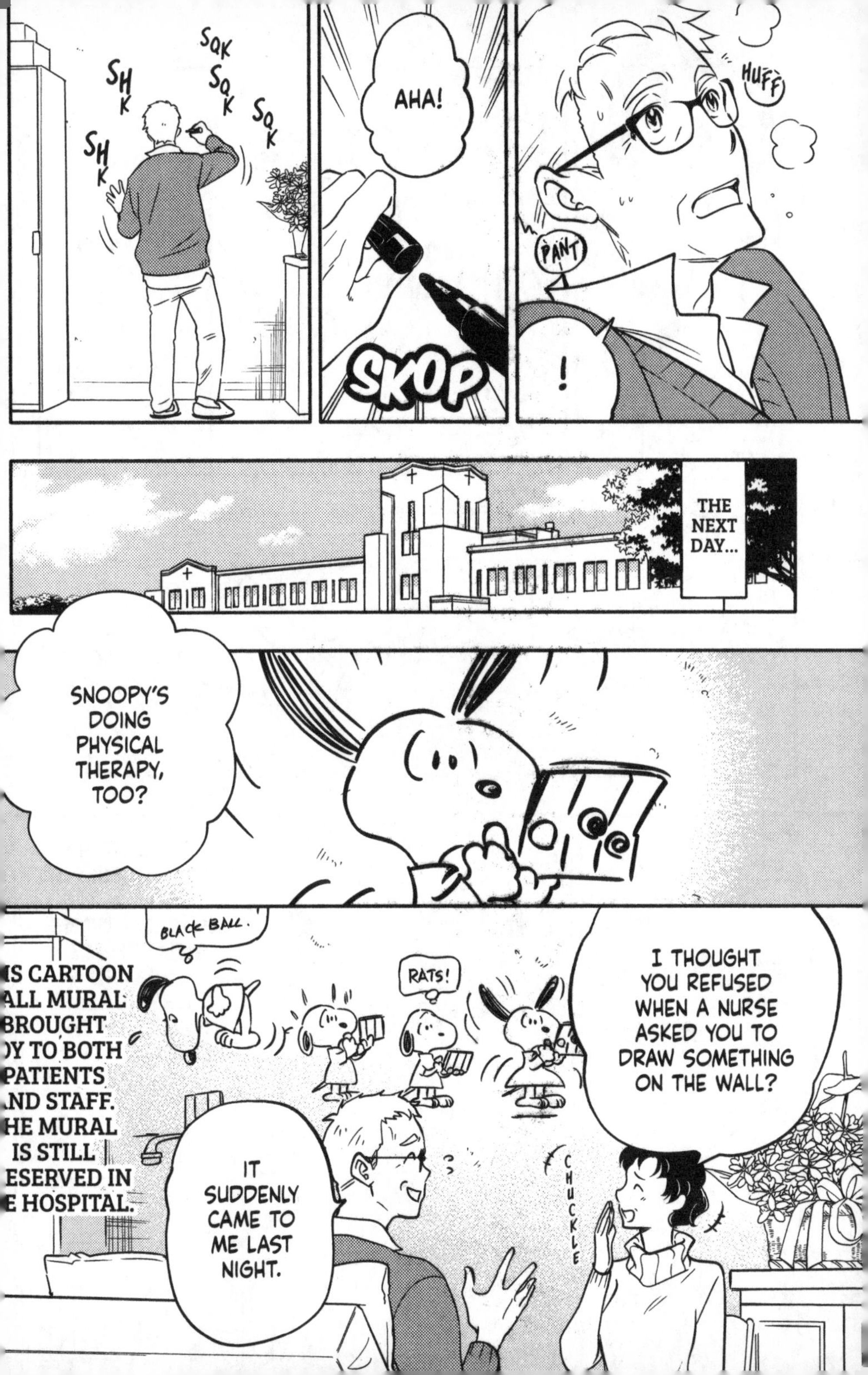
HUFF
PANT
!
AHA!
SKOP
SQK
SQK
SQK
SHK
SHK
THE NEXT DAY...
SNOOPY'S DOING PHYSICAL THERAPY, TOO?
I THOUGHT YOU REFUSED WHEN A NURSE ASKED YOU TO DRAW SOMETHING ON THE WALL?
CHUCKLE
IT SUDDENLY CAME TO ME LAST NIGHT.
RATS!
BLACK BALL.
IS CARTOON
ALL MURAL
BROUGHT
Y TO BOTH
PATIENTS
ND STAFF.
HE MURAL
IS STILL
ESERVED IN
E HOSPITAL.

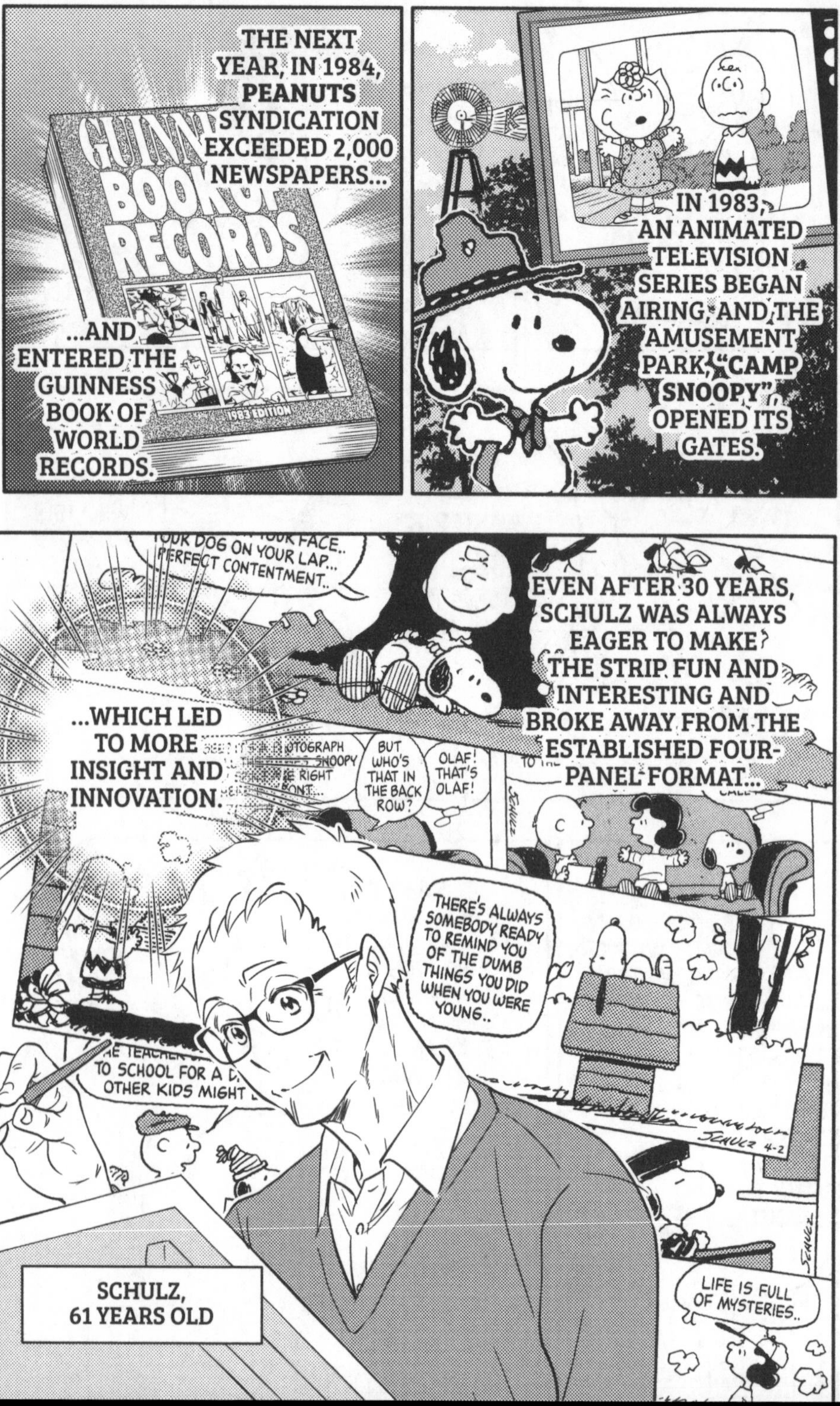
IN 1983, AN ANIMATED TELEVISION SERIES BEGAN AIRING, AND THE AMUSEMENT PARK, "CAMP SNOOPY", OPENED ITS GATES.
GUINNESS BOOK OF RECORDS
1983 EDITION
THE NEXT YEAR, IN 1984, PEANUTS SYNDICATION EXCEEDED 2,000 NEWSPAPERS...
...AND ENTERED THE GUINNESS BOOK OF WORLD RECORDS.
EVEN AFTER 30 YEARS, SCHULZ WAS ALWAYS EAGER TO MAKE THE STRIP FUN AND INTERESTING AND BROKE AWAY FROM THE ESTABLISHED FOUR-PANEL FORMAT...
PERFECT CONTENTMENT..
OLAF! THAT'S OLAF!
BUT WHO'S THAT IN THE BACK ROW?
...WHICH LED TO MORE INSIGHT AND INNOVATION.
THERE'S ALWAYS SOMEBODY READY TO REMIND YOU OF THE DUMB THINGS YOU DID WHEN YOU WERE YOUNG..
LIFE IS FULL OF MYSTERIES..
SCHULZ, 61 YEARS OLD

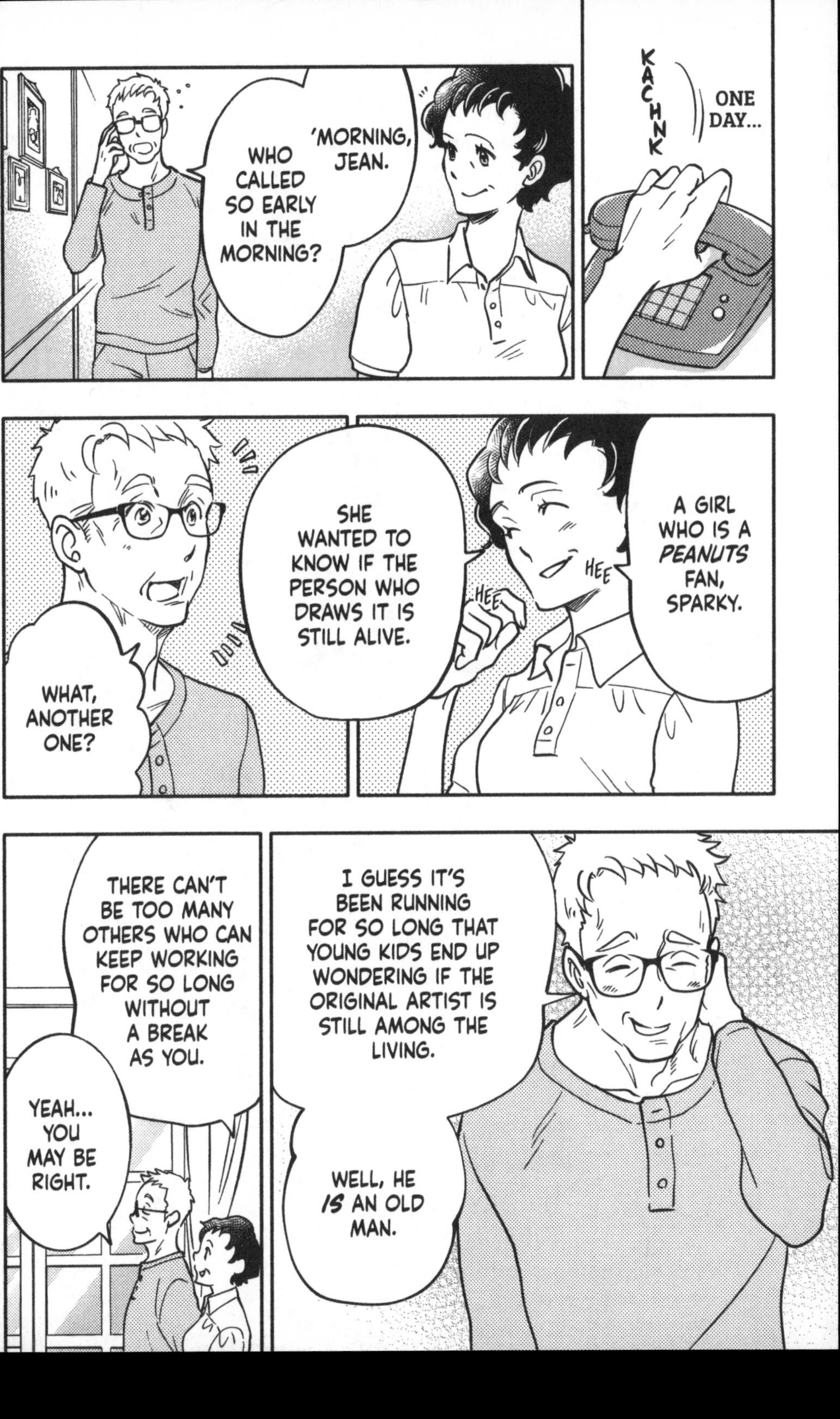
KACHNK
ONE DAY...
'MORNING, JEAN.
WHO CALLED SO EARLY IN THE MORNING?
A GIRL WHO IS A *PEANUTS* FAN, SPARKY.
HEE
HEE
SHE WANTED TO KNOW IF THE PERSON WHO DRAWS IT IS STILL ALIVE.
WHAT, ANOTHER ONE?
I GUESS IT'S BEEN RUNNING FOR SO LONG THAT YOUNG KIDS END UP WONDERING IF THE ORIGINAL ARTIST IS STILL AMONG THE LIVING.
WELL, HE *IS* AN OLD MAN.
THERE CAN'T BE TOO MANY OTHERS WHO CAN KEEP WORKING FOR SO LONG WITHOUT A BREAK AS YOU.
YEAH... YOU MAY BE RIGHT.

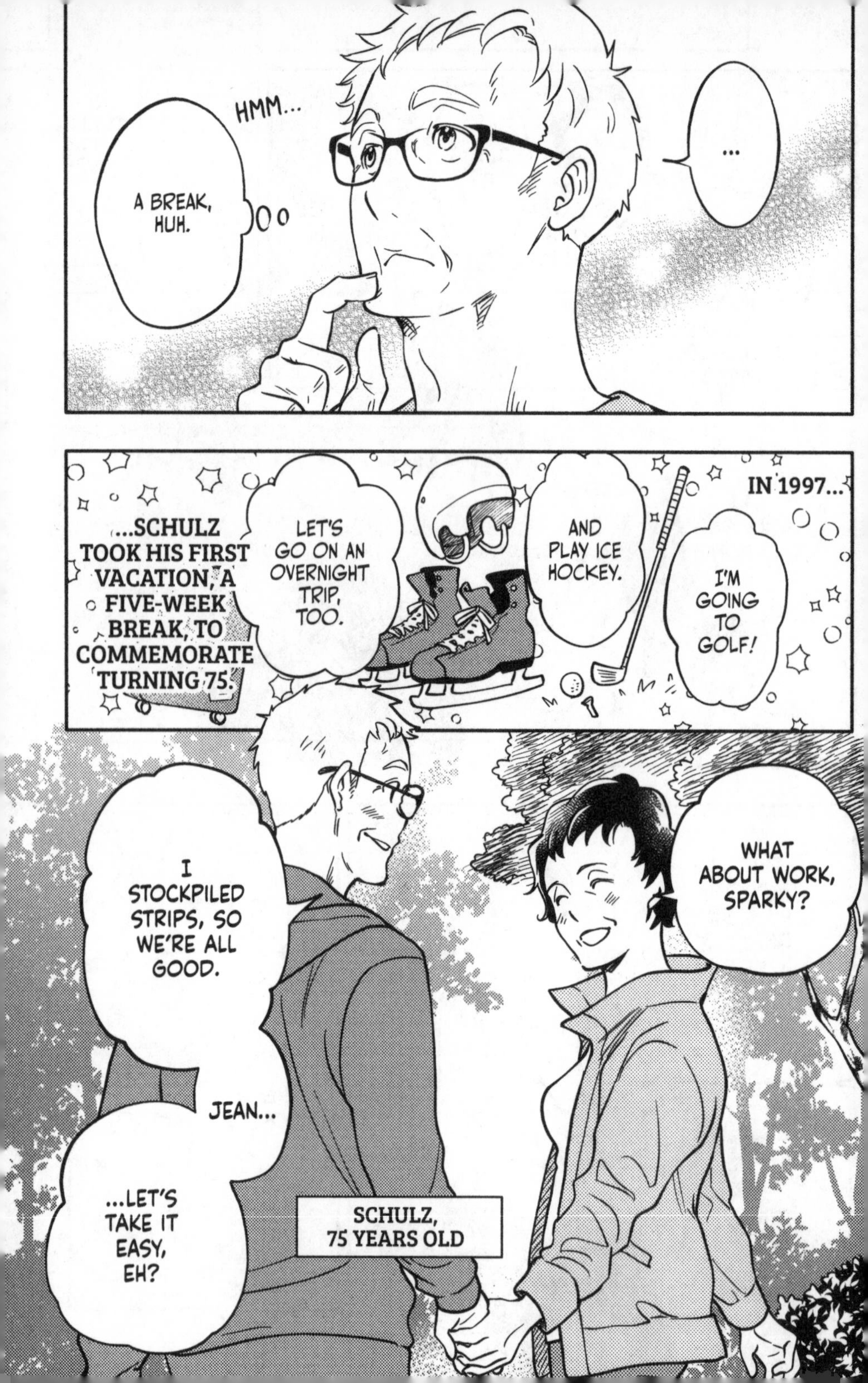
...
HMM...
A BREAK, HUH.
IN 1997...
I'M GOING TO GOLF!
AND PLAY ICE HOCKEY.
LET'S GO ON AN OVERNIGHT TRIP, TOO.
...SCHULZ TOOK HIS FIRST VACATION, A FIVE-WEEK BREAK, TO COMMEMORATE TURNING 75.
WHAT ABOUT WORK, SPARKY?
I STOCKPILED STRIPS, SO WE'RE ALL GOOD.
JEAN...
...LET'S TAKE IT EASY, EH?
SCHULZ, 75 YEARS OLD

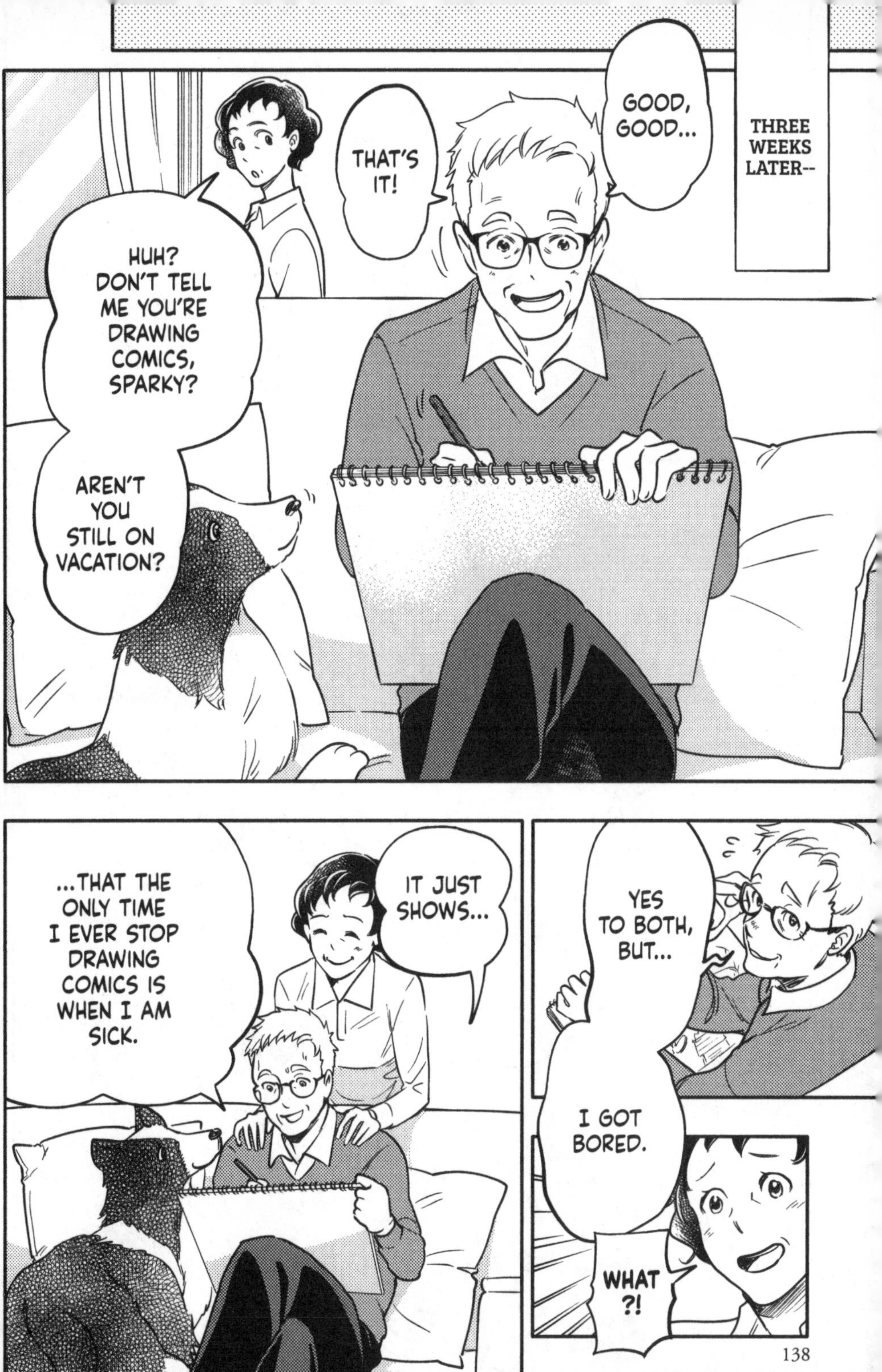
THREE WEEKS LATER--
GOOD, GOOD...
THAT'S IT!
HUH? DON'T TELL ME YOU'RE DRAWING COMICS, SPARKY?
AREN'T YOU STILL ON VACATION?
YES TO BOTH, BUT...
I GOT BORED.
WHAT?!
IT JUST SHOWS...
...THAT THE ONLY TIME I EVER STOP DRAWING COMICS IS WHEN I AM SICK.

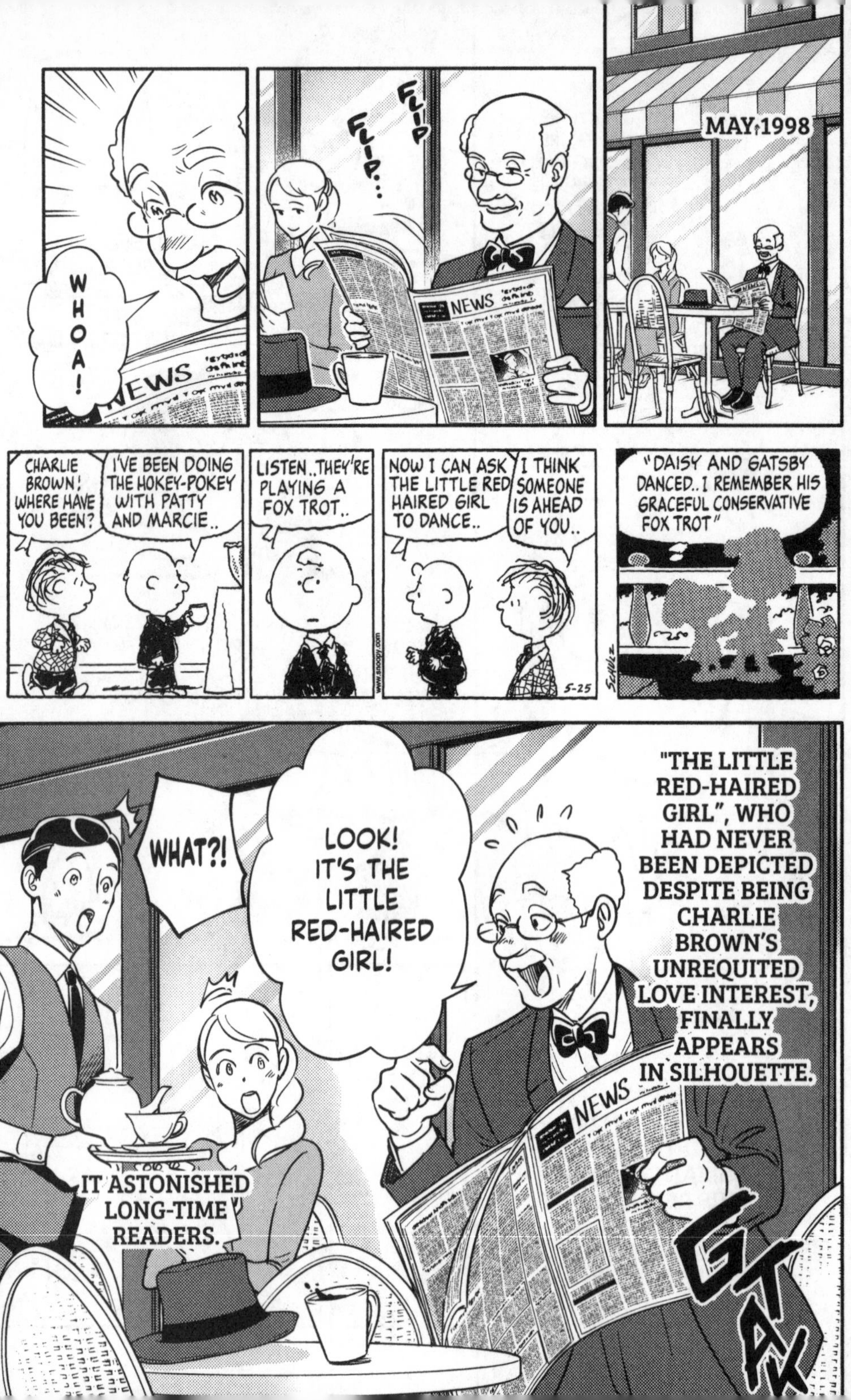
MAY 1998
FLIP
FLIP...
NEWS
WHOA!
NEWS
CHARLIE BROWN! WHERE HAVE YOU BEEN?
I'VE BEEN DOING THE HOKEY-POKEY WITH PATTY AND MARCIE..
LISTEN..THEY'RE PLAYING A FOX TROT..
www.snoopy.com
NOW I CAN ASK THE LITTLE RED HAIRED GIRL TO DANCE..
I THINK SOMEONE IS AHEAD OF YOU..
5-25
"DAISY AND GATSBY DANCED.. I REMEMBER HIS GRACEFUL CONSERVATIVE FOX TROT"
SCHULZ
"THE LITTLE RED-HAIRED GIRL", WHO HAD NEVER BEEN DEPICTED DESPITE BEING CHARLIE BROWN'S UNREQUITED LOVE INTEREST, FINALLY APPEARS IN SILHOUETTE.
LOOK! IT'S THE LITTLE RED-HAIRED GIRL!
WHAT?!
NEWS
IT ASTONISHED LONG-TIME READERS.
GTAK

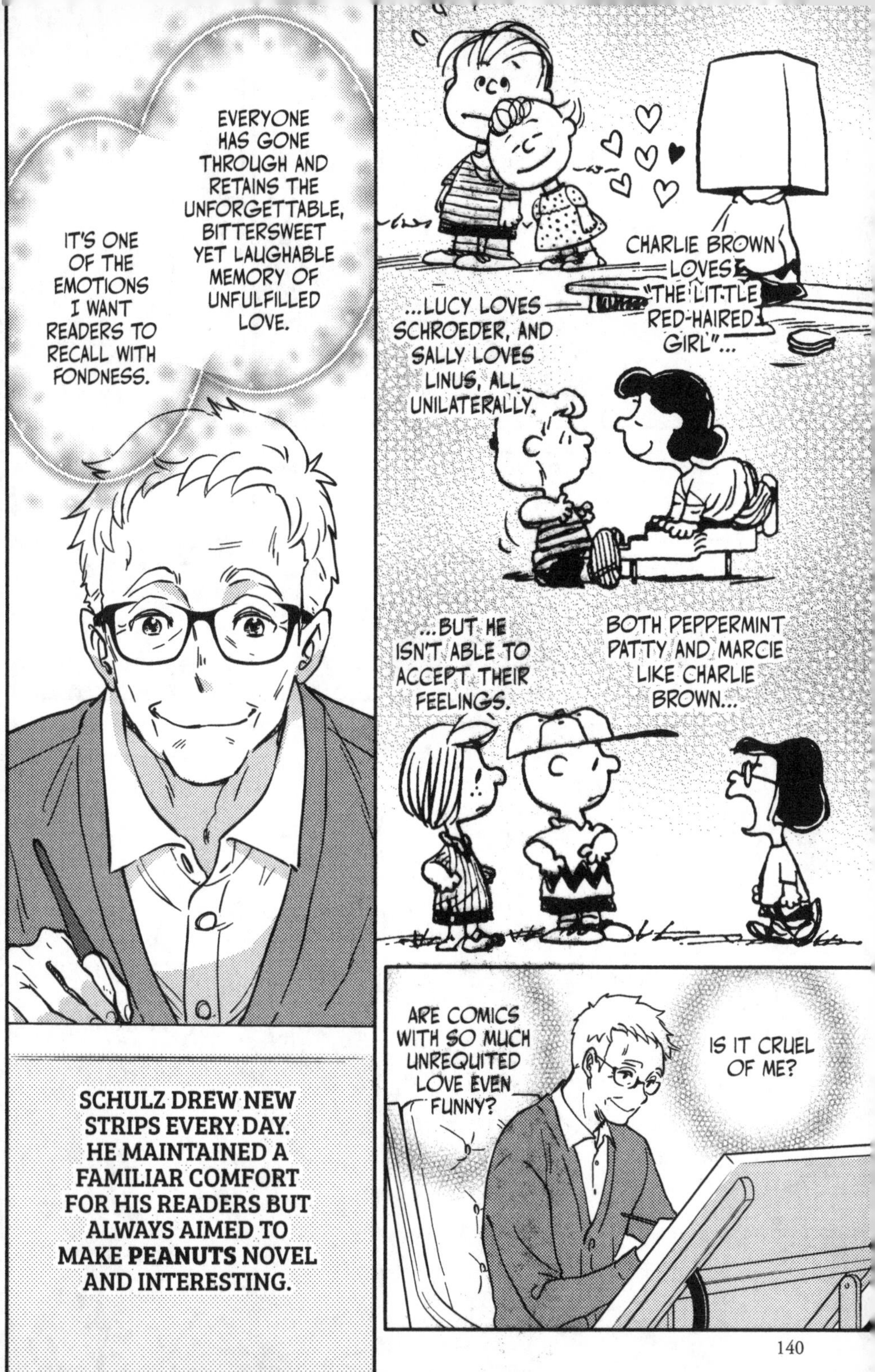
CHARLIE BROWN LOVES "THE LITTLE RED-HAIRED GIRL"...
...LUCY LOVES SCHROEDER, AND SALLY LOVES LINUS, ALL UNILATERALLY.
BOTH PEPPERMINT PATTY AND MARCIE LIKE CHARLIE BROWN...
...BUT HE ISN'T ABLE TO ACCEPT THEIR FEELINGS.
EVERYONE HAS GONE THROUGH AND RETAINS THE UNFORGETTABLE, BITTERSWEET YET LAUGHABLE MEMORY OF UNFULFILLED LOVE.
IT'S ONE OF THE EMOTIONS I WANT READERS TO RECALL WITH FONDNESS.
IS IT CRUEL OF ME?
ARE COMICS WITH SO MUCH UNREQUITED LOVE EVEN FUNNY?
SCHULZ DREW NEW STRIPS EVERY DAY. HE MAINTAINED A FAMILIAR COMFORT FOR HIS READERS BUT ALWAYS AIMED TO MAKE **PEANUTS** NOVEL AND INTERESTING.

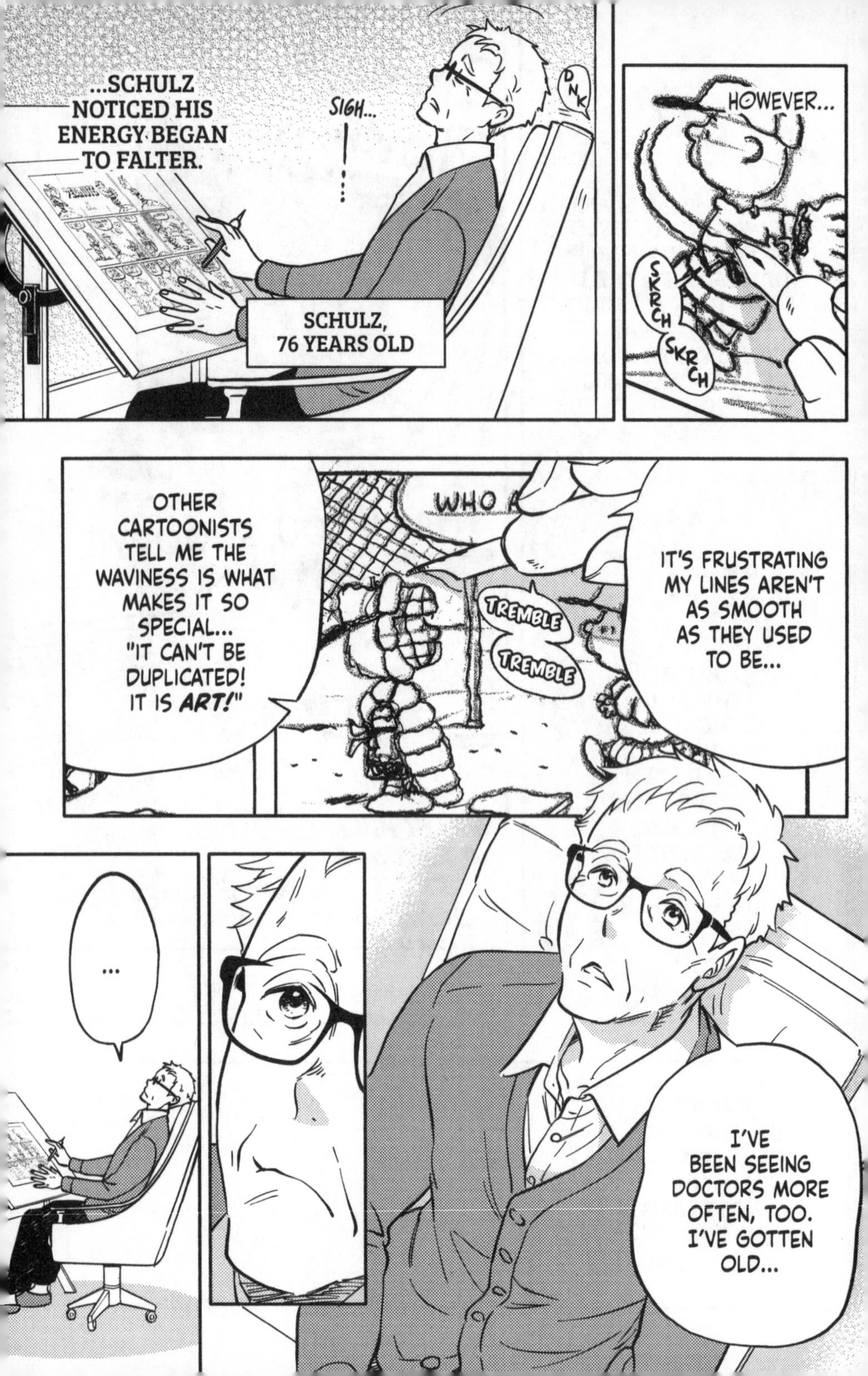
HOWEVER...
SKRCH
SKRCH
...SCHULZ NOTICED HIS ENERGY BEGAN TO FALTER.
DNK
SIGH...
SCHULZ, 76 YEARS OLD
IT'S FRUSTRATING MY LINES AREN'T AS SMOOTH AS THEY USED TO BE...
WHO A
TREMBLE
TREMBLE
OTHER CARTOONISTS TELL ME THE WAVINESS IS WHAT MAKES IT SO SPECIAL... "IT CAN'T BE DUPLICATED! IT IS ART!"
I'VE BEEN SEEING DOCTORS MORE OFTEN, TOO. I'VE GOTTEN OLD...
...

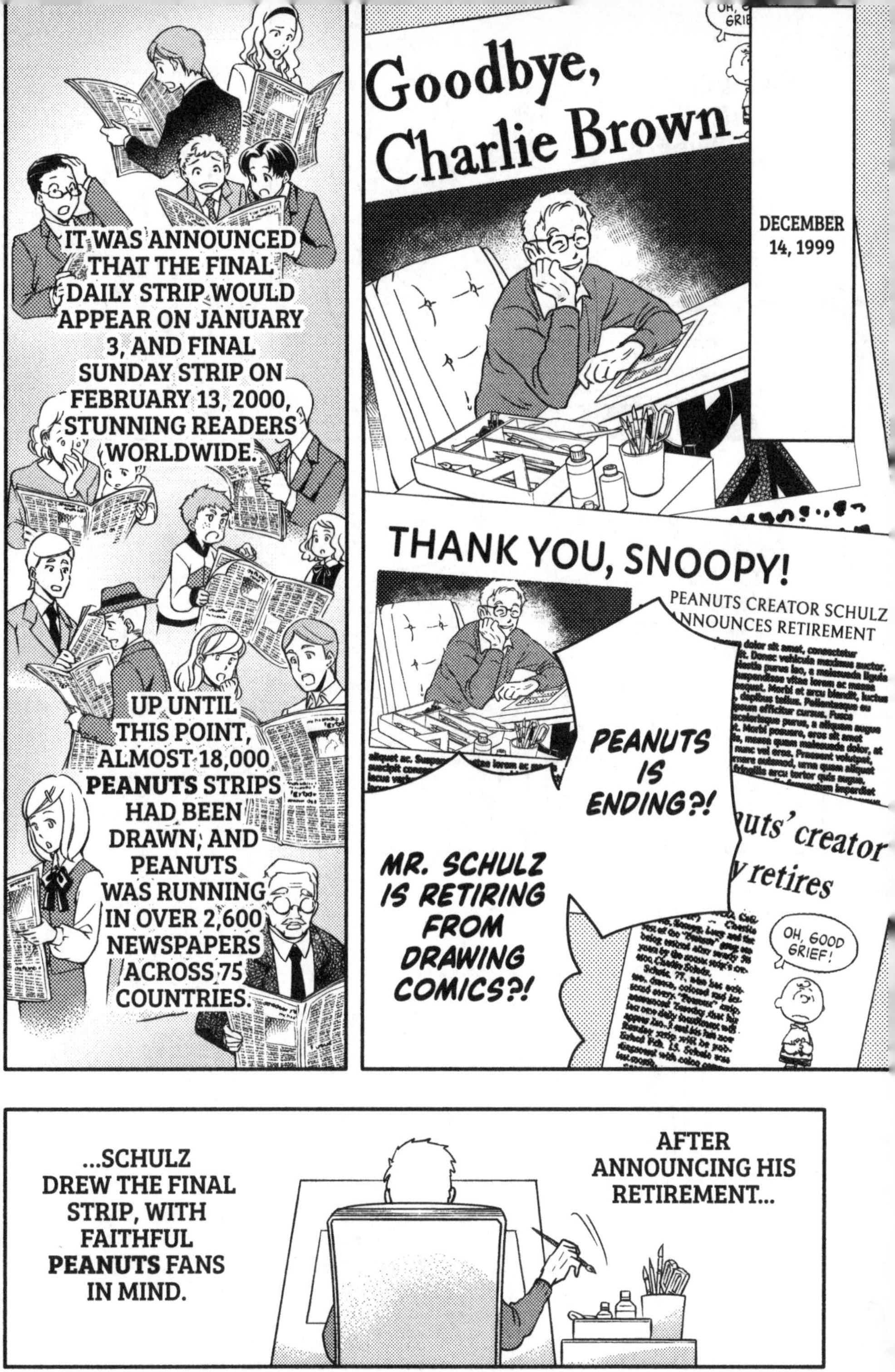

DECEMBER 14, 1999
Goodbye, Charlie Brown
THANK YOU, SNOOPY!
PEANUTS CREATOR SCHULZ ANNOUNCES RETIREMENT
PEANUTS IS ENDING?!
OH, GOOD GRIEF!
MR. SCHULZ IS RETIRING FROM DRAWING COMICS?!
IT WAS ANNOUNCED THAT THE FINAL DAILY STRIP WOULD APPEAR ON JANUARY 3, AND FINAL SUNDAY STRIP ON FEBRUARY 13, 2000, STUNNING READERS WORLDWIDE.
UP UNTIL THIS POINT, ALMOST 18,000 **PEANUTS** STRIPS HAD BEEN DRAWN, AND PEANUTS WAS RUNNING IN OVER 2,600 NEWSPAPERS ACROSS 75 COUNTRIES.
AFTER ANNOUNCING HIS RETIREMENT...
...SCHULZ DREW THE FINAL STRIP, WITH FAITHFUL **PEANUTS** FANS IN MIND.

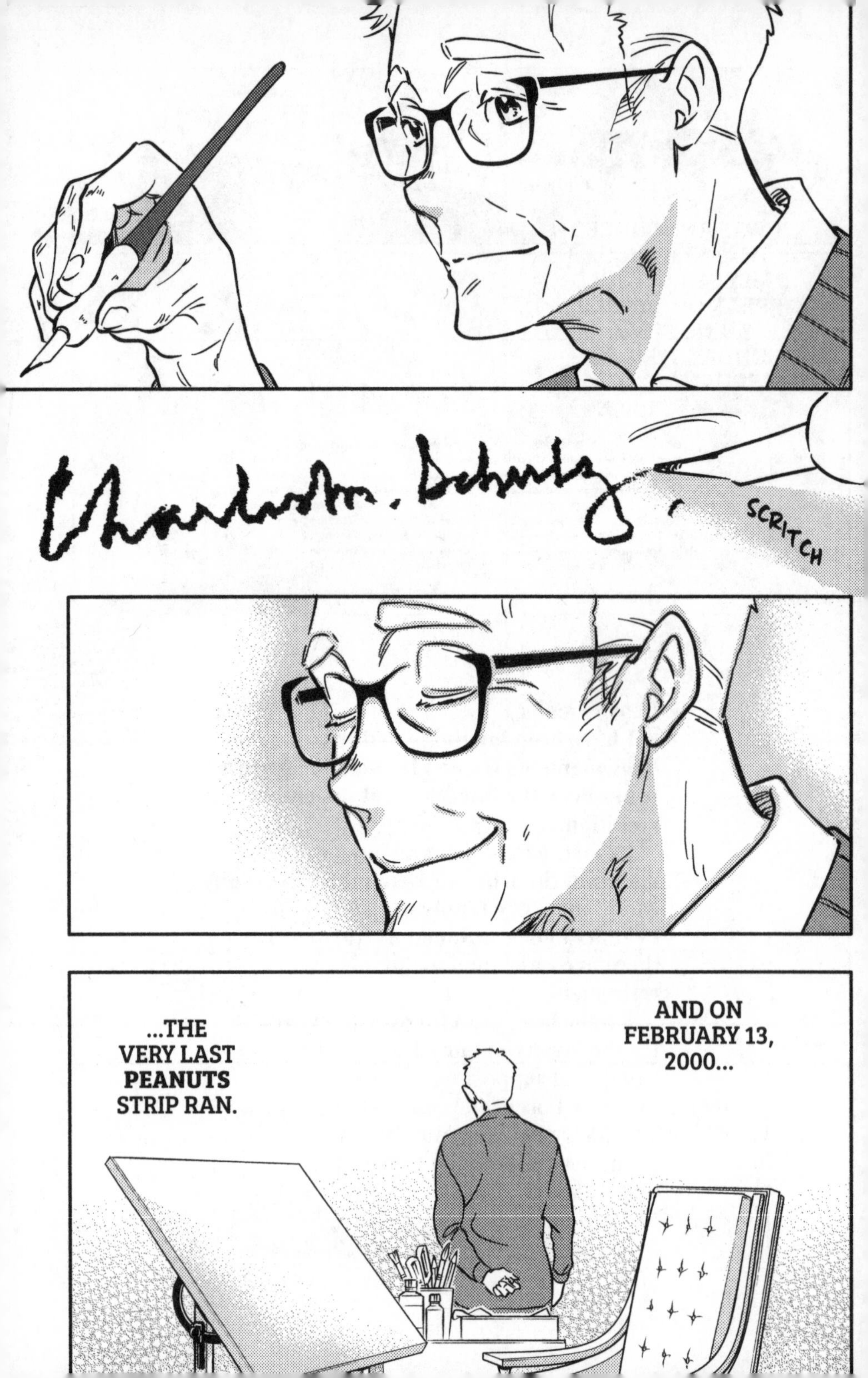
SCRITCH
AND ON FEBRUARY 13, 2000...
...THE VERY LAST PEANUTS STRIP RAN.

Dear Friends...
NO, I THINK HE'S WRITING..
PEANUTS
by SCHULZ
GOOD GRIEF!
CLOMP!
AAUGH!
BONK!
Dear Friends,
I have been fortunate to draw Charlie Brown and his friends for almost 50 years. It has been the fulfillment of my childhood ambition.
Unfortunately, I am no longer able to maintain the schedule demanded by a daily comic strip. My family does not wish Peanuts to be continued by anyone else, therefore I am announcing my retirement.
I have been grateful over the years for the loyalty of our editors and the wonderful support and love expressed to me by fans of the comic strip.
Charlie Brown, Snoopy, Linus, Lucy...how can I ever forget them...
PSYCHIATRIC HELP 5¢
THE DOCTOR IS IN
2-13-00

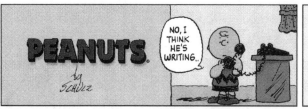

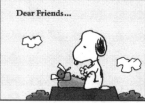

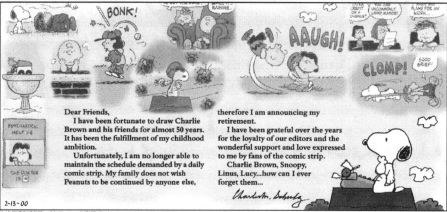

Dear Friends,

I have been fortunate to draw Charlie Brown and his friends for almost 50 years. It has been the fulfillment of my childhood ambition.

Unfortunately, I am no longer able to maintain the schedule demanded by a daily comic strip. My family does not wish Peanuts to be continued by anyone else, therefore I am announcing my retirement.

I have been grateful over the years for the loyalty of our editors and the wonderful support and love expressed to me by fans of the comic strip.

Charlie Brown, Snoopy, Linus, Lucy...how can I ever forget them...

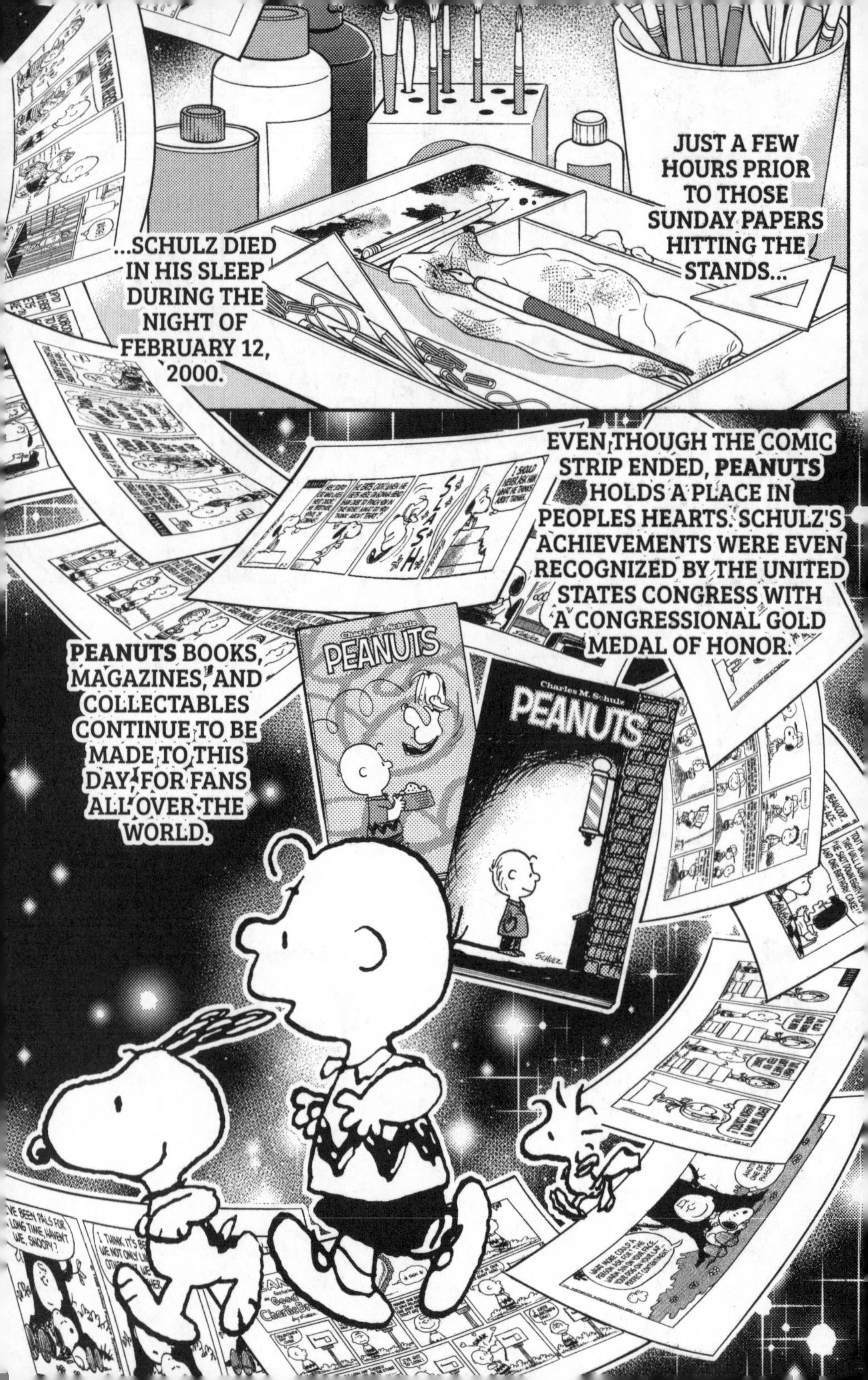
JUST A FEW HOURS PRIOR TO THOSE SUNDAY PAPERS HITTING THE STANDS...
...SCHULZ DIED IN HIS SLEEP DURING THE NIGHT OF FEBRUARY 12, 2000.
EVEN THOUGH THE COMIC STRIP ENDED, **PEANUTS** HOLDS A PLACE IN PEOPLES HEARTS. SCHULZ'S ACHIEVEMENTS WERE EVEN RECOGNIZED BY THE UNITED STATES CONGRESS WITH A CONGRESSIONAL GOLD MEDAL OF HONOR.
Charles M. Schulz
PEANUTS
PEANUTS
PEANUTS BOOKS, MAGAZINES, AND COLLECTABLES CONTINUE TO BE MADE TO THIS DAY, FOR FANS ALL OVER THE WORLD.

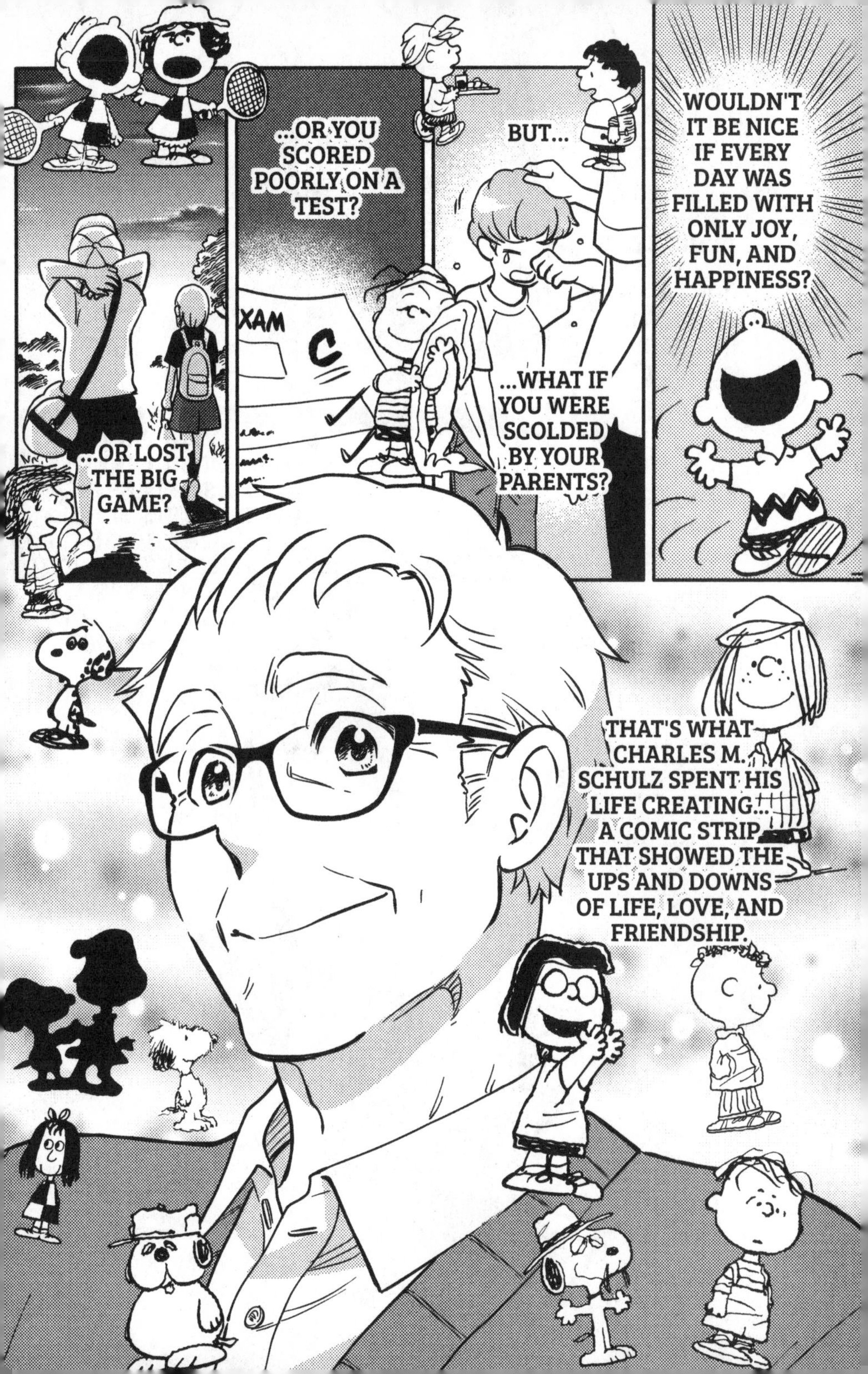
WOULDN'T IT BE NICE IF EVERY DAY WAS FILLED WITH ONLY JOY, FUN, AND HAPPINESS?
BUT...
...WHAT IF YOU WERE SCOLDED BY YOUR PARENTS?
...OR YOU SCORED POORLY ON A TEST?
XAM
C
...OR LOST THE BIG GAME?
THAT'S WHAT CHARLES M. SCHULZ SPENT HIS LIFE CREATING... A COMIC STRIP THAT SHOWED THE UPS AND DOWNS OF LIFE, LOVE, AND FRIENDSHIP.

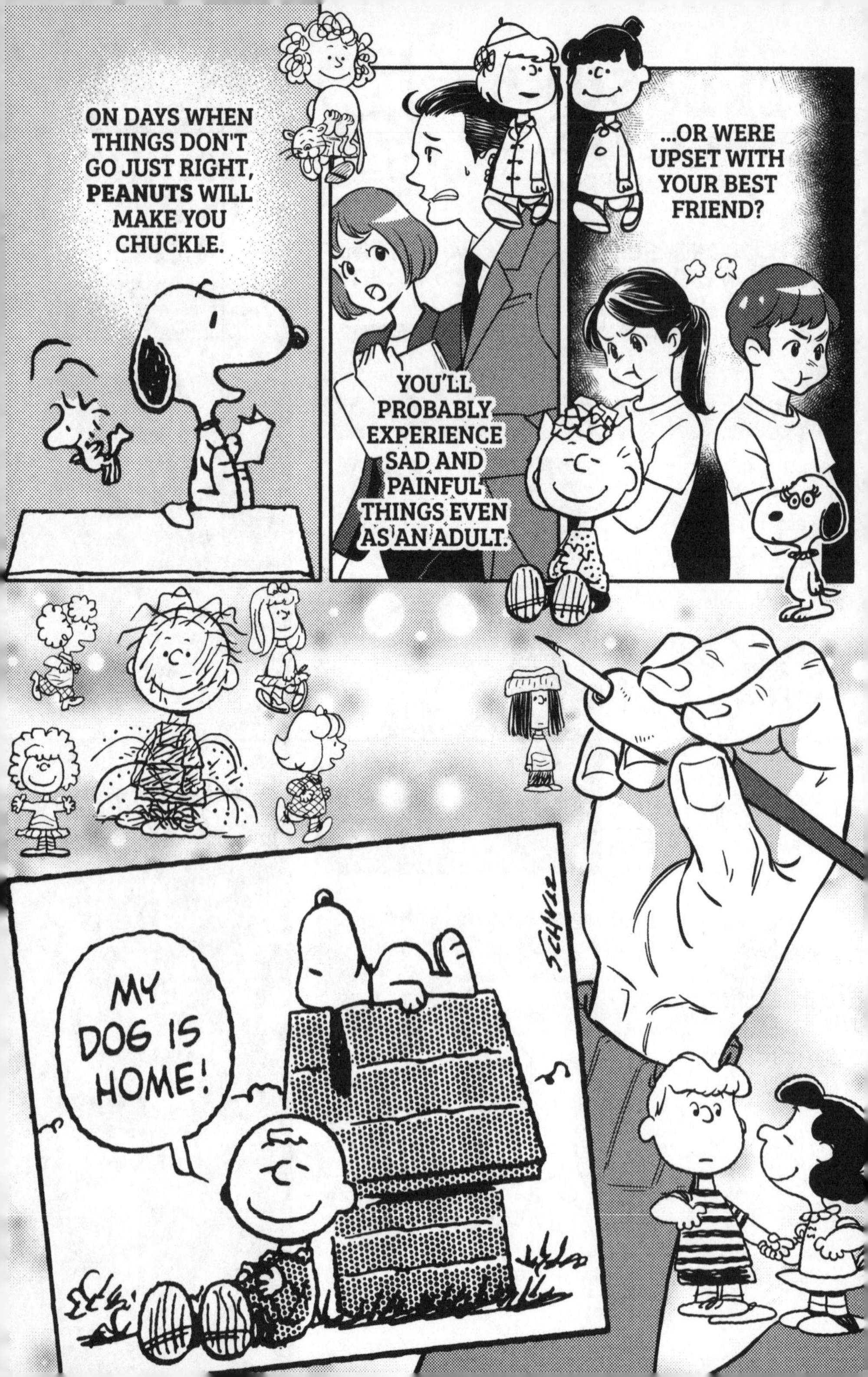
...OR WERE UPSET WITH YOUR BEST FRIEND?
YOU'LL PROBABLY EXPERIENCE SAD AND PAINFUL THINGS EVEN AS AN ADULT.
ON DAYS WHEN THINGS DON'T GO JUST RIGHT, PEANUTS WILL MAKE YOU CHUCKLE.
SCHULZ
MY DOG IS HOME!

The Exciting

SCHULZ IN REAL LIFE

CONTENTS

TREASURE DISCOVERED

INTRODUCING SCHULZ AND *PEANUTS* TRIVIA YOU CAN BRAG TO YOUR FRIENDS ABOUT! A RARE COLLECTIBLE, TOO!

WHERE *PEANUTS* CAME TO LIFE: SCHULZ'S OFFICE

SCHULZ HEADED TO HIS OFFICE AT THE SAME TIME EVERY MORNING. HE DREW COMICS IN THE SAME ORDERLY WAY AS HE LIVED HIS LIFE. HIS TOOLS INCLUDED PAPER, PENCILS, AND PENS.

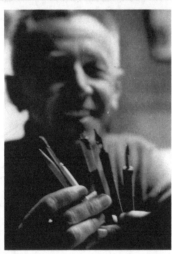

▶ SCHULZ'S FAVORITE PENCILS AND PENS. HE WAS ESPECIALLY FOND OF THE RADIO PEN #914 NIB.

THERE WAS A *PEANUTS* PROTOTYPE!

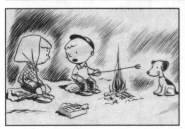

CHARACTERS SIMILAR TO CHARLIE BROWN AND SNOOPY APPEARED IN *LI'L FOLKS*, WHICH SCHULZ DREW BEFORE *PEANUTS*.

▲ FROM *LI'L FOLKS* (*ST. PAUL PIONEER PRESS*, OCT. 31, 1948). IT DEPICTED MUNDANE SCENES OF SEVERAL CHILDREN AND A DOG.

SNOOPY GOES TO THE MOON!

IN 1968, SNOOPY WAS SELECTED AS AS THE OFFICIAL SAFETY MASCOT FOR NASA (NATIONAL AERONAUTICS AND SPACE ADMINISTRATION). THE FOLLOWING YEAR, APOLLO 10, WHOSE LUNAR MODULE WAS NAMED "SNOOPY" AND ITS COMMAND MODULE "CHARLIE BROWN", WAS LAUNCHED TOWARDS THE MOON. THEY CONDUCTED A DRY RUN FOR APOLLO 11'S LUNAR LANDING.

A SPACESUIT-CLAD SNOOPY DOLL WAS CREATED THAT USED ACTUAL SPACESUIT MATERIAL.
▼

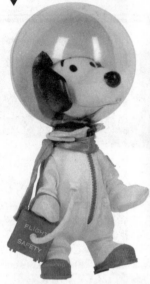

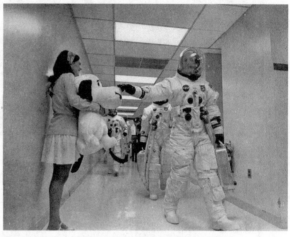

▲ APOLLO 10 ASTRONAUT THOMAS STAFFORD PATTED A STUFFED SNOOPY BEFORE DEPARTING FOR THE MOON.

SNOOPY, HAND-DRAWN ON A HOSPITAL WALL!

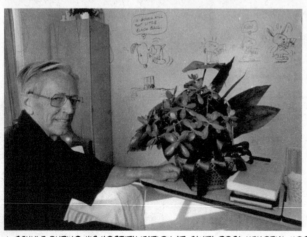

IN 1981, SCHULZ WAS HOSPITALIZED AND UNDERWENT HEART SURGERY. DURING THAT TIME, A NURSE ASKED HIM TO DRAW SOMETHING ON THE WALL. HE INITIALLY DECLINED, BUT GOT A SUDDEN IDEA IN THE MIDDLE OF THE NIGHT AND DREW SNOOPY, DETERMINED TO DO HIS PHYSICAL THERAPY.

▲ SCHULZ DURING HIS HOSPITALIZATION AT SANTA ROSA MEMORIAL HOSPITAL.

ANYTHING & EVERYTHING

GET TO KNOW PEANUTS!

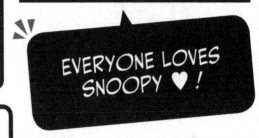

EVERYONE LOVES SNOOPY ♥ !

SNOOPY IS CHARLIE BROWN'S DOG AND THE NEIGHBORHOOD'S FAVORITE BEAGLE. A LEGEND IN HIS OWN MIND, SNOOPY CAN TAKE TO THE SKIES AS THE WORLD WAR 1 FLYING ACE, RULE THE COLLEGE CAMPUS AS JOE COOL, OR WRITE ANOTHER UNPUBLISHED MANUSCRIPT AS THE WORLD FAMOUS AUTHOR. NO MATTER WHERE HIS IMAGINATION TAKES HIM, SNOOPY ALWAYS COMES BACK TO HIS DOGHOUSE FOR SUPPERTIME FROM THAT 'ROUND-HEADED KID', CHARLIE BROWN.

FUN FACT

SNOOPY IS A BEAGLE

SNOOPY WAS BORN AT THE DAISY HILL PUPPY FARM. BEAGLES ARE VERY GIFTED DOGS, ACCORDING TO HIM.

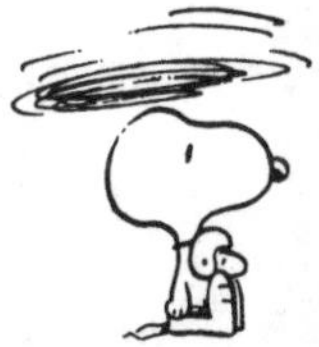

▲ HE CAN EVEN SPIN HIS EARS TO FLY!

FUN FACT

WOODSTOCK IS A SMALL MIGRATORY BIRD

SNOOPY'S BEST FRIEND WOODSTOCK HAS LOTS OF FRIENDS!

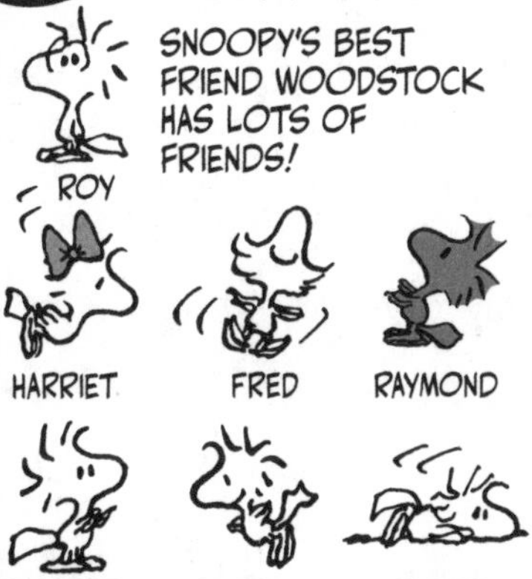
ROY
HARRIET
FRED
RAYMOND
CONRAD
BILL
OLIVIER

THE EVOLUTION OF SNOOPY

[AROUND 1950]

WAS STILL A PUPPY. WALKED AROUND ON ALL FOUR LEGS.

[AROUND 1954]

GOT A BIT BIGGER, WITH LARGER EARS AND A ROUNDER NOSE.

[AROUND 1956]

STARTED STANDING UPRIGHT AND DOING HAPPY DANCES!

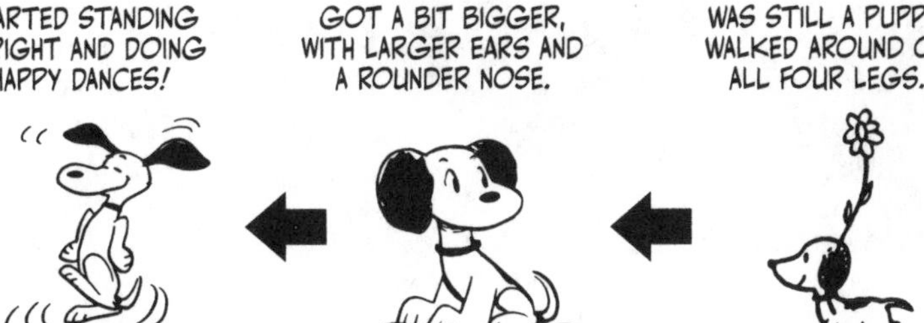

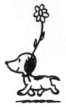

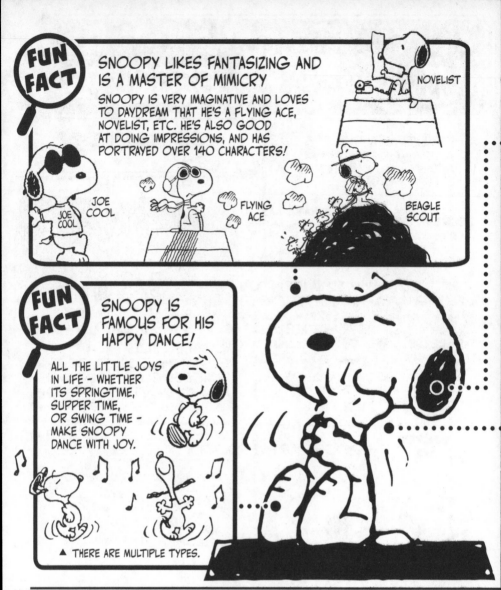

FUN FACT

SNOOPY LIKES FANTASIZING AND IS A MASTER OF MIMICRY

SNOOPY IS VERY IMAGINATIVE AND LOVES TO DAYDREAM THAT HE'S A FLYING ACE, NOVELIST, ETC. HE'S ALSO GOOD AT DOING IMPRESSIONS, AND HAS PORTRAYED OVER 140 CHARACTERS!

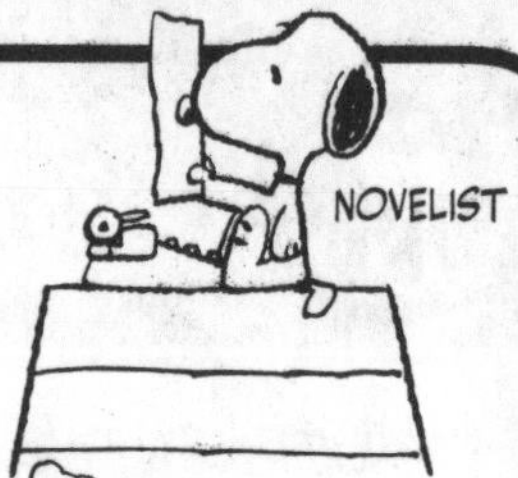
NOVELIST

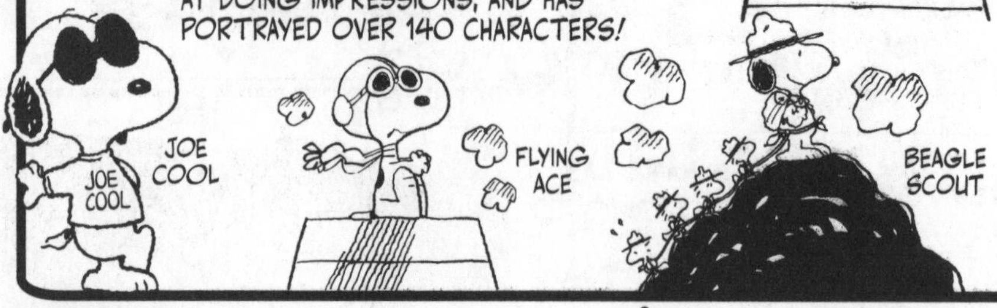
JOE COOL
JOE COOL
FLYING ACE
BEAGLE SCOUT

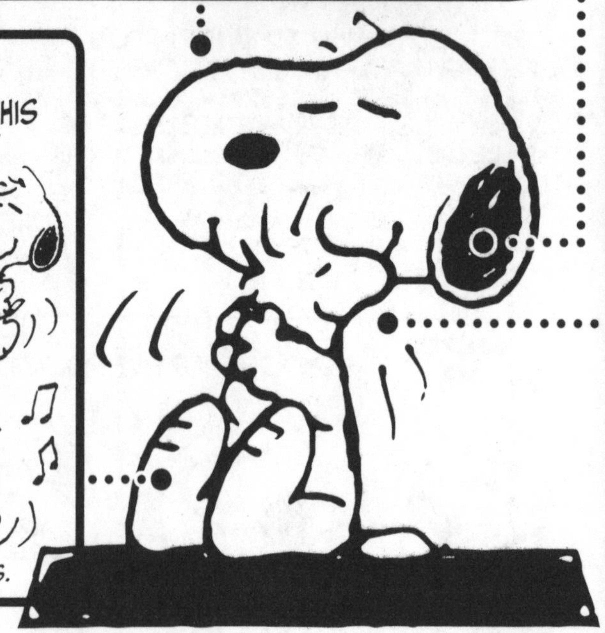

FUN FACT

SNOOPY IS FAMOUS FOR HIS HAPPY DANCE!

ALL THE LITTLE JOYS IN LIFE - WHETHER ITS SPRINGTIME, SUPPER TIME, OR SWING TIME - MAKE SNOOPY DANCE WITH JOY.

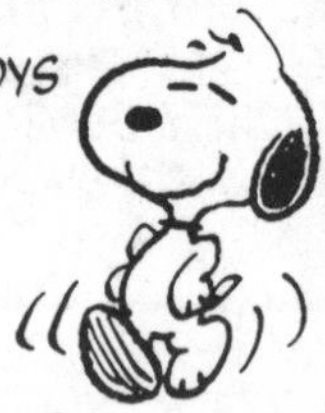

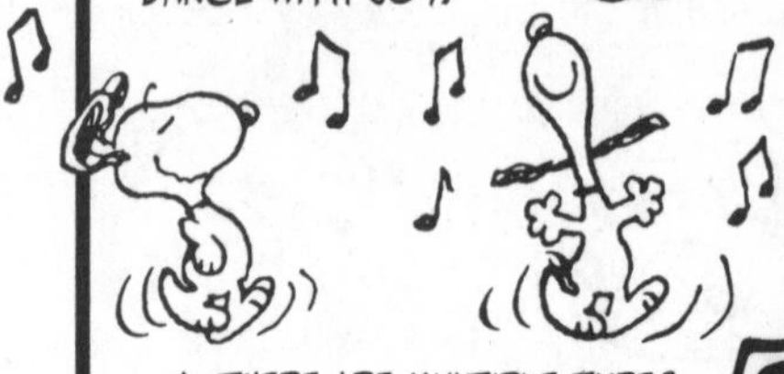

▲ THERE ARE MULTIPLE TYPES.

[AROUND 1960]

STILL REMINISCENT OF EARLIER DAYS, BUT HIS NOSE IS BIGGER.

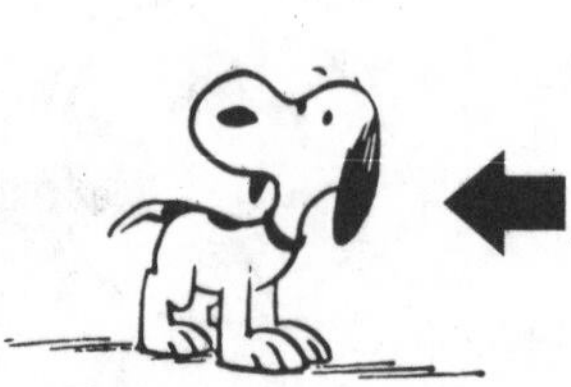

[AROUND 1972]

FACE GOT BIGGER AND EARS A LITTLE SMALLER.

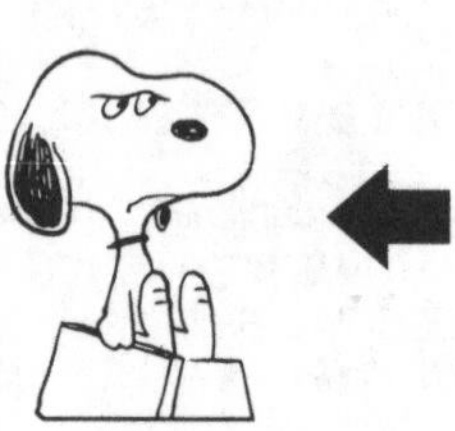

[AROUND 1980]

BECAME THE EXPRESSIVE SNOOPY WE ALL LOVE!

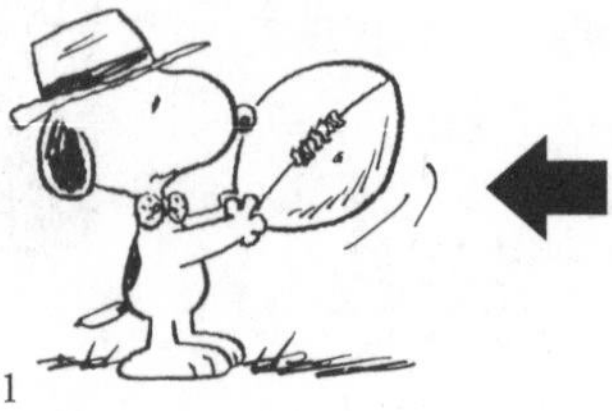

11 *PEANUTS* SECRETS

Eleven Secrets

PEANUTS IS A TIMELESS CLASSIC COMIC STRIP THAT HOLDS MANY SECRETS. HOW MANY DO YOU KNOW?

SECRET #1

SNOOPY'S NAME WAS ORIGINALLY GOING TO BE "SNIFFY"

SCHULZ WAS PLANNING TO NAME THE DOG APPEARING IN *PEANUTS* "SNIFFY". ONE DAY, HOWEVER, HE DISCOVERED THE NAME WAS ALREADY BEING USED IN ANOTHER COMIC. HE THEN RECALLED HIS LATE MOTHER HAD WANTED TO NAME THE NEXT FAMILY DOG 'SNOOPY'"

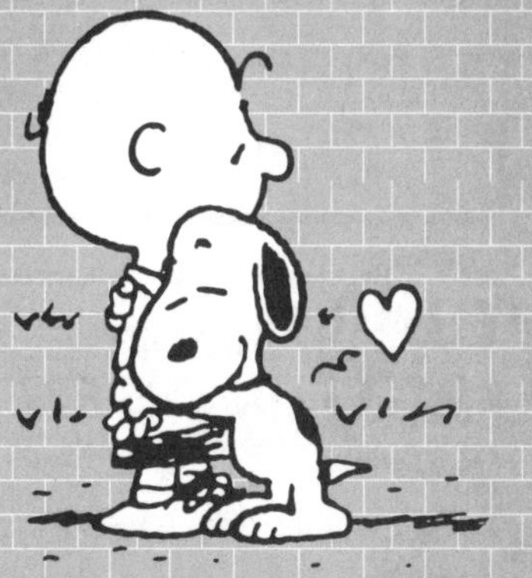

▲ SNOOPY'S NAME IS SPELLED "スヌーピー" IN JAPANESE.

SECRET #2

SNOOPY HAS FIVE SIBLINGS!

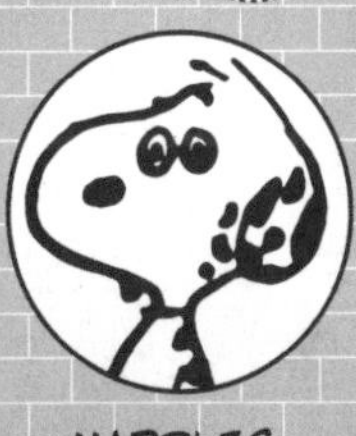

MARBLES

▲ THEIR HOBBIES AND PERSONALITIES APPARENTLY AREN'T COMPATIBLE.

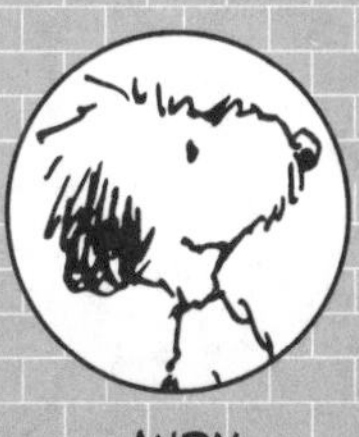

ANDY

▲ HAS NO SENSE OF DIRECTION, SO OFTEN GETS LOST.

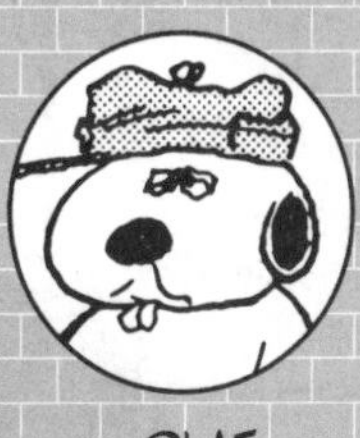

OLAF

▲ GOES ON A LOT OF ADVENTURES WITH ANDY.

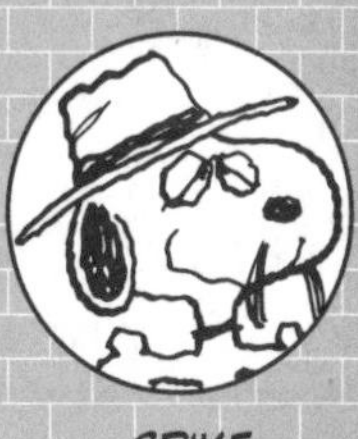

SPIKE

▲ SNOOPY'S OLDER BROTHER WHO LIVES IN THE DESERT.

BELLE

▶ THE ONLY FEMALE SIBLING.

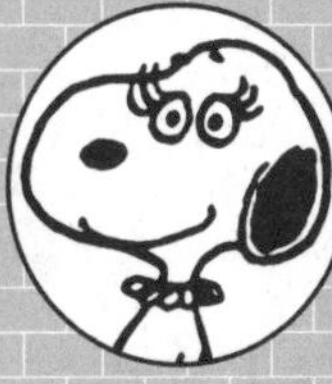

SCHULZ MAY HAVE BEEN AN ONLY CHILD, BUT HE GAVE SNOOPY MANY SIBLINGS. FIVE IN FACT: SPIKE, BELLE, MARBLES, OLAF, AND ANDY. SPIKE LIVES IN THE DESERT, BELLE LIVES IN KANSAS CITY (WITH HER SON), ANDY AND OLAF LIKE TO TRAVEL TOGETHER, AND MARBLES WEARS SNEAKERS. FUN FACT: A SECOND SISTER WAS INTRODUCED IN A TV SPECIAL BUT SHE NEVER APPEARED IN THE COMIC STRIP.

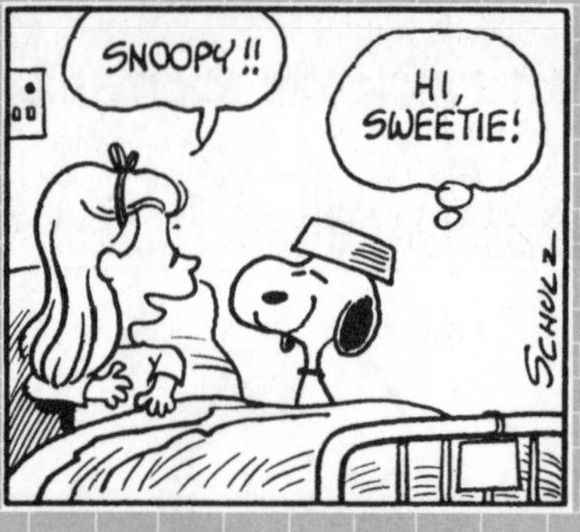
SNOOPY!!
HI, SWEETIE!
SCHULZ

▲ A WORRIED SNOOPY EVEN WENT TO VISIT LILA IN THE HOSPITAL.

SECRET #3

SNOOPY'S FIRST OWNER WAS LILA

SNOOPY'S FIRST OWNER WAS A LITTLE GIRL NAMED LILA. SHE BROUGHT SNOOPY HOME FROM THE DAISY HILL PUPPY FARM BUT WAS FORCED TO PART WITH HIM BECAUSE HER APARTMENT DIDN'T ALLOW DOGS. DID YOU KNOW SHE HAS CONTINUOUSLY WRITTEN LETTERS TO SNOOPY AFTER THEIR SEPARATION?

SECRET #4

SNOOPY ACTUALLY HAD A FIANCÉE BUT SHE RAN OFF WITH SPIKE?!

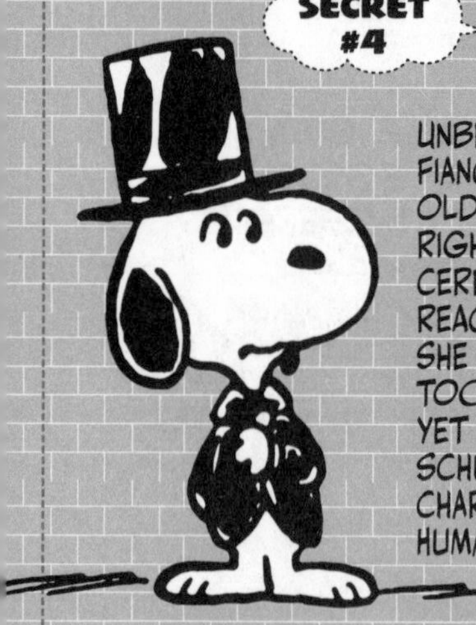

UNBELIEVABLY, SNOOPY'S FIANCÉE RAN OFF WITH HIS OLDER BROTHER SPIKE, RIGHT BEFORE THE WEDDING CEREMONY! AS SOON AS THEY REACHED THEIR DESTINATION, SHE ABANDONED SPIKE TOO, RUNNING OFF WITH YET ANOTHER COMPANION. SCHULZ DEPICTED HIS DOG CHARACTERS IN A VERY HUMAN-LIKE WAY.

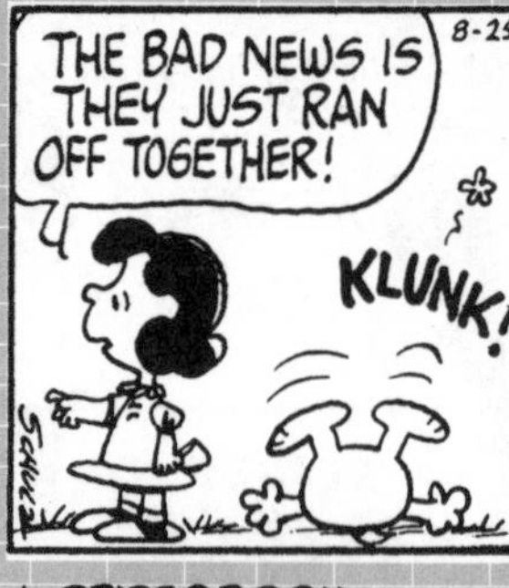
8-25
THE BAD NEWS IS THEY JUST RAN OFF TOGETHER!
KLUNK!
SCHULZ

▲ BRIDEGROOM SNOOPY IS IN SHOCK WHEN HE LEARNS HIS FIANCÉE DESERTED HIM!

SECRET #5

THE INSIDE OF SNOOPY'S DOGHOUSE IS VERY SPACIOUS?!

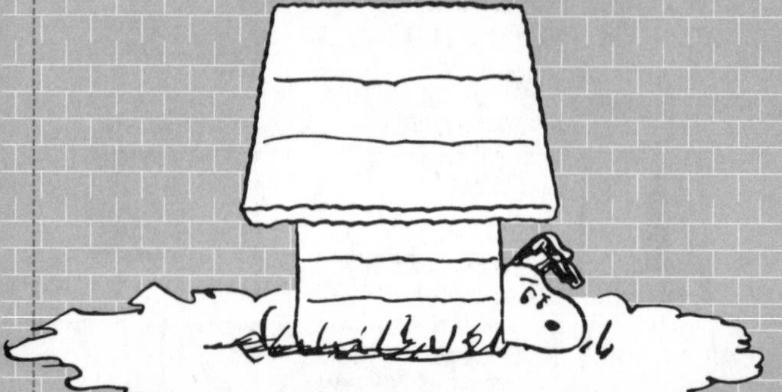

▲ CHARLIE BROWN AND THE OTHERS HAVE EVEN GIVEN IT A GOOD CLEANING.

SNOOPY'S DOGHOUSE IS MORE THAN IT APPEARS! IT'S ROOMY ENOUGH FOR A POOL TABLE, A TELEVISION, A RECORD PLAYER, A REFRIDGERATOR, A LIBRARY, A GRANDFATHER CLOCK, AND A BASEMENT! IT EVEN HAS FRAMED PAINTINGS FROM SOME OF SCHULZ'S FAVORITE ARTISTS.

SECRET #6 CHARLIE BROWN NEVER GETS TO KICK THE FOOTBALL

LUCY ALWAYS PULLS THE BALL AWAY FROM CHARLIE BROWN. THIS PLOTLINE BECAME A FALL STAPLE IN 1956, WITH SLIGHT VARIATIONS EACH TIME. WHEN SCHULZ WAS A CHILD, HE KICKED A BALL AROUND WITH HIS COUSINS, TOO.

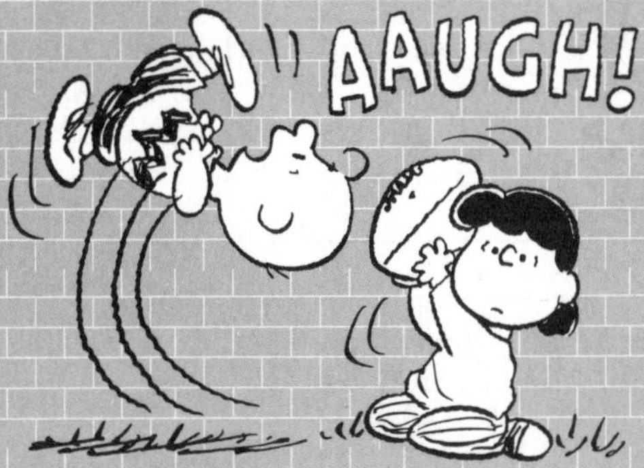
AAUGH!

▲ CHARLIE BROWN HAS FAILED AT LEAST 42 TIMES TO DATE?!

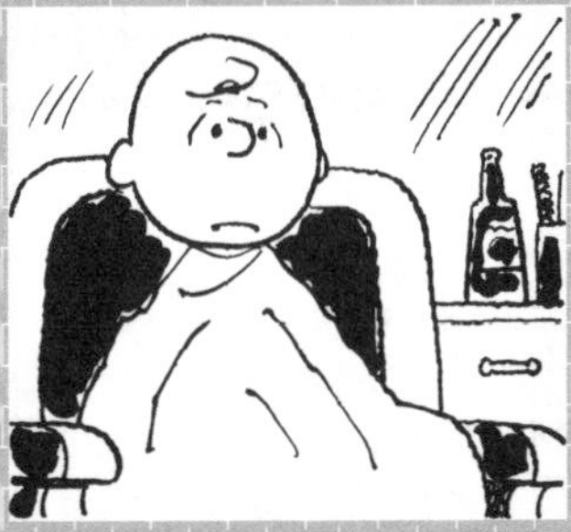

▲ CHARLIE BROWN HAS FINE BLOND HAIR. HE IS NOT BALD!

SECRET #7 BOTH CHARLIE BROWN'S FATHER AND SCHULZ'S FATHER ARE BARBERS

CHARLIE BROWN AND HIS CREATOR SCHULZ: WHAT THEY HAVE IN COMMON IS THAT THEIR FATHERS ARE BARBERS, WHOSE BUSINESSES ALSO SHARE THE SAME NAME, "THE FAMILY BARBERSHOP". BOTH SCHULZ AND CHARLIE BROWN RESPECTED THEIR HARDWORKING FATHERS.

SECRET #8 ADULTS DO NOT APPEAR IN *PEANUTS*

SCHULZ ALWAYS DREW *PEANUTS* FROM A CHILD'S PERSPECTIVE. IN THE RARE INSTANCE SCHULZ DREW ADULTS THEY WERE ONLY SEEN FROM THE KNEE DOWN.

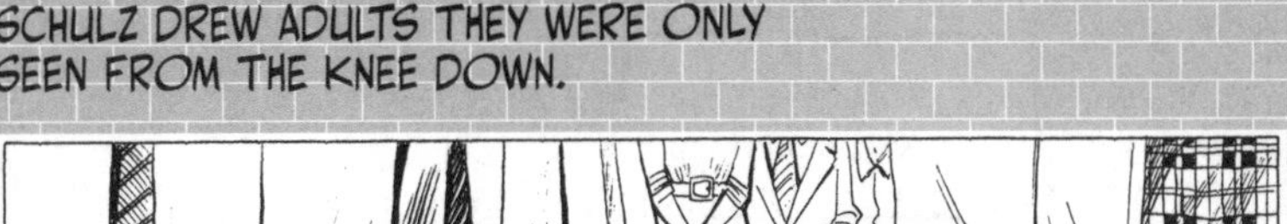
CONTINUED

▶ ADULTS PROTRUDE OUT OF THE PANEL'S BORDER, SO THEIR FACES AREN'T VISIBLE.

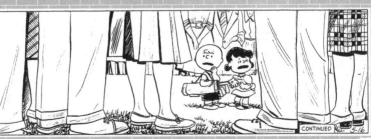

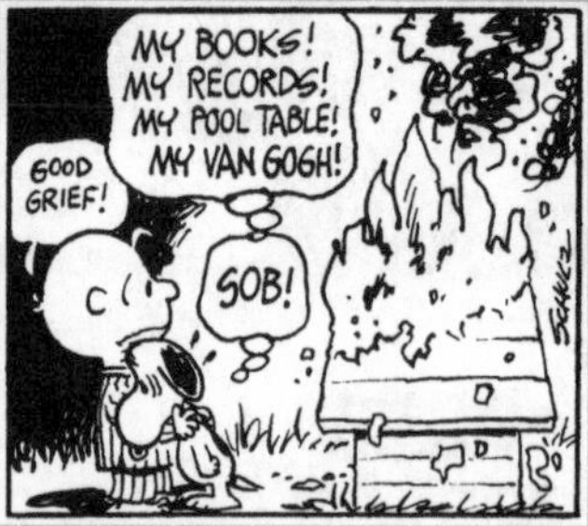

GOOD GRIEF!
MY BOOKS! MY RECORDS! MY POOL TABLE! MY VAN GOGH!
SOB!
SCHULZ

▲ SNOOPY IS IN SHOCK FROM ALL HIS POSSESSIONS GOING UP IN FLAMES ALONG WITH HIS DOGHOUSE.

SECRET #9 DONATIONS WERE SENT TO REBUILD THE DOGHOUSE

IN THE STRIP FROM SEPTEMBER 19, 1966, SNOOPY'S DOGHOUSE BURNS DOWN, LEAVING SNOOPY IN SHOCK. AFTERWARD, READERS FROM AROUND THE WORLD SENT SCHULZ LETTERS OF ENCOURAGEMENT FOR SNOOPY AND MONETARY DONATIONS.

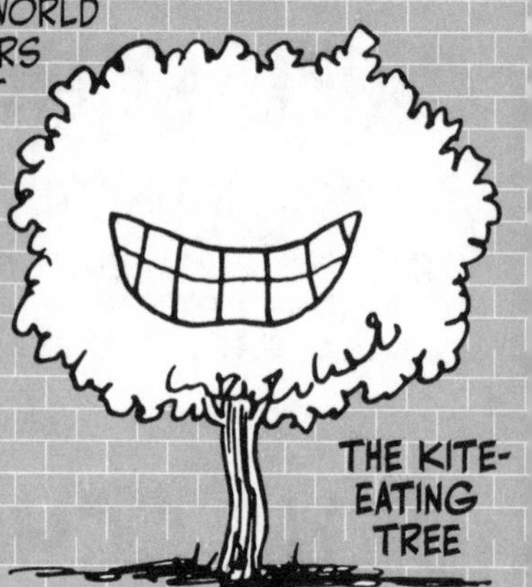

THE KITE-EATING TREE

SECRET #10 A TREE THAT EATS KITES AND A SCHOOL WITH A HEART APPEAR

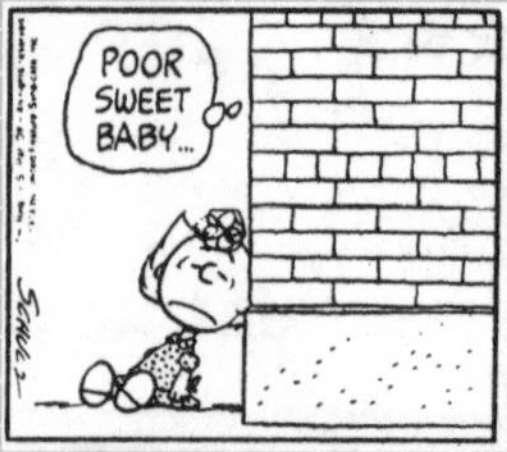

POOR SWEET BABY...
SCHULZ

▲ CHARLIE BROWN'S LITTLE SISTER SALLY LOVES HER RED-BRICKED SCHOOL BUILDING.

THE KITE-EATING TREE THAT GOBBLES UP KITES AND THE SCHOOL BUILDING WHO TALKS TO SALLY ARE JUST SOME OF THE UNIQUE IDEAS THAT MADE *PEAUNTS* LOVED AROUND THE WORLD.

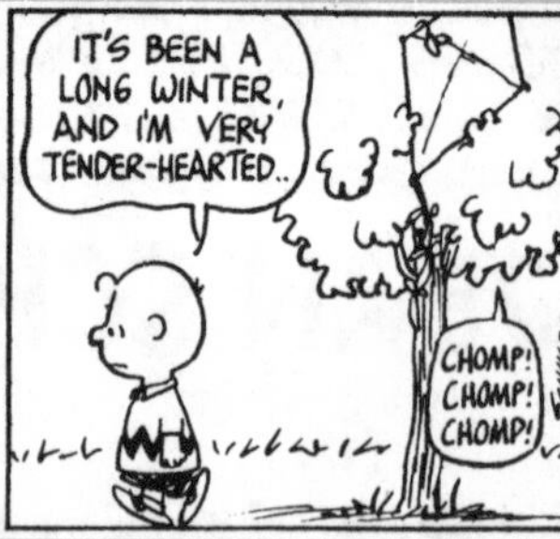

IT'S BEEN A LONG WINTER, AND I'M VERY TENDER-HEARTED..
CHOMP! CHOMP! CHOMP!
SCHULZ

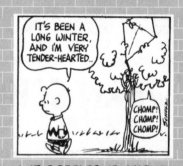

▲ IT GOBBLES UP CHARLIE BROWN'S KITES.

SECRET #11 AUGUST 10TH IS "SNOOPY DAY" AND HIS BIRTHDAY!

SNOOPY'S BIRTHDAY WAS AMBIGUOUS FOR MANY YEARS, BUT IN 2011 IT WAS OFFICIALLY DECLARED TO BE AUGUST 10TH. THERE IS A STRIP FROM AUGUST 10, 1968, WHERE CHARLIE BROWN AND THE OTHERS THROW SNOOPY A BIRTHDAY PARTY. IT IS EVEN RECOGNIZED AS "SNOOPY DAY" IN JAPAN.

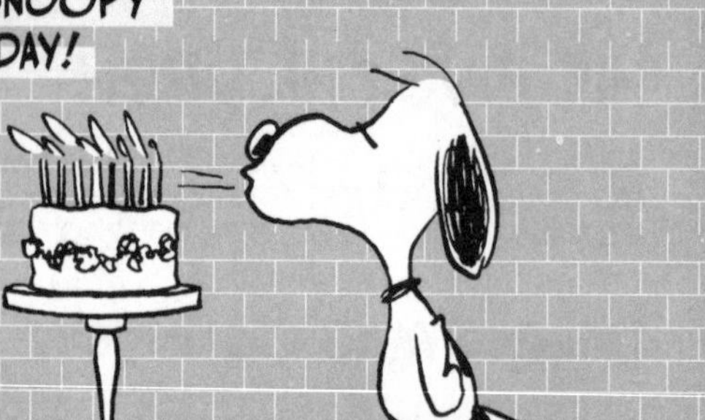

▲ LET'S SEND "HAPPY BIRTHDAY" MESSAGES ON AUGUST 10TH!

AMAZING THINGS ABOUT THOSE WHO SUPPORTED HIM!

INTRODUCING AMAZING THINGS ABOUT THE PEOPLE
WHO SUPPORTED SCHULZ'S EFFORTS!

THE SCHULZ EDITION

CARL SCHULZ

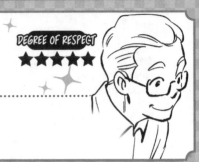

DEGREE OF RESPECT
★★★★★

SCHULZ'S FATHER WAS THE MOST HARDWORKING MAN IN TOWN

CARL SPENT ALL DAY EVERY DAY ON HIS FEET, WORKING AS A BARBER. SCHULZ TOILED WITH EQUAL EARNEST ON HIS COMICS

DENA SCHULZ

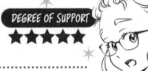

DEGREE OF SUPPORT
★★★★★

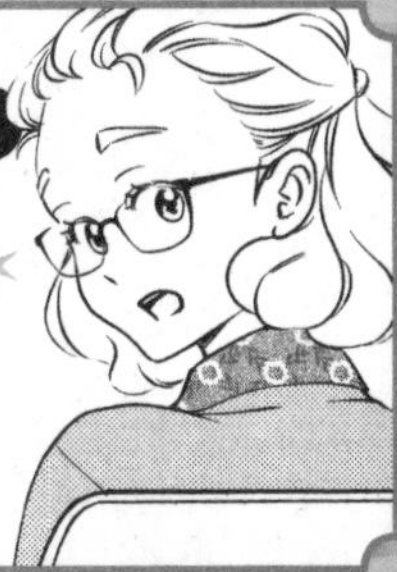

THE MOTHER WHO BACKED HIS DREAM TO BECOME A CARTOONIST

SCHULZ'S MOTHER DENA SHOWERED HIM WITH AFFECTION, AND WAS ALSO THE ONE WHO URGED HIM TO TAKE THE ART INSTRUCTION SCHOOL COURSE.

JEAN SCHULZ

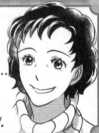

DEGREE OF DEEP AFFECTION
★★★★★

THE PARTNER WHO WATCHED OVER SCHULZ

SCHULZ AND HIS WIFE JEAN WERE A MARRIED COUPLE SO WELL-MATCHED THAT THEY PLAYED TENNIS TOGETHER, AND SHE WAS AT HIS SIDE SUPPORTING HIM UNTIL THE DAY HE PASSED AWAY.

HIS FIVE CHILDREN

THE DRIVING FORCE BEHIND HIS COMICS

DEGREE OF EMOTIONAL NOURISHMENT
★★★★

SCHULZ WAS A KIND FATHER WHO PLAYED WITH HIS FIVE CHILDREN AND ENCOURAGED THEM. THERE WERE TIMES HE GOT IDEAS FOR STORYLINES AND CHARACTERS FROM WATCHING THEM.

DONNA MAE JOHNSON

THE MODEL FOR "THE LITTLE RED-HAIRED GIRL"

DEGREE OF BITTERSWEETNESS
★★★

DONNA WAS SCHULZ'S FIRST LOVE. HE PROPOSED TO HER, BUT SHE TURNED HIM DOWN. THAT BITTERSWEET MEMORY IS WHAT INSPIRED THE "THE LITTLE RED-HAIRED GIRL" VIGNETTES.

THEY'LL RESONATE WITH YOU!

BEST 3 QUOTES

THE SCHULZ EDITION

SHOWCASING THE BEST 3 QUOTES THAT YOU WILL WANT TO USE, FROM AMONG ALL THE FAMOUS LINES IN *PEANUTS*

#1 CHARLIE BROWN

"I WANT TO BE LIKED FOR MYSELF..."

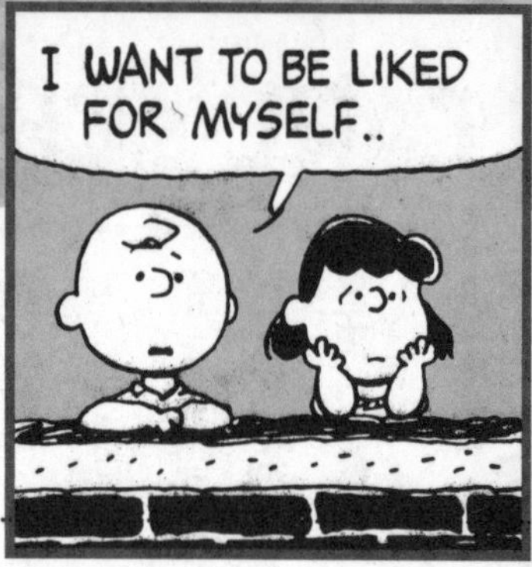
I WANT TO BE LIKED FOR MYSELF..

YOU WANT OTHERS TO LIKE YOU FOR YOUR OWN MERITS AND FOR YOUR WHO ARE.

WHEN TO USE IT? TRY TO RECALL THESE WORDS WHEN YOU'RE UNSURE HOW TO MAKE TRUE FRIENDS.

#2 SNOOPY

"YOU PLAY WITH THE CARDS YOU'RE DEALT..."

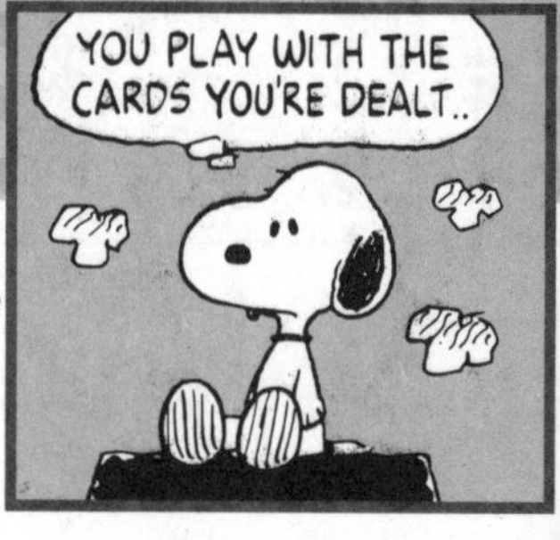
YOU PLAY WITH THE CARDS YOU'RE DEALT..

THERE WILL BE THINGS IN LIFE YOU CANNOT CHANGE. FIND HAPPINESS BY ACCEPTING THE HAND YOU ARE DEALT IN LIFE.

WHEN TO USE IT? YOU MAY HAVE FRIENDS WHO ARE TROUBLED BY THINGS THEY CAN'T CONTROL OR THINGS THAT ALREADY HAPPENED. THAT'S WHEN YOU SHOULD LIFT THEM UP BY SENDING THEM THESE WORDS FROM SNOOPY!

#3 LINUS

"NO PROBLEM IS SO BIG OR SO COMPLICATED THAT IT CAN'T BE RUN AWAY FROM!"

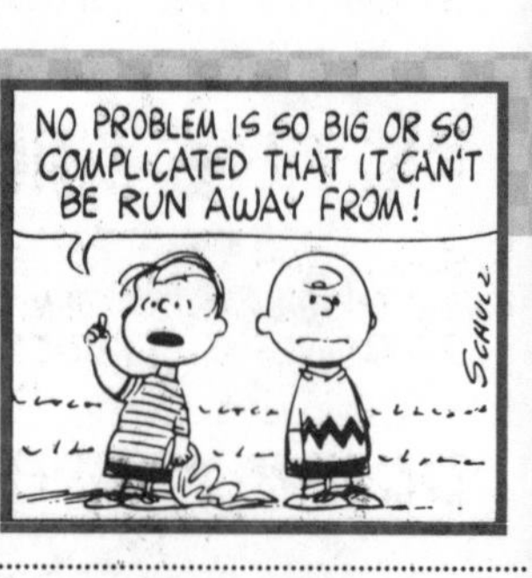
NO PROBLEM IS SO BIG OR SO COMPLICATED THAT IT CAN'T BE RUN AWAY FROM!
SCHULZ

LINUS MIGHT BE JOKING, BUT THERE IS WISDOM IN HIS WORDS! IF YOU GET STUMPED IN LIFE, SOMETIMES THE BEST SOLUTION IS TO STEP BACK AND TAKE A BREAK. A SOLUTION MAY PRESENT ITSELF.

WHEN TO USE IT? LET'S RECALL THESE WORDS WHEN YOU ARE HAVING DIFFICULTIES AND YOU NEED A BREAK.

CHARLES M. SCHULZ TIMELINE

SCHULZ SAT AT HIS DESK AND SINGLE-HANDEDLY DREW COMICS FOR 50 STRAIGHT YEARS, SUPPORTED BY HIS FAMILY AND FANS. LET'S TAKE A LOOK BACK AT HIS LIFE.

YEAR	SCHULZ'S AGE	MAJOR EVENTS
1922	0	IS BORN ON NOVEMBER 26 IN MINNEAPOLIS, MINNESOTA
1937	14	SCHULZ'S SKETCH APPEARS IN A NEWSPAPER, BECOMING HIS **FIRST PUBLISHED WORK**
1939	17	WORLD WAR II BEGINS
1940	18	ENROLLS IN A ONE-YEAR CORRESPONDENCE COURSE THROUGH THE FEDERAL SCHOOL OF APPLIED CARTOONING AND GRADUATES HIGH SCHOOL
1942	20	IS DRAFTED AND UNDERGOES U.S. ARMY TRAINING
1943	21	HIS MOTHER DENA DIES
1945	23	WORLD WAR II ENDS
1947	25	**DEBUTS AS A CARTOONIST** WHEN HIS COMIC STARTS RUNNING IN A LOCAL PAPER
1950	28	*PEANUTS BEGINS SERIALIZATION IN SEVEN PAPERS ACROSS AMERICA*

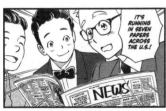

IT'S RUNNING IN SEVEN PAPERS ACROSS THE U.S.!

NEWS

▲ SCHULZ SIGNS WITH A MAJOR SYNDICATE, LEADING TO CHARLIE BROWN, SNOOPY, AND THE OTHERS' DEBUT ACROSS AMERICA.

1951	29	MARRIES JOYCE
1955	33	*PEANUTS* SYNDICATION **PASSES 100 PAPERS; WINS THE REUBEN AWARD**
1964	42	**WINS SECOND REUBEN AWARD**
1965	43	THE FIRST ANIMATED PROGRAM, *A CHARLIE BROWN CHRISTMAS*, AIRS ON TELEVISION
1966	44	*A CHARLIE BROWN CHRISTMAS* **WINS AN EMMY AWARD;** HIS FATHER CARL DIES
1969	47	OPENS A SKATING RINK IN SANTA ROSA, CALIFORNIA; APOLLO 10 LIFTS OFF TOWARDS THE MOON
1972	50	DIVORCES JOYCE
1973	51	MARRIES JEAN
1981	59	DRAWS SNOOPY ON THE WALL OF THE HOSPITAL WHERE HE IS HOSPITALIZED
1984	62	*PEANUTS* SYNDICATION ***PASSES 2,000 PAPERS,*** WHICH IS **RECOGNIZED AS A GUINNESS WORLD RECORD**
1999	77	ANNOUNCES RETIREMENT
2000		PASSES AWAY ON FEBRUARY 12; THE FINAL PEANUTS STRIP APPEARS THE NEXT DAY, THE 13TH, IN SUNDAY PAPERS

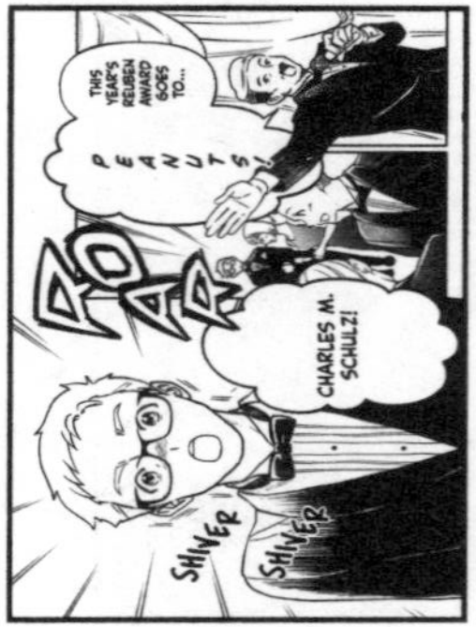
THIS YEAR'S REUBEN AWARD GOES TO...
PEANUTS!
CHARLES M. SCHULZ!
SHIVER
SHIVER
▲ THE REUBEN AWARD, THE HIGHEST HONOR A CARTOONIST CAN RECEIVE. SCHULZ WAS THE FIRST PERSON TO WIN IT TWICE.

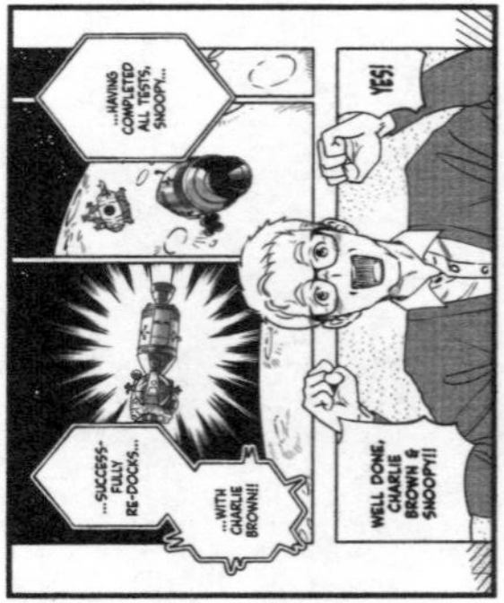
...HAVING COMPLETED ALL TESTS, SNOOPY...
...SUCCESS-FULLY RE-DOCKS...
...WITH CHARLIE BROWN!!
YES!
WELL DONE, CHARLIE BROWN & SNOOPY!!
▲ COMMAND MODULE "CHARLIE BROWN" AND LUNAR MODULE "SNOOPY" PLAYED BIG ROLES IN THE FIRST MANNED LUNAR LANDING.

The Legend's PORTRAIT STUDIO

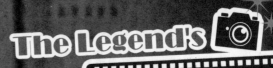

WHAT KIND OF PERSON WAS SCHULZ? LET'S LOOK BACK AT HIS LIFE VIA SOME PRECIOUS PHOTOS!

A COMIC STRIP COMES TO LIFE!

THE *PEANUTS* STRIP THAT RAN ON JUNE 16, 1968

COMPLETED!

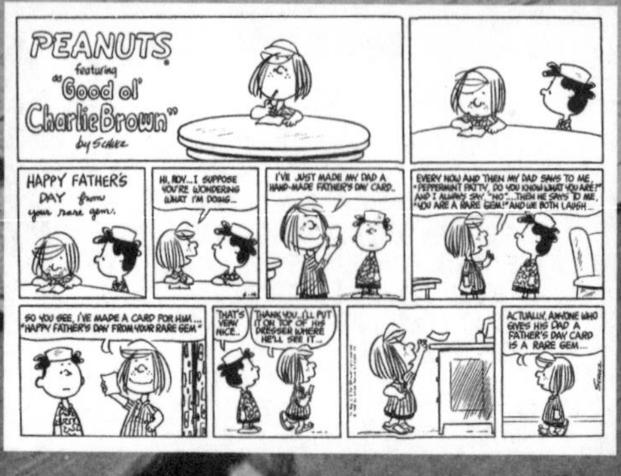

PEANUTS
featuring
"Good ol' CharlieBrown"
by Schulz
HAPPY FATHER'S DAY from your rare gem.
HI, ROY...I SUPPOSE YOU'RE WONDERING WHAT I'M DOING...
I'VE JUST MADE MY DAD A HAND-MADE FATHER'S DAY CARD...
EVERY NOW AND THEN MY DAD SAYS TO ME, "PEPPERMINT PATTY, DO YOU KNOW WHAT YOU ARE?" AND I ALWAYS SAY, "NO"...THEN HE SAYS TO ME, "YOU ARE A RARE GEM!" AND WE BOTH LAUGH...
SO YOU SEE, I'VE MADE A CARD FOR HIM... "HAPPY FATHER'S DAY FROM YOUR RARE GEM"
THAT'S VERY NICE...
THANK YOU...I'LL PUT IT ON TOP OF HIS DRESSER WHERE HE'LL SEE IT...
ACTUALLY, ANYONE WHO GIVES HIS DAD A FATHER'S DAY CARD IS A RARE GEM...

SCHULZ INKING A SUNDAY EDITION NEWSPAPER STRIP. WHAT HE IS DRAWING IN THIS PHOTO IS THE EPISODE TO THE RIGHT. UNLIKE JAPANESE MANGA, ENGLISH COMICS NORMALLY READ LEFT TO RIGHT.

The Legend's PORTRAIT STUDIO

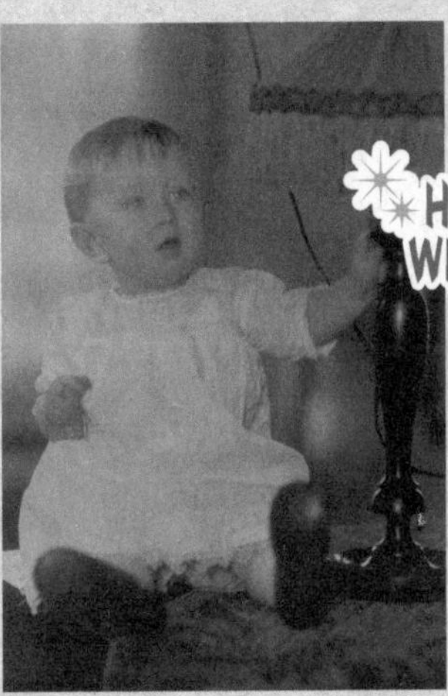

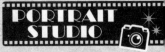

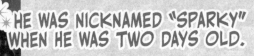

HE WAS NICKNAMED "SPARKY" WHEN HE WAS TWO DAYS OLD.

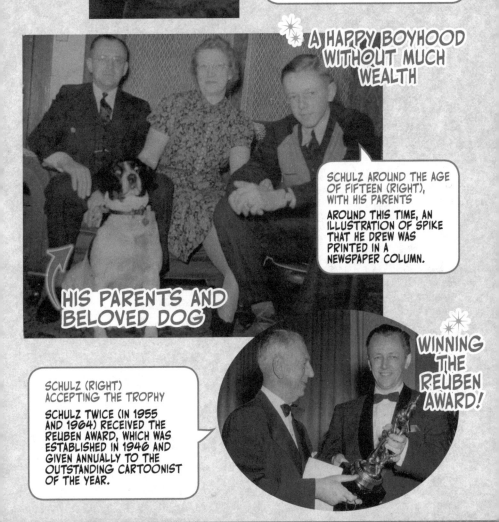

SCHULZ AROUND ONE YEAR OF AGE

SCHULZ AS A CHILD HAD A ROUND HEAD LIKE CHARLIE BROWN. HE WAS NICKNAMED "SPARKY" BY AN UNCLE, AFTER A CHARACTER FROM A NEWSPAPER COMIC STRIP THAT WAS POPULAR AT THE TIME.

A HAPPY BOYHOOD WITHOUT MUCH WEALTH

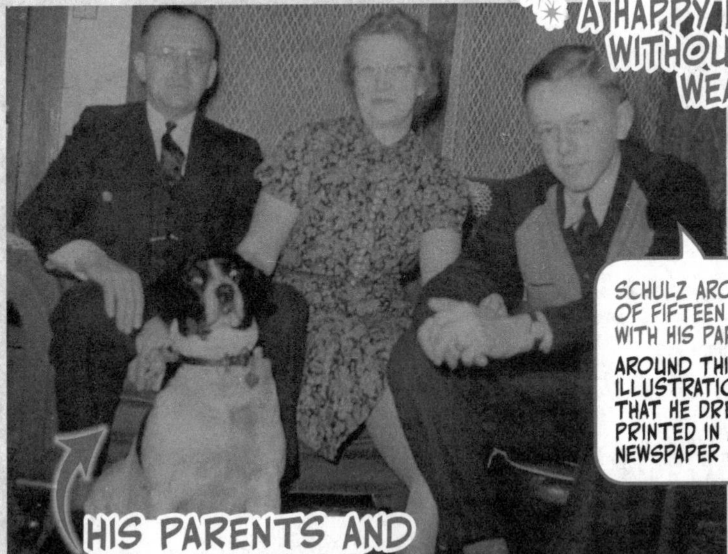

SCHULZ AROUND THE AGE OF FIFTEEN (RIGHT), WITH HIS PARENTS

AROUND THIS TIME, AN ILLUSTRATION OF SPIKE THAT HE DREW WAS PRINTED IN A NEWSPAPER COLUMN.

HIS PARENTS AND BELOVED DOG

WINNING THE REUBEN AWARD!

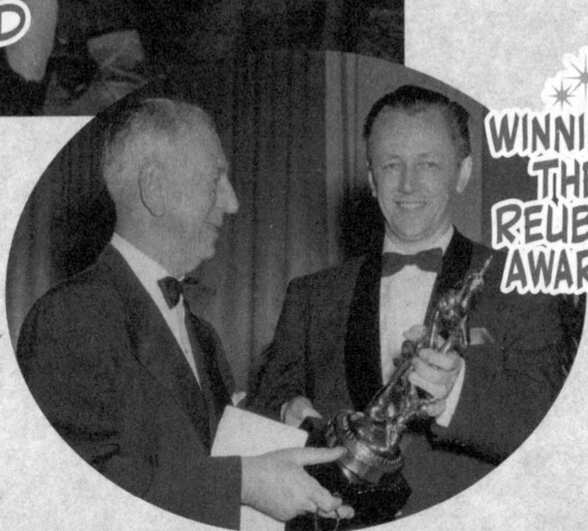

SCHULZ (RIGHT) ACCEPTING THE TROPHY

SCHULZ TWICE (IN 1955 AND 1964) RECEIVED THE REUBEN AWARD, WHICH WAS ESTABLISHED IN 1946 AND GIVEN ANNUALLY TO THE OUTSTANDING CARTOONIST OF THE YEAR.

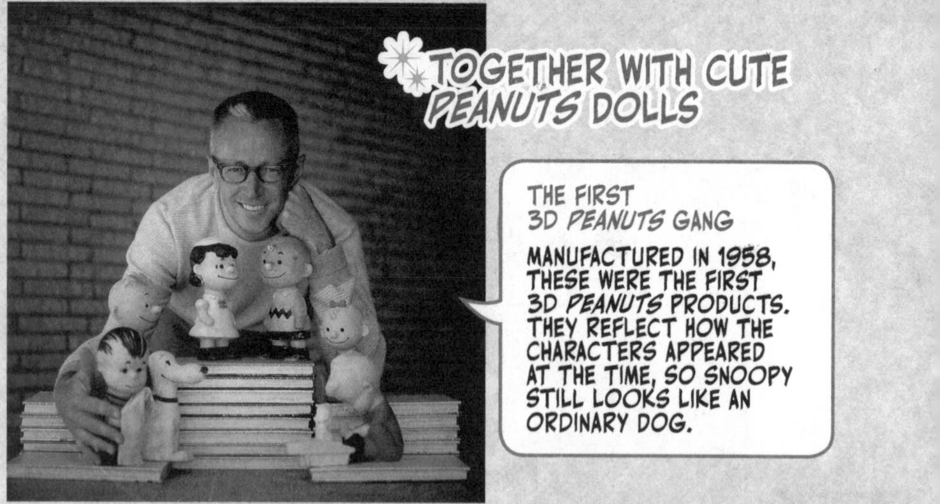

TOGETHER WITH CUTE *PEANUTS* DOLLS

THE FIRST
3D *PEANUTS* GANG

MANUFACTURED IN 1958, THESE WERE THE FIRST 3D *PEANUTS* PRODUCTS. THEY REFLECT HOW THE CHARACTERS APPEARED AT THE TIME, SO SNOOPY STILL LOOKS LIKE AN ORDINARY DOG.

RECEIVES A STAR ON HOLLYWOOD'S FAMOUS WALK

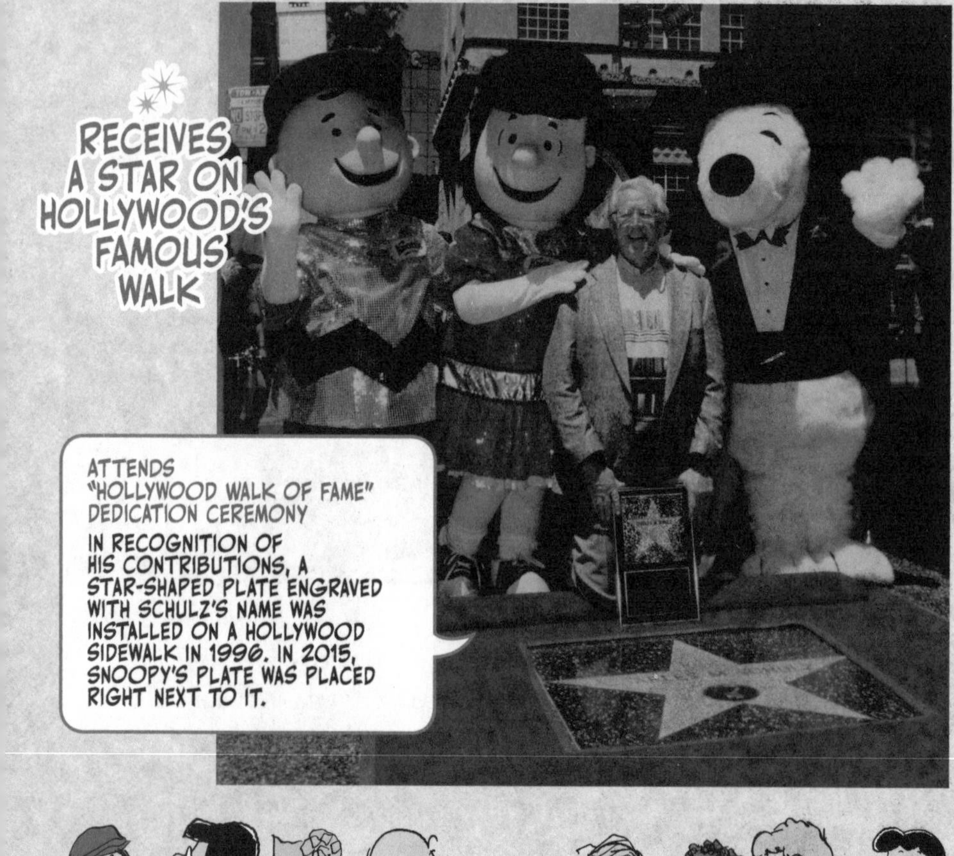

ATTENDS
"HOLLYWOOD WALK OF FAME"
DEDICATION CEREMONY

IN RECOGNITION OF HIS CONTRIBUTIONS, A STAR-SHAPED PLATE ENGRAVED WITH SCHULZ'S NAME WAS INSTALLED ON A HOLLYWOOD SIDEWALK IN 1996. IN 2015, SNOOPY'S PLATE WAS PLACED RIGHT NEXT TO IT.

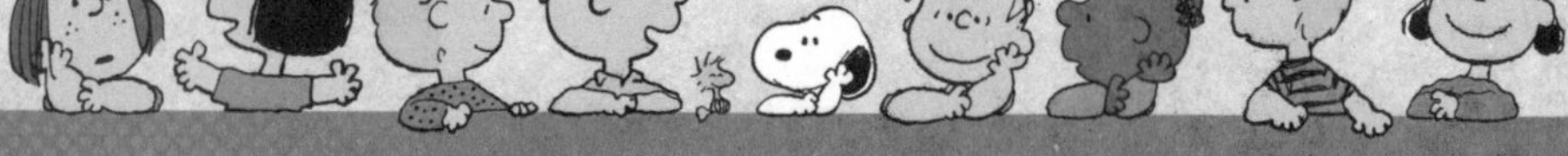

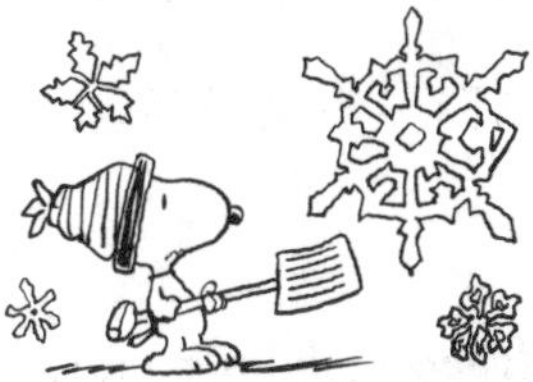

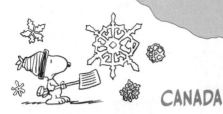

CANADA

MINNEAPOLIS

ST. PAUL

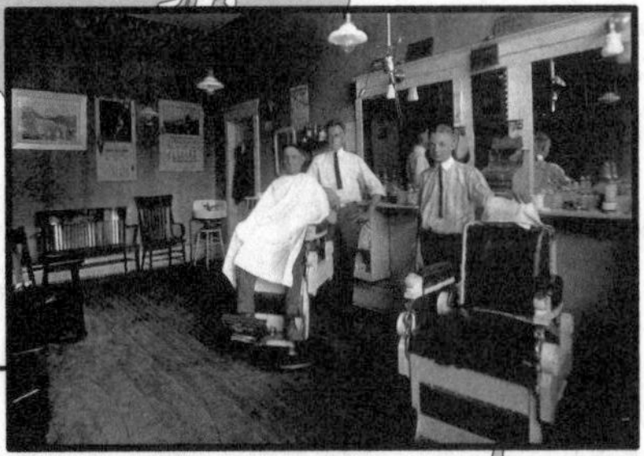

SCHULZ'S FATHER'S BARBERSHOP

ST. PAUL IS A CITY WHOSE WINTERS ARE AMONG THE MOST BITTERLY COLD IN AMERICA. SCHULZ'S FATHER OWNED AND RAN A BARBERSHOP ON ONE BLOCK OF THAT CITY.

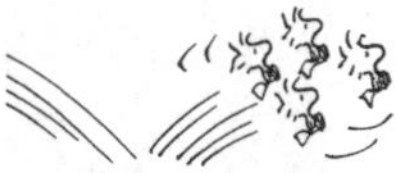

WHERE SCHULZ LIVED FOR A TIME

A SMALL CITY IN CALIFORNIA. SCHULZ LIVED HERE FOR A TIME WHEN HE WAS SIX YEARS OLD. THIS IS WHERE SPIKE LIVES IN *PEANUTS*.

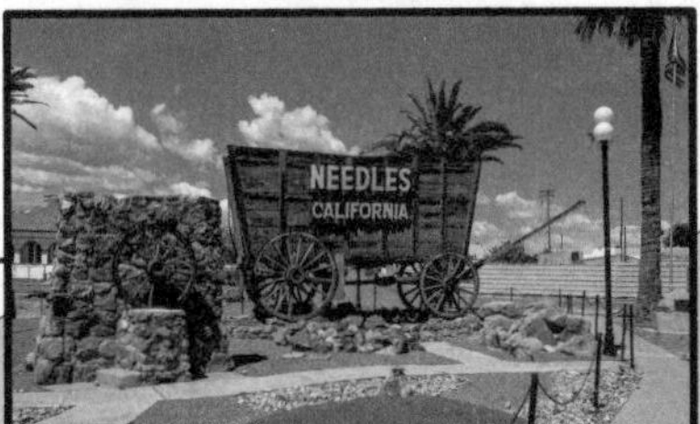
NEEDLES
CALIFORNIA

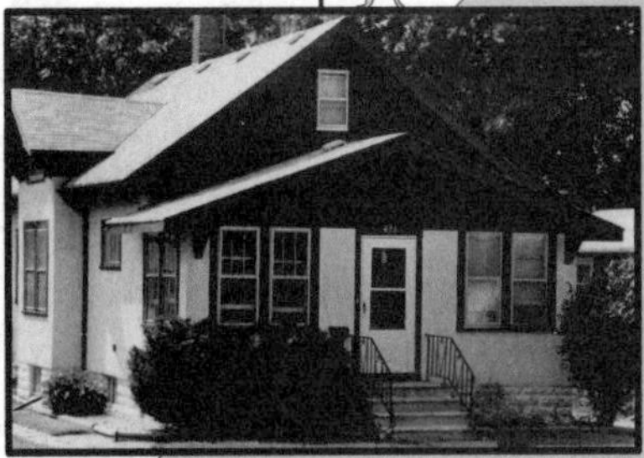

HIS CHILDHOOD HOME

SCHULZ WAS BORN IN MINNEAPOLIS BUT MOVED WITH HIS FAMILY TO THE ADJACENT CITY OF ST. PAUL, WHERE HIS FATHER'S BARBERSHOP WAS, IN 1927.

MAP OF THE LIFE OF CHARLES M. SCHULZ

EACH CITY SCHULZ LIVED IN PROVIDED IDEAS FOR AND SHOWED UP IN *PEANUTS*. LET'S TAKE A TOUR!

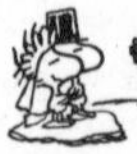

CURRENT PLACE NAMES AND BORDERS ARE USED.

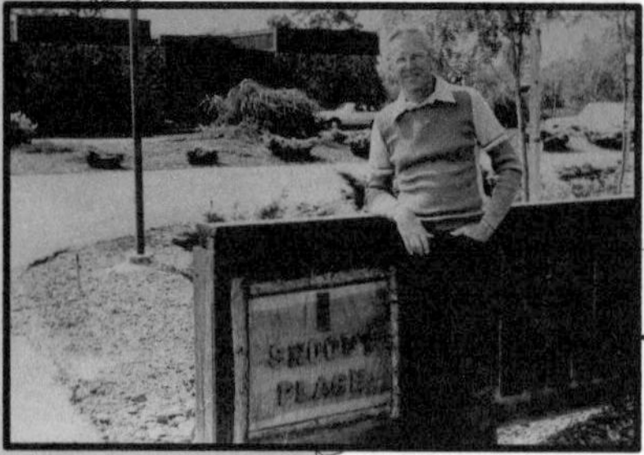

SNOOPY'S PLACE

CREATIVE ASSOCIATES STUDIO

SCHULZ, WHO HAD MOVED TO SEBASTOPOL IN 1958, BUILT A STUDIO THAT WOULD BECOME HIS OFFICE IN NEARBY SANTA ROSA IN 1970.

WHERE SCHULZ LIVED AFTER GETTING MARRIED

THE CITY WHERE SCHULZ LIVED AS A NEWLYWED. LOCATED AT THE EASTERN FOOT OF THE ROCKY MOUNTAINS, SCHULZ SPENT TIME GAZING AT THE MAGNIFICENT VIEW, TOO.

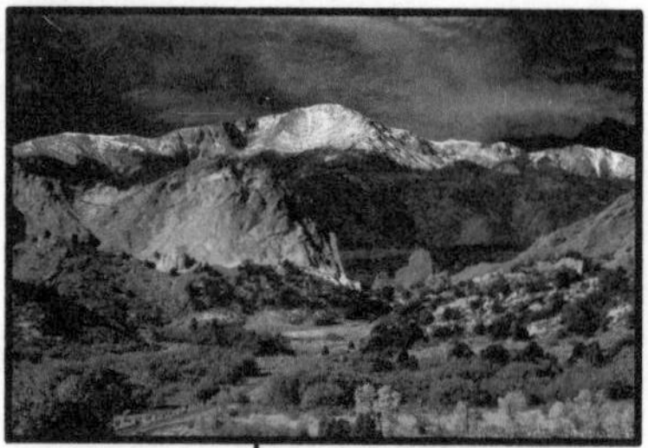

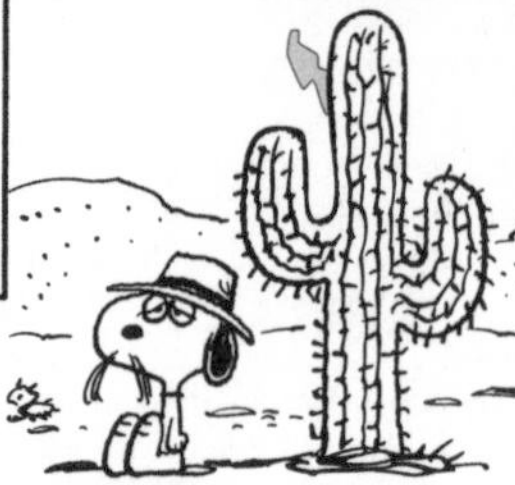

SANTA ROSA

SEBASTOPOL

COLORADO SPRINGS

UNITED STATES OF AMERICA

NEEDLES

MEXICO

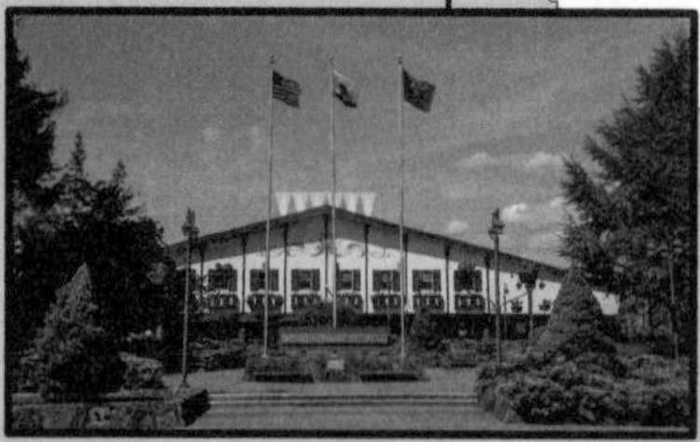

REDWOOD EMPIRE ICE ARENA

SCHULZ, WHO LOVED ICE HOCKEY, OPENED A SKATING RINK IN SANTA ROSA IN 1969.

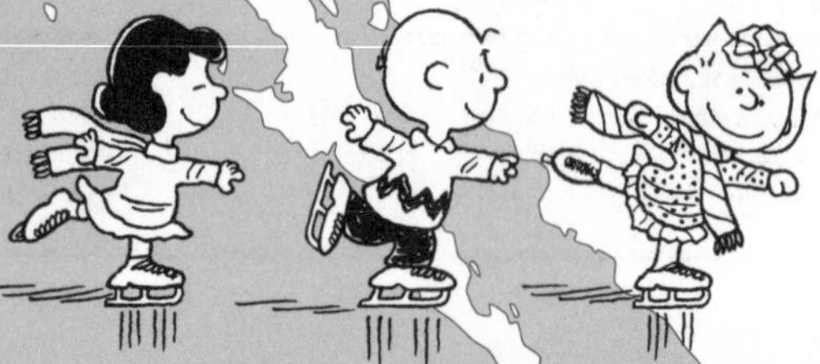

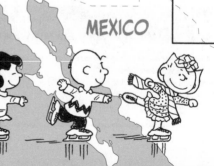

Main Reference Books & Materials

Snoopy Exhibition: Happiness is Getting to Know You Better (Ever and Never: the art of PEANUTS) Exhibition Catalogue
Good Grief: The Story of Charles M. Schulz (Japanese translation), Asahi Shimbun Company
Peanuts: A Golden Celebration: The Art and the Story of the World's Best-Loved Comic Strip (Japanese translation), Asahi
        Shimbun Publications
Charles M. Schulz: Cartoonist and Creator of Peanuts (People to Know) (Japanese translation), Gakken Plus
Bessatsu Kadokawa SUPER SNOOPY BOOK (Kadokawa Mook), KADOKAWA
The reassuring words of Charles M. Schulz, KADOKAWA
50 Years of Happiness: A tribute to Charles M. Schulz (Japanese translation), Kodansha
Snoopy's Secrets: Charles M. Schulz's Fictional World, Geijitsu Shincho October 2013 Issue Special Feature, Shinchosha
Snoopy's Secrets A to Z, Shinchosha
Pen magazine Issue 399, CCC Media House
Snoopy Museum Special Exhibition: PEANUTS GANG ALL STARS! Exhibition Catalogue, Sony Creative Products
SNOOPY, Bijutsu Techo November 2016 Supplemental Issue. BIJUTSU SHUPPAN-SHA
The Complete Snoopy Supplemental Volume: Peanuts Jubilee - 25 Years of Snoopy Comics (Japanese translation of *Peanuts*
        Jubilee: My Life and Art with Charlie Brown and Others by KADOKAWA), Fukkan.com
SPARKY: The Life and Art of Charles M. Schulz, Chronicle Books
Only What's Necessary: Charles M. Schulz and the Art of Peanuts (Japanese translation), DU BOOKS
The Peanuts Collection: Treasures from the World's Most Beloved Comic Strip, Little, Brown and Company

Charles M. Schulz Museum and Research Center website: www.schulzmuseum.org

Photo Credit & Materials Assistance

"Li'l Folks"; Spike the dog, object trios, appointment book doodle: p.30, p.37, p.55, p.148
© Schulz Family Intellectual Property Trust

Peanuts Worldwide LLC: p.149 (top left)
Schulz Family Intellectual Property Trust: p.162 (3 images) , p.163 (lower), p.148 (lower), p.149 (lower, top right),
        p.163 (top, bottom right), p.164 (top left)
Shutterstock: p.2 (3 images), p.164 (bottom left), p.165 (top right)
CBS Photo Archive: p.163 (top left)
Tom Vano, Courtesy of the Charles M. Schulz Museum and Research Center: p.148 (top), p.161
DJ Ashton, Courtesy of the Charles M. Schulz Museum and Research Center: p.165 (lower left)

SPECIAL THANKS TO
Charles M. Schulz Museum and Research Center
Charles M. Schulz Creative Associates
Sony Creative Products

The People Who Made This Book

Editorial Supervision: Charles M. Schulz Creative Associates
Cover & Dust Jacket: Chi-ko
Script and Manga Art: Yuzuru Kuki
Book Design: Musicago Graphics

Proofreading: Sachiko Iikawa, EDiT, Persol Media Switch Media
Planning Department Proofreading Group, Baru Planning
Editorial Assistance: Baru Planning, Koji Mitarai
Japanese Edition Translation Assistance:
    Kevin Gifford, Tomoe Spencer, Rikako Maruyama, Media Egg

manga biographies

CHARLES M. SCHULZ

THE CREATOR OF SNOOPY & PEANUTS

COVER BY
CHI-KO

MANGA STORY & ART BY
YUZURU KUKI

EDITORIAL SUPERVISION
CHARLES M. SCHULZ CREATIVE ASSOCIATES
EDITORIAL DIRECTOR: **ALEXIS E. FAJARDO**
EDITORIAL ASSISTANCE: **SAMUEL SATTIN, BRYAN STONE**
CHARLES M. SCHULZ MUSEUM, CURATOR: **BENJAMIN L. CLARK**
FOR PEANUTS WORLDWIDE: **CRAIG HERMAN, LISA SHIRAI**

SPECIAL THANKS TO **JEAN SCHULZ** AND **THE SCHULZ FAMILY**
FOR THEIR SUPPORT OF THIS PROJECT.

ENGLISH EDITION
Translator: MARI MORIMOTO
Letterer: ANDWORLD DESIGN
Editor: MARSHALL DILLON
English Cover Design: MATT MOYLAN
English Book Designer: MARSHALL DILLON

UDON STAFF
Chief of Operations: ERIK KO
Director of Publishing: MATT MOYLAN
Director of Operations: MARSHALL DILLON
VP of Business Development: CORY CASONI
Director of Marketing: MEGAN MAIDEN
Associate Editor: M. CHANDLER
Japanese Liaisons: ANNA KAWASHIMA

角川まんが学習シリーズ まんが人物伝 チャールズ· シュルツ スヌーピーの生みの親

KADOKAWA MANGA GAKUSHU SERIES
MANGA JIMBUTSUDEN CHARLES SCHULZ SNOOPY NO UMI NO OYA

First published in Japan in 2019 by KADOKAWA CORPORATION, Tokyo.
English translation rights arranged with KADOKAWA CORPORATION, Tokyo
through TUTTLE-MORI AGENCY, INC., Tokyo.

English language version published by UDON Entertainment Inc.
118 Tower Hill Road, C1, PO Box 20008, Richmond Hill, Ontario, L4K 0K0 CANADA

First Printing: July 2024
ISBN: 978-1-77294-344-3
Printed in Canada

manga biographies

MangaBiographies.com
UDONentertainment.com

UDON

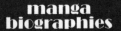